NOTES

ON THE

STATE

OF

AMERICA

Black To The Future, Or White From The Past

Ronald Peden

NOTES ON THE STATE OF AMERICA:
Black To The Future, or White From The Past

Copyright © 2008 by Ronald Peden

Published in the United States by OAU Publishing,
Box 382361,
Cambridge, MA 02138-2361
www.orgamu.com

Printed in Taiwan by
Red & Blue Color Printing Co., LTD.
Cungho City, Taipei

Library of Congress Control Number:
2007930489

ISBN: 978-0-9792910-0-5

In loving memory

For the Gift . . .   *and the Spirit*

of life.

The colored people of
this country are bound to
keep fresh a memory of the
past till justice shall be
done them in the present.

— Frederick Douglass

OAU

Where the mind is without fear and the head is held high;
Where knowledge is free;
Where the world has not been broken up into fragments
by narrow domestic walls;
Where words come out from the depth of truth;
Where tireless striving stretches its arms towards perfection;
Where the clear stream of reason has not lost its way
into the dreary desert sand of dead habit;
Where the mind is lead forward by thee into
ever-widening thought and action--
Into that heaven of freedom, my Father, let my country awake.

--Rabindranath Tagore.

ACKNOWLEDGEMENTS

To the many whose encouragement, assistance, feedback and guidance along the way made this work possible, I say with my deepest sincerity, Thank You a million times.

A special gratitude, however, is owed to Sheuli Nath at OAU Publishing for breathing new life into the work and allowing completion in a way unforeseeable before her influence. She, alone, gave the essential support, encouragement and inspiration that on one else could, or would, give at the most critical time.

A special Thank you is also owed to Mr. Carl Gray, without whose literally lifesaving friendship several years ago I would not have still been on this earth. My debt to him can never be paid.

Research for the book was conducted through the public library system of Massachusetts, primarily in the Cambridge Public library and its Minuteman Network of libraries. For the facilities and services available through this institution, I am grateful.

It is unfortunate, but imperative, however, that the begrudging attitudes and, at times, overtly-discouraging assistance from some of the individual employees at these libraries, up to and including the Cambridge director, must also be acknowledged, because of the potentially chilling effect on the conduct of serious research, not to mention on learning and the dissemination of knowledge, amounting to a subversion of the essential function of libraries, which cannot be ignored.

CONTENTS

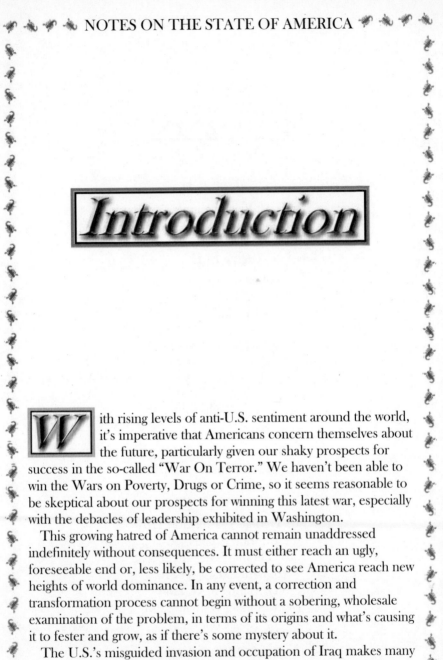

Introduction

With rising levels of anti-U.S. sentiment around the world, it's imperative that Americans concern themselves about the future, particularly given our shaky prospects for success in the so-called "War On Terror." We haven't been able to win the Wars on Poverty, Drugs or Crime, so it seems reasonable to be skeptical about our prospects for winning this latest war, especially with the debacles of leadership exhibited in Washington.

This growing hatred of America cannot remain unaddressed indefinitely without consequences. It must either reach an ugly, foreseeable end or, less likely, be corrected to see America reach new heights of world dominance. In any event, a correction and transformation process cannot begin without a sobering, wholesale examination of the problem, in terms of its origins and what's causing it to fester and grow, as if there's some mystery about it.

The U.S.'s misguided invasion and occupation of Iraq makes many believe a mere change of the political administration is the simple cure.[1] But if we remember the terrorist attacks going as far back as the killing of American servicemen in Beirut, Lebanon during the Reagan administration, or even the taking of hostages in Iran during the democratic administration of Jimmy Carter, in 1979, we can see the problem has been festering for at least a generation or more. In fact, I would argue the demise of American respect and credibility formally began at the time of the failed campaign in Vietnam, which necessarily carried a degree of lost respect for our supposed military invincibility, and only further reinforced by the "Shock and Awe" of our effort in Iraq, the shocking part being the sheer accuracy of Osama Bin Laden's characterization of the U.S. as a "paper tiger."

But I happen to believe America's declining command of world respect even has much deeper roots, and has only crystallized in this Age of Information where perfect knowledge is seemingly absolute, because of our open borders, the availability of transportation, satellite technology, the internet, etc. The informal roots of this new "American Dilemma," as I see it, must be at least, if not wholly, related to the dilemma traditionally identified with this country, most prominently in the nineteenth century by the Frenchman Alexis de Tocqueville, and in the twentieth century by the American scholar W.E.B. Du Bois, and the European Gunnar Myrdal, and symbolized by the recent tragedies experienced in the aftermath of hurricane Katrina, which showed, still, the limited economic acceptance and participation by Black slave descendents in America, screaming out the continued need for equality of opportunity and rights. Whether the largely avoidable, disastrous results were indifferently mishandled out of racist motives or not is irrelevant. The fact is, the tragedy highlighted the embarrassing problem that has existed since the beginning of this, the world's richest democracy: racial inequality.

Although we have traditionally promoted ourselves around the world as a country without class distinctions, where everyone is truly free and equal, that is something we are not and never have been, at least with regard to the country's native Black population. As a descendent of Black American slaves, I find myself constantly bumping into compromising race issues in my daily life, whether in a professional, social, political, educational, economic or civic environment, yet faced with the expectation and pressure to accept the norm that in this country Black is, still, second-class, less than, and subordinate to White. I've come to a place where I now find this increasingly difficult to do, because as someone old enough to remember some of the Civil Rights battles of the Sixties, I understood that, certainly by the twenty-first century, America would be a very different country. To be sure, there has been definite progress from the era of legally segregated public accommodations. But due largely to entrenched stereotypes, and the legacy of Black slavery, the reality is, America still has not fully closed the gap.

Because America's resistance to full racial equality has persisted, I believe it has seeped into our dealings with the outside world, where many countries feel the U.S. does not deal with them as equals but with a condescending arrogance that is off-putting. For that reason, America cannot repair its image abroad without a serious look at its problems at home, particularly with regard to race and the acceptance of diverse communities as equal, viable parts of the whole of the country, rather than as mere appendages to the mainstream. A major part of that introspection, should necessarily include an accounting of the past. As such, a major component of forcing the world community to take notice of American desire to repair its image in a genuine way should, I think, begin with making reparations for past injustices, specifically for Black slavery. By highlighting issues of America's history of slavery and its legacies, this book seeks to contribute to a national dialogue that will be a positive stimulus to that end.

Wondering where it all started and how it came to this, as America proclaims equality for all people, inevitably led me to search independently for answers in the nation's yet unaddressed history of African slavery. The study of that history led me to a different understanding altogether of how the institution affects the lives of Americans today, through its legacy of economics and race, and to find seriously misplaced accountability with regard to what, and how, America came to be.

Namely, like it or not, slavery was a crucial part of this country's economic growth and development, without which America could not claim any semblance of the preeminent position it occupies in today's world order. Yet, not without good reason, we look upon slavery with curiosity, shame, disgust and regret. As a consequence, in my opinion, Reparations are singularly crucial to allowing America to honorably put a period behind that institution, and to change the face of shame to one of ownership and pride. We are now a full-grown nation. It's time to stop pretending slavery didn't happen, or was simply an isolated episode of misfortune in American history, and instead acknowledge its cornerstone contribution to the America we know today — on par with the Founding Fathers.

I have always felt an emotional and spiritual connection to America's African slaves and, although somewhat fearful, have even as a child been curious about their history and lives, possibly because my foster father in Philadelphia, Arthur "Papa" Deas, born 1909, who migrated from South Carolina after World War II, knew his grandfather and great grandfather, both of whom had been born slaves, part of the prominent, slave-owning Deas family of South Carolina (see slave sale broadside, next page). "Papa" Deas, didn't generally talk much, but when old-time family or acquaintances from the South visited there were occasional references to fascinating memories and stories of old slavery customs and experiences handed down to them through the generations. These "old folks" thought their stories were amusing, but it was nevertheless clear the sometimes-chilling truth was in reality no laughing matter. Though I was curious, the thought of asking questions or broaching conversation on the subject was never a realistic possibility, not without risking a serious thrashing afterwards, that is. In the early 1970s, children were supposed to be seen and not heard whenever "cump'nee" came by. Still, I've always known that someday I would have to understand what it all meant. My motivation for this project therefore came in no small part from a curiosity about the truth and the facts. I find it astonishing that such an important aspect of America is virtually ignored in the general history taught in grade schools. What I've learned, however, has helped me understand myself, and my family, in a way that I would not have otherwise. In that sense this has been the most fulfilling thing I have ever done, and, perhaps, ever will do.

During this process of truth seeking, admittedly at times somewhat cynically, I forcefully challenge accepted conventions of what American slavery was and what it meant to this country and the world, as well as what has not been said. As a result, the book will likely be received, or dismissed, largely as polemic. However, I believe a successfully persuasive argument lies not only in the strength of positive promotion, but also in the strength of its rebuttal arguments.

In reading about America's history I identified a widespread interest in altering slavery's unpleasant truth to conform to what seemed a much more palatable un-truth. Slaves are no longer around to speak for themselves, so I found it difficult to ignore or accept what I saw as attempts to interpret slavery independent of the narratives and recordings they left behind, particularly given the fact that those interpretations affect the quality of Black life today, and will continue to do so long into the future.

It is not my intention to offend, but rather to be truthful and accurate about the facts as I see them, though I've been questioned as to whether there exists a single, universal truth regarding slavery, a reference to the many inferences that might be drawn from a particular set of facts. Although, really, there can be only one set of facts. My goals are primarily to distinguish these facts from mere wishful thinking and romanticism, with regard to both the history and the legacy.

I am, however, sensible that the facts regarding slavery are themselves often unpleasant or offensive, particularly when it comes to issues of race. I found it difficult, if not impossible, though, to analyze the many truths of slavery or its legacies without relating much that is unpleasant and distasteful, because slavery was not a nice institution. Moreover, the resulting legacies Blacks have to live with are, for the most part, anything but nice. Those sufficiently tired of revisiting slavery's uncomfortable truths, or more Black perspectives on American racism, particularly from a polemic perspective, should not read on.

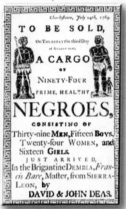

1769 slave sale by the Deas family of S.Carolina.

But in recognition of slavery as the only connection of African Americans to a sense of ownership and belonging in this country, a frank examination is nonetheless critical. For example, when I move around Boston's famous streets and historical landmarks, I feel the precious few signs of any significant Black contribution to the city's history, aside from, 'this individual lived here,' or, 'that event happened there,' are conspicuously subordinated to the celebrated contributions of the city's founders, such as Boylston, Faneuil, Adams, etc. I therefore feel no personal connection to the city and certainly no sense of ownership or belonging, which, no doubt, is the intended effect.

However, after learning Peter Faneuil, of Boston's famed Faneuil Hall, and Thomas Boylston, namesake of the city's prominent Boylston Street, were shipping merchants engaging the African slave trade; or that historic Harvard University, Massachusetts General Hospital and Boston Symphony Orchestra were all, in fact, the largest philanthropic beneficiaries of the profits harvested from the backs of Black slaves, I suddenly have a very different feeling about the city (though I'm more galled at the insultingly low enrollment of native born Black Americans at Harvard). Since the blood of slaves contributed to the fame of its namesake, and not only made an important contribution but, in fact, potentially the most important one — the ultimate contribution, I now strangely feel I belong in Faneuil Hall as much as anyone.

In truth, the very same reality applies to almost every city in America, where institutions and monuments of supposed White genius and industry more appropriately symbolize the inhumanity and depravity of their namesakes. In New York City, for example, the fabled Astors and Tiffany's, for starters, built fortunes gleaned from slavery profits, and in Philadelphia the extensive Wharton and Girard fortunes, among many others, were similarly anchored in the misery and death of Black slaves. I find this subordinated significance of Black slavery in America's brief history, in favor of White supremacy, deeply troubling. Much has been written yet there is still much to be understood, in terms of slavery's history and its legacies. This is an attempt to further uncover these truths

I broach no specific definitions of the terms used, believing the generally understood meanings, even with minor variations, will suffice. Except, that is, with regard to use of the term "White supremacy," because of differing intellectual and emotional connotations understood between many Blacks and Whites. My application of the term is not limited to the extreme, violent factions generally associated with it by many White Americans. Any promotion of the superiority of Whites or, alternatively, the inferiority of Blacks, in any way, consciously or subconsciously, be it of values, intelligence, morals or work ethic, including everyday racism and discrimination, is a belief in the supremacy of the White race and therefore falls within the definition of White supremacy as I use and understand it.

TRUTH

1

All In The Family

CAN'T TRUSS IT!

Public Enemy: "Can't Truss It"
Apocalypse 91...The Enemy Strikes Black
Sony/Def Jam Records

O ne of American slavery's more puzzling aspects, considering how much has been written about it, is the divergence of opinions on exactly what it really was. There is chiefly a conventional view that holds slavery to have generally been an abomination, and an alternate, revisionist view that centers on less objectionable aspects of the institution.

This troubling alternate view, however, seems without significant support in the narratives left by the former slaves and flies directly in the face of calls for accountability for slavery and its devastating legacies. It's therefore hard not to see this as an effort to skew the accuracy of the historical record, in order to evade accountability; an attempt to erase the shocking and embarrassing reality from the American conscience.

Because slavery is the only direct ancestral history most African Americans know, such efforts must be confronted. As noted by the producers of the epic public television series, Africans in America, "slavery is central to who we are as a Black people, it is not some peripheral issue that can remain a footnote of American history," and therefore the truth about it is of vital importance.

Unfortunately, historian James W. Loewen acknowledges, in *Lies My Teacher Told Me*, there have been "startling errors of omission and distortion" in the telling of American history,[2] which are of course the basis for the diverging opinions, and one reason it's been historically difficult for America to come to grips with it. But, ultimately, there will have to be some national, public acknowledgement of slavery's proper position in American history. So far though, because of fear, shame and embarrassment, that hasn't happened.

In this chapter I highlight a few representative examples of slavery's troubling distortion and omission issues, of more or less significance, that serve to bolster the romanticized opinions about the institution's history, and its devastating legacies — examined later in the book — and which facilitate the evasion of accountability.

Honey Suckle

Attempting to highlight a parallel between the slave-era experiences of Black and European American women, in a book titled *Within the Plantation Household*, late author Elizabeth Fox-Genovese presents some interesting examples of the trend towards whitewashing slavery's harsh reality.

A "high level of intimacy" characterized personal relations between slaves and slaveholders, she writes, "Mistresses whipped slave women . . . whose children they *might* have suckled and who frequently had suckled theirs,"[3] no doubt coming across countless references to slaves suckling European American children during her meticulous research, such as this oft cited reference by the former slave, Thomas Cole: "Mah mother was Elizabeth Cole, her bein' a slave of Dr. Cole. She was a family nurse. She nursed all de six chilluns of Master Cole."[4]

Within the Plantation Household is a voluminous writing of four hundred pages — not including bibliography, index and an extraordinary amount of notes. Yet there's no indication Fox-Genovese uncovered a single reference to a European American mistress suckling a slave child, so critical to the book's theme of White and Black, Southern, antebellum women being "bound in a web of intimacy," which no other solitary fact or image can convey with equal effect, particularly for female readers. It is, curiously, the one point lacking *any* supporting authority in the book whatsoever.

Too powerful to be left out for lack of support, however, if her theme
is to be believable, she therefore indulges the inherent creativity of the
writing process by suggesting a strong likelihood, even a probability,
since it's commonly known Black slaves routinely suckled their
European American slave mistress' babies, similar to this account
from Harriet Jacobs:

My mother's mistress was the daughter of my grandmother's mistress.
She was the foster sister of my mother; they were both nourished at
my grandmother's breast. In fact, my mother had been weaned at
three months old, that the babe of the mistress might obtain sufficient
food. They played together as children and when they became
women, my mother was a most faithful servant to her whiter foster
sister. On her death-bed her mistress promised that her children
should never suffer for any thing. . . . [My] mistress possessed but few
slaves; and at her death those were all distributed among her relatives.
Five of them were my grandmother's children, and had shared the
same milk that nourished her mother's children. Notwithstanding my
grandmother's long and faithful service to her owners, not one of her
children escaped the auction block.[5]

And the former slave, Mary Reynolds:

I was born same time as Mis' Sara Kilpatrick. Dr. Kilpatrick's first wife
and my maw [gave birth] right together. Mis' Sara's maw died and
they brung Mis' Sara to suck with me. It's a thing we ain't never
forgot. My maw's name was Sallie and Mis' Sara allus looked with
kindness on my maw. We sucked till we was a fair size and played
together, which wasn't no common thing. None the other li'l niggers
played with the white chillum. But Mis' Sara loved me so good.[6]

   If Fox-Genovese uncovered proof that European American
mistresses had in fact suckled Black slave babies she would have, or
certainly should have, cited it. So, to create the perception without
such definitive authority she instead says they "might" have, as in
maybe they did, or maybe they didn't.
   Still, the mere suggestion is powerful enough to form the image on
its own, which is then, for the most part, substituted for fact. Thus,
through being "imaginative with the evidence," writes reviewer
Christine Stansell, in *The Nation,* Fox Genovese "coaxes new
insights."[7]

What's My Line?

Photos: *Bullwhip Days*

The fact is, White mistresses did not suckle Black slave babies. The very notion is absurd; if they wouldn't suckle their own, then why in hell would they suckle someone else's, especially a Black, slave baby?!

The idea that European American women of the South endured anything comparable to the brutally terrifying experiences of Black slaves is nothing short of romanticism. Slave women lived under the continuous threat of rape, torture, hard labor and permanent separation from family and friends. White women, on the other hand, suffered a life of mere boredom and neglect. Or, as actor Dennis Haysbert reminded his celebrated co-star, Michelle Pfeiffer, in the popular film Love Field, a film about the racial climate of early 1960s America, "being bored and being Black are not the same." To compare the "aimlessness" of southern White women to the often horrific experiences of Black female slaves, says Stansell, is "specious,"[8] at best, not to mention deeply insulting to Black women all across America.

In truth, and more often than not, European American mistresses were some of the most fearsome and deadly abusers of Black slaves.[9] The fact that these White women were neglected and placed on a pedestal while their husbands sought satisfaction in the slave cabins, leaving mulatto babies behind as a constant reminder, infuriated them to no end.

Frederick Douglass wrote:

I know of such cases; and it is worthy of remark that such slaves invariably suffer greater hardships, and have more to contend with, than others. They are, in the first place, a constant offence to their mistress. She is ever disposed to find fault with them; they can seldom do any thing to please her; she is never better pleased than when she sees them under the lash, especially when she suspects her husband of showing to his mulatto children favors which he withholds from his black slaves. The master is frequentlycompelled to sell this class of his slaves, out of deference to the feelings of his white wife; and, cruel as the deed may strike any one to be, for a man to sell his own children to human flesh mongers, it is often the dictate of humanity for him to do so; for, unless he does this, he must not only whip them himself, but must stand by and see one white son tie up his brother, of but few shades darker complexion than himself, and ply the gory lash to his naked back.[10]

The fact that *Within the Plantation Household* has been celebrated with various awards (co-winner of the Julia Cherry Spruill Prize by the

Southern Association for Women Historians) can be seen as symbolic of how desperately some Americans want to get out from underneath the looming reality of slavery's inhumanity.

Noting that author Orlando Patterson "illuminates the dark side of the picture" in his book, *Slavery and Social Death,* Fox-Genovese seems to acknowledge such a desire, apparently convinced slavery in fact had an overlooked light side.[11] And, we learn later, she is not at all alone.

OH, HAPPY DAY

Fox-Genovese's wishful thinking may in fact have been based in similar delusions to those of so-called benevolent slaveholders like Thomas Jefferson, who genuinely thought his slaves loved him and were happy, yet couldn't understand why they habitually ran away. Or like James Madison, also described by contemporaries as a "kind master" to the "happy thoughtless race of people" he owned, who couldn't fathom why his female slaves "preferred by a great deal working in the fields" in the company of the other Blacks to "spinning and sewing" inside the house, in the company of Whites.[12]

Some perspective on the exact magnitude of Mr. Madison's "kindness" may be garnered from the lavish lifestyle he afforded his slaves, which he lamented as a burdensome weekly expense of approximately fifty cents per slave, including meals, clothing, healthcare, lodging, etc., as compared with the overseer's salary of "£60 Virginia currency of £48 sterling per annum" (approx. $300, or just under $6/wk), in addition to "everything he or his family could want."[13]

Fanny Kemble seemed to put the idea of slave happiness into proper perspective when she wrote "slaves of a kind owner may be as well cared for, and as happy, as the dogs and horses of a merciful master; but the latter condition — i.e., that of happiness — must again depend upon the complete perfection of their moral and mental degradation,"[14] which, she later observed, "is very complete, for they have accepted the contempt of their masters to that degree that they profess, and really seem to feel it for themselves."[15]

Desiring to show that complete moral and mental degradation had not in fact been perfected, Fox-Genovese, noting both subtle and extreme resistance, signifies an "absolute rejection" of the slave system, as evidenced by examples of slaves running away, committing arson, poisoning, physical opposition, and even murder.[16] But, of course, large-scale forced labor as existed in America could not have occurred without the complete physical and psychological domination that had in fact become manifest.

Determined, nevertheless, to show the debilitating hegemony of slavery did not prevail, Fox-Genovese cites what she believed was symbolic of the slaves' "total resistance": the Herculean courage of Harriet Jacobs, who hid in a confined, nine-foot, attic crawl space for seven years to escape slavery because her spirit had been broken. "Skeptical" of the story's "improbable" details, including the length of time Jacobs hid and "the size of her hiding space," Fox-Genovese characterizes the story as likely "embellished," to be read as "fiction" rather than factual.[17] One wonders though if the story of Anne Frank hiding in an attic with her family, during World War II, might be similarly deemed "embellished." Somehow, I highly doubt it.

If slavery was so treacherous, she writes, "then it had to have had consequences. If the consequences included, as she claimed, a breaking of the spirit of the enslaved, how could slaves be credited with character and will?"[18] The obvious answer, as anyone who has faced a degree of fear knows, breaking the spirit can heighten emotions to the point where individuals anticipate pain, terror and torture, and then react with great desperation, which, unfortunately, I can relate to from personal experience:

While receiving a whipping once as a child of no more than seven or eight years old in Reading, Pennsylvania, I ran out of the house, naked, into the alleyway behind our house and hid till night fall when my foster mother, Gladys, left for the evening. She had a particularly terrorizing habit of sending you to disrobe while she went to retrieve her long, slender, seemingly razor-thin leather belt that cut with frightening ease from her sweeping, powerfully efficient strokes. One can easily imagine the fear and anxiety that built during the wait — precisely the desired affect.

As I remember it, Gladys, a stout, burly woman, returned flush with fury, and began striking me wildly with the belt. Screaming and thrashing about in vain to avoid the stinging lashes, in the narrow aisle of the small room with standing room only between two single beds, I somehow managed to break free from her vise-like grip, which was tight enough to stop the flow of blood to my hands.

Flying down the stairs, I ran straight through the kitchen and out the back door into the yard. Half naked with only a t-shirt, and what felt like a broken arm and shredded legs, I jumped the short, four foot fence at the back of the yard onto the small paved ravine below.

I stayed there huddled in a crouch against the building on the opposite side of the alley, about fifty feet from the outlet to the street where pedestrians walked casually by. It was early in the evening during the summer so I was not cold, but with no pants still a little chilly. I was terrified and exhausted, but I didn't care. Nor did I care if anyone saw me. It was embarrassing and felt ridiculous, but the only thing that mattered was being free of the terror and torture that seemed unbearably cruel.

Gladys played Bingo every evening, so I waited until dark when I was sure she had left then went inside to get more clothes. Afterwards, I immediately ran away, knowing I would only get it worse if I was home when she returned.

I guess running away can be seen as an act of defiance or rebellion, but desperation and fear are the only emotions that came to me. Defiance suggests boldness and complete disregard for authority, whereas desperation is borne out of despair, hopelessness, and distress, as in one consumed by fear and terror. The former suggests an aggressive, offensive-minded attitude, the latter an entirely defensive posture of last resort.[19] The resulting behaviors, at once both rational and irrational, may in fact be indistinguishable, making the terms somewhat interchangeable, as Fox-Genovese knew, with her background in psychoanalysis.

"It is no easy matter to define rational behavior," writes Peter Wood, in *Black Majority*, but even the most illogical responses "rested upon a rational appraisal of the slave environment."[20] When faced with certain death or extreme cruelty, reactions instinctively take on an courageous character, circumstances not allowing an opportunity to reflect, which otherwise might lead to hesitation, and worse.[21] And although willful, we are informed by Nietzsche, "all mechanical occurrences, in so far as a force is active in them, are forces of will, effects of will."[22]

The enormity of Harriet Jacobs' endeavor is no more improbable than working from sun-up to sun-down in the blazing hot Georgia cotton or rice fields in midsummer, which on most days, no doubt, extracted a super-human toll. And what of the impossibly cramped confines of transport over the Middle Passage endured by those brought successfully from Africa, as described by an eighteenth century slave trader:

I could not conjecture how so many human beings could draw breath in a vessel's hold where her between-decks had only 22 inches height, and as I had stowed them myself, I knew them to be well cramped. As they were not fastened it was found necessary to secure them under deck while the vessel descended the river, to prevent their escaping by jumping over the board. As the height did not admit of allowing them to sit, we made them lie down spoon fashion, one in the other's lap; on the starboard with the left side down, and on the port vice versa.[23]

Consider also the improbability of surviving the following extreme ordeal, fashioned as a sort of sadistic punishment:

A planter who resided about twenty miles from one of those towns in North Carolina, invited the traveler from New York to take a ride with him in his [horse-drawn carriage] to his dwelling. The offer was accepted. About the middle of the day they prepared to start, and the northern citizen was surprised to find a very young woman fast-bound by the arms behind the [carriage]. It appeared that she had been driven into the town after the same manner and put into the slaveholder's "castle of misery," as a punishment for her refractory conduct. In what respects she was rebellious, was not directly mentioned. The whole distance of about twenty miles over the sand and dust was passed over in less than three hours, and the slave was obliged to keep pace with the horse, unless her arms had been separated at the elbows. . . . At a short distance, but out of sight of the family dwelling, the gentleman of New York perceived the same girl who had been driven almost at the full speed of a horse for twenty miles, suspended by the two wrists to the limb of a tree, with her body naked to her hips. With one foot she could just rest upon a small block of wood, while the other leg remained without any support. Without any ceremony, after venting a few of those hideous curses, with which the men-stealers generally salute "the flock of the slaughter," he proceeded to flagellate her with the cart whip, . . . Then leaving her bound to the tree, without the possibility of changing her position, he returned to the house, conversed about all the common topics with no apparent perturbation, dined as usual, and passed away the afternoon with as much external composure as though no evil had ever entered his domicile.[24]

Africans were in fact carefully selected for their likelihood to withstand the cruel physical and mental challenges awaiting them in America.[25] And Blacks in America have continuously had their stamina and will to survive tested and challenged in impossible ways, yet always manage to carry on. But this may in fact be the very reason for the curious characterizations of slaves and slavery by writers like Fox-Genovese.

It's not that difficult to see how one might find the seemingly superhuman story of Harriet Jacobs incredulous. However, what purpose is served with this statement: "slaveholding women could not, in their own persons, embody the physical attributes of a master, who could, if circumstances demanded, whip his strongest male field hand himself?"[26] Truth or falsity notwithstanding, a more shameless promotion of White supremacy would be hard to imagine.

> The Snake, the Rat,
> the Cat, the Dog.
> How you gonna see 'em
> if you livin' in a fog?

DMX: "Damien"/*It's Dark and Hell is Hot*
Rush/Def Jam Records

The Berlin Wall

Slavery's romanticized, revisionist writing is carried one step further by historian Ira Berlin, advancing a view of slavery in direct contrast with the generally prevailing image of the antebellum South.[27] First introduced in the book, *Many Thousands Gone,* Berlin posits slavery as a "negotiated relationship," implying slaves, through hook or crook, essentially bargained their way to whatever station they endured during the institution's first century and a half, while at the same time he concedes the nineteenth century phase where cotton reigned to have been patently non-negotiable, as it were. Again, however, this understanding subordinates a contrary view depicted by slaves in the narratives they left behind, which Berlin seemingly wants to discredit in favor of his latter view.

In *Remembering Slavery,* for example, a compilation of written and recorded memories of former slaves edited by Berlin, he devotes a fairly lengthy thirty-five page introduction to explaining exactly what the slave experience was — to him — even though the book is intended to feature the slaves' own perspectives. Not coincidentally, those perspectives are mostly at variance with his own, an inconsistency he explains by apologetically accusing slaves of being selective in their choice of experiences to recount. He writes:

Rather than recalling the experience of their parents, grandparents, and great-grandparents [the supposed open-bargaining era of slavery], former slaves preferred to dwell on the immediate past . . . partly because those stories were the ones their descendents wanted most to hear and partly because they were the ones the ex-slaves themselves wanted most to tell. Slavery's memory thus became increasingly short-term, with the direct, personal confrontations with slaveholders in the foreground.[28]

The first part of this chapter recognized this as a suggestion that slavery's non-confrontational, or "lighter side" has been selectively omitted, the very thing lamented by Elizabeth Fox-Genovese. It is an attitude illustrative of a level of arrogance, presumption, audacity and contempt that is nothing short of astonishing.

TRUTH OR DARE

Berlin has written or contributed to a significant body of work now widely accepted as the enlightened authority on slavery. With very few critics, if any, his work has also influenced a considerable number of historians. It would, in fact, be hard to find anything written recently on the subject that doesn't substantially echo his perspective, showing the impact one person can potentially have on the telling of history. He has therefore positioned himself to surreptitiously influence and — single-handedly — preempt or derail the push for slavery accountability, if he so desires. For these very critical reasons, the revisionist history originating from this single source deserves particular scrutiny. A cursory effort at which, such as follows, reveals the romantic theories advanced to be, at the very least, troublingly suspect.

Ira Berlin, it just so happens, has in fact revealed to *The Washington Post* a desire to counter the effort seeking an apology and Reparations for slavery, saying "If labor once expropriated should be compensated, what shall we collect for the gains in creativity?" Slavery, "without doubt," was "a period of extraordinary creativity," giving rise to a "cultural cornucopia" today.[29] He feels the real truth lies not in the harsh despair reflected by former slaves, but rather in the "material" benefit outweighing the devastation. In fact, Blacks may even be indebted to America for their two-hundred-and-fifty-year bondage.

In *Remembering Slavery*, Berlin writes "slaves engaged in the meanest sort of labor," but the work was also "a source of personal satisfaction,"[30] which is the premise he unfolds in *Many Thousands Gone* where his theory of slavery as a "negotiated relationship" is announced. It becomes bolder and bolder as the book progresses, until the reader actually begins to feel positive about slave life. With dramatic, empowering words and phrases to describe slaves, such as how they "demand[ed]" days off (p. 34); were "partners," "lending and borrowing" money from their owners and moving "freely" around the country (p. 35); had "substantial holdings" of assets and were "unrestrained by the confines of plantation life," building "networks of clients and customers," and enjoying "modest comforts" (p. 36); exhibited "extraordinary entrepreneurial audacity," and "a facility for shrewd trading" (p. 37); the deadly, horrifying carriage over the Atlantic's Middle Passage is casually described as a "trek" (p. 112), it is welcome and refreshing to those interested in slavery's *lighter* side, of course, but grossly misleading nonetheless, readily apparent upon an inspection of some of the supporting references.

In the case of slave girl paid to spin cotton for an indentured servant named John Harrower, for example, Berlin suggests a professional arrangement wholly unfounded by the facts. Although the girl is a slave, he characterizes her as both an "employee" and "subcontractor" of Harrower's for-profit "enterprise," receiving a small "income."[31] At best, however, the description is mere innuendo. At worst, it's outright fabrication. And is used to support a conclusion with only a loose theoretical foundation.

To his wife, in December 1774, Harrower wrote this about his supposed enterprise:

I have at this time a great high Girl Carline as Black as the . . . spinning some [cotton] for me for which I must pay her three shillings the pound for spinning it for she must do it on nights or on Sunday for any thing I know notwithstanding she's the Miller's wife on the next plantation. But I'm determined to have a webb of Cotton Cloath According to my own mind, of which I hope you and my infants shall yet wear apart ...[32]

He clearly has no commercial intentions as suggested, but rather sentimental ones. He wants his family, so far away, to have a few items designed by him, presumably to lessen the feelings arising from the long distance separating them.

The point Berlin wants to convey is that the slave girl is being paid for her work. But why embellish the fact? The answer is of course the need to support his negotiated relationship theory, best portrayed through such business terms as "subcontractor," "enterprise" and "employee."

This liberal interpretation of the facts is what's seen by colleagues and reviewers as Berlin's "magisterial synthesis," and an "admirable ability" to take a particular circumstance and "synthesize it with his own fresh interpretations"[33] It appears, however, that, like Fox-Genovese, Ira Berlin molds facts to fit his theory rather than letting the facts, however uncomfortable, simply speak for themselves.

Black is Beautiful

A great deal of *Many Thousands Gone* is devoted to the slave economy as a source of independence and wealth for slaves. Although, far from being empowered, slaves who earned money on their own time were at the mercy of the European Americans they worked for and, as often as not, failed to receive proper value for the work they performed, if they received anything at all.

Did a slave economy in fact exist? Without question. Did it bear the romantic face given to it? Highly suspect, made more clear by the absurdity of Berlin's shockingly insulting scheme to extend the slave economy to the sexual exploitation of female slaves, the-straw-that-broke-the-camel's-back. European Americans, he writes, "inevitably translated the license slave women enjoyed in the marketplace into the metaphor for sexual freedom ... But such activities were always more than opportunities for market women and laundresses to add to their income, for the demand for black sexuality promised new *power*."[34]

Is he kidding? He done lost his mind? How dare he exploit the degraded condition of Black slave women simply to assuage the guilt of European Americans. There is nothing empowering about prostitution, especially in slavery! The demand for Black sexuality did not "promise new power," for female slaves, it promised new power for slave-*owners*. For Black women, prostitution promised *further* degradation, indignity, subjugation, objectification, inhumanity and abuse.[35] "The marketplace" may have addressed those restrictions in the short term, but that is a far cry from empowerment. To quote from Coco Fusco, in *Ms.* magazine, "obviously, there is something fundamentally wrong with[in] a society [when] sex work is the best paying job for women."[36] Slavery, of course, was "fundamentally wrong." Prostitution was, and is, a practice born of the inhumane limits to which women have been, and are, driven to by men. And, during slavery, particularly, that meant European and European

American men. As Beth Day noted in *Sexual Life Between Blacks And Whites*:

> The body of the black female slave was the master's for the taking. Sexual rights over the body of the black woman also became the privilege of the master's sons, the plantation overseers, and, by extension, to any white male around. It was rare to find an overseer who did not avail himself of free black sex . . . [37]

Reverend Francis Hawley who spent fourteen years in the slave culture of the Carolinas during the nineteenth century noted "It is so common for the female slaves to have white children that little or nothing is ever said about it. Very few inquiries are made as to who the father is."[38]

From Slavery Illustrated:

> It is the oracular decision of the men-stealers, that it is not only for their interest, but also for the *benefit* of the female slave–in fact, that it is not only expedient and proper, but just and indispensable, that every "colored girl" at an early period of life, should first admit to her embraces her master or his son . . . they urge that it secures the lasting affections of the young woman, and especially if her first child should be the known off-spring of her owner. . . . [39]

The sister of President James Madison also reportedly exclaimed "We southern ladies are complimented with the names of wives; but we are only the mistresses of seraglios.[40] Yet the only mention of White men in connection with this supposedly empowering business of slave prostitution is a sanitized reference to the "patrons" as some of the nation's leading "gentlemen."[41]

This is essentially the same supply-side logic used by European Americans to convince themselves that Africans were chiefly responsible for the slave trade, in offering fellow countrymen for sale. I don't buy it. Just as White demand for Black sex drove slaves into prostitution, the European demand for labor drove the slave trade. "The willingness of European traders to buy large numbers of captives eventually stimulated slave-raiding in the interior and encouraged African chiefs to [sanction] enslavement," writes Robin Blackburn, in *The Making of New World Slavery*, "[t]he ability of the European traders to offer an impressive range of trade goods [was] a fundamental circumstance" of the trade, which "seemed to come with

its own commercial justification."[42] Captain Theophilus Conneau,
who purportedly spent twenty years in Africa buying and selling Black
slaves, had this to say about the European role as the engine driving
the trade:

> three quarters of slaves shipped are the product of native wars, which
> are partly brought about by the great inducement and temptation of
> the white man. . . . all the principal nations have had a share in
> fomenting the slave traffic and introducing wants, desires, and
> luxuries, with a view to encourage the then humane trade. These
> wants, desires, and luxuries have become an indispensable necessity
> to the natives and the traffic a natural barter.
> England today sends to Africa her cheap Birmingham muskets and
> Manchester goods, which are exchanged at Sierra Leone, Accra, and
> the Gold Coast, for Spanish or Brazilian bills on London. France sends
> her cheap brandies, her taffeta reds, her Rouen cottons, and her
> *quelque-chase*, the United States their leaf tobacco, their one-F
> powder, their domestic spun goods, their New England rum and
> Yankee notions, with the same effect or the same purpose. Therefore I
> say it is *our* civilized commodities which bring the cause of the wars
> and the continual, now called inhuman, traffic.[43]

An additional perspective on this apparent chicken-or-egg
conundrum, by a researcher of the Portuguese trade in slaves at
Angola, shows it was clearly the demand — the money — that set the
process in motion. Eighteenth century mercantilism, according to
Joseph C. Miller,

> contributed to an apparent overextension of credit from merchants to
> the caravan operators, or *sertanejos*, and others who brought slaves
> down from the interior to Luanda or Benguela. To these *sertanejos*,
> also known as *aviados*, or *funantes*, they sold trade commodities on
> credit to be repaid in slaves upon their return to the coast 6-8 months
> or even years later. Ownership of both goods and slaves resided with
> the *sertanejos*, and the Luanda merchants, either as principals or as
> agents, purchased the slaves from them after their arrival on the coast.
> . . .
> [African] kings . . . would first accept the *sertanejo's* goods on the
> promise to provide an agreed number of *pecas* [slaves] and then
> despatch messengers throughout their kingdom and beyond in search
> of people to be sold. As slaves gradually trickled into the royal
> residence in response to these directives, they were handed over as
> quickly as possible to the *sertanejo*, thereby making their maintenance

his responsibility. . . . The collection of a full coffle of slaves (*libambo*, or *quibuca*, as it was sometimes known in Angola) involved weeks and months of delay for the *sertanejo*, as he waited for a return on the loan he had extended to the king, watched the expenses of maintaining a half coffle of slaves rise, and paid higher and higher prices to an African monopolist who understood very well his haste to complete his business.[44]

Also, llustrating the competitive force of this European demand, Miller writes

no matter how carefully slavers planned their departures from Luanda, the availability of slaves for sale often delayed captains hastening to clear port. Since merchants kept as few slaves as possible on hand in Luanda, and since the slaves reached the city in small lots spread throughout the year . . . most ships spent 2-3 months or more acquiring a full cargo of slaves. In a typical year, in which 10,000 slaves left Luanda, they would have entered the city at a mean rate of less than 30 each day, and an average of five ships competing to purchase them would have lain at anchor in the bay. A captain did well, therefore, if he could acquire slaves at the rate of a half dozen each day until he made up the 400-600 that he would need before he would leave.[45]

Source: Black, *Atlas Of World History*

"Down to the steamy ports of the Slave Coast," wrote Thomas Pakenham, in *The Scramble For Africa*, "came the lines of shuffling slaves, to be unshackled and graded, marketed, reshackled, loaded and dispatched with minimum loss in transit (perhaps a third died)."[46]

Sadly, there is no shortage of offensive, contemptuous perceptions of slavery throughout *Many Thousands Gone*, ostensibly advanced to bolster the negotiated relationship theory Ira Berlin so desperately promotes. "The essence of the slaves' history," he writes, "can be found in the ever-changing music to which slaves were forced to dance and in their ability to superimpose their own rhythms by ever so slight changes of cadence, accent, and beat," as if slavery was an allegro, dance production with slaves whimsically ushering on and off stage. One next expects to read about slaves reveling in a celebration of bondage — with their owners, no less. And, sure enough, he later cites from a published account — written by a European American male, no doubt — of a 1775 slave celebration that purportedly included, among other things, "Hams, Beef, Turkies [sic], and . . . bottled liquors of all sorts."

Well, hell. I guess slavery was just one big happenin' party!

But, horror of horrors, there is still more contempt to heap upon the image of Black women who, Berlin matter-of-factly surmises, "elevated the trade, . . ."

And he is not, by the way, referring to the slave trade.

There's not really a clean way to describe my reaction to this outrageous tribute so, in short, I'll just say Ira Berlin is full of shit! Just whom is he trying to kid? The "essence" of slavery was a life and death struggle where human beings were, at best, abused, humiliated, emasculated and dehumanized; at worst, tortured, maimed, raped, killed and torn from family, often on a whim.

The *Journal of Southern History*, however, interprets Berlin's questionable characterizations as a unique "sensitivity to nuances of the power struggles between master and slave." And other than esteemed Princeton historian, Nell Irvin Painter, who in fact labeled Berlin's negotiated relationship theory "overstated," in the *African American Review*, a veritable Who's Who of historians all expressed glowing approval of his revisionist suppositions, using such superlatives as "masterly" (George Fredrickson), "a stunning achievement" (Douglas Egerton), "profound" (Graham Hodges), "superb" (Edward Ayers), and "impressive" (Sheldon Hackney).

Well, in a word, here's my own ghetto-nigger assessment of Ira Berlin's revisionist slavery theory: Bullshit!

With such imaginative storytelling, it's not at all hard to see how history can be, and is, crafted to reflect whatever individual historians desire. And what many desire is for history to discount the fact that European Americans simply used brute force and terror to secure their preferred position in contemporary America and the world, much more so than any superior morality, work ethic or intelligence. To be sure, there is truth to the romantic stories presented by revisionist historians. But rather than an objective historical accounting, they are clearly more interested in feel-good stories that European and European-American readers will find pleasingly palpable.

According to one early philosopher, "No history is good for anything except as it is interpreted correctly; and it is in the interpretation that the chance is offered for all the old arbitrary elements of philosophy and personal prejudice to come in, as well as some new ones." This "'postmodern' refusal to distinguish fact from fiction" in history, as Edmund Morgan describes it, is a sobering reminder of exactly why modern racism is so entrenched.

I think it's high time we broke down the "Wall" of deception about American slavery — and racism — and started telling the ugly truth, no matter how painful.

It's time for Reparations!

2

Negotiations

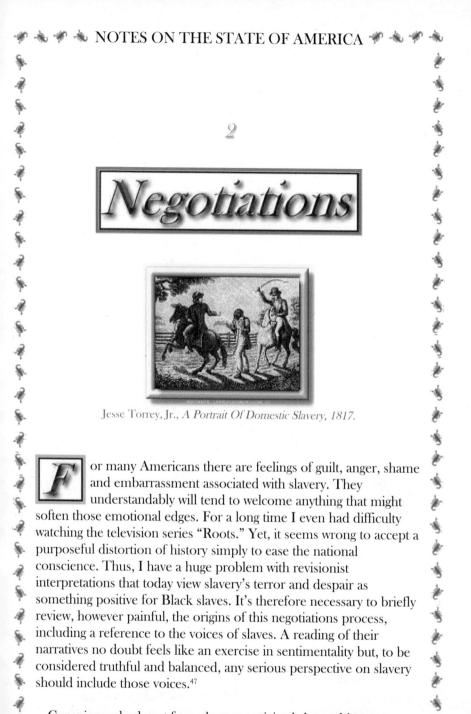

Jesse Torrey, Jr., *A Portrait Of Domestic Slavery, 1817.*

For many Americans there are feelings of guilt, anger, shame and embarrassment associated with slavery. They understandably will tend to welcome anything that might soften those emotional edges. For a long time I even had difficulty watching the television series "Roots." Yet, it seems wrong to accept a purposeful distortion of history simply to ease the national conscience. Thus, I have a huge problem with revisionist interpretations that today view slavery's terror and despair as something positive for Black slaves. It's therefore necessary to briefly review, however painful, the origins of this negotiations process, including a reference to the voices of slaves. A reading of their narratives no doubt feels like an exercise in sentimentality but, to be considered truthful and balanced, any serious perspective on slavery should include those voices.[47]

Conspicuously absent from the romanticized slavery history reviewed in the previous chapter is any prominent voice of the former slaves, effectively amounting to a further indignity to their inhumane existence, not at all consistent with the respect due their sacrifices. In 365 pages of text, for example, *Many Thousands Gone* includes no less than twenty references to such slaveholders as George Washington, Thomas Jefferson, Henry Laurens, and Robert "King" Carter -- each. The only slaves identified were Charles Ball and Sojourner Truth, and neither is quoted as saying anything remotely supportive of slavery being a negotiated relationship. *Within The Plantation Household*, as has been noted, also included a "paucity of firsthand reports of individual slaves," while citing "more than 150 diaries and collections of family papers" from slave owners.[48] This imbalance will necessarily reveal only part of the story of slavery. In addition, there is more than ample reason to question the veracity of much of what has been left behind by slave owning families who, with an eye towards posterity, were more than a little averse to full disclosure, as we see in later chapters.

But, this imbalance of historical perspective inevitably invites speculation about what Frederick Douglass, Harriett Jacobs, William Wells Brown or Harriett Tubman might think about the romantic claims of slavery being a "leveling up of relations" between "partners." And it just so happens that with Ira Berlin's reference to the man who may have employed Douglass' owner in Talbot County, Maryland, Colonel Edward Lloyd, we're provided an opportunity, albeit unwittingly, to read exactly what Douglass might say about this supposed partnership between slaves and owners, in his own words.

Berlin makes the assertion that practical business decisions influenced Chesapeake planters in their sale and purchase of slaves. "Planters not only collected quick cash from the sale of 'excess' slaves," he writes, such sales also "provided them an opportunity to reconfigure their labor force in ways that improved productivity. Edward Lloyd, the largest slave owner on Maryland's eastern shore, regularly sold a portion of his holdings," says Berlin, "to keep his plantation workforce at what he believed to be the appropriate level." "Even the most conscientious masters found it necessary to reduce the size of their holdings periodically," he concluded.[49]

Frederick Douglass, however, saw an altogether different motivation underlying the sale of slaves. Namely, terror. According to Douglass, Lloyd

owned so many [slaves] that he did not know them when he saw them; nor did all the slaves of the out-farms know him. It is reported of him, that, while riding along the road one day, he met a colored man, and addressed him in the usual manner of speaking to colored people on the public highways of the south:

"Well, boy, whom do you belong to?" . . .

"Lloyd," replied the slave.

"Well, does [he] treat you well?"

"No, sir," was the ready reply.

"What, does he work you too hard?"

"Yes, sir."

"Well, don't he give you enough to eat?"

"Yes, sir, he gives me enough, such as it is."

After ascertaining where the slave belonged, [Lloyd] rode on; the man also went about his business, not dreaming that he had been conversing with his master . . . until two weeks afterwards. The poor man was then informed by his overseer that, *for having found fault with his master*, he was now to be sold to a Georgia trader. He was immediately chained and handcuffed; and thus, without a moment's warning, he was snatched away, and forever sundered, from his family and friends, by a hand more unrelenting than death. This is the penalty of telling the truth, of telling the simple truth, in answer to a series of plain questions.[50]

It's certainly fair to say Lloyd meant business when he sold slaves, but it's just as clear it often had little to do with making dollars, or sense, for that matter.

The question of which motives commonly govern an owner's slave sales was, coincidentally, also described by the former slave William Wells Brown. A slave trader, one Mr. Walker, Brown wrote,

soon commenced purchasing to make up the third gang, bought a number of slaves as he passed the different farms and villages. After getting [several] men and women, we arrived at St. Charles, a village on the banks of the Missouri [river]. Here he purchased a woman who had a child in her arms, appearing to be four or five weeks old. . . . Soon after we left St. Charles the young child grew very cross, and kept up a noise during the greater part of the day. Mr. Walker complained of its crying several times, and told the mother to stop the child from crying, but she could not. We put up at night with an acquaintance of Mr. Walker, and in the morning, just as we were about to start, the child again commenced crying. Walker stepped up to her, and told her to give the child to him. The mother tremblingly obeyed. He took the child by one arm, as you would a cat by the leg, walked into the house, and said to the lady,

"Madam, I will make you a present of this little nigger; it keeps such a noise that I can't bear it."

"Thank you, sir," said the lady.

The mother, as soon as she saw that her child was to be left, ran up to Mr. Walker, and falling upon her knees, begged him to let her have her child; she clung around his legs, and cried, "Oh, my child! my child! master, do let me have my child! oh, do, do, do! I will stop its crying if you will only let me have it again." When I saw this woman crying for her child so piteously, a shudder — a feeling akin to horror — shot through my frame. I have often since in imagination heard her crying for her child.... After the woman's child had been given away, Mr. Walker commanded her to return into the ranks with the other slaves. Women who had children were not chained, but those that had none were. As soon as her child was disposed of she was chained in the gang.[51]

Not only does this not represent a sound business decision, in no way does it resemble a leveling of relations, much less a negotiated relationship.

Process

Slavery was not a negotiated relationship. Nothing could be further from the truth. Slaves struggled within the limits of the institution and against the indignity, inhumanity, heartache and terror that comprised their daily reality, just so as not to commit suicide from utter demoralization.[52] To characterize those life and death struggles as a negotiation suggests they freely accepted slavery as part of some agreement.

Indentured servitude, where terms and length of service were, in fact, largely negotiable, might properly have been called a negotiated relationship. Slavery, however, was "a *power* relationship"[53] whose "state of war" as John Locke described it,[54] was universally lamented by almost all slaves, including the generally better-treated house servants,[55] yet that truth has been rejected and displaced by those having difficulty accepting the institution as it was remembered by the former slaves.

As Edmund Morgan laments:

what slaves remembered most vividly about slavery was not the degree of autonomy they were able to negotiate. What stands out in all these interviews in grim monotony is the unrelenting dominance of masters, maintained by regular whipping and torture, sometimes by exemplary murder. What former slaves remembered about their work . . . was the lash that set the pace for it. . . . What they remembered about their family structure was the whippings they had to watch one another endure . . .[56]

"Enslavement was captivity," explained historian Winthrop Jordan, "the loser's lot in a contest of power."[57] Countryman echoed "there was no place in early-eighteenth-century America where being black did not also mean being enslaved, stripped of all honor, and subjected to some European's absolute, total power."[58]

Enemies,
Feel my energies;
four centuries of anger.
Remember me?
The field Niggah?

REDMAN: "Well All Rite Cha"
DOC'S DA NAME 2000 /Rush/Def Jam Records

PRELIMINARY NEGOTIATIONS

Early coercive measures designed for servants were adjusted to motivate slaves who "could not be made to work for fear of losing liberty," explains Morgan, "so they had to be made to fear for their lives," to no avail unless masters were free from criminal liability for going too far.[59] The Virginia assembly therefore passed, in 1669, an Act that officially gave birth to what we refer to today as terrorism:

An Act about the casual killing of slaves:

Whereas the only law in force for the punishment of refractory servants resisting their master, mistris or overseer cannot be inflicted upon negroes [extending the time of service], nor [can] the obstinacy of many of them by other than violent means [be] supprest. Be it enacted and declared by this grand assembly, if any slave resist his master (or other by his masters order correcting him) and by the extremity of the correction should chance to die, that his death shall not be accompted Felony, but the master (or that other person appointed by the master to punish him) be acquit from molestation, since it cannot be presumed that prepensed malice (which alone makes murther Felony) should induce any man to destroy his own estate.[60]

Such punishments included the following, requested by Robert Carter, in a court order from 1707, the period claimed by Berlin to have been comparatively mild:

Robert Carter Esq. Complaining to this Court against two Incorrigible negroes of his named Bambarra Harry and Dinah and praying the order of this Court for punishing the said Negroes by dismembering them It is therefore ordered That for the better reclaiming the said negroes and deterring others from ill practices That the said Robert Carter Esq. have full power according to Law to dismember the said negroes or Either of them by cutting of their toes.[61]

The Law referred to was the Virginia Code of 1705, widely adopted and utilized among the several slave states. Maryland, for example, "passed a law in 1723 providing for cutting off the ears of blacks who struck whites, and that for certain serious crimes, slaves should be hanged and the body quartered and exposed."[62] I felt a particularly horrific chill upon learning fire was among the favored instruments of punishment and coercion used against slaves, as codified in a 1798 Virginia law intended to deter runaways, providing that an offender be "burned in the hand."[63].

As a child of approximately five-years-old, I was sent to the corner store to pick up a loaf of bread and was given the exact amount of change. I arrived to find the bread already bagged and waiting to be picked up. Gladys, my foster mother, had apparently called ahead with the order. As I remember it, I reached up with both hands to place the change on the counter and at the same time pulled the bread down, while slyly, I thought, also grabbing a piece of candy from the counter top, an irresistible temptation. I headed out the store without saying anything and without paying for the candy.

Gladys had apparently already been told of the theft, the storeowner having saw it and called her right after my exit. As soon as I opened the back door and stepped into the kitchen, Gladys furiously grabbed my arm and snatched me inside, sending the bag with the bread flying across the room. She then rifled through my pockets and, discovering the candy, asked if I'd just taken it from the store without paying for it. Horrified, I shouted, "No Ma'am! No

Ma'am!," using the formal, respectful address she demanded at all times.

With a death grip on my slight arm, she angrily dragged me, kicking and screaming, around the kitchen to the cooking area, while screaming repeatedly: "Oh Yeah! You wanna steal? Ahma teach you to steal alright!" I frantically cried out that I didn't mean it and wouldn't do it again. I was of course terrified being unable to physically fend off such a strong, big-boned, burly woman full of rage. I had no idea what was about to happen, except that my punishment would be swift and fierce, as usual.

In an instant, Gladys snatched my hand over the stove and quickly turned one of the gas burners on to a high, flickering, angry blue fire, clutching my arm with both her hands and holding it over the flame, seemingly with all her might while I screamed and tried in vain to free myself; the tips of my toes barely touched the floor and didn't allow me the necessary leverage to pull myself free. As my arm and body were yanked powerfully forward, I could literally hear the fire ferociously blowing and roaring.

The crazed focus of Gladys' eyes and her vice-like grip on my arm made me believe she seriously meant to burn me, sending me into even more hysterics as I fought with the desperation of a trapped wild animal to free myself. The frantic struggle, along with the heat built up in the small alcove, caused both Gladys' hands and my arms to sweat, making it difficult for her to maintain the death grip on my hand and steady it over the flame without slipping, thus saving me from serious injury. When she finally tired and released me I burst out the back door into the yard, ran down the alleyway after hopping the fence, and collapsed.

There is, moreover, some evidence that such depraved behavior is in fact passed down through generations.[64] No less than Thomas Jefferson foretold of slavery's inevitable consequences in his much-quoted description of slavery's tyranny from his *Notes On The State Of Virginia*:

the whole commerce between master and slave is a perpetual exercise of the most boisterous passions, the most unremitting despotism on the one part, and degrading submissions on the other. Our children see this, and learn to imitate it; for man is an imitative animal. This quality is the germ of all education in him. From his cradle to his grave he is learning to do what he sees others do . . . The parent storms, the child looks on, catches the lineaments of wrath, puts on the same airs in the circle of smaller slaves, gives a loose to the worst of passions, and thus nursed, educated and daily exercised in tyranny, cannot but be stamped by it with odious peculiarities. The man must be a prodigy who can retain his manners and morals undepraved by such circumstances.[65]

No, slavery was no negotiation. It was a system of laws and practices designed to instill maximum terror, the only system that could guarantee success. No method of compulsion was too horrific or inhumane for many slaveholders, if not most, who would then stop at nothing.

To be sure, not all slaveowners were murderous rapists, and to characterize them all as such is also not the complete truth. However, no morality exemption should be given to so-called *kind* masters, many of whom, such as the supposedly benevolent James Madison, for example, apparently also believed slavery to be a negotiation. During a visit to his plantation by British author Harriet Martineau, he acknowledged having sold a dozen slaves just the previous week, an event that no doubt generated several thousand dollars of income. "He accounted for selling his slaves," relates Martineau, "by mentioning their horror of going to Liberia, a horror which he admitted to be prevalent among the blacks," referring to Madison's participation in the American Colonization Society, as a means to alleviate his "despair" for having owned slaves over the entire course of his lifetime, the despair being heightened, no doubt, by the impending sense of his own death.[66]

Founded in 1817, The Society established Liberia on Africa's west coast, adjacent to Sierra Leone, as a home for emancipated American slaves, because, according to Madison, "If the blacks, strongly marked as they are by physical & lasting peculiarities, be retained amid the whites, under the degrading privation of equal rights political or social, they must be always dissatisfied with their condition as a change from one to another species of oppression."[67] And, according to Martineau, he mentioned "how the free states discourage the settlements of blacks; how Canada disagrees with them; how Hayti shuts them out; so that Africa is their only refuge," although, she added, "he did not assign any reason why they should not remain where they are when freed."[68]

An important consideration by the Society was that placement ought to be "equitable and satisfactory to the individuals immediately concerned," which, as to the slave, meant "his condition in a state of freedom, be preferable in his own estimation, to his actual one in a state of bondage,"[69] a "willing mind" being, of course, "the first requisite to the emigrant's success."[70] If, however, emigration to Africa was not "satisfactory" to the slave, it apparently meant he or she would have to be sold, undoubtedly accounting for the "horror prevalent among the blacks." As a simple "yes or no" proposition, going to Liberia doesn't seem, in itself, very frightful. But when you add to that proposition the prospect of being immediately torn from family and home to be sold into the deep South if you refuse, well, that's some scary shit! The simple fact is, for Black Africans in America, a "negotiation," slavery was not.

If European Americans want to separate from the undignified and inhumane legacy of slavery, which, apparently, they desperately do, extending Reparations are therefore crucial.

RACE

3

Racism Matters

My life -- Do you feel what i feel?
My life -- Do you see what i see?
Have you been where i been?
Can you go where i go? -- My life.
Do y'all know what it feels like?
Do y'all know what it be like?

Foxy Brown: "My Life"
Chyna Doll /Violator Records

As one of slavery's more recognizable legacies, race has been as much a fixture of American identity since Emancipation as before, despite many curious claims to the contrary, morphing into an intractable infection trapping many Americans in an embarrassing state of agonizing confusion, manifest partly in this desire to romanticize the history of slavery. This section represents some cursory examples of just how deeply this legacy is ingrained into the minds and institutions of America, including academia, the media, government and business.

The Balls Of Academia

Showing he too has the disease, Ivy league historian Edmund Morgan laments the slaves' seeming uniform focus on slavery's brutality. Outside of his support for the promotion of a lighter side of slavery, Morgan doesn't exactly articulate his reasoning. His feelings, however, are easily understood from the thoughts he offers in a review of four books on slavery for the *New York Review of Books*:

Many Thousands Gone, by Berlin; *Slave Counterpoint*, by Philip D. Morgan; *Remembering Slavery*, edited by Berlin along with two others; and *Africans in America*, by Patricia Smith and Charles Johnson. The reviews are noteworthy because they have a particular bearing on popular perceptions of slavery's meaning and value — and therefore on the merits of Reparations — and because they highlight troubling aspects of race relations in America today.

The two books Morgan reviews unfavorably, *Remembering Slavery* and *Africans in America,* are told from a Black perspective. That is, without the overlaying sugarcoated theories, aside from a lengthy Introduction in *Remembering Slavery* written by Berlin. The other two books, by Ira Berlin and Philip Morgan, share the undertone of slavery as a negotiated relationship, discussed above, allowing them to be comfortably read by European Americans who would rather understand slavery without the associated "guilt trip," which, Morgan acknowledges, offers support to present-day racism, as the authors themselves well know. He writes,

> Whatever guilt we may feel for slavery stops short of repudiating our national heroes . . . Their sins have to be attributed to a system in which everybody was involved, including the slaves, whose necessary participation was an embarrassment to men like Washington and Jefferson. Guilt feelings are a continuation of that embarrassment, and racism is a way of exorcising it by blaming the victims and their descendents. [71]

By essentially assigning slaves the responsibility for their own inhumane, degraded station, through their "participation" in the system, the motives behind Ira Berlin's, "negotiated relationship," based on the logic of Edmund Morgan, must therefore be attributed to racism. Not surprisingly, however, Morgan stops short of an indictment. In fact, he is so averse to the claim that he instead encourages us, in what seems an amazing contradiction, to believe Berlin's motives are actually "to induce a greater respect by whites for the 'Negro Past' and a greater pride in it on the part of blacks."[72] "If slave culture was a mode of opposing slavery," he reasons, then "the study of it is surely a mode of opposing racism."[73]

And it very well may be, depending on who's doing the studying and how they interpret it, but it certainly could just as well *promote* racism. In any event, as has been appropriately recognized by one reviewer, "History should not be written with the intent to help: it is scholarship, not social work, and its only criterion of success is truth."[74]

But in light of his rather bold observation about guilt and racism, which ring all too true, Morgan's avoidance of accountability in his reviews seems somewhat curious. A close reading of his opinion on the books, however, offers some interesting insight. He writes:

> The resuscitation of slave culture by . . . historians should ultimately gain its exponents the respect that slave owners could not grant. But that respect requires the sophisticated understanding that *only* books like [Philip D.] Morgan's and Berlin's can supply. Understanding *requires* a recognition . . . , that slavery was a negotiated relationship.[75]

Here, we find Edmund Morgan brazenly designating Berlin's romantic theory as the "only" respectable standard through which to view slavery. Never mind that Berlin has altered the truth to support his claims; that fact simply qualifies his work as "sophisticated," and gives it "scholarly integrity."[76]

Why does accepting the truth about slavery "require" it be told from Berlin's romanticized perspective? Obviously, the truth is a blow to the European American claim to a superior morality. Preserving that claim seems to be Edmund Morgan's chief objective. He readily describes slavery as America's "Big Crime," so why then the indignation at seeing the "criminals" implicated? Furthermore, why would he even care since, as he says, slavery "is over."[77]

It's hard to read the stories the former slaves tell in *Remembering Slavery* without feeling pity, he says, but evidently, the ones to be pitied are himself and other European American readers. That is why he "requires" historians to place their slavery writings in the context he finds most comfortable, to be considered worthy of "respect." He is little concerned for Washington's legacy, and less for the dignity of Black slaves and their tormented lives. His major concern is upholding a notion of White moral supremacy — something the truly inhumane details of slavery makes very difficult. Thus we have Ira Berlin presenting slavery as a "partnership" and, essentially, "blaming the victims."[78] And that is also why virtually all the reviewers of *Many Thousands Gone* bought every bit of Ira Berlin's theory of a "negotiated relationship." Not because it's the truth, but because they desperately want to, need to, maintain the feeling of European American moral superiority, welcoming anything supporting it.

That is also why European Americans generally do not support slavery Reparations. As an inherent indictment of White supremacy,

Reparations is generally deemed "polemic"[79]; Affirmative Action "divisive." To quote *Wall Street Journal* editor Dan Henninger, the mere discussion of Reparations creates "acrimony" between the races.[80]

No amount of context can make a slaveowner a humane, moral individual. All European Americans were not slaveowners, even among the Southern European American population, although some of those, no doubt, would have liked to[81] but didn't because of moral misgivings. And many who did own slaves freed them for the same reasons.

We're not talking the Ice Age here. This was the era of the Enlightenment. The intelligent minds of early America, including Jefferson, Madison, Hamilton and Franklin, must be judged by the same standards of intelligence and morality as others of their time. No excuses. You cannot on the one hand praise them for being highly sophisticated, intelligent and courageous, and then excuse their terrorist transgressions on the ground that a small minority of contemporaries were doing the same thing. The fact that so many of America's founding leaders were slaveholders, men supposedly of high moral character, is a testament to the critical importance of slavery to this country. There can be no doubt that Washington, Jefferson and Madison, who all made clear their deep personal misgivings about owning slaves, understood the depraved moral implications of it. Jefferson was in fact reportedly ashamed to have his name publicly associated with the institution. None, however, used his power or stature to bring the institution to an end — because their lives depended on it. Patricia Smith was therefore right on to present what Cornell West might refer to as a "morally mature view" of both Washington and Jefferson in *Africans In America*,[82] but Edmund Morgan found this to be problematic. "The very quaintness of the language in which we hear of unspeakable tortures, casually related as they were casually given, serves to aggravate the horror," he says, and "it only requires a few words from Smith to twist the knife,"[83] referring to Smith's work as an "exercise in sentimentality."

The moral issue simply comes down to this: did they know the wrong in what they were doing and did they have opportunities to prevent or stop it? True, Washington and Jefferson were both born into slavery. Yet, that alone is not a sufficient excuse. Once they became old enough to learn what it entailed they made a conscious decision to continue their involvement, including in its gruesome terrorism and trafficking aspects.

Maintaining the rhythm of labor, moreover, also required discipline and punishment, which meant the threat of being sold away from family and loved ones always existed, terrorizing enough in itself. Despite a perceived lenient policy or mandate of an owner, severe coercion was commonly the resort of overseers whose remuneration was tied to levels of productivity, set by the owner/planter. No matter how benevolent Washington may have thought he was, or how happy Jefferson may have thought his slaves were, purchases, sales, resistance and recalcitrance were always a part of the business. There is no "context" that can supercede, mitigate, or qualify this reality.

On every slave ship crossing the Atlantic, large numbers of slaves, sometimes all, died from disease, suicide, murder or any host of other causes, including sheer exhaustion. Those who owned the ships, as well as those who bought and sold the slaves, are all then personally implicated in those deaths — essentially murder. As David Landes explained, in *The Wealth And Poverty Of Nations*, "To lose one in seven was considered normal; one in three or four, excessive but pardonable. Every day's sail cost lives — no slave ship [was] without its escort of sharks."[84]

Patricia Smith, in my opinion, was not only justified, but obligated to present Washington and Jefferson in their true light: avaricious and immoral. Those Black African souls who perished on the Atlantic and in slavery were all mothers, fathers, sons, and daughters — human beings — not inanimate objects. I never fail to grieve when reading the narratives that tell so vividly of the endless despair and torment the slaves suffered. Edmund Morgan also grieves when he reads the slaves' narratives, but, apparently, not for the slaves.

The fact is, from Columbus to the Founding Fathers, immoral people established America upon immoral principles. They were not all outstanding leaders, many were not even respectable human beings. No credit should temper that truth. But the "passive voice" Morgan seems to be promoting "helps to insulate historical figures from their own unheroic or unethical deeds."[85]

Is there any wonder why America's minority students tune out to history in schools today?[86] With twenty-five years' experience teaching in public schools, Julie Landsman, in *A White Teacher Talks About Race*, writes "in order to hold our students' attention, I believe that the continuum of history — its influence on present-day economics, politics, neighborhoods, and the law — must be presented in all its multifaceted complexity. . . I speak here about nothing less than presenting the truth, in its difficult and troublesome entirety."[87]

Instead, we have Edmund Morgan explaining to the "exponents" of slave history that the "only" way their work will be respected, i.e. credible and acceptable, is if it conforms to the theories of Ira Berlin. Such a mandate effectively ensures a continued distortion of history.

DIVERSE MISCONCEPTION

With this seeming mandate to rewrite history, it's not at all difficult to see how we get to the point reached by author Peter Wood, in a book titled *Diversity: The Invention of a Concept*. As garden variety, anti-diversity fare the book is unremarkable, except that it posits "Diversity" as, among other things, unconstitutional and, well, essentially un-American.

Says Wood: "A well designed republic might have the capacity to thwart the naturally destructive tendency of diversity," which "is a challenge to higher virtues and greater goods. We jeopardize liberty and equality by our friendship with this new principle. It is an unruly guest in our house, and the time has come to call a cab and send it home."[88] Aside from the fact that the statement makes no sense (equality is irrelevant sans diversity), the "We" Wood refers to is, of course, obvious. He believes he is addressing patriotic Americans, but since he is expressly anti-Diversity the America he identifies with is decidedly non-diverse. The "hither virtues" of "our" house, he reminds fellow patriots, will be ruined unless America's less-virtuous, diverse elements are sent "home," although he doesn't say exactly where "home" is. Most clearly, however, Wood's intent is to spur a surge of anti-diversity patriotism, in opposition to Affirmative Action and immigration. His is a loyal, though misguided, contribution to a significant groundswell of energy dedicated to the same effort.

Woods conflates James Madison's promotion of protections for diverse interests with a denunciation of diversity. At best, this is just plain wrong. At worst, it's intellectually dishonest. Madison, in fact, promoted republican government precisely because it provides for a diversity of interests — including minority interests — which generally are overrun in democracies, a.k.a. "popular government," by what Madison saw as the most dangerous "faction": the majority. At the Constitutional Convention, he stated:

> In all cases where a majority are united by a common interest or passion, the rights of the minority are in danger. What motives are to restrain them? . . . we have seen the mere distinction of colour made in the most enlightened period of time, a ground of the most oppressive dominion ever exercised by man over man. What has been

the source of those unjust laws complained of among ourselves? Has it not been the real or supposed interest of the major numbers?[89]

And in *The Federalist*, no. 10, he wrote:

As long as the reason of man continues fallible, and he is at liberty to exercise it, different opinions will be formed. . . . The diversity in the faculties of men, from which the rights of property originate, is not less an insuperable obstacle to a uniformity of interests. The protection of these faculties is the first object of government. . . .
   When a majority is included in a faction the form of popular government . . . enables it to sacrifice to its ruling passion or interest both the public good and the rights of other citizens. To secure the public good and private rights against the danger of such a faction, and at the same time to preserve the spirit and the form of popular government is then the great object to which our inquiries are directed.[90]

Although there is often disagreement on the meaning of much in the Constitution, the writings left behind by Madison are so voluminous it would be difficult to be mistaken as to exactly what his views were. But one thing almost every American should know is that Madison was a champion of republican government, the very reason we do not have a pure democracy. Madison knew having a check on the majority was an essential feature of the new government and not having such a check would make the Constitution unacceptable to the people, and thus could not be ratified. Wood's interpretation, however, is in direct conflict with this idea.
   Determined to use Madison to sanction his racist bent, Wood nevertheless states, "The most that Madison could say in favor of diversity was that if the republic were sufficiently large and the 'variety of parties' sufficiently great, the chances of 'one party being able to outnumber and oppress the rest' would be diminished."[91] However, "Controlling" that oppressive "evil," as Madison referred to it, was, in fact, the Framers' main objective. "Every *peculiar* interest . . . ought to be secured as far as possible," said Madison. "Whenever there is danger of attack there ought be given a constitutional power of defense."[92] Although, the Constitution has seemingly left minority interests powerless against non-governmental institutions, such as academia. But "where a majority are united by a common sentiment," wrote Madison,

and have an opportunity, the rights of the minor party become insecure. In a Republican Gov[ernment] the Majority if united have always an opportunity. The *only* remedy is to enlarge the sphere, & thereby divide the community into so great a number of interests & parties, that in the 1st place a majority will not be likely at the same moment to have a common interest separate from that of the whole or of the minority; and in the 2nd place, that in case they sh[ould] have such an interest, they may not be apt to unite in the pursuit of it. It was incumbent on us then to try this remedy, and with that view to frame a republican system on such a scale & in such a form as will controul all the evils w[hich] have been experienced.[93]

Wood, might rightfully question whether race was ever contemplated within Madison's "sphere" of diverse interests, however, since Madison himself was a lifelong slaveholder. But even as to this apparent dichotomy the "Father of the Constitution" seemed more clear, in his late years. Addressing the Virginia Convention, in December, 1829, he stated

In Republics, the great danger is that the majority may not sufficiently respect the rights of the minority. Some gentlemen, consulting the purity and generosity of their own minds, without adverting to the lessons of experience, would find a security against that danger in our social feelings; [and] in the aggregate interests of the community. . . . We all know that conscience is not a sufficient safeguard, besides that conscience itself may be deluded; many being misled by an unconscious bias into acts which an enlightened conscience would forbid. . . . The only effectual safeguard to the rights of the minority must be laid in such a basis & structure of the Government itself as may afford, in a certain degree, directly or indirectly, a defensive authority in behalf of a minority having right on its side.
To come more nearly to the subject . . . I mean the coloured part of our population. . . . if we can incorporate that interest into the basis of our system, it will be the most apposite and effectual security that can be devised. . . . It is due to justice: due to humanity: due to truth; to the sympathies of our nature: in fine, to our character as a people, both abroad and at home, that they should be considered, as much as possible, in the light of human beings; . . . As such they are acted upon by our laws; and have an interest in our laws. . . . the mere circumstance of complexion cannot deprive them of the character of men.[94]

Madison was not, of course, advocating the elimination of slavery, explaining in a subsequent letter to the Revolutionary War hero, Lafayette: "I scarcely express myself too strongly in saying, that an allusion in the Convention to [abolition], would have been a spark to a mass of Gunpowder."[95]

Madison: Diverse disposition.?

WHY RACE MATTERS

Another interesting manifestation of this racist, anti-diversity attitude, to say the least, is from Michael Levin, who proudly goes to astonishing lengths in denigrating Black Americans with unabashed hubris in a book titled *Why Race Matters*. He lays out justifications for racial inequality in pro-slavery style arguments that would no doubt make Thomas Jefferson proud, entirely dismissing Blacks from having played any significant role in history and mixing what he supposes to be irrefutable science with more than a little personal bias, and a generous heaping helping of distorted historical fact about why Blacks do not deserve consideration as the equal of European Americans, and thus why White Americans should oppose Affirmative Action, proving, contrary to the assertions of many concerning its demise, racism is alive and flourishing in America.

In his defense, however, Levin's distortions are merely an indictment of an American educational system that teaches a ridiculously biased perspective of history.[96] Although, he is a university professor, so he really has no excuse, even if his expertise is Philosophy.

Levin:

As [every White] knows but has become reluctant to say, the world as a whole would hardly have noticed had sub-Saharan Africa not existed or never been contacted by Europeans and Asians. No important discovery, invention, or world leader emerged from Africa.

The art, music, architecture, literature, and political history of Eurasia owe virtually nothing to Africans. Trade with black Africa (as opposed to European exploitation of the mineral wealth of the African continent) has always been negligible. Afrocentrists point to or, . . . exaggerate, the contributions of Egypt, but in any event Egyptians were not black.

Blacks in the United States . . . played no role in the construction of the major American cities, and had little contact with the nineteenth century immigrants who influenced the country's character . . . Benjamin Banneker's design of the District of Columbia, seem to be fiction . . . While the patent office keeps no racial statistics, it seems likely that blacks hold disproportionately few patents. . . . Few blacks have achieved eminence in areas other than sports, entertainment, the demand for rights, or writing about race itself.

Afrocentrists accuse conventional white authorities of inventing these facts. But white historians, who freely acknowledge the attainments of Asians, have no reason to lie about blacks. The truth is that, until recently, most whites gave blacks relatively little thought, and would not have cared enough about blacks one way or the other to invest energy in obscuring their achievements. Blacks simply have not mattered as much to the white world as Afrocentrists implicitly claim they did — and perhaps wish they did, for having powerful enemies is considerably more flattering than being ignored. The limited interest in blacks shown by conventional historians is best explained by the belief that further interest was unwarranted.[97]

Upon reading this interesting bit of wishful thinking I had to sit back and wonder, incredulously, after a good laugh out loud, "Can it actually be true that an entire sub-continent has made absolutely no significant contribution to the advancement of civilization and mankind?" Such a people must necessarily have perished from an inability to even sustain themselves, absent some capacity to adapt and evolve,[98] or have been entirely dependent upon other cultures for their evolution and survival — the very point Levin is attempting to sell readers.

Black Africans and those descended from the pan-African Diaspora, however, most certainly have not perished. On the contrary, we are a vibrant, lively and prolific people the world over, having survived, indeed thrived, despite suffering through generations of unconscionable terror, torture, and inhumanity, unlike the many proud, mighty Native cultures who succumbed to the sadistic barbarity of avaricious Europeans, which in itself would seem to be an unparalleled contribution to the advancement of civilization. And

European Americans certainly cannot claim Africans were wholly dependent on them for survival because, if anything, we know the exact opposite to be true. The premises offered by Levin therefore are entirely unsupported by the facts of history. But then, making a statement of historical fact is not the goal. His aim is purely to promote the notion of White supremacy, and in the process pollute as many hearts and minds as possible with his personal race bias. As James Loewen highlights, "[i]t is always useful to think badly about people one has exploited, or plans to exploit."[99]

Unfortunately, as evidenced by Thomas Jefferson's *Notes On The State Of Virginia*, and so many others, generations of Americans, both White and Black, are affected by these ideas, which of course is the desired affect: make Blacks believe they are not the equal of European Americans so that they don't earnestly push for equality, believing themselves to be unworthy[100]; at the same time, reinforce the notion European Americans want so desperately to believe: they are the sole contributors to the progress and development of civilization, especially America and the West, and are therefore entitled to and deserving of supreme status over people of color, particularly Africans and Americans of African descent.

The passage cited on the previous pages comes from just one and a half pages of Levin's book, which is chock full of similar ranting, equally extolling the supposed majestic accomplishments of European Americans and the comparatively pathetic, non-accomplishments of Blacks. Suffice it to say that after reading this particular bit of "history," I was positively seeing red. If a single factor can be said to have motivated me to write this book, *Why Race Matters* is it. In the twenty-first century, Blacks simply cannot afford to allow the clock to be turned back to the eighteenth century where Levin's brand of thinking flourished and led to the destruction of countless Black lives. Levin doesn't exactly call for the extermination of Blacks, but his attitude, seen as "chutzpah" by some European Americans,[101] suggests that may be proper. Those who lack an understanding as to why "White Pride" carries a negative public connotation need look no further than Levin's mentality. History reveals all too painfully where such notions of a master race lead. But, sadly, many European Americans, led by influential academics, nevertheless continue to roil against the presence of Blacks and other diverse cultures in this country and around the world.[102]

4

Media & Politics

First ship 'em dope

and let 'em deal to brothers.

Then give 'em guns,

step back,

and watch 'em kill each other.

Tupac Shakur: "Changes"/*Greatest Hits*
Death Row/Interscope

Meet The (full court) Press

Much has been made in America of a supposed liberal bias within the mainstream media. A certain conservative ideology, however, particularly with regard to race, gets plenty of traction on the national networks and cable television, even PBS, but is largely unacknowledged. One example of this can regularly be seen on none other than television's Meet The Press with Tim Russert, who, as the lauded all-American, family man, speciously uses the show to promote his personal race bias and influence American racial politics. Seemingly every Black politician visiting his Sunday morning show must address supposed problems of social morality in the Black community, but rarely, however, is he seen confronting Whites on his show about racism, that age-old staple of European American immorality.

In August, 2002, for instance, Russert questioned then prospective presidential candidate Al Sharpton about , among other things, the disproportionately high percentage of single-parent, Black households and out-of-wedlock pregnancies in the Black community. It is, I would learn, by far the favored race topic on his Sunday talk show. However, the questions rather troublingly struck me as a seeming biased indictment of Black morality not raised with other so-called mainstream politicians, in that election or since, as he is invariably selected to moderate elections of national and statewide importance. however, But when interviewing newly elected Senator Barack Obama prior to the 2004 Democratic National Convention, one of the first questions to come out of Tim Russert's mouth centered on a reported seventy-five percent of African American children in Illinois born out of wedlock.

Choosing his words carefully in his first Meet The Press appearance, Obama appeared to play both sides, acknowledging the "problem" while also asserting that the solution should be economic as well as one of "individual responsibility," surprising, given his stated "inten[tion] to give voice to those [Black] men on the street corners who have no work and very little hope,"[103] the very subjects of Russert's ire. Obama also appeared to contradict his later, though wildly popular, nationally-televised Convention statement asserting "there's no Black America, no White America and no Latino America," which, if true, would mean we've finally reached the promised land of Dr. King's Dream. But, ironically, even the conservative, tragically-subservient Colin Powell has acknowledged "we ain't arrived."[104] Introducing soon-to-be president, George W. Bush, at the podium of the Republican National Convention in 2000, Powell said, "The issue of race still casts a shadow over our society. Despite the impressive progress we have made over the last 40 years to overcome this legacy of our troubled past, it is still with us."[105] Obama, at the risk of being at odds with White America, had no such courage.

In questioning the Reverend Sharpton and Barack Obama on the issue of illegitimate childbirths, Tim Russert, it seems, was ostensibly judging the Black community morally responsible for its own perpetually subordinate economic and social status. He is interested mainly in influencing the "collective imagination" of Whites inclined to support national policy solutions, and relieving them of any responsibility for seriously engaging the problems, as Angela Davis described it, "especially those produced by racism."[106] Through demonization, the country can look on with a clear conscience at the

continued marginalization of Black America, to the benefit of the
dominant hegemony of White supremacy.

To quote Jewell Handy Gresham:

> whenever blacks get restless (or show strength); whenever whites in
> significant numbers show signs of coming together with blacks to
> confront their mutual problems (or enemies), the trick is to shift the
> focus from the real struggle for political and economic empowerment
> to black "crime," degeneracy, pathology and . . . "deterioration" of the
> black family.[107]

News personalities like Tim Russert are, of course, "more famous
than most movie stars and more powerful than most politicians."[108]
"Like it or not," explained former CBS anchor Dan Rather, "people
key off you."[109] With his considerable television experience and
exposure, no one knows this better than Russert. As the so-called
"most respected man in America," he had the power to single-
handedly compromise the appeal, if any, of Sharpton's message to
White voters, and, no doubt, to more than a few Blacks as well. But
the effort was conspicuous for the very reason that it was unnecessary.
Sharpton's chances of actually securing the Democratic party's
nomination were only slim, at best, though he knew, as did Russert, a
Black presence in the election would assure at least some attention to
issues of importance to the Black community. He was therefore
willing to be the bad guy. As Hall Of Fame basketball player Charles
Barkley might describe it, he was "willing to be ridiculed," the result
of advocating for racial equality.[110] In my opinion, however, that
sacrifice alone made the Reverend more qualified to be President
than Bush Jr. or Sr. In hindsight, could he have fared any worse?

On the urgency of moving into Iraq, the President, in fact, stated,
"We owe it to future generations to deal with this problem,"[111] though
the astronomical price tag of that conflict has considerably strapped
future generations. But what about America's Black, Native
American, or Latino youth who stand a greater likelihood of going to
prison than to college?[112] Nothing over in Iraq or that region of the
world addresses their dilemma here at home. Diverting some of the
money spent in Iraq to educate youth in America seems a much more
effective and secure investment for future generations.

"When an 18 year old Palestinian girl is induced to blow herself up,
and in the process kills a 17 year old Israeli girl, the President was
also quoted saying, the future itself is dying."[113] However,
disenfranchised Black and Latino youth are blowing each other away

on the streets of urban America in increasingly shocking numbers.[114] A mere percentage of the $400 billion-plus — and counting — spent in Iraq most certainly would make a difference, and maybe save some lives here at home. Yet the President is unconcerned. Such indifference is why it was crucial to have the Reverend Sharpton in the election, even if he realistically had no chance of winning. Tim Russert's demonization can therefore be seen as an tyrannical attempt, on the part of the majority, to undermine Black America's ability to seek political redress.

It's not surprising then to see Russert cleverly getting powerful Representative Charles Rangel of NY to begrudgingly state on national television, in April 2007, that Barack Obama is "not as qualified as Hillary Clinton" to be president, and that he supports Mrs. Clinton for their party's nomination, even after personally encouraging Obama to enter the race. To be sure, coming from the Black Congressman from Harlem, the statement carries an entirely different weight with Whites than, for example, *The Washington Post* curiously saying that given the "dialogue of race" they're engaged in, and its "parsing of perceptions and expectations, Hillary "has a more high-powered political resume than the former state legislator and first-term senator," even though, in fact, Mrs. Clinton has not held elected office longer than has Mr. Obama."[115] She's no doubt been credited with the experience of her husband's eight years in the White House, though it's doubtful many other women across America are considered amply qualified for a job based solely on the related experience of their husbands. Unless, of course, their main competition for the job happens to be a Black man.

Chagrined, with polls showing, in December 2007, that Obama might actually win the party nomination, Russert asks him "Why don't you wait? Why'd you have to run now?"

It's also then not surprising an entire hour of Meet The Press was devoted to the demonization of Black youth in October of that year by the dreadfully confused Bill Cosby, he of the infamous I Have To Scream speech, promoting a book written with, also predictable, a Harvard academic, presumably to give intellectual credibility to Cosby's blathering nonsense. It was a supreme hour for Russert, gushing in all his White pride glory for having gotten a famous, though borderline senile, Black man to do his dirty work for him. Mission accomplished.

On the other hand, Tim Russert invites comment about Don Imus ("nappy-headed Ho's") from Senator Joe Biden of Delaware, who famously described Barack Obama as the "first clean, articulate, mainstream African American candidate" to run for the presidency. Go figure. Effectively, Biden's comments were the mirror image of Imus's; describing Obama as "clean" and "articulate" is really just a P-C way of saying he's *not* a nappy-headed Ho. He apparently thought otherwise of previous Black presidential candidates, however, like Jesse Jackson, for instance.

As ignorant as his comments were, Imus' job, after all, is to talk. His comments therefore carry only the significance of so much hot air. But Senator Biden is a powerful voice in our nation's public councils (Yikes!). And "leaders of the country," to use his own words, "cannot engage in this kind of talk and the way we characterize people . . . and think it doesn't permeate society."

I CAN ONLY GUESS WHAT'S HAPPENIN' YEARS AGO HE WOULDA BEEN A SHIP'S CAPTAIN.

Public Enemy: "Can't Truss It"
Apocalypse 91...The Enemy Strikes Black
Sony/Def Jam Records

Reparations

It so happened that Tim Russert also aggressively pressed the Rev. Sharpton on what Blacks may or may not be owed from centuries of slavery, abuse, discrimination and disenfranchisement in America, seemingly implying that Blacks dissatisfied with their status represent enemies of the State, or, presumably, that Blacks in fact owe a debt to America. Rightly or wrongly, I interpreted the exchange as an indictment of Reparations advocacy, and an attempt to use the Reverend to further steel White America against the idea.

With respect to patriotic accountability, Blacks owe America the same responsibility as all other citizens: the duty to see to it the country lives up to its guarantees of liberty and equality for all. Tim Russert, of course, isn't concerned one bit about citizens being shortchanged on America's promise of equality. He expects unequivocal allegiance regardless, showing what might fairly be described as a serious "failure of the historical imagination," to borrow a term from journalist/author Michael Ignatieff.[116]

Conservatives, both Black and White, readily place the causes of Black illegitimacy on some moral deficiency. Few seem willing to trace the history of the problem back to its slave origins and, in fact, are adamantly opposed to such thought, apparently because of its moral implications for Whites.[117] There's no hesitation, however, to harken back to America's founding settlers for anything having to do with the origins of perceived greatness in American society. This "ahistorical" perspective, as Cornell West describes it, is of course what allows Whites to claim to be a breed apart.[118] Black women's increased risk of pregnancy-related death associated with live-births, for example, is four times higher than for European American women, according to public health experts, and "cannot be explained by available sociodemographic and reproductive variables."[119] This would seem to reference a potential genetic connection to the hegemony of slavery, where miscarriages, stillbirths, and the pregnancy-related deaths of slave women were multiples of European American women, while infant mortality was double.[120] And given the horrors regarding the harsh treatment of slaves during pregnancies, recounted by slavery contemporaries like Fanny Kemble, and others,[121] it seems probable these grave effects stretched far into future generations, particularly considering health care services to the Black community significantly lag those to European Americans.[122] Black American women, it's been acknowledged, "may have risk factors not traditionally considered by health care providers, especially psychological and social stress."[123]

> **"Do do do do, do do do do, the twilight zone calls."**

–Emily Rooney
Greater Boston

LESSER BOSTON

An example of this conservative race bias manifest in the local media can be seen on **PBS** where, at **WGBH** in Boston, Emily Rooney, daughter of Andy Rooney of **CBS** television's 60 Minutes, is the long-time hostess and managing editor of the daily Greater Boston television talk show. A one-time executive producer at **ABC News**, briefly (very) in the early 90's, Ms. Rooney was shown the door, in part for her determination to introduce a more conservative perspective into the Nightly News. In Greater Boston, however, she's seemingly found the perfect vehicle for her conservatism. Despite being on public television in a city with a non-White population greater than 50 percent, she doesn't feel the need "to be evenhanded," saying, "in a talk program it's impossible to be even."[124]

In November, 2002, Rooney interviewed the late attorney Johnny Cochran, who appeared on the show to promote his new book, *A Lawyer's Life*. But, aware of his work on behalf of slavery Reparations, she wants viewers to know that in her mind America's history of slavery is irrelevant, cynically asking Cochran why we should be concerned about something that took place "so long ago?" Likely perceiving his book sales may be affected by his remarks promoting Reparations, Cochran quickly mentioned that the issue wasn't about "a paycheck" for anybody.

Rooney moved on, though she wasn't exactly done promoting her views on race or, I should say, promoting her racist views. Referring to Cochran's client, the embattled, pioneering pop star Michael Jackson, who had recently charged his record label with racism in connection with the way it failed to promote one of his music releases, Ms. Rooney stated how much she hates "people who use race as an excuse for failure," apparently believing racism either doesn't exist or should be ignored. I nearly fell out of my chair.

In a July 2003 segment devoted to the racial profiling of Americans of Middle Eastern descent, in the wake of September 11, Emily Rooney again took the opportunity to assert her firm belief in the degeneracy of Blacks. Citing the recent outbreak of gun violence in Boston's Black Roxbury and Dorchester neighborhoods after a decrease during the 1990's, she anxiously described, with a level of conviction that would have made Dinesh D'Souza extremely proud, the resulting criminal stereotyping of Black males as all but proper.

Exasperated, I informed Ms. Rooney by E-mail that I thought expressions of race bias on public television were inappropriate, unwelcome and unprofessional. She defiantly replied that such "intemperate" objections were potentially "actionable," closing her response with "Do do do do, do do do do — the twilight zone calls."

FOOLS RUSH IN

To avoid the impression that the conservative influence of the media on America's social psyche is solely the fault of Whites, we are obliged to show that Blacks who've found a cushy home among the dollars and non-sense that is the American media monster will also sing the tune, when prompted, lest they find themselves on the outside looking in.

Long-time television talk and sport show host, James Brown, for instance, gave a dutiful, on-air editorial response to the controversy created by conservative radio personality Rush Limbaugh, who, in 2003, said the heralded, oft-injured, professional football quarterback, Donovan McNabb, was a public relations beneficiary of the media's desire "that a Black quarterback do well." The Harvard-educated Brown thought Limbaugh's comments opened up "old wounds," noting that, in his estimation, race relations in America had been "moving along quite nicely."[125] It's hard to know whether the offering was his own idea, but no matter, Fox, his employer at the time, would, in any event, certainly have been pleased. If he'd said anything remotely critical of American race relations on national television he'd no doubt find himself in the unemployment line so fast it would make his head spin.

James Brown did not exactly qualify the basis for his "nice" on-air assessment, though we know the Harvard indoctrination seems to demand an obligatory loyalty to White supremacy from even the most staunch opponents of racism in America — or else. Both former Harvard professors Cornell West and Derrick Bell, in fact, fell on their swords recognizing race inequity inside and outside the school. The silence of some others, on the other hand, is deafening.

How is it, for example, the Secretary of Homeland Security, Michael Chertoff, can show up at Harvard Law School's Institute for Race and Justice, founded by professor Charles J. Ogletree, Jr., on a public relations tour one year after the hurricane Katrina disaster and not face a barrage of criticism about the mismanagement and incompetence at FEMA that compounded the devastation and misery, and cost so many folks in New Orleans everything? By his own admission, the Secretary expected he was entering a hostile environment, no doubt anticipating race questions at the Institute, which likely was seen as the safest such forum to patch the department's shaky public confidence going into the 2006 mid-term elections. Though Republicans lost soundly nevertheless. But to characterize the Secretary's reception as an old-fashioned butt-kissing would be putting it mildly.

Professor Ogletree has, however, criticized his indomitable employer since his stinging literary misstep that, no doubt, was likely engineered by disloyal Harvard factions. His public criticism of the school's pathetic lack of diversity in its athletic administration and coaching ranks seemed in stark contrast to the pass given the school in *All Deliberate Speed* where, discussing his experiences as a law student and faculty member, he avoided not coloring the school or anyone connected with it as racialized. In 1975 Boston, at the height of the notorious school busing furor, Ogletree wrote, those problems were limited to "just across the river."[126]

The precariously fine line between militancy and subservience is a particularly difficult one for those associated with America's leading academic bastion of racism who, rightly, feel they have Harvard to thank for everything they are and have. The experiences of professors Bell and West must also loom quite large. Then, of course, there are also those such as the Indian professor, Mahzarin R. Banaji, whose ethical fortitude and intentions appear to have been seriously clouded by the Harvard mystique. Her unsettling research into subconscious attachments to racism and discrimination cause one to wonder about the seeming detachment of her work from the Black community, which is itself based in a negative stereotype. Though inexcusable, such fine lines are commonly navigated by Black leaders, however.

THE POWELL PERPLEX

The day after the 2000 Republican National Convention, Colin Powell said, on NBC's "Today" show, "This is the time for the party to be challenged. . . we now have a leader in the party, in George W. Bush, who truly is committed to inclusion and diversity. . . . He puts a new face on the party, so I wanted to challenge the party to get behind Governor Bush's message of inclusion."[127]

But Powell did not challenge the party, or George W. Bush, when the United Nations Conference Against Racism was held, the perfect opportunity to prove America to be "that shining city on the hill the world looks up to." His failure to step up and be counted was a particularly stinging slap in the face, not only to Black America, but to all oppressed minorities of the world who would have gained added hope by seeing a Black American leading the Conference.

It should be noted that Powell made his pledge to challenge the party before he was selected by George W. Bush to be Secretary of State. In fact it was before Bush had even been (s)elected to the Presidency, so he would have been on notice of Powell's "challenge" when he chose him as Secretary of State. It must therefore be assumed, that he expected to be challenged!

I wouldn't expect Bush to value a high profile American presence at the Conference Against Racism. But it was the job of Powell to warn him of further erosion of the U.S. image as a supposed moral leader of the free world, particularly on the heels of the U.S.'s snuff of the Kyoto Treaty on the environment, the International Criminal Court, the Biological Weapons Convention, the Geneva Conventions on prisoners of war, the Comprehensive Test Ban Treaty for nuclear weapons testing, the global problem of land mines.[128] Rather than dismiss attendance outright, Powell might have "challenged" the President on why it was in America's best interest to not only be there but to lead the conference. "Our greatest strength is the power of our example to be that shining city on the hill that the whole world looks up to," he stated at the 2000 Convention, "to continue to be that place, we must all work to show the world what our American family can do. That is the challenge. This is the time."[129]

To not atend the Conference, said former National Urban League president Hugh Price, "sends a terrible domestic signal to this country that we don't take these issues seriously."[130] "This is a moment for engaged diplomacy," observed Harold Koh, the former Assistant Secretary of State for Human Rights in the Clinton administration, "the reason that he's Secretary of State is so that he can engage in it, and this is potentially a defining moment for him."[131]

By his own admission, Powell was afraid to confront the race bias of Reagan and Casper Weinberger early in his White House career when they slighted him to his face. "The problem with Reagan and Bush and Weinberger and their ilk," he rationalized, is they never knew, "they never had to live with it."[132] Ever the dutiful soldier, he would much rather tell Black Americans to go to hell, than to say or do anything to cause Whites to think him disloyal. By dutifully accepting those blatant racial slights from Reagan's cronies with a "Yes sir," "Thank you, sir," and a smile, Powell showed his loyalty. That, and only that, is how he was *allowed* to advance as far as he did.

Powell told Henry Louis Gates, Jr. his appeal with Whites was apparently attributable to the fact that he is not visibly "threatening" since he comfortably engages them by not going "off in a corner" somewhere at parties. "There's more to it than that," he said, "but I don't know what it is,"[133] thoroughly brainwashed to believe Blacks are "off in a corner" because they're not comfortable around Whites, or because, unlike himself, they can't hold an intelligent or sophisticated conversation (i.e., they're dumb).

On the contrary, Whites accepted him for the simple reason that he had no real interest in Black equality, or he knew well enough to keep his mouth shut about it, which, of course, is why he's seen as non-

Colin Powell

At the 2000 Republican National Convention
Photo: Mark Humphrey

threatening. I don't care how engaging or charismatic he thinks he is, or how comfortable he may be around Whites, if he were to suddenly begin openly advocating for Black equality, he would most certainly find himself "off in a corner" somewhere. He was, nevertheless, easily convinced he had something that set him apart from other Blacks. And, of course, he swallowed it all, hook, line and sinker.

In the atmosphere of the monumental difficulties engulfing America's Iraq occupation, Powell, for his pivotal role in securing congressional authorization, now finds himself isolated off in a corner somewhere. Though currently enjoying an apparent lucrative demand for his public speaking and lecturing presence, a report of a 2005 Iraq strategy session of statesmen and advisors, convened by the president, depicted Powell as conspicuous by his deafening silence.

The notion that Blacks are not representative of mainstream America unless always, first and foremost, promoting White supremacy, as seemingly articulated by the Delaware senator Joseph Biden, is what directly and indirectly leads to the unscrupulous jailing, unemployment and disenfranchisement of Blacks who don't, or won't, dutifully act and think like Colin Powell and James Brown. This places America at a grave crossroads in this critical stage of its third century. Black America collectively Refuses to go back down that road!

We happen to live in a time when, at the touch of a button, people anywhere can tune into what's going on everywhere. Why would Iraq buy into a new government based on American style democracy when they know very well how Blacks and other minorities are treated here, and have been from the very beginning? If our example is the model of democracy, then it is seriously flawed.

We like to think the world hates America because of its wealth. The ways in which that wealth was immorally obtained and developed is a factor, to be sure, but, as virtually all polls affirm, many also hate America's arrogant, self-indulgent, self-righteous hegemony of White supremacy that seeks to impose its will and image on the entire non-White world — still.[134] What, for example, should they think of America's claims of tolerance and respect for diverse cultures when they can tune into American media and see Diane Sawyer of ABC News asking women in North Korea if they wouldn't "want to dye their hair blonde," as if blonde hair is the absolute ideal of feminine beauty every non-European woman would naturally want to emulate if given the choice.

5

Employment

Nowadays,
if you can't say a rap,
or play sports,
you might just
come up short.

Too Short: "Money In The Ghetto"
Get In Where You Fit In/Zomba Records

Affirmation In Action

Based on national test scores, Stephen Thernstrom and wife, Abigail, mention "cognitive skills" and the "need to learn basic literacy and good diction" in their book, *America In Black And White,* as the chief reasons Blacks are denied even low-wage, entry-level employment, "for which they are barely prepared," they say, apparently unaware that national test scores are not consulted in employment screening. But the Thernstroms, nevertheless, praise immigrants for landing these same jobs with "very little education," while having "no command of English."[135]

In fact, according to research, 82 percent of immigrants between 16 and 24 without a high school education are employed, whereas only 37 percent of African Americans have a job.[136] Moreover, the lack of educational achievement and/or cognitive ability also never manages to limit job opportunities for European Americans, who are routinely exempted from even minimum educational requirements for employment, under the presumption that a supposed superior White intelligence inherently justifies their selection, particularly over a Black candidate who is often subjectively presumed less qualified.[137]

The claim that Blacks are denied jobs because of inadequate education and cognitive skills is as false as the claim that immigrant labor fills a need Americans won't otherwise supply, as if somehow the want of immigrants to eat and support their families is greater than that of non-immigrants. As a practical matter, Black Americans are routinely denied fair opportunities to compete for the jobs supplied to immigrant laborers who, for example, are often exempted from the screening of any application process altogether, particularly if they don't understand English. For the same jobs, by comparison, Blacks are screened more harshly, turned away, or their applications are either ignored or discarded. This, obviously, will have a chilling effect on the likelihood of individuals to apply.

Moreover, citing an October 2006 study of more than 400 U.S. executives and human resource professionals, the online business journal of the University of Pennsylvania's Wharton Business School, *Knowledge@Wharton*, found that, across all races, "entry-level employees, including graduates of four-year colleges, lack critical skills" and "the vast majority of high school graduates are deficient in written communications, professionalism and problem-solving, among other areas" but, because of the meaningless yet ominous, so-called "achievement gap," Black Americans are uniquely disadvantaged as a result.[138]

Figure I is a telephone order taken at Bruegger's Bagels located at Porter Square, Cambridge, MA, where I worked part-time, briefly in Summer, 2002. The note is for an actual order of ten dozen bagels to be cut, bagged and held for pick-up by a customer, written by Carlos, a *supervisor* and Portuguese national. The note, shown in its entirety, except for the last name and complete phone number of the customer, in Carlos' own handwriting, was given to me to fill. It clearly shows, if nothing else, that education may not be the all-important factor in employment as suggested by the Thernstroms, but merely a plausible excuse to mask underlying racism.

The baker at Bruegger's, moreover, a 50+ year-old, Brazilian national and grandmother, for some years, worked seven days every week in front of a blazing hot oven baking bagels, a difficult job that began at 5am each day. The store avoided running afoul of labor restrictions by dividing her weekly hours between her married and maiden names on the schedule, scheduling her for weekday hours under one name, and weekend hours under another. To add insult to

Figure I

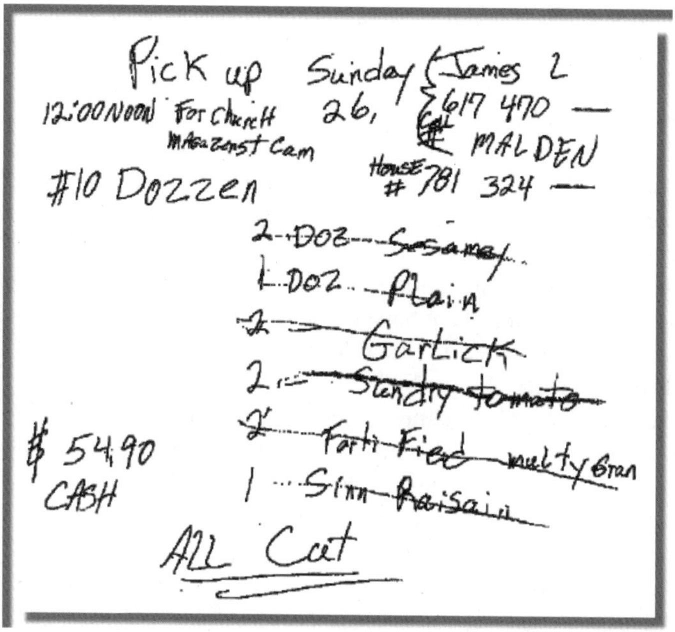

Pick up Sunday { James 2
12:00 NOON For Church 26, { 617 470 —
MAGAZINES Cam MALDEN
#10 Dozzen House # 781 324 —
2 DOZ Sesamey
1 DOZ Plain
2 Garlick
2 Standry tomato
2 Farti Fied multy Gran
$ 54.90 CASH
1 Sinn Raisain
ALL Cut

injury, the manager, Sandra, would go so far as to manipulate the woman's hours between the two names so as to avoid having to pay overtime wages for work exceeding 40 hours in a given week (which, as the store's only baker, she invariably did), or if the store's overall payroll was considered too high, a practice not at all as uncommon as we might think, or hope, since immigrants are often at the mercy of any and all employer demands, no matter how unreasonable, or unlawful.[139] This susceptibility to abuse and exploitation is then one difference, if any, between immigrant and native-born, American labor.

Due to overwhelming White ownership of the nation's employment and capital resources, Black Americans are, nevertheless, also at the mercy of White supremacy's hegemony, a reality that precludes European Americans from claiming race is meaningless with regard to employment. As the Harvard academic, David Landes, reminds us, "when one group is strong enough to push another around and stands to gain by it, it will do so."[140]

Border's Bookstore, where I worked briefly around the Fall of 2001, had a staff of approximately thirty, nearly a third carrying supervisory or management responsibility, filled, of course, by Whites. The general manager, Paul, was a likeable, low profile guy who, in terms of sales and personnel management, might accurately be described, albeit harsh, as an incompetent. As a personnel manager, however, he was absolutely clueless and as a sales manager he was even worse. During the five months or so I was there, the store fell short of its sales projections on a daily and weekly basis without fail, the exception being on holidays when the mall was so overrun with traffic that the only way the store could fail to meet its quotas was if it had no product whatsoever to sell. This, with no significant bookstore competion within ten minutes of the surrounding Cambridge, MA vicinity, and situated in a highly popular urban mall where the foot traffic might have made the store profitable with no management staff at all. As one Border's supervisor said, "a monkey could run this store at a profit."

Nevertheless, Paul remained a highly respected manager at the company and therefore thought of himself as a sophisticated, highly intelligent, competent manager. During Christmas, when the store was crowded with customers standing elbow to elbow, Paul generally left about 5pm, at the peak of the stores busiest period, as if he worked in a 9 to 5 office job, even though the shelves were sometimes nearly empty and the shipping and receiving room was overflowing with thousands of unshelved books ready to be sold but unavailable to customers. It was both shocking and embarrassing to have to repeatedly tell customers that we were "sold out" of a book, knowing full well there were thousands of unpackaged books in the back that likely included the ones they were looking for. But Paul was utterly overwhelmed (admittedly, the store was understaffed) and actually at a loss to get books onto the sales floor and available to customers, the basic function of the store. As a result, customers were forced to go on line or further out of their way for books or other items they might have obtained at our location. Still, the store reached its goals for the period, covering up the fact that sales were only a fraction of what they might have been. Thereafter, I made it a point to inquire about the sales performance from each previous day to compare against what I saw as mismanagement. I noticed that the only days the store achieved its goals was on some irregular occasion such as a holiday. My inquiries of course were met with indignation for asking about sophisticated matters presumed to be way over my head.

Another example of questionable management, and there were several, was evident when local author, Gary Bender, came to the store to do book signings. Paul thought his aggressive style of setting up a table by the store entrance and greeting each customer as they entered was too confrontational, saying the hard sell was a turn-off. I asked if any books were sold during the signings and the response was yes. According to Paul, Bender actually sold between ten to fifteen books. As it turned out, that was more books than were sold at all others combined in a given year at the store, anywhere from a couple to a half-dozen signings at that time. I recall only two such events during the five months I worked there. Instead of bitching about what he perceived as Mr. Bender's over-the-top style, I thought, Paul should apply that same success to the other less successful signings.

But the big question for me was: how does a guy who knows nothing about sales end up as the manager of a major retail store, particularly given the alleged "high standards" supposedly undermined by Affirmative Action? Of course, these jobs are not brain surgery, requiring only a minimum of skills, but if we think lower standards for Whites applies only to menial labor, we need only evidence the corruption and incompetence witnessed at FEMA in the wake of Katrina, or Boston's Central Artery debacle, known as the "Big Dig," (presumably for the way construction contractors dug into the pockets of taxpayers). In fact, corporate America is rife with such evidence of similar incompetence. The bumbling, dumbfounded responses of air-traffic controllers to the attacks of 9/11 come painfully to mind here.

A fallacy maintained by many employers who are inclined to use immigrant labor is they can't find native-born, American workers in sufficient numbers. But I've been to a few day labor pick-up sites over the years, in Boston, Dallas, New Orleans, and Washington D.C., seeking work at places frequented by small employers needing help, and by immigrants looking for work. If employers were seriously interested in American workers, many could just as easily recruit at locations or from groups they often have to pass on the way to the day labor sites. However, they know American workers, particularly Blacks, given their history in this country, will not long suffer being exploited and abused. Employers will generally drive to different locations where they know potential workers assemble, until, more or less, they attract the help needed for a given day. When they say they don't know whether the workers are legal or not, they're likely lying. One reason they settle on this option in the first place, is to save on the administrative expenses associated with personnel and payroll. Employing a sort of "don't ask, don't tell" policy, they are specifically looking for the workers who hope and expect the paperwork, i.e., documentation, will not be a necessary hurdle to overcome in order to get hired. Specifically, both parties are uninterested in questions about legalities.

While working for construction contractors, I've also been on the other end looking to hire temporary labor. I learned from these experiences that it is a desperate bargain, with the employer holding all the cards. Some guys will do anything for a dollar, and employers know it. Workers have to be sure they understand exactly what the expectations and promises are beforehand. Nobody wants to spend eight, ten, or twelve hours at hard labor and not get paid, so you gotta know what's up. There's pressure though because there are only a limited number of jobs to be had, often just one or two for each employer, and sometimes just one or two each day. Reputation and loyalty play a big part here. Straight-up employers are obviously the most popular, but opportunities are usually rare with them because they might also have their favorite workers and ask for them by name. If one's not there then somebody else may get a chance. Needless to say, much bad blood is created over these early morning tussles. The shadiest employers, generally the most desperate who nobody wants to work for because of their reputation for stiffing workers, will go to places far and wide, sometimes covering as much as a sixty to seventy-five mile radius to get workers — up to a ninety minute drive — without having to go to the same location twice within several months' time. The makeup of workers at a given location generally turns over during that period, for a myriad of reasons, so an employer's bad reputation will not have materially survived if he's not been seen more than once inside that time frame.

Another clumsy excuse used for employment discrimination is what the Thernstroms call "spatial mismatch," the geographical difference separating suburban jobs from urban workers. Hispanics and Asians, however, who the Thernstroms in fact say are from the same neighborhoods and "often live on the same block," are not equally affected by this circumstance.[141] What, moreover, could be a bigger "spatial mismatch" than jobs in America filled by workers from Mexico and South America? Well, the reason immigrant workers are willing to travel so far is because they are certain they'll be hired once they arrive. In fact, some have been "promised jobs in the United States" before they ever embarked upon their thousand-plus mile journey.[142]

The Thernstroms cite a Chicago area survey in which employers admit "reluctan[ce] to hire" Black Americans from the "inner city," because of concerns about criminal behavior,[143] and they are less attractive than immigrant labor, according to experts, because of also "fathering children out of wedlock." The Thernstroms, apparently, are unaware, or unconcerned, that such an admission of selectivity based on stereotyping is in fact still nothing more than race discrimination, a.k.a. racial profiling, "covert bias," "reasonable racism," or whatever you prefer to call it.[144] But, as a practical matter, employers don't concern themselves with the criminal records or parental status of immigrants. Indeed, administrative costs make it almost prohibitive in lower-levels of employment where immigrants may predominate.

> Now who's the real victim?
> Can you answer that?
> The Nigga that's jackin'
> or the fool gettin' jacked?

Warren G.: "Do You See"
Regulate, The G-Funk Era

The heightened scrutiny attaching to Black employment applicants gives racism the color of promoting so-called "high standards," when, in truth, as the preferred candidates, minority immigrants are not more qualified or harder working — and neither are White Americans — they simply are not screened as thoroughly as are Blacks. Indeed, the higher up the ladder one goes, the tighter the scrutiny for Black Americans, and the greater the presumption of competency for Whites, evidenced in part by the determined resistance to Blacks and other minorities rising above an ever-present, corporate glass ceiling, coupled with the seeming ease with which European Americans navigate the ladder to powerful employment on bogus credentials, such as the former dean of admissions at MIT, Marilee Jones, and the former CEO of RadioShack, David Edmondson, among others.[145]

In fact, the comparison of Blacks with immigrant labor is seemingly indicative of an inherent belief that the proper place for Black Americans, who are only "barely" qualified, say the Thernstroms, is at the entry-level, and that higher-level employment should be reserved for European Americans,[146] presumed uniquely qualified to skip the entry-level or quickly pass through to more lucrative and *suitable* middle and higher management positions.[147]

The legacy of Black slavery, combined with the fact that Whites supposedly founded America all by themselves, has of course contributed to European Americans believing they not only are inherently superior, but are therefore entitled to forever maintain their traditionally superior social position, which they assiduously endeavor to assert and affirm, what I like to call "Affirmation In Action."

> "WHAT A WASTE OF POTENTIAL,"
> IS WHAT MY TEACHERS USED TO TELL ME.
> "YOU CAN ALWAYS GET A JOB . . . !"
> THAT WEAK SHIT THEY TRIED TO SELL ME
> GOT ME NOWHERE BUT BROKE,
> AND FUCKED UP IN THE GAME . . . !

DMX: "Crime Story"/*It's Dark and Hell is Hot*
Rush/Def Jam Records

The reality of this dilemma facing Black Americans effectively places them in a perpetually compromised citizenship status, as shown in *Yet A Stranger,* by Deborah Mathis, and differently in the journal *Theoretical Inquiries in Law,* which explains how

> birthright citizenship largely shapes the allocation of membership entitlement itself (the "gate-keeping" function of citizenship). But no less significantly, it also distributes opportunity unequally (the "wealth-preserving" function of citizenship). . . upholding the legal connection between birth and political membership benefits the interests of some . . ., while providing little hope for others. . . . It is this slippage between an abstract right to membership and its concrete materialization that demonstrates how the focus on formal equality of status makes invisible the *inequality of actual life chances* attached to membership in specific political communities.[148]

Author Ayelet Shachar, interestingly, finds the roots of this intentional compromise to citizenship "in the inheritance regimes of property that date back to medieval England." "Whereas the archaic institution of hereditary transfer of entailed estates has been discredited in the realm of property," a similar "structure" continues to exist, he writes, "in the conferral of citizenship."

Inherited entitlement to citizenship not only remains with us today; it is by far the most important venue through which individuals are "sorted" into different political communities. Birthright principles strictly regulate the "entail" of political membership for the vast majority of the population. They secure the transmission of membership entitlement to a limited group of beneficiaries — those who gain access to the property on the basis of bloodline or birthplace. These beneficiaries, in turn, gain the right to pass it on to the next generation by inheritance, and these children will then pass it on to their children, and so forth: this structure effectively recreates the "fee tail" in the transmission of citizenship.[149]

The practical affect on the workplace is that there are countless numbers of people who get, and keep, their jobs, for no other reason than the fact that they happen to be White. Many undeserving and unqualified Whites would be unable to find work, certainly not at the same levels they currently enjoy, but for that fact, which, in effect, amounts to a racial preference for Whites, possibly explaining why so many European Americans oppose changes designed to level the playing field, such as Affirmative Action.

The 2001 census by the American Society of Newspaper Editors (ASNE) showed that approximately 45% of 956 daily newspapers surveyed had absolutely no minority staff, and 12 percent of overall newsroom staffing is comprised of minorities. According to then ASNE President Tim McGuire, executive editor of the *Minneapolis Star Tribune*, the goal was to have minority newsroom staffing nationwide match the percentage of the minority population as a whole, though, shockingly, not until the year 2025![150]

Why wasn't 2005 the goal?

Well, when ASNE's first census, in 1978, revealed just a 4 percent minority employment in newsrooms, the Association designated the year 2000 as its target for parity but subsequently saw only an 8 percent increase over the next twenty-plus years. So, according to ASNE's executive director, the current sobering goal of 2025, "clearly," is also "a stretch."[151]

The percentage of minorities comprising newsroom staffing increased a half percent in 2002, to 12.1, from 11.6 percent in 2001, "only because payrolls shrank in the recession, with more white journalists taking buyouts," the *Boston Globe* reported, amounting to "a net increase nationwide of four minority journalists."[152] By 2004, minority employment in newsrooms had risen to 12.9 percent,[153] and to 13.4 percent in 2005, while Black journalists have increased their total number in newsrooms across the whole of America by less than seven per year over the five years ending in 2005.[154] At this rate employment for minority journalists over the next two decades will still be astonishingly disproportionate to that of Whites.

The UNITY: Journalists of Color President has said "ASNE will not reach its goal of achieving parity in the newsroom by 2025 as long as this remains an institutional goal and not a personal one for its hundreds of members."[155] Declining revenues at many large city newspapers also makes the ASNE goal less likely to be realized.[156] This is what might be described as "inequality by design."[157] Yet, according to observers, mainstream groups like ASNE "are deeply devoted to (or mired in) the diversity movement."[158]

> I gots to get the fuck up in here,
> and formulate a caper!
> 'Cause a nigga's straight sufferin'
> from lack of havin' paper!

Tupac Shakur: "picture me rollin"
All Eyez On Me: Death Row / Interscope

Of course, since under-employment for minorities means over-employment for Whites, many European Americans will have newspaper jobs who otherwise might not and, conversely, by virtue of simply being Black, Latino, Asian or Native American, many journalists will be unemployed or under-employed.

Why should Whites occupy a disproportionate share of jobs in the newsroom, or in any profession for that matter? Where are minority journalism majors — twenty-seven percent of all students in those majors, according to the *Globe* — supposed to find work after graduation? McDonald's, of course, which explains why the gap in earnings between Black and White males with college degrees is greater than the gap between a Black male with a college degree and a White male with only a high school diploma, in fact nearly 50 percent greater by some estimates.[159] Yet the NCAA wonders why Black athletes have low graduation rates, obviously failing to recognize that maybe athletes aren't motivated academically because they don't see a job available for them when they graduate,[160] regardless of whether they have a degree or not, particularly when they see the exact opposite applies for European Americans who, degree or no degree, generally can get a decent-paying job anytime they want, just by virtue of being White.

As a practical matter, the only way minority employment will reach parity will be if you start hiring more minorities than Whites. But as soon as that happens Whites start crying that "less qualified" minorities are being hired strictly because of their color, which brings a prompt end to minority hiring so Whites can resume their normal favored status.

Is unemployment harsher for Whites? No. But largely because of the biased history taught in America's schools, European Americns believe they are entitled to forever occupy a favored economic and social position in this country.

> *I hit the Highway,*
> *makin' Money the Fly way.*
> *But there's got to be a better way.*

Li'l Troy: "Wanna Be A Baller"/*Sittin' Fat Down South*
Short Stop/ Uptown/Universal Records, Inc.

An interesting example of this Affirmation In Action can be seen on the evening news each night. In 2002, former NBC News anchor, Tom Brokaw, anticipating retirement, announced, to no one's surprise, his successor would be long-time heir apparent Brian Williams. Never mind that at the time of the announcement Williams' own hour-long cable news show was being summarily trounced by the competition at the Fox News Channel,[161] or that declining viewership for network news over the previous twenty years, by some 50 percent, suggested the American public may be interested in something besides the old White male, talking-head format, or even that Williams at the time was reportedly considered not particularly "good for business" by network affiliates, a concern that hits directly at the bottom line.[162]

The most striking factor in Williams' selection, however, was his lack of objective qualifications — he had not earned a bachelor's degree from college. "He was an inattentive student," Marjorie Williams explained in *Vanity Fair*, he "went to a local community college, then transferred to Washington's Catholic University and, later, George Washington University," where he "attended only two classes," and "never finished."[163]

Qualifications? Well, for starters, Williams "watched the news assiduously, and performed stand-up reports with a toy microphone," as a child.[164] And he is as "smart and funny as a stand-up comedian," according to a close friend.[165] "A perfectly fine news reader,"[166]

Williams, also has "the strange package of talents it takes to deliver the news, live, on the air."[167] But with respect to what really matters for television anchorpersons he is most qualified — "how they look."[168] "The suspicion," according to a *Vanity Fair* source, was that NBC "wanted somebody younger and prettier."[169] Ahhhhhhh...! The pretty-boy exception (Well, hey, that's the way it is!). The beautiful, talented consummately professional — and Black — Carol Simpson, on the other hand, a former university journalism *professor*, remained firmly planted at ABC news on weekend broadcasts where, columnist Frank Rich noted, anchors who don't fit "the mold" of the middle-aged, White male are assigned.[170]

Despite not having finished college, Brian Williams "wanders" into a coveted White House internship, during the Carter administration, and then another choice job at the National Association of Broadcasters where he "hooked up" with the general manager of a station in Pittsburg, Kansas.[171] Then, after reportedly just over a year, Williams returned to a "technical job" in Washington where the news director "saw something in him and *gave* him a chance to be a reporter," from where, *Vanity Fair* notes, it was "a straight shot up the ladder."[172] But, get this, "he didn't come from the kind of background where your parents' friends will make a phone call for you, or get you that internship," said his wife, "*one way or another*," according to her, "he got himself everywhere he went."[173]

My mother would say that was "by hook or by crook."

Okay, so if it wasn't his parents' money, and he didn't get it "the old fashioned way," then what was it? He played on his good looks? Come on! Granted, he's not Mat Lauer, but as "Weezy" Jefferson might say, "He ain't all *that* good lookin'!" and I can think of a lot of other people I'd rather spend twenty minutes looking at (and Katie Couric ain't one of 'em).

Both Ann Curry and Robin Roberts, on the other hand, have got more smarts, style, class and personality individually than Williams, Couric and Lauer put together, in my opinion, and they're not bad to look at. But, of course, being minorities, neither Curry nor Roberts has *otherwise* got the right stuff (wink, wink).

Clearly, Brian Williams didn't get to the top the way Blacks are constantly being told is the way to succeed in America: education. In fact, if he were Black, European Americans would be up in arms, saying he got the job because of his color, pointing to his lack of formal education as proof that Affirmative Action lowers "standards."

According to John Fernandez, in *Race, Gender & Rhetoric*, the competitive, capitalist marketplace makes success based on merit impossible because there are overwhelming numbers vying for the top who are all deserving, and therefore the message of America as a meritocracy, is, for the most part, "a myth," and seriously "flawed." Conformity inevitably becomes the deciding factor, observed Fernandez, particularly when decision-makers were themselves beneficiaries of that standard.[174]

Okay then, so let's keep it real. Brian Williams got his position for no other reason than the color of his skin. If anyone thinks he would have had the same success if he were Black or Latino, they're hopelessly delusional. Like many European Americans, he is simply the beneficiary of a racially biased system that discriminately facilitates success independent of merit.[175]

Consider also that the late Peter Jennings, who purportedly never even finished high school, considered it "a joke" that he was "handed" the anchor position at ABC news,[176] and was supposedly instrumental in bringing Emily Rooney, to work at ABC.[177]

When asked about her entry into television Rooney confided, "I was never sure I wanted to be a journalist," but "well, my father was in the TV business"[178] where, surprise, surprise, two of her siblings also landed successfully.[179] In another seeming example that a career in television journalism has little to do with so-called standards, Rooney reportedly survived what was described as a "tough grilling" as part of her screening at ABC, Jennings recalled, with questions about her opinion of "various correspondents," including himself and "her brother."[180]

She was fired in just over six months.

We continually stress over the so-called "achievement gap" in America, trying to figure out why Black youth aren't more excited about academics, when the short answer, quite simply, is they've got two eyes and can see what's really going on. Do we really think the frustration of Black parents who've been jilted professionally doesn't manifest itself in their homes and affect their children, and, in turn, those children's attitudes towards education? Young people are not stupid, they know what's real and what's not, so telling them things are really different from what they see in their everyday lives only makes them lose more confidence in the system. And "rarely," Landsman writes, "do they see what happens outside of school as connected to school itself."[181]

Moreover, nothing brings home the value of a college education to Blacks more than having a bachelor's or even a graduate degree and earning nearly the same or even less than a White co-worker performing the same job who only has a high school diploma. "Racial and class differences in the payoff to human capital," wrote Rhonda Williams two decades ago, "affect investment decisions" as much as a lack of either interest or ability.[182]

This then is the reality likely fueling America's skyrocketing high school dropout rates. Young people are motivated to excel by the legitimate hope of realizing success commensurate with the time and energy they've invested, instead of having their professional fate in the

> *There's hunger*
> *in the streets*
> *that's hard to defeat.*
> *Many steal for sport,*
> *but more steal to eat!*

Mos Def: "Got"
Black On Both Sides /Rawkus Records

hands of those inclined to arbitrarily frustrate their efforts. It is "[t]he power of the visual," according to Julie Landsman, that "transport[s] students into the realm of possibilities for themselves. . . . Once they have talked with and seen such people," she observes, they can conceive of such a future for themselves.[183]

Getting better test scores is much more a function of time than of money, contrary to the theory mainly promoted in the Black community. Study harder — put in more time — and test scores will improve, it's as simple as that. But what incentive do Black youth have to put in the extra study time, knowing, in the end, grades are irrelevant. Because of entrenched stereotypes, European American employers subjectively assume Black applicants are dumb regardless of education. And, moreover, they'll also conveniently assume a White candidate is smarter or better educated. And if you've gotten straight A's they'll conveniently say, from the disingenuous belief employers are falling all over each other to hire 'qualified' Blacks, "I'd like to hire you but you've got so many other options. I can't afford to invest in someone who's not going to stick around."[184] That's reality.

In *No Excuses*, however, Stephan Thernstrom audaciously lists education as the number one impediment to full social and economic equality in America, as if the employment screening process objectively rests on grades and test scores. Americans are beating themselves to death trying to figure out how to close the gap in test

scores between Blacks and Whites, while obviously in denial about
the endemic, controlling force of racism.

> Hard to understand,
> but a helluva man.
> This cat of the Slum
> had a mind, wasn't dumb.

Curtis Mayfield: "Superfly"
Warner Brothers

In *No Shame In My Game: The Working Poor In The Inner City*,
author Katherine S. Newman looks at the struggle for survival among
the poor and readily acknowledges the role of race in limiting the
ability of Blacks to secure employment and rise up from poverty.
Blacks, writes Newman,

face higher hurdles and more scrutiny because of their skin color, the
assumptions employers make about the neighborhoods they live in or
the schools they graduated from. ... What employers seem to see
coming in the front door is a black face, and they fill in the negative
assumptions accordingly. . . . employers carry around a set of beliefs
about job applicants from the inner city that are deeply ingrained and
fundamentally prejudicial. African Americans meet a wall of suspicion
from employers and managers who believe they are more trouble than
they are worth.[185]

Curiously though, Newman, skips right over the race issue when
summarizing what might be done to alleviate their impoverished
plight, focusing instead on "Wage subsidies," "tax breaks," and, a la
the Thernstroms, "Moving people to jobs." But these other would-be
solutions are drowned out by her deafening silence on race, a sad
reflection of contemporary America, placing our refusal to confront
the truth front-and-center.

Question: If Affirmative Action was such a policy of racial
preferences in favor of Blacks, why has it been so ineffective in
bringing about racial equality? Answer: Because it is no such thing.
But the continued characterization of it as such assures it never will be
effective.

"Americans remain deeply divided over whether America should be race-blind or race-conscious," Samuel Huntington concludes, based on the recent University of Michigan Supreme Court case.[186] The division, however, lies not in whether America *should* be race-blind, but in whether we are in fact race-blind, and whether or not we can get there absent a policy of so-called "racial preferences." Huntington and many others seem to think the country is color-blind. Many others, Blacks and Whites, disagree.

With deep European American opposition, even among those responsible for its implementation, Affirmative Action is not the proper vehicle for achieving American racial equality. Although the U. S. Supreme Court seems to naively think twenty-five more years of it will accomplish something forty previous years has not, the very definition of "with all deliberate speed." Affirmative Action merely encourages inclusive consideration, but, as Huntington highlights, "elites in most major American institutions — government, business, the media, education — are white," making it virtually impossible for Blacks to be comparatively evaluated independent of entrenched, subjective stereotypes, particularly over European Americans at higher levels of employment.[187] Huntington nevertheless claims corporate America is "lined up in support of racial preferences," but fails to show the hiring records of these supposed Affirmative Action champions, particularly with regard to "appointments to professional and managerial positions." The reality would of course inspire only laughter, not the fear he seeks to promote. But he's aware that if people read non-truths often enough they'll eventually begin to believe them.[188] Therefore, Huntington's claims, as Michael Elliott wrote in *Time*, "should not be accepted without challenge."[189]

"The question is whether Americans will go the extra mile and adopt the logic of *Who Are We*," offers Lazare. "My guess," he says, "is that a growing number will," with the effect of "substitut[ing] tradition for popular sovereignty . . . the past triumphing over the present."[190] Although, based on the anti-diversity rhetoric being openly promoted across America institutionally, it seems an alarming number of people already have.

The Chief Justice of the U. S. Court of Appeals for the Fifth Circuit, Edith H. Jones, for example, could be heard in March, 2006, openly denouncing "multiculturalism" and diversity at, where else, Harvard Law School. But that, she believes, "is not a prescription for intolerance."[191] She, of course, is the very Justice who affirmed the death penalty conviction for a gay defendant whose attorney infamously slept during trial, saying it was impossible to determine whether the representation had been compromised. Not surprisingly, for this and other questionable decisions, such as condemning a mentally retarded man to death, and discounting the seriousness of a sexual harassment claim because the guilty co-worker, who, among other things, allegedly pinched the breast of the claimant, had reportedly apologized for his behavior, Jones was voted one of the five worst justices in Texas by *The Texas Observer*.[192]

Chief justice Jones, in fact, believes "our legal system is way out of kilter" because the courts are used as vehicles through which to achieve social justice. Go figure. "There are better ways to achieve social goals than by going into court," she claims, apparently unaware of the federal courts' unique, constitutionally-mandated role as a check on government infringement of individual rights, and upholding justice.[193] "The crowning counterweight to 'an interested and over-bearing majority,'" according to an Constitutional historian, "was secured in the peculiar position assigned to the judiciary, and the use of the sanctity and mystery of the law as a foil to democratic attacks."[194] As an officer of the court, the chief justice is sworn to uphold the Constitution, but it seems her interest lies more in subverting it. With the power she and others wield professionally, and with the sway they hold over young minds, like the captive minds at Harvard, there is ample reason to be concerned about the future direction of America.

Virginia Congressman Virgil H. Goode Jr.'s public opposition to a Black American taking a seat in the Congress, and presidential hopeful, Senator Joe Biden of Delaware's less than becoming perspective on Black participation in mainstream American politics, both show that racial ignorance and intolerance within America's most powerful policymaking institutions is not at all as isolated as we may want to think.

Lamenting Representative Goode's biased remarks against Muslims in government, a *Washington Post* editorial correctly surmised: "the real worry for the nation is that the rest of the world might take him seriously, as proof that America really has embarked on a civilizational war against Islam."[195] The Post of course, is too late. The president himself has already affirmed as much.

6

Criminal Just-Us

It ain't a secret or concealed.
In fact,
the penitentiary's packed,
and it's filled with Blacks!

Tupac Shakur: "Changes"
Greatest Hits: Death Row / Interscope

Stereotypical

nside the Dorchester District Court in Boston, a European American ADA and fellow NESL alum once told me that, in his opinion, "99 percent of the people who come in here are guilty." Maybe so, I thought, but are they guilty of what they've actually been charged with and hauled into court for? And, what happened to "innocent until proven guilty?" Having been on the receiving end of that zeal, the ADA's confidence seemed to me utterly arrogant and biased, at best. Not coincidentally, a significant percentage of the defendants at Dorchester just happened to be Black.

A professor in law school also once stated in open class that, as Boston's former Chief of Homicide, he invariably prosecuted cases on what he perceived to be fabricated and improbable police evidence, often gaining convictions. But there seems to be something wrong with having a hand in causing someone to be carted off to jail on evidence you believe to be questionable.[196] Prosecutors will say it's not their job to do a defense councilor's work for her. It is unquestionably their job, however, to see that justice is done. The willingness to tolerate, much less pursue, injustice is troubling considering the disproportionate representation of Blacks and Latinos in America's prisons. If a substantial number of capital convictions is suspect, as has recently been revealed through the use of DNA evidence, one can just imagine how much greater the number of suspect non-capital convictions must be. Since minorities are disproportionately caught up in the criminal justice system, the institution consequently becomes a facilitator of social inequality.

Law enforcement officials use the perception of greater violence in minority communities to justify steering greater resources there.[197] Although when rates of violence subside Black Americans are still herded off to prisons in disproportionate numbers.[198] Whatever the truth may be, there's no doubt the perception of a greater predisposition towards criminal behavior — a stereotype — has for some time heavily influenced the allocation of law enforcement resources disproportionately towards Black American communities.[199] Who can forget the statement from long-time Philadelphia District Attorney, Lynne Abraham, that 85 percent of the crime in the city was committed by African Americans, while the percentage of Black defendants held in the city's jails at the time just happened to be, yep, 85 percent. The Black criminal stereotype is so thoroughly ingrained into the minds of society as a whole that one wonders if it can ever be fully eliminated. Some amusing observations revealed to me the daunting prospects of this improbability.

At a downtown Boston drugstore, not long after my arrival in the city to attend law school, I noticed a twenty-something, White female casually walking down the aisles ahead of me, taking what appeared to be candy or other snack items from the shelf, unwrapping them, and sticking them in her mouth as she nonchalantly moved along. As I slowed to make sure I was seeing correctly, she looked over her shoulder and noticed me staring, then angrily picked up her pace and moved to another aisle, not so much worried that I'd seen what she was doing, but that my proximity to her might draw unwanted attention from store personnel and security cameras focused on *me*. Fully aware of the irony, I turned and proceeded to shop, shaking my head.

At the checkout counter I told the employee, also a European American, what I'd seen, to see what his reaction would be. He just looked at me incredulously, as if to suggest he wasn't fooled by my clever attempt to divert his attention from what he seemed convinced were my own thieving designs. Apparently, thinking my behavior was suspicious, he had been watching me the whole time, never bothering to take his eyes off me even as I stood beside a girl who actually was stealing!

Another funny incident happened in a downtown Philadelphia photolab where I worked several years earlier. One of my co-workers, a bohemian looking European American, happened to live in the same apartment building as I did. We worked the second shift so we walked home together afterwards, usually stopping at a convenience store on the way to pick up something cold to drink. One day he asked me to buy him some cigarettes, but I was just as broke and said I didn't have enough for both the cigarettes and the drink. He proposed that I instead buy the cigarettes and let him get the cold drink.

"But I thought you didn't have any money?" I said.

He didn't, but said he could still get the drinks.

"How?" I asked, pretending to be coy.

"Just take it," he said, dead serious.

Neither of us had on jackets and there was nowhere for him to hide it but he said he could easily get the stuff out of the store in his hands. "And what about the employee?" I asked.

The attention would be so focused on me that the clerk wouldn't notice him, he said. "I just get it and walk out."

I laughed and told him he was "fucked up in the head." But he insisted that Blacks were the perfect cover for him to steal. He let a giggle out of the sheepish smirk on his face and said, "I'm serious man, I do it all the time."

I can see he thinks he's endearing himself to me by being candid, but by assuming I'm even down with stealing in the first place, a stereotype, he's unwittingly revealed an altogether different side of himself. But it's no secret that when you're a Black male they sweat you in damn near every store you enter. I just wasn't aware White folks would exploit that. But then, I thought, why wouldn't they?

Now, I know some serious thieves, cats who steal all the time — every day of the week. As a group, they're generally the smartest of all criminals, which really ain't that bright. But real thieves are sneaky; cunning; they do their homework. I'm sizin' my co-worker up, and, yeah, he's got that sly, greasy look about him. He ain't courageous — no stick up kid. But he's definitely got the look. Like a fiend under control, one step ahead, maybe two steps.

I'm somewhat sick to my stomach, but part of me wants to throw him a bone and see what happens, hoping it's not really true, so I can feel this racist profiling shit is all in my mind, though I know otherwise. I look inside the store and notice the clerk is a guy I jawed with one afternoon on my way into work. He got upset at a time when the store was crowded with other customers because I waited at the counter demanding my two cents change, instead of just chalking it up, which is what I guess most people would do. He looked at me and rolled his eyes as if to say, "cheap bastard!," and threw the pennies down on the counter. I promptly scooped them up and sarcastically said "Thank you!" and strolled out.

I turned to give my "partner" a closer goin over, to make sure he wasn't packin' — I didn't need no late night surprises — then said, "Fuck it, lets go, it'll give us something to laugh and talk about on the way home." I ask what kind of cigarettes he wants. He doesn't care. "Whatever you can afford," he says. We walk inside and I go over to the counter, to the left of the entrance, while he heads straight to the refrigerated cases at the rear of the store, to the right.

I ask the clerk for a pack of cigarettes.

"What kind?" he replies. It's after midnight and the place is empty, so it seems there's no way he can miss what's going down.

"Whatever's the cheapest," I answer back.

Right away, he's noticeably suspicious — of me. No bravado, so I sense he doesn't recognize me from our previous "encounter." I'm not a smoker, but I suddenly realize I've made him suspicious because smokers aren't indifferent about what brand they get, when they're buying, that is. He doesn't want to turn his back to pick out the cigarettes. I'm keeping my eye on him at the same time, 'cause this is Philly where, as they say, "shit be happenin'," which I know all too well, having been shot only blocks from this very location a little more than a year earlier.

He steps to the side so I can see and calls out some brands and prices. I pick one and count the money out on the counter as he rings it up. Meanwhile, I notice my co-worker calmly exits the store to my left. And, sure enough, he's carrying not one, but two drinks in his hands, down by his side. The clerk is oblivious. His eyes are fixed dead on me, even though I'm standing right in front of his face! After giving me my change he looks me up and down while I head out the door, to see if I've got anything in my hands, possibly candy from the racks on the customer side of the counter. He's certain I'm up to something, but he just doesn't know what. I say "thanks" and exit shaking my head. His eyes never stop searching me all the way out the door. I glance back with a dirty look of my own before disappearing onto the street outside. My co-worker is waiting about half-way down the block, and sure enough, he's got two ice teas *plus* an apple pie. I'm half angry and half stunned; partly angry at myself because I realize I could've gotten killed over these sophomore antics, and stunned at how easily and confidently he pulled it off. It was only petty theft, but even as a fearless, naïve juvenile I probably wouldn't have been so bold, and this is a grown man! He's obviously done this many times before. Like just another routine convenience store transaction.

Another story? Like practically every other Black American, if I've got two, I've got twenty. These may be small incidents, but you multiply them by the entire Black population and it's easy to see stereotyping and racism have got a firm grip on America, and how it just as easily, and inevitably, affects law enforcement, to a degree that has come to be considered normal. A truly objective, color-blind perspective, is hard to find.

A recent study by Northeastern University in Boston, sponsored by the Sate of Massachusetts — which has only a six percent Black American population — found that 249 out of 341 police departments state-wide, or two thirds, practiced some form of racial profiling. But, shockingly, the state secretary of public safety said the disparity in treatment for African American motorists could very well be the result of good police work.[200] Yet people wonder why residents of Boston's Black communities don't have positive impressions of the service they get from police.[201]

Persistent stereotypes, inevitably, some might say, too often accompany the unscrupulous manipulation of the system and its resources in order to get convictions. Sometimes it's the police, sometimes the DA, sometimes the Judges, and sometimes all three, or any combination. Simply put, careers are measured by success, and success is measured by convictions, period. And too often, unfortunately, an easy way to secure a conviction "beyond a reasonable doubt," is by manipulating the process in some way. Thus the zealous, disproportionate investment of time and resources in pursuit of the groups most widely perceived as criminally-minded, which the general public (jurors) will more readily be willing to convict — Blacks and Latinos.

Police pursue Black suspects more enthusiastically and are more apt to testify falsely or fabricate evidence; jurors, commonly inculcated with prevailing stereotypes, will be more apt to believe them; prosecutors more apt to withhold exculpatory evidence, and to make damning, sometimes unfounded, inferences that a judge will be more apt to tolerate or ignore; and defense attorneys will even be less apt to vigorously defend, all from the belief that the Black accused is more likely to actually be guilty. And this is all outside of the deliberate, overtly biased acts some officials are daringly willing to indulge simply out of race hatred.

One former big city police chief described this unscrupulous manipulation of the system this way:

Last year, state and local police made somewhere around 1.4 million drug arrests. Almost none of those arrests had search warrants. Sometimes the . . . officer reaches inside the suspect's pocket [and finds nothing, but] testifies that the suspect "dropped" it as the officer approached. It's so common that it's called "dropsy testimony." The lying is called "white perjury." Otherwise honest cops think it's legitimate to commit these illegal searches and to perjure themselves because they are fighting an evil. In New York it's called "testilying," and in Los Angeles it's called joining the "Liar's Club."[202]

In Miami, where police officers who were part of an "elite" patrol known as the "Jump Out Boys" were convicted of planting a handgun on an unarmed suspect the officers shot, a retired officer testified that planting guns at crime scenes "was a commonly known practice."[203] In one case, two Black robbery suspects were fatally shot in the back by police who then planted guns on the victims. Separate state prosecution and police internal investigations nevertheless determined the shootings were justified.[204]

The fact that investigations come up empty only serves to sanction shady police practices. And when the cases brought behind these actions ultimately result in convictions, the dirty dealing is then sanctioned by the judicial system, further fueling the presumption of Black guilt. The issue, Susan Sontag wrote, "is not whether a majority or a minority" of individuals are engaged in the behavior, "but whether the nature of the policies prosecuted" by government and society "makes such acts likely."[205]

Infamous former Los Angeles police detective Mark Furman, whose race bias and overzealous police work, possibly more than any other single factor, sank the O. J. Simpson prosecution, has become somewhat of a cult hero, appearing regularly in television and print media expressing esteemed opinions on law enforcement matters of local and national interest. His profile has in fact risen so high that merely offering his opinions on criminal matters — to the media —

caused at least one reporter to see him as "central" to the proceedings.[206] Law enforcement officials seemingly see his sudden celebrity status as a public sanction for their own over-zealousness. This kind of public affirmation, combined with the ambition to be similarly recognized as a champion of the public cause, helps to breed arrogance in law enforcement officials who interpret it to mean the end result therefore justifies the means.

TRIED TO MAKE IT MY WAY
BUT GOT SENT ON UP THE HIGHWAY.
WHY THEY GOTTA DO ME LIKE THAT?

JadaKiss: "Why"/*Kiss Of Death*
Ruff Ryders/Interscope Records

AFFORDABLE HOUSING

The budget for the Federal Bureau of Prisons in 1980 was $330 million, with 44 prisons. In 2002 it was $4.6 billion covering 102 prisons with eleven more under construction, a fourteen-fold increase in spending on more than twice the number of facilities. Conversely, over roughly the same period, median net worth for Whites more than doubled from $54,644 in 1984 to $120,900 in 2001, while actually *decreasing* for Blacks, from $17,627 to less than $17,000, as reported by the Federal Reserve Board.[207] Overall, America spends $54 billion on state and federal prisons combined. This investment has spurred a five-and-a-half fold increase of Black men in prison from 143,000 in 1980, to an astronomical 791,600 in 2000, a whopping 40 percent of the nation's jailed population, according to figures cited from the Justice Policy Institute.[208]

The poorest State in the American union, Mississippi, having built 15 prisons within a recent seven year period, is a good example of economic policy tying itself into this issue. On a tour of one of its prisons, says the *Wall Street Journal*, Mississippi State Rep. Linda Coleman told the state's corrections commissioner, Robert Johnson, they "needed more inmates so the county wouldn't default on $7.8 million in debt it took on to build the facility," then "pointed to a guard and said, 'If we don't get [more inmates], she might get laid off.'" Prisons

spawned a new set of vested interests with stakes in keeping prison full and in building more. In Mississippi, those interests include private prison companies and their lobbyists, legislators with prisons in their districts, counties that operate their own prisons and sheriffs who covet convicts for local jails. The result has been a financial and political bazaar, with convicts in stripes as the prize.[209]

Professional lobbyists, moreover, can earn in excess of a quarter of a million dollars a year, in essence, "begging for inmates" for the prisons. The president of the private corrections corporation known as Wackenhut told one of its lobbyists it "needed at least 900 inmates to cover costs and generate a 'reasonable' profit." State officials, including "legislators, wardens and county supervisors" then "deluged the corrections department with pleas for prisoners."[210]

Is it at all possible such tremendous economic and political pressures could not find their way into the State's police departments and courthouses? Individual police officers, for example, would certainly be mindful that more arrests might at least increase their chances to earn promotions and higher salaries. More arrests would also likely consume greater courthouse resources, potentially increasing prosecutorial budgets — and employment — for judges and prosecutors, and in turn for defense lawyers. Reportedly, "even as lawmakers were cutting state budgets for classroom supplies, community colleges, mental-health services and other programs," Mississippi was paying private prison companies for beds they did not have enough prisoners to occupy, though crime rates were in fact falling.[211]

Fueled partly by tougher drug laws, the federal government was also a major player, "agree[ing] to pay above market prices," according to the *Journal*, and "big cash bonuses" to private prison companies to operate federal facilities.[212]

The flip side of the presumption of Black guilt, of course, is a presumption of White innocence, where European Americans choose not to view their behavior as criminal, facilitating the disproportionate allocation of law enforcement resources by rationalizing the crimes they mostly prefer to identify themselves with, so-called white-collar crimes, as victimless, and therefore not deserving of the most serious punishments. An analysis offered by one New York attorney typifies this attitude:

It's my experience that the preponderance of individuals caught up in criminal investigations in the white-collar arena are not what people would call evil. They do not get up that morning and decide, today

I'm going to commit a crime. Most of these are normal people who end up just getting caught in something that spins out of control.[213]

This suggests there's no such thing as a predisposition to criminal behavior, and so-called white-collar offenders should not, in fact, even be considered criminals. But, more disturbing, it seems to suggest inherent "evil" in those engaged in crime that is not white-collar, but I ain't gonna take it there. According to Bruce Porter, writing in *The New York Times Magazine*, a "bright prospect starts off in career, works hard to build successful enterprise," he explains, "then one day, as if contracting a moral virus, turns from solid corporate citizen into closet criminal."[214]

If you're an everyday hustler,
then get your money,
Cause what they do to Black men
ain't funny,
All the time tryin' to put us in the pen,
you get paroled,
then they send you again!

Too Short: "Money In The Ghetto"
Get In Where You Fit In/Zomba Records

On the contrary, a white-collar crime is not what might be classified as a crime of passion or something that just "spins out of control." It is, by definition, a crime that requires great planning, calculation, cunning and stealth. Indeed, elements one might fairly associate with an "evil" mind. And, in fact, when part of a crime such as murder, the law considers those elements to be evidence of a depraved mind, aggravating the nature of the offense and commanding a more serious penalty, including even capital punishment. In practice, white-collar crimes regularly include such aggravating elements, yet perpetrators are seen as "normal people" and shown leniency, while those whose crimes really arise from events "spinning out of control," most often aided by a mind-altering controlled substance, are considered the most depraved or evil. However, not only do white-collar criminals get up thinking "today I'm going to commit a crime," but they go to bed the night before thinking it, and even several days, weeks, months or years before as well. Setting up skeleton corporations, tax schemes and other types of fraud, as we learned in the experience of Enron and other corporate fraud cases, are highly complex, sophisticated activities requiring tremendous amounts of time, energy and expertise to devise and carry out, and generally are milked over long periods of time. From beginning to end, when they finally get caught, those responsible walk around as "normal people," sometimes for years, mindful of their ongoing criminal behavior. They do not suddenly "contract a moral virus."

Sam Waksal, the former CEO of Imclone and Martha Stewart infamy, explained to Steve Croft of CBS television's popular "60 Minutes" program, how he would "glibly do something [criminal] and rationalize it." He was finally charged

> with telling his father and his daughter to lie for him, and directing an ImClone employee to destroy documents. He also forged the signature of a corporate officer to fraudulently obtain a bank loan, and he avoided more than $1 million in New York State sales tax by shipping $15 million in artwork he'd bought to an ImClone address in New Jersey,

Incredibly, he says "I could sit there thinking I was the most honest CEO that ever lived,"

Fraud? says Jay Jones, the former high-flying executive, now a convicted, white-collar felon, "honestly, the first time I ever looked at that squarely in the face, in that light, was when the government brought it up. . . . I certainly knew it was nefarious, a little wormy, unethical, make no mistake about that," he says, "but criminal?"[215]

Worse is, their transgressions do not materially limit future opportunities for these offenders and incompetents.[216] Maureen Dowd asks, of State Department defect and World Bank reject Paul Wolfowitz, "Once you've helped distort W.M.D. intelligence to trick the country into war, shouldn't you be banned for life from ever having another top-level government post concerning W.M.D.?"[217]

But not only the white-collar offenses of European Americans are given less attention. As a former police chief concluded, the war on drugs also is "an assault on the African-American community. Any police chief that used the tactics used in the inner city against minorities in a white middle-class neighborhood would be fired within a couple of weeks."[218] Another law enforcement agent, formerly with the Drug Enforcement Agency (DEA), the Bureau of Alcohol Tobacco and Firearms (ATF), and the Customs Service, stated, "I've spent much of my life in these ghetto neighborhoods watching drug dealers. I would say 95 percent of the customers are white."[219] "I put a hidden camera on a street corner where I knew they sold heroin," another told *The New York Times*, "You wouldn't believe the customers we got on film: [White] lawyers, doctors, teachers."[220]

The fact that ten times as many Blacks between the ages of 25 and 30 are incarcerated than Whites, and that virtually half America's prison population is Black, while only twelve percent of the total population is African American, suggests race bias plays a very real part in this country's criminal justice system.[221] With devastating impact, criminal convictions have become the ultimate weapon in the formula securing a permanent European American political and economic domination over Black Americans, at once compromising employment options, political empowerment and social freedoms.[222] No question many White police, prosecutors and judges take their roles in this design seriously. And because of this reality, there must at some point be greater public accountability within America's criminal justice system, in terms of a more equitable application of law enforcement resources and greater accountability for prosecutorial discretion, which, unchecked, weighs heavily against Black American equality.[223]

7

Why Racism Matters

> Wake up in the morning and i ask myself,
> is life worth living?
> Or should i Blast myself?
> I'm tired of being poor,
> and, even worse, i'm Black.
> My stomack hurts,
> so i'm lookin' for a purse to snatch.

Tupac Shakur: *"Changes"/Greatest Hits*
Death Row/Interscope

One Nation

I f not for the painful truth underscored by catastrophic events like hurricane Katrina and its aftermath, America's omnipresent inculcation of White supremacy might credibly be regarded as insignificant, if not a thing of the past. But the lasting legacy of this country's unfortunate acceptance of slavery in its formative centuries has been the accepted discount of the Black race in the century-and-a-half since Emancipation, manifest through the careful, institutional management and control of government policy, in addition to, as we've seen, the collective workings of economic and social institutions. Imbalances of wealth and power in this country are therefore still overwhelmingly drawn, not coincidentally, along lines of race, highlighting a major shortcoming of the democratic model the U.S. arrogantly seeks to replicate the world over, Black Americans are virtually powerless to affect the all too deliberate pace of change. As I was matter-of-factly reminded by the Massachusetts State Representative, Alice Wolf, a long-time European American public servant, "discrimination will always exist" in this country. This absence of a true meritocracy, due to racism, means Blacks are permanently foreclosed from enjoying the equality promoted in America's creed.

When Black contributions to American and overall world development are discounted, social disparities are then seen by the overbearing majority as proper and just, causing the march towards full equality to assume a pace of "all deliberate speed," as advocated by the United States Supreme Court in the landmark *Brown v. Board of Education* de-segregation case.

In short, thanks to the determined efforts of academics holding sway over the captive minds of America's youth and significant elements of popular opinion, many European Americans simply do not, in fact, believe Blacks are their equal or deserving of equal status. We do not have full equality in America, therefore, because of staunch opposition to it by a majority that believes it alone contributed everything of substance to the making of America, and which sees Black Americans as demanding something simply on the basis of skin color, but have not earned and do not deserve.

Since the balanced truth is obviously not taught in America's educational system, Black youth, overwhelmed by White supremacy indoctrination and believing, understandably, the American ideal does not include a place for them, inevitably succumb to intractable self-loathing and nihilism that lasts a lifetime.[224] From the moment he's born, noted Tocqueville after his 1835 visit to America, a Black youth is told "his race is naturally inferior to the white man and almost believing that, he holds himself in contempt. He sees a trace of slavery in his every feature, and if he could he would gladly repudiate himself entirely."[225]

Portions of the intellectual community advocating White supremacy believe racism, though not completely dead, is ironically no longer responsible for America's persistent social and economic disparities. These academics were inspired, no doubt, by the ridiculous book written by Dinesh D'Souza titled *The End of Racism*, which suffers from the same failures as many other intellectual offerings on race, particularly those from recent immigrants whose knowledge of America is gleaned exclusively from a book: it evidences an acute disconnection from reality. D'Souza, for instance, claims "discrimination against black men can be fully eradicated only by getting rid of destructive conduct by the group that forms that basis for statistically valid group distinctions," an assertion separating discrimination from race and positing it as a function of statistical observations, an embarrassingly short-sighted, uninformed perspective.[226]

As mentioned, however, most advocates of White supremacy stop short of saying racism is dead altogether but, nevertheless, still characterize it as suddenly irrelevant. For example, in *Culture Matters*, a book of essays examining how cultural values are primarily responsible for economic success or failure, co-edited by Harvard professors Lawrence Harrison and Samuel Huntington, Harrison states that although "*some* racism and discrimination" still exist, they are "no longer viable" as an explanation for black *underachievement* as at mid-twentieth century.[227]

What proof is offered for why racism is suddenly harmless? None. Except, of course, for kudos to White folks for the "sweeping changes" in their attitudes about race. America has experienced "a racial revolution" over the last fifty years of the century, writes Harrison. The evidence, as he sees it, is that immigrants from Latin America have also been discriminated against, "but surely less than blacks and probably no more so than Chinese and Japanese immigrants, whose education, income, and wealth substantially exceed national averages." Besides, he adds, higher poverty and high school dropout rates also exist in Latin America where racism and discrimination are presumably irrelevant. "Hispanic underachievement," he notes, "is now a greater problem."[228]

Ouch! The fact that Hispanics have *underachieved* with comparatively less discrimination or, in the case of Latin America, with none at all, as he describes it, means racism is of no effect for the plight of Blacks in America? Well, one conclusion invited by this of course is that Blacks brought the devastating, yet containable, effects of hurricane Katrina on themselves and, a la former first lady Barbara Bush, actually enjoyed a net benefit from the incompetence, indifference and outright bias that magnified the damage and destruction. What should have been nothing more than an inconvenient storm instead became a devastating, permanently-life-altering event.

Okay, so rich, White corporate-types needn't feel bad because they don't want Blacks working or living near them. It's their own fault if Blacks can't pay rent, feed their kids or otherwise pay their bills; or if Katrina victims don't have sufficient means to re-settle their uprooted lives, or can't independently weather the insurance company shell game. Black Americans don't subscribe to America's "core culture," which, although "contributed to and modified" by many generations of immigrants, says Huntington, in *Who Are We?* is, for the most part, still defined as the traditional Anglo-Protestant values of America's founders, comprising "the Christian religion, Protestant values and moralism, a work ethic, the English language, British traditions of law, justice, the limits of government power, and a legacy of European art, literature, philosophy, and music."[229] Despite the omission of a few other traditional values even more critical to America's success, ones that don't exactly support the theory of an inferior culture as the reason for "underachievement," such as murder, torture, terror, theft, brutality, inhumanity, rape, avarice, bigotry, exploitation and racism, Huntington, nevertheless, has the gall to say the setllers' *traditional* Anglo-Protestant values have been the source "of liberty, unity, power, prosperity and moral leadership," during three and a half centuries, for "Americans of all races."[230]

For his part, Lawrence Harrison doesn't explain the development of Hispanic underachievement since the time when racism *did* influence economic disparities between Blacks and European Americans. Nor does he explain the exact nature of the supposed "racial revolution" that led to such "sweeping changes in attitudes about race on the part of whites." It obviously includes improved White values over those from just fifty years ago, a truly historic shift that reverses more than a millennium of behavior. Though he can't very well advocate pure values while at the same time hanging the age-old, putrid, decayed albatross of racism and discrimination around the necks of Whites, now can he?

The supposed change, referred to as a "renaissance of culture" by Huntington and Harrison, and Thomas Sowell, among others, merely shifts the focus of responsibility for America's social disparities to "cultural factors," such as "the behavior of ethnic groups,"[231] and Shazam! racism is banished. "First marginally weakened by the outcome of the Civil War," it was "drastically eroded by the civil rights movement in the 1950s and 1960s," says Huntington,[232] proudly explaining how the country "eliminated the racial and ethnic components that historically were central to its identity" and became a "society in which individuals are to be judged on their merits," owing, get this, to "the Anglo-Protestant culture and the Creed of the founding settlers."[233]

What?

Huntington is of course referring to the death of Jim Crow & policy initiatives such as the Voting Rights Act, etc., but he is also promoting a White-washing of American history that eliminates any acknowledgement of Black slavery, assigning its fruits to the virtues of White supremacy. Protestantism, he says, "stressed the work ethic and the responsibility of the individual for his own success or failure in life."[234] The same work ethic, of course, supporting George Washington and Thomas Jefferson's virtuous legacies as champions of America's all-important agrarian industry, while both heroes, not coincidentally, were among the largest slaveholders of their time.

The impact of this racist indoctrination, which bookstores, libraries and schools are full of, should be obvious to every American. Nothing is more complete in American history than the promotion of White supremacy on the backs of Black slaves. Slavery, after all, while recent enough to not be forgotten, is far enough in the past to be effectively transformed in the public mind, as many historians are well aware. Journalist Cokie Roberts, for example, pompously includes "the successful cultivation of indigo" among the "many accomplishments" of South Carolina matron Eliza Pinkney, in *Founding Mothers*, knowing full well the woman never personally lifted a finger to cultivate indigo, relying instead on hundreds of Black plantation slaves.[235] Such an oversight is an inexcusable and intolerable insult.

LABOR PAIN

It shouldn't be necessary here to reiterate the fact that American slavery was, for the most part, the exclusive domain of Blacks. But I'm genuinely confused as to how any American, particularly a European American, can possibly tout the work ethic of early settlers. That is simply an affront that must be challenged.

The first European settlers in America, we understand, had "only rudimentary familiarity with arable farming"[236] and, moreover, were mostly the English and Irish poor facing starvation in Europe, more than a few of whom were convicts and therefore "must have proved incorrigible," remarked Lewis C. Gray, in *History of Agriculture in the Southern United States To 1860.*[237] "All the available evidence," writes another historian, "tends to show that average servants were at best irresponsible, lazy, and ungoverned, and at worst frankly criminal."[238] The European "must above all be a white man and maintain the superiority of the white race, largely by a careful refusal to do any work," records another, E.T. Thompson, in the journal *Agricultural History.*[239] Yet, Tocqueville observed,

many Americans maintain that below a certain latitude it is fatal for them, whereas Negroes can work there without danger, but I do not think that this idea, with its welcome support for the southerner's laziness, is based on experience. The south of the Union is not hotter than the south of Spain or of Italy. Why cannot the European do the same work there? . . . I do not think that Nature has forbidden the Europeans of Georgia and the Floridas themselves, on pain of death, to draw their sustenance from the soil.[240]

In *Economic and Social History of New England*, by contrast, William B. Weeden, explains that the Black and Native American "dependents" of New England "soon dwindled in numbers, or dropped out from a life too severe for any but the hardiest and firmest-fibred races,"[241] apparently forgetful that Native peoples survived in North America long before the arrival of Europeans, and that so-called "hardy" Europeans were initially able to survive here only with their aid. But because of the support they provide for institutions of racism, such as White supremacy and slavery, "It is significant," wrote Thompson, "that the various climatic theories of human society, from Aristotle to Huntington, are closely associated with the various racial theories."[242]

RACIAL PREFERENCES

Although widely shared, pride in the supposed unique Anglo-Protestant work ethic is, however, inherently problematic in the face of America's 200-year record of Black slavery, requiring historians to speciously discount slavery's value. In *Tobacco and Slaves,* for example, historian Allan Kulikoff maintains Chesapeake planters had a "preference for white servants over slaves for much of the late seventeenth century," and only reluctantly became "reconciled" to black labor following the turn of the century when they had "exhausted the supply of white laborers."[243] And in *From Tobacco To Grain,* Paul Clemens similarly asserts that seventeenth century "Eastern Shore planters showed no distinct preference" for African slaves over European laborers.[244]

When the number of servants declined in the 1670s and '80s, colonists "turned first to English women" and then to Irish men, says Kulikoff, and only *after* the supply of European labor ran low, did they "reluctantly" turn to Africans.[245] This seems a bit of a stretch since throughout the seventeenth century women were in short supply in the colonies due to "[h]igh mortality and predominance of males among immigrants."[246] According to Edmund Morgan, "conspicuous" among the early American settlers, was "an extraordinary number of gentlemen" who were unskilled and "could not be expected to work at ordinary labor."[247] "Footloose younger sons and gentlemanly adventurers usually lacked stamina and discipline," notes Blackburn, "and expected routine labour to be performed by menials."[248] "In quality, as well as in quantity, white indentured labor clearly left something to be desired," concludes Peter Wood, in *Black Majority*, "general lethargy and laziness," he writes, "seemed prevalent among whites (and which was by no means confined to servants)."[249]

The Price Is Right

Kulikoff writes,

when the supply of servants began to diminish during the 1670s and 1680s, the price of white men increased, both absolutely and relative to the price of full field hands. Planters in southern Maryland could buy three white men for the price of a single prime-age black male field hand in the early 1670s, but the same slave was worth only two servants by the end of the decade. This pattern strongly suggests that planters wanted servants more than slaves, for if they had believed that slaves were more profitable, the relative price of servants would have diminished.[250]

This is followed by the seeming contradiction that servant to slave prices rose at the turn of the century, "and again reached nearly three servants per slave by the 1710s, despite the near-total disappearance of servants."[251] Blackburn similarly observed a steady rise in the prices for African slaves over the course of the eighteenth century, explaining, "in the years1676-1679 a slave could be purchased on the African coast for trade goods worth a little over £3; by 1698-1707 this had risen to £8-£12, and by 1763-1788 to £12-£15."[252] Lewis Gray notes that South Carolina offered a bounty to importers of European male immigrant labor in 1712, and increased in 1716, in "an effort to enlarge the very limited market for European servants,"[253] due, "unquestionably," he concludes, to a "preference for slaves."[254] Consequently, planters were additionally "required" to purchase one European laborer "for each ten slaves owned by him as his turn came by lot," to counter the "increasing preponderance of slaves, the terror of slave revolts, and the continual menace of the French and Spanish influence among frontier [Indian] tribes."[255]

The temporary drop in the cost of African slaves noted over the last quarter of the seventeenth century might also be explained by an increased supply from England's Royal African Company, chartered in 1672. The Company "established seventeen forts or factories on the coast of Africa" and "dispatched some 500 ships" between 1672-

1713 — one ship a month over the 40 year period — in exchange for "exported goods worth £1.5 million."[256] Ninety-seven percent of Black slaves brought to Virginia in the first decade of the eighteenth century were transported directly from Africa, rising from 18.2 to 29.5 percent between 1712 and 1755, "in spite of the large immigration of small white farmers."[257] Slave prices, nevertheless, rebounded at the turn of the century — and increased — suggesting a clear preference for African laborers, even at higher prices. "According to Gray,

as compared with about the middle of the seventeenth century the level of slave prices had increased from 25 to 30 percent by the beginning of the eighteenth century, had approximately doubled by the middle of the eighteenth century, and in the years just preceeding the Revolution was probably three times as high.[258]

Average prices quoted for slaves in the 1670s was at £23, while in the first decade of the eighteenth century, quotes show prices rising as high as £30 to £35. Indentured servants, by comparison, were worth an average of £10 in 1672, but were being supplied by contractors in Virginia and Maryland for £10 more than a century later, in 1779, despite the relative short supply, indicating an actual *decrease* in the real prices, given inflation and costs of farming equipment, land, transportation, supplies, etc.[259]

Productivity

Seventeenth century entrepreneurs calculated profit by "returns in productivity," therefore when tobacco prices dropped in England, colonial planters compensated by acquiring *more* land and labor and increasing production.[260] Productivity gains lowered costs and produced profits for planters in the face of falling prices.[261] From the 1620's to the 1670's tobacco production increased from less than 300 pounds per worker to over 1000 pounds per worker.[262] Increased productivity helped tobacco exports from Virginia and Maryland to grow six-fold during the last third of the eighteenth century.[263] The reason for the increased productivity, according to Eric Williams, "lay in two words": "Negro slavery."[264] Black slaves "made most of the largest individual crops recorded," observed Lorena Walsh, "not White servants."[265]

Worker output "peaked during the years in which the proportion of slaves in the bound labor force rose to half or more.[266] Tobacco was largely raised on small, owner-operated farms in the seventeenth century with the help of an occasional servant. In the eighteenth century, large plantations worked by slaves dominated production, although "yeomen planters remained important throughout the colonial period."[267] Large Eastern Shore estates, worked by slaves, experienced production output per worker of more than 50% greater than smaller estates worked by slaves in combination with servants. [268]

With the supposed superior work ethic of Whites and the dubious value of Black labor, a legitimate question therefore exists as to exactly how or why African slavery developed in America in the first place, and that it was not exactly the "unthinking decision," as is generally promoted.[269] In fact, according to some of the evidence, there may have been a distinct desire and/or preference for African laborers from the very day the first Black slaves arrived at Jamestown, in October, 1619.

In *Business & Capitalism*, N.S.B. Gras "wonders," whether the charter of the second Dutch West India Company, formed in 1618, "stress[ing] the welfare of the settlers," may have inspired the design of a new policy to make the Virginia Company more profitable after its 1619 restructuring by the new treasurer of the Company,[270] a policy that likely would have included the introduction of Black slaves into the colony. Despite the Dutch ambition to disrupt Spain's West India trade, wrote Gras, they would nevertheless have "had no silly notion about the ease of making money" and "expected hard earned profits."[271] Distinguished for their "businesslike methods," they "did not allow military expenses to outweigh the profits of trade."[272]

But whatever the influence, it seems England, with the newly formed Company of Adventurers to Guinea and Benin receiving its Royal charter in 1618, reportedly "to supply slaves for tobacco plantations" in Virginia, may have already determined to introduce Black slavery into the colony.[273] In any event, the first Blacks landed at Jamestown would have quickly betrayed their value if, as Lerone Bennett, Jr. states, "[n]ot a single black died in the first three years," a peculiarity that surely would not have been lost on the colony's organizers, given the mortality rate for European laborers in their first year of at least 66 percent.[274]

After the arrival of those first Blacks in 1619, tobacco cultivation using African slaves increased steadily until Black slavery was established as the dominant form of plantation labor, a transformation that seems to have become manifest relatively quickly.[275] Records indicate tobacco exports from Virginia alone grew "from 20,000 pounds in1619," the year the first Africans arrived at Jamestown, "to nearly 20,000,000 pounds less than a century later," and Chesapeake production reached 100,000,000 pounds just prior to the revolution,[276] an increase having an inverse relationship to the ratio of indentured and free labor used in tobacco cultivation over the same period.

The progression of Chesapeake slavery, conclude John McCusker and Russell Menard, in *The Economy of British America, 1607-1789*, "can be approached by assuming that planters chose their work force by comparing costs and output among the alternatives in order to maximize net returns and by focusing on shifts in the supply and demand for labor."[277] The Royal African Company "had to respect market principles, and learn the precise wants and needs of hundreds of suppliers on the African coast and thousands of purchasers in the American colonies," wrote Blackburn, "the evidence of rational responses to market stimuli," he found, "is a picture of a series of closely connected competitive economic markets, in Africa and America, in which large numbers of traders and planters responded promptly and shrewdly to economic incentives."[278] "As the slaves could make more tobacco than the indentured servants," writes Thomas Wertenbaker, in *The Planters of Colonial Virginia*, "it became the settled policy of the Crown to encourage the African trade in every possible way."[279]

Ask him his dream,
what does it mean?
He wouldn't know.
Can't be like the rest
is the most he'll confess.
But the time's runnin' out
and there's no happiness.

Curtis Mayfield: "Superfly," Warner Brothers

INDIVISIBLE?

Although Samuel Huntington believes he exemplifies America's traditional Anglo-Protestant values, he, no doubt, would vehemently object to being identified with a "racist, divisive and provocative spirit."[280] But therein lies a key to understanding the mantra against diversity of Huntington and the rest of his endless legion of academics who see this country's acknowledgement of its diverse population as a threat to what has traditionally been viewed, both at home and abroad, as a country built by and for Whites. They long to return to the days when the White race reigned without any acknowledgement whatsoever of anything other than the supremacy of having been born White, proving that Racism has been central to America's so-called core culture from the beginning.

To be sure, Huntington's influence, unmatched in stature, can help normalize indifference to the suffering and displacement experienced following hurricane Katrina, and therefore should not be underestimated. "There's no question that his influence has been growing," *The Nation* says of Huntington, since the seemingly prescient attacks of September 11, which he loosely anticipated in *Clash of Civilizations.*[281] Indeed, *Foreign Policy* magazine listed him among the top four "Winners In Iraq," behind Iran, the Shiite cleric Moqtada al-Sadr and Al Quaeda. And the collective influence of Huntington, Harrison, David Landes and Stephen Thernstrom, among others, shows exactly why Harvard is more than deserving of its well-earned reputation as the leading bastion of White supremacy in America. This despite Harvard's having been the beneficiary — more so than any other single educational institution in America and, truly shocking, potentially more than all others combined — of millions of dollars from the shredded, bloodied backs of Black slaves, to become a viable institution.

Huntington knows the on-rush of diversity, in the form of immigration from Latin America, will eventually dilute the ability of Whites to indefinitely impose their tyrannical, Eurocentric will over America. He therefore seeks to unify the majority in opposition to immigration, and Affirmative Action, by claiming the pure and righteous American identity established by the Founders is irreversibly changing for the worse. His M.O., "so favored by fascist mentalities," observes Mexican novelist Carlos Fuentes, "is fear of the 'other.'"[282] He knows that only fear itself will urgently move the as yet greater numbers of Caucasians to stem the rushing tide of immigration from south of the border while continuing a vigil over the rising power fortunes of Blacks and other minorities through Affirmative Action, which he exerts an especially desperate effort to discredit by making a great deal of the fact that a majority of Americans oppose that so-called policy of "racial preferences." But he gives the last word on the subject to the infamous Stephen and Abigail Thernstrom. Led by Huntington, however, the anti-diversity faction appears to entirely discount the fact that one of the central features of American government is (supposed to be) the protection of minority interests — from a unified majority.

With the strong belief that superior or inferior cultural norms are primarily responsible for social and economic inequality, Stephen Thernstrom and wife Abigail wrote an impassioned opposition to Affirmative Action, which they believe is undeserved, in *America in Black and White, One Nation Indivisible: Race in Modern America*. They ostensibly attempt to illustrate how Blacks are responsible for their own *underachievement*, and if they would just change certain cultural habits they would of course realize prosperity in America equal to that of European Americans.

Calling *America in Black and White* the most "comprehensive" study of Black America since Gunnar Myrdal's historic *An American Dilemma* more than sixty years ago, the Thernstroms hoped to displace that work as the seminal intellectual authority on Black America, and, most importantly, its conclusions that racism and discrimination are the major reasons for American economic and social inequality. Apparently inspired by D'Souza, they seek to conclusively establish that Black Americans are not constructively doing something that European Americans are, and doing destructive things European Americans are not. In essence, as the Thernstroms see it, Black Americans are in fact lazy, stupid and promiscuous to a degree European Americans apparently are not, the classic White supremacy premise that Myrdal termed "the defense ideology of slavery."[283] By inviting comparisons between their work and Myrdal's, however, the Thernstroms inevitably paint themselves, a la D'Souza, as prime examples of why some intellectuals who spend the majority of their time in a classroom or with their heads in a book aren't credible when addressing social issues that require a practical understanding of the real world.

Myrdal for instance, removed himself to the Black community to understand first-hand what life was like for Blacks where they lived, worked and socialized, and conducted extensive original research while also using Black assistants and associates to help compile his data. The Thernstroms had no such courage. Their work and opinions therefore carry no similar integrity. In fairness, it is an example followed – surprisingly, and inexcusably – even by opinionated Black intellectuals such as Orlando Patterson and John McWhorter who, not surprisingly, claims the Thernstroms as "good friends," allowing them to now happily make the claim that "some of our best friends are black."

Another shortcoming distinguishing the Thernstroms' book is the fact that it's analysis of Black America begins in the Jim Crow era, whereas *An American Dilemma* begins with an examination of

American slavery. The Thernstroms, however, would have us overlook this difference as immaterial, even practical. Omitting any discussion of slavery most obviously spares European Americans a guilt trip, but the attempt to separate Black Americans from their slave roots is entirely unacceptable. It is no more appropriate than separating White America from the Founding Fathers. Just as Samuel Huntington and the Thernstroms, et. al. seek recognition of the importance of Anglo-Protestant settlers to creating America, Black Americans similarly demand a reckoning for the legacies born of slavery.

Black Poverty

It's difficult to get beyond the picture of the Thernstroms as anything except angry racists because their arguments contradict themselves at almost every turn. For example, relying on statistics for unemployment, the so-called achievement gap, lower marriage rates and crime as proof- positive support for their objectivity, they summarize Black men "are most likely to be living below the poverty line either because they are jobless or work less than full-time throughout the year,"[284] a stunning contradiction to an earlier

Wanna know the secret to how you stay on me? You gotta get on, stay on, your J-O-B!

Foxy Brown: "J-O-B"
China Doll/Violator Records

declaration that poverty rates among African Americans nevertheless approached 90 percent even during the period of relative stability for Black families headed by two parents.[285] "A generation ago," they acknowledge, "a good many black men and women labored full-time, year-round without being able to earn enough money to keep their families out of poverty."[286] Then they ridiculously conclude "it is the unwillingness of a growing number of black men to accept family responsibilities that has reduced their incomes,"[287]

In any event, it seems clear that the lack of two-parent families in the Black community is less likely a cause of poverty, than an effect. Few men can successfully take on the responsibilities of a family if they can barely feed themselves. And women are less interested in having, or keeping, a man who has no job or earns less than they do.[288]

According to sociologist Pamela Smock, as quoted in the *Wall Street Journal,* "it's more likely that a couple will marry if they have money, and if the man is economically stable."[289] "Wives out-earning their husbands," wrote Ralph Gardner, Jr., in *New York* magazine, "is causing havoc in the home." Basically, one woman explains, "it's hard to be the power broker every day and then be the femme fatale. I'm not going to pay the bills," she says, "and then come home and suck his dick."[290] Should it be a surprise then that the groups with the highest unemployment, Black males, and the lowest earnings, Black females, are having serious difficulties maintaining viable unions?

The most relevant questions concerning the higher poverty rates of Black America should more properly revolve around the reasons for higher Black unemployment, since European Americans disproportionately control the vast majority of American business, capital, and employment resources, thus controlling Black access. It therefore still remains true, as Myrdal wrote sixty years ago, that questions about "equality of opportunity, fair play, and free competition — independent of race, creed or color, ... must direct every *realistic* study of the Negroes' economic status in America."[291]

Regarding Black females, the Thernstroms again float some rather curious conclusions that seem to make little sense. "For adult Black women who fall below the poverty line," they say, "the problem has more to do with family circumstances than with their position in the labor market — which is essentially the same as that of White women." But how can that be, since poverty is measured as a function of income, seemingly implicating one's "position in the labor market?" No matter how you slice it, any attempt to separate poverty from income and employment is asinine, because, sadly, there are also married couples living in poverty, and a disproportionately high percentage of those also exists in the Black community.[292] Nevertheless, say the Thernstroms, "it's tempting to think that white women have higher-paying jobs than black women, but they don't, on the average."[293]

Oh, really? On what authority?

None, of course. In fact, it's been reported that White women hold 15 percent of higher-paying corporate officer positions in Fortune 500 companies, while Black women hold just 1 percent,[294] a far cry from their respective positions in the labor market being "essentially the same." Across virtually all occupations of the work force you will not find Black women in high paying jobs comparable to White women, and at Harvard, that bastion of American racism where Stephen Thernstrom is employed, that fact is plain enough for anyone to see, unless of course their eyes are closed to reality, as the Thernstroms' obviously are. And the reason their eyes are closed is because the painfully obvious disparity in employment between Black and White females illuminates the very issue the Thernstroms are trying to obscure: racism.

Under the disingenuous guise of concern for Black children living in poverty, Stephen Thernstrom says the fact that an overwhelming percentage of them happen to live in single parent households "is a problem."[295] But their real interest is to denigrate Black women for exercising their God-given, Constitutionally protected right to bear children. Black mothers raising children on their own is not, in any event, a new phenomenon. It stretches all the way back to slavery so it would seem that if he, they, were so interested in a comprehensive study of Black America they would be compelled to go back to analyze the "problem" at its roots. They are, of course, unwilling to do that because they would then have to climb down off their high horses and paint themselves with the same brush of immorality they are attempting to paint Blacks with. Is it possible to fix a problem without analyzing its origins? Well, one thing is for sure. The normalization of single motherhood, irresponsible fathers, and the low levels of marriage among Blacks all had a healthy influence from Whites during slavery. Yet Whites have never, ever made any attempt to take responsibility for that.

In *Two Nations: Black and White, Separate, Hostile, Unequal,* written in the wake of the Los Angeles riots of the early 1990s, Andrew Hacker argued that assigning responsibility to slavery should be done with "some care," suggesting changed social norms, in the form of liberal attitudes towards relationships and single parenting, may instead explain the causes.[296] These shifting influences, however, have not had staying power comparable to the indoctrination and practices spanning three centuries, "such is the infinite power of custom."[297] As Sumner notes, in *The Challenge of Facts*, "It will take centuries of scientific study of the facts of nature to eliminate from human society the mischievous institutions and traditions" that "statesmen, philosophers, and ecclesiastics have introduced into it."[298]

OH, BABY!

In *Why Race Matters*, Michael Levin intellectualizes the staying power of slavery's immorality through the scientific evolution of cultural reinforcement. To value something from a behavioral standpoint is to be reinforced by it, he explains, "[m]oral approval, then, is a categorical reinforcement tendency, and the morality of a group [is] its shared categorical reinforcement tendencies."[299] Not all categorical tendencies are moral ones, Levin acknowledges, but

> Moral rules are distinguished by sign-change and multiplier effects: the value of adherence to them tends to become positive when the number of other adherents passes a minimum, and then increase rapidly with number of adherents. . . . Hence one can expect to find categorical reinforcement of precisely those rules the benefits of following which increase with the number of followers . . . . So we may say that morality consists mainly of rules that are categorically reinforced because they tend to benefit all when obeyed by all. [300]

Such a "benefit" existed as a reprieve from slavery's oppressive hegemony. Fanny Kemble put it into perfect perspective in the journal she kept during her brief visit to the Georgia Sea Island plantations of her husband, Pierce Butler: "it seems to me that there is not a girl of sixteen on the plantations but has children," she wrote, "nor a woman of thirty but has grandchildren."[301]

> There are certain indirect premiums held out to obey the early commandment of replenishing the earth which do not fail to have their full effect. . . . [Slaves] enjoy, by means of numerous children, certain positive advantages. In the first place every woman who is pregnant . . . is relieved of a certain portion of her work in the field, which lightening of labor continues, of course, as long as she is so burdened. On the birth of a child certain additions of clothing and an additional weekly ration are bestowed on the family; and these matters, small as they may seem, act as powerful inducements . . . Moreover, they have all of them a most distinct and perfect knowledge of their value to their owners as property; and a woman thinks, and not much amiss, that the more frequently she adds to the number of her master's livestock by bringing new slaves into the world, the more claims she will have upon his consideration and good will. This was perfectly evident to me from the meritorious air with which the women always made haste to inform me of the number of children they had borne, and the frequent occasions on which the older slaves would direct my attention to their children, exclaiming: 'Look, missis! Little niggers for you and massa; plenty little niggers for you and little missis [the plantation heiress]!'[302]

Legitimate childbearing among slaves, one might argue, never developed because no benefit accrued from it. European Americans, on the other hand, heavily valued the illegitimate offspring of slaves for economic reasons. They therefore encouraged and directed, not to mention indulged, Black illegitimacy over the course of the entire two-hundred-fifty-plus-years of America's peculiar institution, controlling both slave life and its values, enjoying a sexual as well as a financial boon in the process — justified, no doubt, as return on investment and, in the case of sale of offspring, capital gains.

Slave marriages, on the other hand, were not legally sanctioned and in fact only existed through the permission or will of a White master, whose interest must be consulted first and foremost.[303] Consider, for example, the following:

> . . . [when] an attachment is formed between the young woman and one of her male [slave] associates, . . . she is instantly doomed to examination, and [forced to] betray her secret . . . The young woman is shut up in the appointed place, and when the deeds of darkness can be perpetrated without discovery, her lover is introduced. Before her eyes he is mercilessly scourged for having dared to interfere with the prior right, as they allege, of the slave-driver, or his son, or the overseer . . . Then in her delicate condition she is divested of her clothing, and her only friend, . . . is obliged to whip her, and if he does not strike hard enough, and draw sufficient blood, the deficiency is measured out upon himself. After their rage is glutted with this display of wrath, he is bound fast, and those sons of [Bitches] complete their master's abomination by defiling her before her lover's face. . . . As quickly as possible the stripes are healed, and he is then sold to the slave-trader, to be transported to a distant plantation.[304]

The former slave Harriet Jacobs described her owner's reaction to her desire to be married this way:

> "So you want to be married, do you?" Said [master Flint], "and to a free nigger."
> Yes, sir."
> "Well, I'll soon convince you whether I am your master, or the nigger fellow you honor so highly. If you must have a husband, you may take up with one of my slaves."
> I replied, "Don't you suppose, sir, that a slave can have some preference about marrying? Do you suppose that all men are alike to her?"
> "Do you love this nigger? said he, abruptly.
> "Yes, sir."
> "How dare you tell me so!" he exclaimed, in great wrath. After a slight

pause, he added, "I supposed you thought more of yourself; that you felt above the insults of such puppies."

I replied, "if he is a puppy, I am a puppy, for we are both of the Negro race. . .

He sprang upon me like a tiger, and gave me a stunning blow. . . . "Do you know that I have a right to do as I like with you,–that I can kill you, if I please?" . . . Never let me hear that fellow's name mentioned again. If I ever know of your speaking to him. I will cowhide you both; and if I catch him lurking about my premises, I will shoot him as soon as I would a dog. Do you hear what I say? *I'll teach you a lesson about marriage* and free niggers! Now go, and let this be the last time I have occasion to speak to you on the subject.[305]

And the former slave, William Wells Brown, observed this lesson:

There was, also, among the servants, a girl whose master resided in the country. Her name was Patsey. Mr. Colburn tied her up one evening, and whipped her until several of the boarders came out and begged him to desist. The reason for whipping her was this. She was engaged to be married to a man belonging to Major William Christy, who resided four or five miles north of the city. Mr. Colburn had forbid her to see John Christy. The reason of this was said to be the regard which he himself had for Patsy.[306]

> I'm tryin' to play but,
> she tryin' to have my daughter.
> But I can't blame her,
> for what her momma taught her.

Lloyd Banks: "On Fire"
HUNGER FOR MORE / G-Unit Records

Well, certainly there's nothing about irresponsible parenting that can be tied to slavery, right? Upon visiting James Madison's plantation in the year before his death, 1835, Harriet Martineau observed how "every slave girl [is] expected to be a mother by the time she is fifteen," noting that a third of Madison's approximately two hundred slaves were in fact, "under five years of age."[307]

"The slaveholders' assault fell particularly heavily on slave men: equating manhood with control over an independent household," notes Ira Berlin regarding Black fatherhood, "the masters of the great plantation contested their right to choose a wife, discipline their children, and care for their aged parents, thus relegating slave men to a lesser roles [sic] within their own families."[308] As Tocqueville observed, "the Negro has no family; for him a woman is no more than the passing companion of his pleasures, and from their birth his sons are his equals."[309] "In the first place," Fanny Kemble wrote,

none of the cares, those noble cares, that holy thoughtfulness which lifts the human above the brute parent, are ever incurred here by either father or mother. The relation indeed resembles, as far as circumstances can possibly make it do so, the short-lived connection between the animal and its young. The father, having neither authority, power, responsibility, or charge in his children, is of course, as among brutes, the least attached to his offspring; the mother, by the natural law which renders the infant dependent on her for its first year's nourishment, is more so; but as neither of them is bound to educate or to support their children, all the unspeakable tenderness and solemnity, all the national, and all the spiritual grace and glory of the connection, is lost, and it becomes mere breeding, bearing, suckling, and there an end.[310]

According to Levin, "adaptiveness transposes the benefits of categorical reinforcement into a *genetic* key," making it additionally possible for reinforcement to be carried forward into future generations.[311] "If the pressures that select a socializing regimen also select responses to it," he explains, "children in groups that evolved the regimen have been shaped to internalize it more readily than children of other groups."[312] Racism, discrimination, bias, hatred and stereotypes Blacks are faced with everyday in America certainly cause emotional stresses. Generations of children experiencing dehumanizing oppression might then, for example, evoke internalized behavioral responses such as a desire for affirmation of humanness through reproduction and intimacy, the "product of unconscious processes" preserved by evolution.[313] Therefore, Levin concludes, where "lower levels of male engagement in child-rearing were differentially adaptive" historically, higher levels of single parent homes and children being raised without a father, as supposedly exist within the Black community, are to be expected.[314]

The U.S. government, moreover, acknowledges some impact of slavery's legacy on the lives of contemporary Black Americans. A

Report of the Surgeon General on Mental Health: Culture, Race, Ethnicity stated

> . . . the legacy of slavery, racism, and discrimination continues to influence the social and economic standing of [African Americans]. These and related findings have prompted researchers to ask how racism may jeopardize the mental health of minorities. Three general ways are proposed:
>
> (1) Racial stereotypes and negative images can be internalized, denigrating individuals' self-worth and adversely affecting their social and psycho-logical functioning;
> (2) Racism and discrimination by societal institutions have resulted in minorities' lower socioeconomic status and poorer living conditions in which poverty, crime, and violence are persistent stressors that can affect mental health (see next section); and
> (3) Racism and discrimination are stressful events that can directly lead to psychological distress and physiological changes affecting mental health.[315]

Lacking the courage to even contemplate the implications of slavery in the root "problems" of the Black family, while at the same time feigning ignorance to the unique role of race in employment and poverty, Stephan Thernstrom, nevertheless, has the gall to say the "enormously close correlation between being born out of wedlock, growing up without a father in the household, and being poor," would not, in his opinion, "be ameliorated one wit if every white racist dropped dead tomorrow,"[316] to which my hopeful response to him would be: "Drop Dead!"

In my opinion, as a major reason for America's hypocritical, immoral image, racism is one of the most crucial issues this country must come clean about. Acknowledging our slave history, and its legacies, is a major component of that. We cannot afford to continue demonstrating that we still believe people of color are less-than, immoral and ignorant, particularly as we seek to export American-style democracy abroad. As the late Arthur Schlesinger, Jr. observed, "Our problem is not rejection of the white majority by minorities, but rejection of minorities by the white majority."[317]

I don't believe America can reach its tri-centennial with that attitude, and I'm doubtful whether just half that time, a generation or two, will see this country in its current state, particularly with the growing forces bent on our destruction. The world is constantly changing. In the last century there have been major political and cultural upheavals in virtually every nation of the world, but America has for the most part been spared. The odds are not good that we can or will remain so.

Whether White America likes it or not, the world is, and always has been, culturally, ethnically and racially diverse. I happen to believe the survival of America lies not in a return to its artificial traditions but in an understanding that we are but one part of a diverse world community that must acknowledge the equality of all other parts. To be sure, if the rest of the world collectively decides it wants regime change in America, there's gonna be regime change in America. We cannot defeat the whole world. Our arrogant, isolationist, anti-diversity attitude pushes us closer and closer to that eventuality. In which case, if we are not respectfully unified (as opposed to forcefully so), we stand no chance. In short, whether angry Anglos like it or not, the strength of America lies in its diversity, not vice-versa. Despite popular rhetoric, Europeans did not build this country alone, and it most certainly will not survive the challenges of the future by a reversion to the supposed traditional supremacy of an Anglo-Protestant ideology.

American debacles in Vietnam and Iraq might fairly be measured as a rejection of supposedly superior Anglo-Protestant values, in favor of indigenous cultural traditions. If America had a better understanding of, and respect for, those cultures and traditions we would have, no doubt, met with much greater success.

What, for example, would have been the savings in money and lives if, instead of sending a hundred-thousand-plus troops into Iraq, we were able to introduce into the country half as many Arabic-speaking, culturally-versed businessmen and civilian ambassadors? Ditto, Vietnam? The results certainly could not have been worse than what actually occurred. Those possibilities, however, could only have been realized if America learned to embrace, study and share in the diversity of the world, rather than rejecting, changing or attempting to displace it. That would of course mean embracing and promoting multiculturalism at home, including multilingualism, the very things much of White America opposes, no small thanks to the considerable effort to push America culturally back into the seventeenth and eighteenth centuries, with the help of powerful and highly influential institutional efforts in education, led by Huntington and company. Given the fact that so many of America's government officials emanate from Harvard, for instance, is it any wonder that with the isolationist, anti-diversity rhetoric taught there ("the West and the Rest") the world hates the policies and attitude of the U.S. The country, clearly, is in need of a new image. Harvard University, it also seems, may be largely to blame.

The relative importance of America's domestic priorities is the main implication of Reparations for Black slavery, however, because the salvation of the nation as we know it, or any similarity thereof, likely rests upon a fast and true realization of the national principles always espoused, but never fully lived up to.

True equality, we now know, will never be realized in this country with "all deliberate speed." Rather, it will require a single act, a sweeping stroke as bold as Emancipation itself. But not, hopefully, requiring the same bloodshed accompanying the Civil War.

MONEY

8

Africa

Query I

ccording to Michael Levin: "the world as a whole would hardly have noticed had sub-Saharan Africa not existed or had never been contacted by Europeans and Asians. Trade with black Africa (as opposed to European exploitation of the mineral wealth of the African continent) has always been negligible."

On the surface, the statement appears nothing more than the elementary world history popularly disseminated to Americans from a young age.[318] Given the relative wealth of America and the West it seems easy to believe and promote a certain cultural superiority that cuts Africa out of having played any significant role in world history whatsoever. The reality, however, is not nearly as sexy as this delusional fantasy of the White race being uniquely all-capable, who alone were responsible for creating the modern world as we know it. There is, nevertheless, a plethora of historians promoting exactly that, albeit mostly with infinitely greater degrees of sophistication and tact than Michael Levin. But because of the devastating influence on American racial equality and the true merits of historical accountability for Black slavery, it is imperative that such wishful thinking not go unaddressed.

TRADE

Most interesting about Levin's popularly held position is the
attempted separation of Africa's mineral exploitation by Europeans
from supposedly "negligible" legitimate trade. In fact, what made
Europeans return to Africa — and keep returning until they eventually
occupied and colonized the entire continent — was, of course, gold
and slaves. Although European interest in gold seems acknowledged,
it's doubtful Levin contemplates the true scope of that interest. It's
equally doubtful his assessment of trade with Black Africa is intended
to encompass the slave trade — at one time the most lucrative interest
of Europe in the continent. But, if so, it is the first time I've known
the trade referred to as "negligible," although it certainly would not be
unusual as an attempt for Americans to distance themselves from it.
As Weeden informed us, "Massachusetts writers have always been
especially sore at the point where the trade in African negroes is
touched."[319]

What should we think, therefore, when historian Ralph D. Paine,
in *The Ships And Sailors Of Old Salem*, attempts to separate Salem,
MA from the slave trade by explaining how the city generally engaged
in more respectable avenues of ocean trade during the depression that
followed the Revolutionary War, despite a predominately maritime
economy and the potential for enormous profits in transporting Black
Africans across the Atlantic. Well, Weeden cites a general
understanding among contemporaries that "almost every vessel"
engaged in the Caribbean trade returned with at least "a few" slaves,[320]
which included all Salem vessels and, indeed, virtually all those from
New England, while the trade in Africans was at one time the most
profitable branch of commerce between Africa and the West Indies.
Paine, nevertheless, concludes slavers from Salem were
"inconsiderable," while adding, "most of the family papers which
dealt with slave trading have been purposely destroyed."[321]

In *Salem And The Indies*, James Duncan Phillips similarly explains
that, previous to establishing the U.S.'s foreign, post-Revolutionary
War trade, Salem's mariners and merchants turned to "inland
adventures," such as land speculation in the Northwest Territory.[322]
He references a pioneering voyage of the ship *Commerce* that is
documented to have sailed for Newfoundland, following peace with
Great Britain, in June, 1783, but "Where she went next" is
mysteriously "not evident in the records," though she "came sailing in
from St. Petersburg," Russia, on October 4, 1784, by way of Elsinore,
Denmark.[323] The Russian cargo would have been largely procured
with West Indian sugar, most probably bartered for African slaves,

always a valued commodity in the West Indies where, according to Samuel Eliot Morison, in *The Maritime History of Massachusetts*, "a large discretion was left to shipmasters and supercargoes,"[324] undoubtedly accounting for the gap in the *Commerce's* log.

In *Yankee Traders, Old Coasters & African Middlemen*, however, historian George E. Brooks, Jr. places "the Boston **slaver** *Commerce* under the command of John Dudley Staltonstall" who, in April 1784, was "offering a generous distribution of rum" to the natives on the Gold Coast of Africa, where the British regarded the Americans as "interlopers" attempting to supplant their exclusive West African trade. They complained he "used every Argument to inflame the minds of the Blacks," with whom "no arguments are so powerful . . . as a plentiful supply of Rum, of which he has not been sparing," causing "an affray with the British garrison" that lead to the ship's departure in May 1784,[325] to open U.S. trade "to the Baltic and St. Petersburg."[326]

Paine offers Elias Hasket Derby, one of the so-called "merchant princes" known for his legendary privateering during the Revolution, and for initiating American commerce with India,[327] as an example of Salem's supposed higher trading morals. He describes a frustrated triangular voyage of *The Grand Turk*, loaded with a cargo of New England rum, among other things, to be exchanged at Cape Town, South Africa, for Chinese Black Tea, and then to the Guinea coast for ivory and gold dust "without taking a single slave," ahem! and proceeding to the West Indies for sugar and cotton before returning to Salem.[328] Unable to obtain the tea because of restrictions on trading in Chinese goods at intermediate locations with ships bound for Europe, we're told, get this, that captain Ingersoll otherwise completes the trip and

> notwithstanding the disappointment in the principal object of the voyage and the consequent determination to go to the coast of Guinea, his resolution not to endeavor to retrieve it by purchasing slaves did the captain great honor, and reflected equal credit upon [Derby], who, he assured me, would rather sink the whole capital employed than directly or indirectly be concerned in so infamous a trade.[329]

What? Return home empty handed from a harrowing eighteen month, ten thousand mile journey, whose "principle object" is to realize a profit, simply for the sake of scruples? When the profits are right there for the taking? Uh-huh. Right. To believe all this we first must believe the captain, who generally had at least a vested minority interest in his voyages, was himself indifferent to the tempting profits on his own account, as well as to the five per cent commissions "on the profit made on goods that may be purchased . . . in any other [transaction] that may arise on the voyage,"[330] all in addition to his 100 percent take from transactions completed outside the knowledge of the ship's owner, whose written orders to the captain were, in fact, expressly "not meant as positive" and afforded the discretion "to break them in any part where you by calculation think it" in the interest of profits.[331] In fact,

> The captain was *expected* to 'break [Derby's] orders in any part,' if he could drive a better bargain than his employer had been able to foresee at a distance of ten thousand miles from the market. Merchants as well as navigators, the old-time shipmaster found compensation for these arduous responsibilities in the 'privileges' which allowed him a liberal amount of cargo space on their own account as well as a commission of the sales of the freight out and back. His own share of the profits of two or three voyages to the Far East might enable him to buy and ship and freight a vessel for himself. Thereafter, if he were shrewd and venturesome enough, he rose rapidly to independence and after a dozen years of the quarterdeck was ready to step ashore as a merchant with his own counting house and his fleet of stout ships.[332]

Well, this makes that mysterious gap in the log of the *Commerce* look more and more like a "Don't ask, don't tell" situation. And in light of the chagrin of having one's name associated with slave trading, the circumstances outlined above, as much as any other, and seemingly more than any lack of interest, likely underlie the "negligible" trade record with Black Africa.

American rum "sold well along the entire length of the coast," Brooks writes, though "by far" the greatest amount was traded in the prime slave trading areas "on the Gold Coast and to leeward."[333] New England merchants as a result "dominated" the commerce of West Africa, where both tobacco and rum were staples.[334] "The greatest [shipping] tonnage of Salem merchants for twenty years following the Revolution," was their large fleet of vessels trading to the West Indies, whose homebound cargoes consisted of sugar for home use, and molasses to be converted into rum for export. By 1791, Salem had seven rum distilleries and "probably distilled 500,000 or 600,000 gallons of rum every year."[335]

Salem's trading voyages, observed Morison, generally began with a cargo assembled in Virginia, Charleston or Savannah, or the Baltic, the West Indies, and New England, to be sold at Africa, India, Indonesia and even China, "making three or four turnovers before returning home."[336] So-called "legitimate" West African trade, consequently, cannot be separated from the slave trade. "The two coexisted side by side in a relationship that is best described as symbiotic," according to Brookes.[337] "All the maritime interests of New England were in reality one interest that must stand or fall together," Morison writes, "no one of her sea-borne industries was self-sufficient, and many of the greater merchants were directly concerned in all of them."[338] But even if the total volume of trade with Black Africa had been negligible, two generally discounted factors deserve consideration for any bearing they may have had on the issue: smuggling, and the degree to which West Africa was economically self-sufficient.

The impact of smuggling on official trade figures is age-old and obvious. Consider, for example, that in 2006 the producer of Kent, Pall Mall and Lucky Strikes cigarettes shipped more than a million pounds of cigarettes from South Carolina to Iran, but due to trade restrictions over Iran's nuclear ambitions, and alleged ties to terrorism, some 70 percent of cigarettes sold there are said to be smuggled in from the U.S., allowing tobacco companies to avoid both tariffs and the unsavory stigma of sleeping with the enemy, as well as dramatically skewing the picture of the exchange actually taking place between the two countries.[339] Trading in human lives, or supporting the practice, would have had no less an impact on official trade figures to Africa.

Also, as Brooks recognized, many of the goods Europeans traded in Africa were non-essential luxury items. "Of the four principal articles of commerce," he explained,

> the staples of European and American trade with West Africa until late in the nineteenth century – namely cloth, tobacco, spirits, and arms and powder, cloth was everywhere produced from locally-grown cotton, bark or other fibers, tobacco was grown in many parts of West Africa, and palm wine was to be had for the tapping on most parts of the coast and can be fermented to make a liquor. Gunpowder was manufactured in some parts of West Africa, only the guns had to be imported.[340]

It would be just as easy to conclude, therefore, that trade figures for Africa were relatively low due to circumstances other than a lack of interest on the part of Europeans and Asians.

Early trade with Black Africa was of course conducted through organized caravans with thousands of camels crossing the Sahara "on the two month passage to the Mediterranean . . . from Jenne and Timbuktu,"[341] or through Arab merchants in India prosecuting an Asian trade with the east coast of Africa.[342] Through these Indian Ocean trade networks the Swahili city-states of Mogadishu, Malindi, Mombasa, Zanzibar, Sofala and Kilwa Kivinje exported copper, iron, cloth, tortoise shells, rhinoceros horns, amber, leopard skins, ivory and gold, in addition to slaves and large amounts of "coconut-palm, orange, sugar-cane, rice and sesame" to Arabia via the Red Sea, the Persian Gulf and Indonesia, and even as far away as China up to the 10th century.[343] This was significant to the trade of the eastern Mediterranean and the Levant, at modern day Israel, Syria, Lebanon and southern Turkey, all-important routes for the South Asian and Far Eastern goods entering Europe.[344] Most important, however, was the trade of the southern Mediterranean Barbary coast connecting the Muslim empire at Spain with Morocco, Tunisia, Egypt and Syria.[345] North Italian merchants who organized and controlled large amounts of the trade "in Spanish silk, West African gold, metals and olive oil" along this route,[346] were resident in colonies known as *funduks* in all of North Africa's major commercial ports.[347] In *The Merchant of Prato*, medieval historian Iris Origo identifies three routes as the "main currents of Mediterranean trade" during the latter fourteenth century, in all of which the sub-Saharan trade between Arab and North Italian merchants would have figured prominently: the Far East, the Levant and southern Europe; the Mediterranean and the North Atlantic; and two "minor" channels including the Adriatic Sea between Italy and the Balkans, and the western Mediterranean routes linking Italy, Spain, and North Africa.[348]

MINERAL EXPLOITATION

The attempt to distinguish Black Africa's mineral exploitation from its otherwise legitimate trade is at least an acknowledgement of the historical importance of African resources to the West. But, it's doubtful the intent was to include the entire scope of that significance, such as, for example, the critical contribution of the estimated two-thirds of Europe's gold supply in the Middle Ages originating from Africa to the development of Western capitalism.[349] According to Peter Spufford, in *Power And Profit: The Merchant In Medieval*

Europe, Western Europe was not producing exports nearly equal to the value of the silk and spices obtained from India and the Far East, so accounts were balanced through transfers of gold and silver coin. The amount of gold available from Europe was "insignificant in comparison with west African gold" prior to about 1320, when deposits were discovered and mined at Kremnica in the German-speaking kingdom of Hungary.[350] Up to an estimated half-million ducats were struck there through the end of the century, diminishing thereafter so that by 1440 only about 24,000 ducats were struck at Kremnica, ceasing altogether within a few years, and coinciding with a "silver famine" at the turn of the century.[351]

The precious metals that came into Europe from North Africa[352] had been transported across the Sahara by caravan from the West African regions of the river Niger, and from Ethiopia down the Nile to Cairo.[353] For centuries this was "the principal source of gold for North Africa, the Middle East, and Europe," also exporting slaves, hides and ivory partly through Ghana, "the oldest of the Sudanic kingdoms," and through Takur, a major eleventh century state controlled by Mali that later "disintegrated."[354] Songhay then "took control of the trans-Saharan trade" in gold, salt, slaves, and weapons from the middle Niger and western Sudan region to Tripoli and Cairo, supporting the development of societies in the central Sudan areas of Lake Chad at Kanem and Bornu from the ninth to the fifteenth centuries.[355]

As Europeans understood it, part of the trade "goes by the caravan route towards Syria, the other two thirds go to Timbuctoo, part going to Tunis, and part to the regions of Marocco, and to those parts come Christian merchants, and especially Italians, to buy the gold in exchange for merchandise of every sort."[356] Upon arrival in North Africa "the gold was coined into dinars and double dinars," and, along with the gold dust "in sealed leather bags" received by resident Italian merchants, "paid across the Mediterranean from either Tunis to Sicily, the Balearic islands to Barcelona, or Morocco to Andalusia and Valencia."[357] After being minted it was exchanged from across Central Asia to the East for silk and spices.[358]

The "enormous growth" of the money supply, largely facilitated by the infusion of African gold, produced a "commercial revolution," according to Peter Spufford,[359] which saw the perfection of many components of modern capitalism, such as standard business practices like trading companies; insurance; courier correspondence; bookkeeping and accounting; local and international banking, including the use of bills of exchange, "cheques," usury and interest rates, transforming the entire foundation of medieval European trade, Spufford says.[360] The evolution benefited the North Italian trading and banking centers of Venice, Florence and Genoa, as well as the manufacturing centers of the southern Netherlands. Europe's population, consequently, "nearly doubled" between the 10th and the 14th centuries.[361]

"As money increased in quantity, it could be used more freely for a wide range of activities in which it had previously played a minimal role," and therefore changed many of Europe's social, civic and political institutions and customs. Rulers who previously moved "incessantly" between their estates were able to remain static, from the ability to receive regular money from subjects in lieu of goods and labor rents, allowing for the creation of capital cities where the ruling administration and houses of nobles were located. These cities then became "magnets of demand," increasing "local, regional, national, international and even inter-continental trade." Such "centers of consumption" arose at Naples, Milan, Venice, Palermo, Florence, London, Barcelona and even Avignon, France, which, as the "centre of the trade between Italy and Flanders," was the residence of the Pope and one of Europe's most important cities.[362] This "almost inexhaustible luxury market" was "a swift road to fortune."[363]

Gold ducats of Medieval Venice

Clain-Stefanelli, *Beauty And Lore Of Coins*

The demand for manufactures like glassware, textiles, and metalwork led to the growth of northern European "industrial centers" at Scandinavia, Germany and Poland, and "to the growth of a thriving network of trading centers,"[364] as Italian merchants linked the commerce of North Africa, Egypt and the Levant eastward across the Baltic region from Germany.[365] These networks also facilitated better food distribution. African, Middle Eastern and Asian foods and spices were available in Sweden from the confederation of north German cities, known as the Hanseatic League, whose merchants operated in Stockholm with goods obtained outside the Mediterranean at the North Sea port of Bruges, Belgium, and at Paris and London, where merchants from Venice, Florence, Milan, Genoa, Lucca and Siena were in residence.[366] "It was worthwhile for Italian companies to maintain branches in London from the mid-thirteenth century through the middle ages," according to Spufford, but "six of the seven highest tax payers in Paris" at the end of the thirteenth century "were Italian businessmen," while thirty business houses from Lucca alone were represented there a century later.[367] Merchants obtained goods from their agents abroad at the half dozen or so annual or semiannual, regional commodity fairs lasting some six weeks each. These developed separately into "a continuous cycle of fairs throughout the year, so that there was almost always an international commodity fair being carried on" in one of the various alpine regions separating France and northern Italy.[368]

THE BEGINNING

It was the tightening of the direct European trade routes to Asia, however, that was the impetus for the so-called Age of Discovery, with the Portuguese first venturing down the West African coast seeking the source of sub-Saharan gold to break the Muslim monopoly of the Sudan traffic, while converting the local peoples to Christianity in the process to allay the Portuguese conscience of its purely avaricious, nefarious motives, leading to African enslavement. The Portuguese ventures were of course followed nearly a century later by the Ferdinand and Isabella-sponsored voyages of Christopher Columbus, Spain having banished the final Muslim stronghold from the kingdom mere days before Columbus set sail.[369]

Although trading in Africans as a distinct line of commerce dates to the Portuguese ventures of the fifteenth century, Italian, Arab and Spanish merchants managed to conduct a healthy trade in Blacks as an adjunct to the North African-Mediterranean trade, and to the trade in slaves from the region of the Black Sea which, decreasing in profitability, was seeing its last days. It was learned that tithes, taxes and rents "brought greater revenues from the labor of freemen than from serfs," Kettell reminds us, the soil of England and, indeed, all Europe, being judged "unfitted for slave-labor."[370]

Arabs had in fact held Black slaves as early as the seventh century.[371] In addition to their use in the Muslim armies of the early middle ages, many were sold to European traders operating in the trans-Saharan trade of the Mediterranean, for which Black slaves and other commodities of sub-Saharan Africa were critical. In the eleventh and twelfth centuries, "Spain had been the great slave-market of western Europe," when "traders from Barcelona were selling Moslem slaves in northern Italy" where they could be "found in most prosperous

Genoese and Venetian households."[372] "By the end of the fourteenth century," according to Origo, "there was hardly a well-to-do household in Tuscany without at least one slave," though "not all from Spain and Africa." It strains the bounds of credibility, however, to think a significant number were not sub-Saharan Blacks.

"Only a very few [slaves] brought to Christian Europe were black," says Spufford, describing a dozen slaves "picked up" in Spain, in the spring of 1467, by traders from Florence on their way home from the North Atlantic.[373] Presumably they were African, he writes. But a dozen slaves in one scoop seemingly indicates a more robust demand for Blacks in Europe than say, one, two or a few, which, no doubt, is the quantity intended in this context. Yet an estimated "one thousand slaves were exported annually to Europe from the African coast by the mid-1450s" from Portuguese excursions.[374] It therefore seems reasonable on the evidence to conclude picking up twelve slaves at once was not an aberration but instead quite common at that time. In which case considerably more than "a very few" of the slaves brought to Christian Europe, would have been Blacks.

15th century mural by Mantegna

Spufford, *Power And Profit*

The medieval Florentine merchant, Francesco Datini, obtained slaves for service in his own home, while separately supplying friends and trading in slaves for profit, sometimes raiding the Barbary coast from his agencies in the Balearic Islands off the Spanish Mediterranean where African and Eastern slaves bound for Italy and Spain "were collected and sold." As Spanish and African trade bases in the Mediterranean, the islands of Majorca and Ibiza "thronged with traders of every Mediterranean race." Ibiza was a regular port of call for Venitian vessels en route to France, Belgium, and Holland, while Majorca was a stop for Spanish vessels returning from trading at the Levant on the eastern Mediterranean coast.[375]

Datini founded three trading companies in Spain in the year 1393, in Barcelona, Valencia, and the island of Majorca, locations that "long possessed an undisputed monopoly of the trade of Northwest

Africa."[376] The largest import from the region into north Italy for his lucrative cloth business, according to Origo, was wool, "both African and Spanish." He seems to also have been interested in silk and saffron, in addition to "leather and wax from Barbary, Moroccan vernice and grain from both Spain and Barbary," as well as "ivory tusks and ostrich-feathers and ostrich-eggs," also from Barbary. Returns included "dyes and spices from the Black Sea and the Levant."[377] Datini's, trade activities, says Origo, were "entirely characteristic of his time."[378]

From this trade, of course, Black Africans found their way to all the corners of Europe; if not as a distinct "commodity" then certainly as valuable necessities of the agents abroad who oversaw international trading and commerce for their principals at home. These men "had to live abroad for the best part of their lives, striving against the mistrust of foreign rulers and the competition of foreign trade — without home or family — and no one but a black or yellow slave to nurse them."[379]

But lest we make the mistake of thinking Blacks may have held any real value in medieval Europe, we're promptly reminded to think otherwise by Spufford, giving in to the irresistible temptation of White historians to discount Blacks, and thereby cloud the accuracy of the facts. "In general," he tells us, Asian girls were "much preferred" in Europe to Africans.[380]

Wait a minute. What's that, again?

Uh-huh. "Mongol girls were particularly appreciated for their loyalty and hard work," he says.

What the . . . ?

But, wait. Circassians were also preferred over Black women, says he, get this, for "their beauty."

Oh, Snap! So, not only were Blacks not much valued as slaves, but Black women were also lazy — and ugly to boot! Ho-ly Sh_t!

The White supremacy bullshit found in some of these books is not to be believed. And so damn blatant! Is it any wonder European Americans think they alone created the world? Everything they read about history says they were the hardest working, the most intelligent, the most beautiful, . . . the ones that "mattered."

Oh. That's not promoting White supremacy, you say? Yeah. Right.

This is the same period of history, mind you, when White slavery was being seen in Europe as increasingly unprofitable, while the procurement of slaves direct from Africa was in its earliest stages, although, since Blacks were supposedly so lazy and undesirable, it's not clear why. Historians have been falling all over themselves to show circumstance rather than race established Black slavery in the New World, where both European servants and Natives first worked the plantations and mines that, in the end, writes Pakenham, "were unworkable without Black African labor."[381] "Everyone knows that the [African] slave trade is the source of the wealth which the Spaniards draw from their Indies," cites Thomas, adding, "he who knows how to supply the slaves will share this wealth with them."[382]

What about medieval Europe, though? What value would Black laborers have there if they were lazy? Who would pay for such a servant since slaves obviously didn't come cheap? The answer, of course, is only if they were obtained for *other* services, obvious in the case of women, especially Black women, long desirable as sex objects by White men. But even in this area Spufford seems to be suggesting Black women were not as desirable as Asian and White women, which, if true, the long-standing European obsession with Black sexuality would seemingly have died out centuries ago. We might here make note of a transplanted Datini partner who supposedly kept, in his medieval Barcelona fondaco, "a Moorish slave woman who acquired so much power over him that she became the real mistress of the place," reportedly costing him his life when he "contracted a disease."[383] Datini's own life was, of course, "subject to strict rule," explains Origo, notwithstanding a slave described as "the exception," whose "role," ahem!, was "tacitly admitted."[384]

Arab Slave market c. 13th century.

Source: Black, *Atlas of World History*

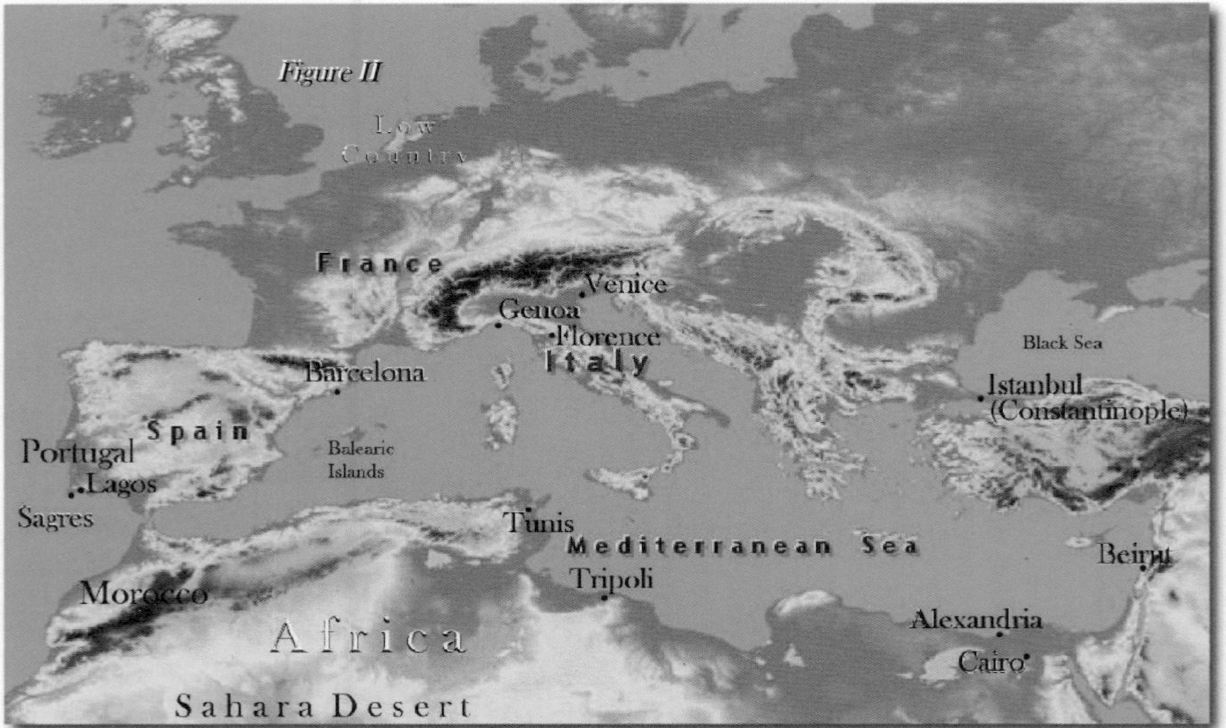

Figure II

Africa

Low Country

France

Venice
Genoa · Florence
Italy

Portugal Spain
Barcelona

Balearic Islands

Lagos
Sagres

Morocco

A f r i c a

Sahara Desert

Tunis

Mediterranean Sea

Tripoli

Black Sea

Istanbul (Constantinople)

Beirut

Alexandria
Cairo

128

Sixteenth century painting of Venice

Spufford, *Power And Profit*

9

The Virgin Prince

THIS IS HOW YOU GET GOT!

Mos Def: "Got"
Black on Both Sides /Rawkus Records

D iscussion of the origins of Portugal's trans-Atlantic commerce in Black human beings[385] should necessarily focus on the "Duke of Viseu, Master of the Order of Christ, and Governor of the Algarves," born March 4, 1394, the third son of John the Great and Philippa of Portugal, more popularly known as Prince Henry the Navigator for his financial and logistical sponsorship of ventures to the Guinea coast of Africa, although he never navigated anything personally.[386] Prince Henry is historically regarded as "the Hero of Portugal, as well as of discovery, the chief figure in his country's history, as well as the first leader of the great European expansion," the spirit that "underlay the exploration of one half of the world's surface, the finding of a new continent in the south and in the west, and the opening of the great sea routes round the globe."[387] These results are credited to others, writes C. Raymond Beazley, in *Prince Henry the Navigator,* but "if Columbus gave [Spain] a new world in 1492, if Da Gama reached India in 1498, if Diaz rounded the Cape of Tempests or of Good Hope in 1486, if Magellan made the circuit of the globe in 1520-2, their teacher and master was none the less Henry the Navigator."[388] The discovery "schemes," Beazley informs us, including maps, instruments and

notes from previous expeditions, were all created by the Prince at
Sagres, or Cape Vincent "with the Atlantic washing the land on three
sides," and from there given to the captains of his caravels leaving
Sagres for the coast of Africa beginning in 1418.[389]

Ostensibly, the Prince's objectives were threefold: scientific,
economic and religious, all of which boiled down to solving the
mysteries and myths of Africa as an alternate route to the riches of the
Indian spice trade, circumventing the economic and political
vicissitudes of Islam. So committed to this eventuality was Henry, he
is said to have eschewed even female companionship, building and
manning his ships from the port of Lagos.

The seminal obstacle occupying the first two decades of the
Prince's exploration was the rounding of Africa's Cape Bojador, "a
promontory that stretched, men said, fully one hundred miles into the
ocean," where tides and shoals formed a "furiously surging" current
twenty miles across that frightened crews and required "seamen to
strike into the open sea out of sight of land" in "a long circuit" that
"forbade all coasting."[390] Bojador was the limit of Europe's knowledge
of the continent since mid-fourteenth century and "an effective if
wholly illusory psychological barrier" to exploration of the African
coast, which Russell believes "almost certainly" to be that shown on
modern maps as Cape Juby.[391]

Even more foreboding than the ocean, no doubt, was the tropical
legend that said "any Christian who passed Bojador would infallibly
be changed into a black, and would carry to his end this mark of
God's vengeance [for] his insolent prying," attributable to Arab
geographers who,

> fringed the coast of Africa with sea monsters and serpent rocks and
> water unicorns, instead of place names, and had drawn the horrible
> giant hand of Satan raised above the waves to seize the first of his
> human prey that would venture into his den. If God made the firm
> earth, the Devil made the unknown and treacherous ocean—this was
> the real lesson of most of the medieval maps, and it was [in] this
> ingrained superstition that Henry found his worst enemy, appearing as
> it did sometimes even in his most trusted and daring captains.[392]

Nowhere, Beazley informs us, did the imaginations of medieval
cartographers and voyagers "revel in genies and fairies and magicians
and all the horrors of hell, with more enthusiastic and genial interest
than in Africa" where, in its southern and desert regions, "the sun
poured down sheets of liquid flame upon the ground and kept the sea

and the rivers boiling day and night with fiery heat. Sailors would of course be boiled alive as soon as they got near to the Torrid zone."[393]

Sent out "under the strongest charge not to return without a good account of the Cape and the seas beyond," one Gil Eannes finally conquered Bojador in 1434, the success of which "proved the salvation of the Prince's schemes."[394] A second dispatch in the year 1435 received "orders to go as far as he could along the coast" till he found some natives, reportedly reaching to an estuary some 390 miles beyond Bojador, believed to be the hopefully named Rio d'Oro,[395] the fabled river first labeled by an anonymous Castilian in his "bogus author-as-traveller," *Libro de Conoscimiento*, accounts of world exploration.[396] Referenced by Henry in the instructions to his captains, the landmark waterway, says Russell, proves the search for gold "was perhaps uppermost in the Prince's mind when he first ordered the exploration of the Saharan coast."[397]

The river was where, in "this first landing of Europeans on the coasts of unknown Africa since the days of Carthaginian colonies," two scouts with "no body-armour, but only lance and sword," were sent on horseback up into the country "to look for signs of natives, and if possible to bring back one captive to the ship,"[398] either "by force or deception."[399] Some twenty miles in, they "came suddenly upon nineteen savages armed with assegais, rode up to them and drove them out" into the open, but were unable to capture any.

Two more unsuccessful attempts were made before the expedition returned to Lagos early in 1436, but the rounding of the prohibitive Cape Bojador and finally landing a European onto African soil was "one of the great moments in the story of Western expansion and discovery," trumping even the journeys of Marco Polo, which established only the eastern limits of European expansion, "and that there would have to be a deadly struggle before European influence could be restored on th[at] side to what it had been under Alexander." However, after passing Morocco to the west, wrote Beazley, "there were only scattered savage tribes to be dealt with."[400]

Between 1436 and 1441, four more expeditions traveled to Africa. One turned back, another failed to reach as far as previous voyages, while two others, in 1440, "met with contrary fortune,"[401] which Russell interprets to mean either a probable loss of vessels and/or "a mutiny."[402] But a 1441 expedition did in fact return to Portugal with Black captives, silencing the skeptics of Prince Henry's "new fangled" African ventures, as "it was only when cargoes of slaves began to arrive in Portugal from Guinea that his critics changed their tune."[403] "Science had its own aims," Beazley noted, "but to gain an income for its work it must promise some definite gain," making the kidnapping of Africans, from the start, "a matter of profit and money returns," since "negro bodies would sell well [and] Negro villages would yield plunder."[404] And because "further discovery depended on trade profits,"

> discoverers who were not disposed to risk anything, and only went out to line their own pockets, would hang about the well known coasts till they had loaded all the plunder they could hold, and would then simply reappear at Sagres with so many more souls for the good Prince to save, but without a word or a thought of "finding of new lands." And this, after all, was the end.[405]

After Portuguese "reprisals" for African resistance had begun, Beazley characterizes the ventures as "an affair of vengeance," with all notions of discovery abandoned: "A village had been burnt, a score of natives had been killed, and twice as many taken. Revenge was satisfied."[406] The coastal peoples of Senegal, however, "forcibly made the point that to make war on the peoples living on or near the sparsely populated Saharan coast was one thing," says Russell, but challenging Black Africa's coastal inhabitants, able to quickly assemble "large numbers of warriors who were usually not in the least intimidated by the small forces the Portuguese could put ashore," was quite another.[407]

> The Portuguese, on the other hand, were much frightened by the effectiveness of the poisoned arrows and lances fired or hurled at them by the massed African warriors. A wound from one of these, . . . usually meant death. Sometimes during these actions the Portuguese had to retreat so fast that they were unable to recover the bodies of their dead comrades. Nor did the Africans always wait to be attacked. They were liable, using dugout canoes, to launch themselves against caravels lying at anchor. In these various encounters some [Portuguese] knights and squires and a considerable number of soldiers and sailors were killed.[408]

The first native captures, however, were given to the credit of two captains sailing separately from Portugal to Africa. One, Antam Gonsalvez, a mere "stripling" of the Prince's household, was given a small ship and ordered "to load a cargo of skins and oil,"[409] valuable because of Prince Henry's soap monopoly in Portugal.[410] How noble it would be, he thought, to be "first to bring a native prisoner" to

Prince Henry, and so devised a plan to attempt a search "in the night."

With a group of nine men landed on the African coast, he followed a path a few miles up from the shore and came across "a track of some forty or fifty men and boys." Tracing it back towards the sea they encountered "a man stark naked, walking after and driving a camel with two spears in his hand." Although alone, "he stood on his defence, as if wishing to show that he could use those weapons of his," but frightened and wounded by "a dart" (a what?), he "threw down his arms like a conquered thing and so was taken, not without great joy of our men."[411] Heading back to the ship "they came upon a blackamoor woman, a slave of the people on the hill," and

> some were minded to let her alone, for fear of raising a fresh skirmish, which was not convenient in the face of the people on the hill, who were still in sight and more than twice their number. But the others were not so poor spirited as to leave the matter thus, Antam Gonsalvez crying out vehemently that they should seize her. So the woman was taken and those on the hill made a show of coming down to her rescue; but seeing our men quite ready to receive them, they first retraced their steps and then made off in the opposite direction. And so Antam Gonsalvez took the first captives.[412]

The other captain, Nuno Tristam, a noble knight "brought up from boyhood at the [Prince's] court," we're told, "came to that place where was Antam Gonsalvez, bringing with him an armed caravel with the express order" to "try and make some prisoners by every means in his power." Imagine what was the joy of the two captains, writes Beazley, "both natives of one and the self-same realm and brought up in one and the self-same household, thus to meet so far from home."

The two determined to "take twenty men, ten from each of the crews, and go up country" in search of the groups of natives from where those already captured had been taken, "as soon as it was night."[413]

> And such was their good fortune that they came early in the night to where the people lay scattered in two dwellings, and our men divided themselves in three parties and began to shout at the top of their voice "Portugal! St. James for Portugal!" the noise of which threw the enemy into such confusion, that they began to run without any order, as ours fell upon them. The men only made some show of defending themselves with assegais, especially two who fought with Nuno

Tristam till they received their death. Three others were killed and ten were taken, of men, women, and children.[414]

One of the captives, "Abahu," reportedly a chief, "shewed full well in his face that he was nobler than the rest" so the place of the capture was promptly named "Port of the Cavalier," while Nuno Tristam afterwards knighted Antam Gonsalvez, "by the instant demand of all others."

Prince Henry was so excited upon viewing the captives he thought "how it would be necessary to send to those parts many a time his ships and crews well armed,"[415] eager to show "crusading for the Faith against Islam" could indeed be carried on profitably in Africa.[416] He wrote the Pope seeking salvation of the Portuguese souls "who in this conquest should meet their end."

Henry's brother, Regent Don Pedro, thereafter granted the Prince a charter allowing him a fifth of the profits accruing to the King from the captures. It also gave him an exclusive license for the right of travel and trade to Guinea so that no one could make the journey without his permission and, of course, a fee, considering "it was by him alone that the whole matter of the discovery was carried out at infinite trouble and expense."[417] Nothing was said in the grant about "Christian evangelization,"[418] strange since it was only as grand master of the Order of Christ that Prince Henry was able to attract funds for his professed voyages of conversion.[419]

Subsequent Prince Henry expeditions brought additional firsts. Gonsalvez, for instance, made the first "ransom," after Henry learned from his African "chief" that "five or six blackamoors" would happily be exchanged for himself and two other boys among the captives. Henry, naturally, was game, deciding it "better to save ten souls than three." But as soon as the chief's feet touched African soil again he took off, and so "by this deceit all our men got warning that they could not trust any of the natives save under the most certain security." Go figure.

As ransom, Gonsalvez received ten Africans in addition to some gold dust, "the first ever brought by Europeans direct from the Guinea Coast," and which, Henry learned, originated from the same sources utilized by the Muslim merchants trafficking in the Mediterranean, from the caravans crossing the Sahara. After seven hundred years under Muslim control it seemed this lucrative trans-Sahara trade finally "was broken in upon by the Europeans," who, in just fifty more years' time would break into "the greater monopoly of the Indian seas" when Vasco Da Gama would sail from Lisbon in

1498 around the Cape of Good Hope to Africa's eastern Malabar coast, and on to southwest India.[420]

"With a caravel manned in great part from the Prince's household," meanwhile, Nuno Tristam seized fourteen natives at Arguin island, "the starting point" for the European Senegambia trade, at a fort built seventy-five miles beyond Cape Blanco by Prince Henry in 1448, one of the first permanent settlements of "new Christian exploration," and "one of the first steps of modern colonization."[421] The location was the first of the "fortified trading factories (feitorias)" from where the Portuguese later ran their overseas commerce in the south Atlantic and the Indian Ocean.[422] Although, as we're reminded by Sugata Bose and Ayesha Jalal, in *Modern South Asia*, "even at the height of their power" during the so-called Portuguese century, they "never came close" to their goal of monopolizing Indian ocean trade and, owing to Muslim naval prowess, also failed "to close the Red Sea to Turkish, Persian, Arab and Indian trade."[423]

A "contradictory" interest arose early on among the merchants who helped fund Henry's excursions, forcing him "to choose between making war on the inhabitants of Mauritania or seeking to trade with them."[424] By mid-century they had resigned themselves to negotiations, the balance of power ruling

Bronze Portuguese soldier, from Benin, West Africa
Black, *Atlas of World History*

out conquest "on any but the most modest scale." Unable to subdue the interior the Europeans were therefore "confined to coastal entrepots."[425]

Approximately three miles in length, Arguin Island sits some two miles off the Mauritanian coast. From here the Portuguese could restock their fish supplies

> and dry their catches on shore in complete security. Arguin offered a relief from a fish diet as well. The spawning fish in the shallows of the Arguin Bank attracted large numbers of . . . pelicans, flamingos and the like. . . . [T]his wildlife was to prove important later on, when Arguin Island became one of the centres in West Africa where slaves were held for shipment to Portugal and the Portuguese had to try to feed them as cheaply as possible until the slave ships arrived.[426]

Owing to the demand from Spain's colonies in the New World, the main trade of the island "continued to be black slaves and gold" into the sixteenth century. [427] But after people bore witness to the first slaves and gold to arrive in Portugal, however, numerous additional volunteers for Henry's future ventures immediately rushed forward.

The view that Henry knew "more of the hundreds taken than of the hundreds more Africans killed, maimed and made homeless in the taking" is not persuasive.[428] Exploits of African "man-hunts," Beazley informs us, were "the main thing in their stories when they got home," the chief instruction from the Prince being, upon granting a license to travel to Africa for slaves, to give a full account of everything seen and done,[429] whereupon he would have heard the following:

> the sailors landed and rushed upon the villagers and saw the Moors with their women and children coming out of their huts as fast as they could, when they caught sight of their enemy; and our men,crying out "St. James, St. George, Portugal," fell upon them, killing and taking all they could. There you might have seen mothers catch up their children, husbands their wives, each one trying to fly as best he could. Some plunged into the sea, others thought to hide themselves in the corners of their hovels, others hid their children underneath the shrubs that grew about there, where our men found them.[430]

If the numbers of injured Portuguese brought back or left dead in Africa didn't convey the true nature of this nefarious business, the Africans themselves certainly would have. "What heart [could be] so stern as not to be pierced with pity to see that company," asks Beazley, relating a written account of the landing and sale of the first African slaves to arrive in Portugal:

> For some held down their heads, crying piteously, others looked mournfully upon one another, others stood moaning very wretchedly, sometimes looking up to the height of Heaven, calling out with shrieks of agony, as if invoking the Father of Nature; others grovelled upon the ground, beating their foreheads with their hands, while others again made their moan in a sort of dirge, in their own way, for though one could not understand the words, the sense of all was plain in the agony of those who uttered it.
> Most terrible was . . . when came the partition and each possessor took away his lot. Wives were divided from husbands, fathers from sons, brothers from brothers, each being forced to go where his lot might send him. Parents and children who had been ranged opposite one another, now rushed forward to embrace, if it were for the last time; mothers, holding their little children in their arms, threw themselves down, covering their babes with their own bodies.[431]

"AWULETH UMSHINI WAMI"[432]

President Jacob Zuma,
African National Congress

"As a part of European commerce," the African slave trade, from this point forward, was officially on,[433] marking, not coincidentally, the dawn of modern times — and the rise of the West.

Conducted on the coast through the many "agencies of Guinea,"[434] the business of buying and selling Africans "earned substantial profits for the Portuguese at the start, before "pass[ing] into the hands of the French at Senegal and at Dahomey, into the hands of the English in Gambia, the Dutch at Gorée and Cape Verde, the Courianders and Danes even, on the Gold Coast,"[435] eventually engaging some six hundred ports on the African coast.[436]

Ironically, the infamous Dutch West India Company had initially sworn off the trade, concentrating instead on the exchange of gold, ivory and other products for its European manufactures. Gold comprised 75 per cent of Dutch returns from Africa, at a profit of 115 per cent, while Portuguese slave traders of the same period realized a mark-up "very much higher" at "983 percent."[437] Heavier expenses in the trade of Indonesian spices and China silks limited net profits to "some 30,000 ducats," whereas net proceeds from West African slaving contracts, "at 80,000 ducats," were more than twice as large as the trade of the East.[438] All Europe, particularly the Dutch, whose "commercial intelligence" was generally considered excellent, was, history shows, very keen to these facts.[439]

According to W.E.B. Du Bois, in *Suppression Of The African Slave Trade*, the private trading companies that merged in 1621 to form the Dutch West India Company "sailed from Holland to Africa, exchanged their goods for slaves, carried the slaves to the West Indies or Brazil, and returned home laden with sugar," sending some 15,430 Black slaves to Portuguese Brazil over four years and "supplying even the English plantations" through a monopoly of the American trade, leading to their status as "the great slave carrier of the day."[440] This "commercial supremacy" Du Bois continued, "early excited the envy and emulation of the English," leading to two wars to place the slave-trade in their hands and, under the final terms of peace, the surrender of New York to England, which then become "henceforth the world's greatest slave-trader."[441]

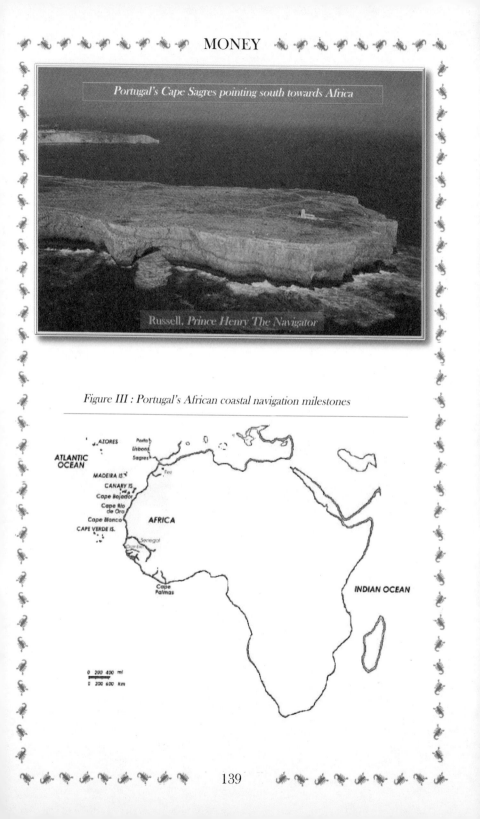

Figure III : Portugal's African coastal navigation milestones

Table I

Atlantic Slave Trade, 1701-1800

Carrier	Total
English	2,532,300
Portuguese	1,796,300
French	1,180,300
Dutch	350,900
North America	194,200
Danish	73,900
Other (Swedish, Brandenburger)	5,000
Total	6,132,900

Source: Blackburn, *The Making of New World Slavery*

10

Sir John Hawkyns

Wearin' red, white and blue,
Union Jack and his crew,
the guys authorized
to beat down for the Brown.

Public Enemy: "Can't Truss It"
Apocalypse 91...The Enemy Strikes Black
Sony/Def Jam Records

egarding the greatest slave trading nation of them all, Great Britain, it's important to note the first to indulge the trade for that nation, Sir John Hawkins. "No understanding of the origins of the English slave trade," writes Nick Hazlewood, in *The Queen's Slave Trader,* should forebear an examination of his early slaving voyages,[442] which set the example for what it would take for England to become a military, economic and political force after the globe had been, willy-nilly, divided between Portugal and Spain. The slave trade was a direct cause of the explosion of wealth and stability of Britain's American colonies, and therefore responsible for the rise of Great Britain to a preeminent economic and military power.[443]

It was through his trade with the Spanish and Portuguese colonists that Hawkins supposedly "learnt" the unfamiliar customs of the New World, writes Blackburn, including that of "holding slaves."[444] But describing Hawkins as a trader suggests a businessman of general character dealing in arms-length transactions. In reality, Hawkins was nothing more than a pirate — albeit of the first rank — likely the most significant thing he learned from the Spanish and Portuguese. His slaving adventures to the Guinea coast of Africa would symbolize "the rise of modern capitalism," which David Landes, citing the German scientist Max Weber, characterized as "sanctioning an ethic of everyday behavior that conduced to business success."[445]

On the first of his three infamous African "trading" expeditions, Hawkins, in October, 1562, not quite thirty-years-old, "got into his possession, partly by the sworde, and partly by other means, to the number of 300 Negros at the least, besides other merchandises, which that country yieldeth" and, with the proceeds from his "praye," according to Hakluyt, "hee did not onely lade his owne 3 shippes with hides, ginger, sugars, and some quantitie of pearles, but he fraighted also two other hulkes with hides and other like commodities."[446] Before returning to England in September, 1563, Hawkins and his men overran a Portuguese ship, beat and clubbed the crew, carting off "between two hundred and five hundred [Black] captives . . . , along with the ship and its cargo of ivory, wax, and gold."[447] All in all, the expedition net an enormously profitable windfall that proved how lucrative this *business* could be.

For his second voyage to the Guinea coast, in October 1564, Queen Elizabeth, obviously anticipating mammoth cargoes and profits far in excess of Hawkins' first excursion, authorized the use of her 700 ton ship, *Jesus of Lubeck.* By comparison, the largest ship on the previous voyage was a mere 120 tons. In addition to the *Jesus*, the fleet included four ships with a crew and company of some one hundred and forty men, plus a number of African women, "almost certainly slaves that Hawkyns had not sold on his previous voyage, but why they were on board, and what function they were being forced to perform, is open to speculation," says Hazlewood, although they were "confiscated" by the Portuguese during a stopover at the Canary Islands.[448]

Having "ankered at one of the Islands called Sambula," on December 12, off the coast of Sierra Leone, the expedition "stayed certaine daies, going every day on shore to take the Inhabitants, with burning and spoiling their townes."[449] "Having taken certaine Negros, and as much of their fruites, rise, and mill, as we could well cary away," they remained on the coastal island until December 21, "whereof there was such store, that wee might have laden one of our Barkes" and departed, but for a just encounter involving a drunken English straggler who recklessly went from the ship to retrieve some previously stashed "pompions" (pumpkins?) when "the Negros" suddenly "came behinds him . . . and straight cutte his throate, as he afterwards was found by his fellowes."[450]

At the Callowsa river, probably in the area of Senegambia, Hawkins visited Portuguese forts some sixty miles inland and "returned with two Caravels, loaden with Negros," which Hazlewood estimates amounted to about six hundred slaves, likely plundered from Portuguese ships.[451] It would be a while before the English learned, as the Portuguese had a century earlier, that taking slaves by force might not be the most efficient method of obtaining them.[452] Hearing of a lightly defended town with a "great quantitie of golde," and "an hundred women and children," Hawkins' men hysterically descended upon it, and in the frenzied disorganization, afforded the Africans a prime opportunity.[453] "For the hope that they had to finde golde in their houses," wrote a member of the expedition, "our men [were] scattering themselves . . . ransacking the same, in the meane time the Negros came upon them, and hurte many,"

and being driven downe to take their boates, were followed so hardly by a route of Negros, who by that tooke courage to pursue them to their boats, that not onely some of them, but others standing on shore, not looking for any such matter by meanes that the Negros did flee at the first, and our companie remained in the towne, were suddenly so set upon that some with great hurt recovered their boates; othersome not able to recover the same, tooke the water, and perished by meanes of the oaze. While this was doing, the Captaine [Hawkins] who with a dozen men, went through the towne, returned, finding 200 Negros at the waters side, shooting at them in the boates, and cutting them in pieces which were drowned in the water, at whose coming, they ranne all away: so he entered his boates, and before he could put off from the shore, they returned againe, and shot very fiercely and hurt divers of them. Thus wee returned backe some what discomforted. . . . having gotten by our going ten Negros, and lost seven of our best men, whereof M. Field, Captaine of the Salomon, was one, and we had 27 of our men hurt.[454]

This was the 27th of December 1564. After some difficulties obtaining fresh water and food at various areas of the coast, they departed January 29 for the West Indies where they would offer their African cargo for sale to Spanish colonists. An interesting description of the Indians encountered at Santo Domingo, on March 23, was given thus:

These Indians being of colour tawnie like an olive, having every one of them both men and women, haire all blacke, and no other colour, the women wearing the same hanging downe to their shoulders, and the men rounded, and without beards, neither men nor women suffering any haire to growe in any part of their body, but dayly pull it off as it groweth. They goe all naked, the men covering no part of their body but their yard, upon which they weare a gourd or piece of cane, made fast with a third about their loynes, leaving the other parts of their members uncovered, whereof they take no shame. The women also are uncovered, saving with a cloth which they weare a hand-breath, wherewith they cover their privities both before and behind. . . . They delight not when they are yong in bearing of children, because it maketh them have hanging breastes which they account to bee great deforming in them, and upon that occasion while they bee yong, they destroy their seede, saying, that it is fittest for olde women. Moreover, when they are delivered of childe, they goe straight to washe themselves, without making any further ceremonie for it, not lying in bed as our women doe.[455]

After venturing as far as Venezuela to dispose of all but fifty of his several hundred slaves, Hawkins' second expedition ended September 20, 1565, with eventful experiences at both Florida and NewFoundland during the return to England. "God be thanked," wrote a companion, "in safetie, with the losse of twentie [White] persons in all the voyage, and with great profit to the venturers . . . , as also to the whole realme, in bringing home both golde, silver, pearles and other jewels. His name therefore be praised for evermore."[456]

The fifty unsold Africans were added to the outbound cargo of Hawkins' troubled third venture that began October 2, 1567, with a fleet of six ships. Two vessels supplied by the queen entitling her to "a third share of the profits."[457] The voyage, however, met with calamity, having been pushed to the brink of cannibalism. Hawkins and a mere fraction of the original fleet and crew were barely able to make it back to England with their lives after armed Spanish opposition to their illegal trafficking in Mexico. Still, Hawkins reported, before the conflict "the Spanish resorted to us by night, and bought of us to the number of 200 Negros."[458] A "final reckoning" of the expedition, however, concluded it had sustained losses "in the region of £30,000," including an itemized accounting of "57 black Africans, . . . each worth 400 pieces of gold in the regions of West India."[459]

NEW BEGINNINGS

The legacy of Hawkins' slave trading voyages for England is of course one of the biggest stories of world development. A microcosm of that story was that by 1752, two hundred years after Hawkins, Liverpool, England employed 53 sailing vessels in the slave trade. In 1786 the city "sold 31,690 slaves for £1,282,690," a 25 percent profit, casting its "phenomenal" development as "one of the most spectacular" commercial circumstances of the eighteenth century.[460] With its proximity to the cotton textiles manufacturing center of Lancashire, England, Liverpool, "reaped the advantages accruing from the marked expansion in the receipts of American cotton and other agricultural commodities in the nineteenth century,"[461] all produced, not coincidentally, by Black American slaves. Liverpool is just one of the many cities around the world that quite literally can be said to owe its very existence to Black slavery.

At about 1700, the African slave population in the Chesapeake colonies numbered approximately less than 15,000. A quarter-century later that total had tripled to more than 50,000.[462] "From 1718 to 1727 Virginia imported slightly over 11,000 Negroes from Africa in 76 vessels," 70 of which, carrying over 10,000 Africans, "were from Bristol, Liverpool and London."[463] Between 1700 and 1740, approximately 54,000 Black slaves entered Virginia, "all but 5,000 of them imported from Africa, while Carolina had almost 40,000."[464] "Death was so great and the rates of childbirth and infant survival were so low," writes Edward Countryman, in *Americans: A Collision of Histories*, the slave population grew "only because fresh Africans were entering even faster than other Africans could die.[465]

Lewis Gray approximates that in 1768 alone the British exported 60,000 African slaves to her colonies, "the French carried 23,500, the Dutch 11,300, the Portuguese 8,700, and the Danes 1,200."[466] In *History of Domestic and Foreign Commerce of the United States*, economic historian Emory R. Johnson, citing Du Bois, estimates the number of "Negroes brought annually to the continental American colonies must have averaged 10,000 . . . with English ships import[ing] about 3,000 into South Carolina each year from 1733 to 1766,"[467] compared to an investigation by Britain's Board of Trade, from 1726, concluding that slaves sold in the American colonies numbered approximately 30,000 annually. Du Bois in fact observed that prior to the Revolution, the average yearly trade in slaves to America was "variously estimated as between 40,000 and 100,000."[468] By 1800, Howard Zinn estimates, "10 to 15 million blacks had been transported as slaves to the Americas, representing perhaps one-third of those originally seized in Africa."[469]

The slave trade, according to Zinn, paid Europe as much as "double the investment on one trip,"[470] although competition and mortality caused profits to vary widely. Long-term, investors in the trade were competitive. Blackburn cites "an annual average profit of 9.5 per cent accruing to British slave traders in the years 1761 to 1807," while "investment in the French slave trade brought a return of 7 to 10 per cent annually," as compared with "real-estate mortgages which yielded 4.5 per cent, or investment in West Indian plantations, which might yield 6-11 per cent."[471] The simple ledger in Table II, below, from an early nineteenth century slaving voyage, gives a picture of returns that could be realized.[472]

"Eagerly sought after by colonial merchants and planters," writes Middleton,[473] the slave trade was by far regarded the most profitable

Table II

Income	
Sale of cargo (217 slaves)	$77,469
Proceeds from sale of vessel	3,950
Total	$81,419
Expenses	
Vessel, fittings, cargo, wages	$39,700
Net Profit	$41,719

Conneau, *A Slaver's Log Book*

trade of the Chesapeake colonies, and "profoundly affected economic relations" with Great Britain.[474] Since 90 percent of colonial slaves were imported by British vessels, "the slave trade represented an invisible export for England to the extent of nearly half a million pounds (£472,500), reducing the adverse trade balance with the colonies to a third of a million pounds" (£333,000) from £804,000.[475] Records from Charleston South Carolina between 1804-1807, inclusive, the last legal years of the trade, "shows a total of 197 ships engaged in the slave trade to Africa, including 70 from Great Britain, 61 from Charleston, and 59 from Rhode Island,"[476]

As profitable as it was for Britain and her colonies, however, it was that much more devastating for Africans, as is well documented. Typical of the cost in African lives during a crossing of the Atlantic was a vessel to Virginia in 1702 carrying 230 Africans that lost 100 at sea.[477] W.E.B. Du Bois in fact identified the percentage of deaths lost over the middle passage in 249 vessels of the Royal African Company, during the period between 1680-88, as greater than thirty percent: 14,387 of the estimated 60,783 shipped from the African coast.[478] Loss of life varied widely but it was not at all unheard of to lose an entire cargo. That is, of course, if they even survived the harrowing ordeal of making it to the coast after months of travel on foot, chained together, from the interior.

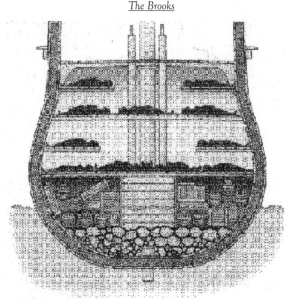

The Brooks

Source: "Northeast," *The Hartford Courant*

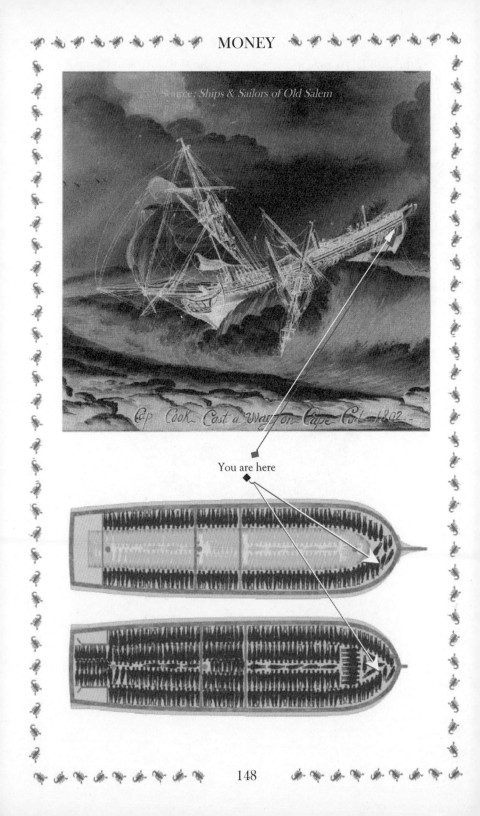

Source: Ships & Sailors of Old Salem

Cap Cook Cast a Way on Cape Cod 1802

You are here

11

Rich Land, Poor Land

Don't believe the Hype!

Public Enemy: "Fight The Power"
Do The Right Thing (A Spike Lee Joint)
Motown Records

Guns, Germs & Still Racism

The question of the impact of Blacks on overall world development, relative to that of Europeans, is being continuously addressed, as we've seen, by historians, philosophers, economists and even scientists. Answering this question "is not of just academic interest," acknowledges Jared Diamond, author of the acclaimed and widely read, *Guns, Germs, and Steel: The Fates of Human Societies*, it is "also of overwhelming practical and social importance. The history of interactions among disparate peoples that shaped the modern world [has] created reverberations that have still not died down after many centuries, and that are actively continuing" in "current political and economic reverberations."[479]

A question of such profound concern and importance to present day America should therefore not be overlooked here, nor should the influence of some of the more popular works on the subject be discounted. Such as *Guns, Germs, and Steel*, for example, which looks at the question from the evolutionary impact of geography and biology on agriculture, technology and, you guessed it, culture.

To support the premise that disparate contributions are unrelated to differing intellectual capacities, Diamond ostensibly wants us to believe he sees the traditionally primitive and uneducated natives of New Guinea as actually more intelligent than European Americans, like himself, who divides his energy between "molecular physiology on the one hand, and evolutionary biology and biogeography on the other."[480] "I do not assume that industrialized states are 'better' than hunter-gatherer tribes," he disingenuously states, "or that the abandonment of the hunter-gatherer lifestyle for iron-based statehood represents 'progress.'"[481]

This would, of course, mean he believes the brutal displacement and exploitation of proud, native peoples in North and South America, Africa, Australia, India and other parts of Asia by Europeans, in the name of so-called "civilization," to have been strictly misplaced, backward and ineffective. Yet it is from this unconvincing proposition that Diamond proffers what he presumes to be a "non-genetic," race-neutral response to the central question of why it is Europe and its ancestors have developed the abundance of the world's advanced goods and technology, while Black descendants of African ancestry have been responsible for so relatively little. He spends a great deal of time explaining how the domestication of crops and animals, and the lack thereof, due mainly to the more suitable climate and geography of the Eurasian fertile crescent, facilitated the diffusion of technology and culture more readily than in Africa and the Americas, whose lengths are divided by the equator and, therefore, more varied in climates and arable farming lands suitable for supporting life.

Diamond, however, completely ignores the exploitation of African labor in the gold mines of Central and South America, and in the cotton, sugar, tobacco and rice fields of North America, as the single most important factor in the explosion of wealth in the modern world, in favor of a "truly classic argument of Eurocentric world history," writes one reviewer, in which "Europe alone, therefore, has had the historical basis for intellectual innovation and social progress,"[482] through the "development of a merchant class, capitalism, and patent protection for inventions, failure to develop absolute despots and crushing taxation," according to Diamond, and, oh! of course, the "Greco-Judeo-Christian tradition."[483] Never mind that these critical institutions he credits were all, for the most part, built up on the bowed backs of African and Black American slaves.

Guns Germs and Steel, James M. Blaut writes,

is influential in part because its Eurocentric arguments seem, to a general reader, to be so compellingly "scientific." . . . But [Diamond] claims to produce reliable, scientific answers to [questions of human history] when in fact he has no such answers, and he blithely ignores the findings of social science while advancing old and discredited theories of environmental determinism.[484]

As with other historians (Berlin, Morgan), Diamond wants us to believe discounting the role of race in world development is actually a promotion of racial equality, since, presumably, individuals will be dissuaded from thinking a supposed lesser contribution equates with racial inferiority. But the true history of modern world development is literally the history of slavery, which has been "peculiarly associated with darker pigmentation or 'black' skin."[485] Therefore, any serious study of world development and relative wealth "must center on early and late African colonialism"[486] — and slavery — because, as Blackburn correctly notes, "Captive Africans and their descendants paid with their blood and sweat and incarceration for the phenomenal expansion of human possibilities in the Atlantic world."[487] This truth, by its very absence, is notably conspicuous throughout *Guns, Germs, and Steel*. The more one gets into the book, therefore, the more clear it is that *Guns, Germs, and Steel* is anything but race-neutral. The chapter titled, "How Africa Became Black," for example, is no doubt welcome reading for European Americans whose skin crawls thinking the origins of man all trace to Black Africa.

By ignoring the import of African slave labor, and the unparalleled, disparate impact of tobacco, cotton, sugar, rice, coffee, wheat and indigo on the world's economic and political development, particularly since Europeans first entered the Western Hemisphere, *Guns, Germs, and Steel* amounts to little more than another shameless promotion of White supremacy. Unfortunately, for non-Whites, the idea that White is and has always been the best, brightest, most important, indeed, the only presence that mattered to world development is very much welcomed and well received — not to mention pervasive.

Wealth & Poverty From Slavery

In *The Wealth And Poverty Of Nations*, Harvard professor emeritus David Landes essentially pulls up a chair to the table set by Diamond — and Michael Levine — serving, as Alexander Hamilton might say, "pork, still, with a little change of the sauce." His is another book intended to engender White pride through a supposed superior European contribution to the development of the modern world.

Critiques of his "politically incorrect" posture are duly noted, but the intellectual and institutional influence of Landes, and the book, is nevertheless significant. As it relates to America's history of Black slavery, and Reparations particularly, *The Wealth And Poverty Of Nations* warrants further critical comment.

Landes doesn't overlook the value of Black slavery in world development but, as one of the "consequence[s]" that followed Christopher Columbus' New World conquest, he simply dismisses it as comparatively "irrelevant." The "exchange" between New World and Old, he says, was "asymmetrical," meaning, of course, the benefits to Europeans outweigh any and all other consequences, including the devastation of Native peoples and the subsequent torture and trafficking of Black slaves. "The European *epiphany*," as he calls it, "was the one that mattered," because Europe "initiated the process, responded to the discovery, and set the agenda for further developments."[488]

Okay, but since the so-called "opening" of the New World did not begin with Columbus' conquest, but instead with the Portuguese ventures down the Atlantic coast of Africa, how 'bout I say Muslims initiated the process, by limiting Europeans' direct routes through Asia, forcing them to seek alternate routes to the Indian spices that killed the taste of their rotten meat? Or, that Africans initiated the process by keeping the sub-Saharan sources of the gold Europeans coveted a mystery? A shortage of gold and the prospect of setting down to a daily plate of warm maggots were in reality the circumstances Europeans responded to that "set the agenda for further developments."

Such "nomenclatorial dissents" from the Eurocentric worldview of history, says Landes, lamenting a waning universal pride in Columbus' infamy, are merely "a form of expiation and political mobilization," designed, he says, "to impute guilt, provoke consciences, [and] justify reparations."[489] But, he audaciously concludes, in an unwitting admission of his own bias, "A *good* historian," like himself, presumably, "tries to keep his balance,"[490] apparently unaware the very definition of "asymmetric," is unbalanced.[491] The "balance" referred to is of course a view of history that does not hold Europeans accountable for their historical evil.

Should we then emphasize a view of the Jewish holocaust that says Hitler was good for the German economy, so as to have balance? The real job of historians in fact is to try and tell the unpleasant truth, however unbalanced it may be, because we all know that history has seldom been balanced. Otherwise you get the kind of purposeful romanticizing done by Ira Berlin or, worse, Michael Levin. Yet Landes no doubt distinguishes his Eurocentric, White-pride perspective from overtly biased arguments like Levine's.

I beg to differ. There's little difference. If history's roles were reversed, one wonders if Landes would deem the decimation of ninety percent of the European population, as was the case with the indigenous populations of the New World, to be similarly irrelevant, particularly if "the process of depopulation was hastened by massacre," as it were.[492] Somehow, I doubt it.

Moreover, as one might easily imagine, a different welcome for Columbus would likely have changed the entire perception of his historic voyage to *India*, where he believed he had traveled to right up to his death, thereby killing all enthusiasm for New World discovery. "No sooner had we anchored than dugout [canoes] began to come to the ships. They brought us water and all manner of things," Columbus wrote, "At 9 o'clock in the morning I sent the ship's boat ashore for water, and those on the island, with very good will, showed my people where the water was. They even carried the full casks to the boat and took great delight in pleasing us."[493] Seemingly already thinking of sugar cultivation, Columbus marveled "I cannot get over the fact of how docile these people are." "With 50 men you could subject everyone and make them do what you wished. [They] ought to make good and skilled servants, for they repeat very quickly whatever we say to them."[494] Yet, this is the guy Hugh Thomas describes as a "serious Christian"[495]; a true American hero?

As for Black slavery, unlike Jared Diamond, Landes finds it difficult to ignore the displacement of African laborers to the tune of "some 10 million over the course of three centuries," although precise estimates, he says, "have grown over the years by way of aggravating the crime."[496] Well, of course. We know the supremacy of Eurocentrism is right and honorable so it's not possible earlier estimates were low by way of mitigating the crime. Right? Sure.

However, the relevant question, according to Landes, imagining the world essentially unchanged from its present state had Black slavery never occurred, is "whether the Industrial Revolution," the cornerstone for modern development and wealth, "would have taken place without it." His answer, predictably, is "clearly yes," but "more slowly,"[497] reiterating Levin's claim that "the world as a whole would hardly have noticed had sub-Saharan Africa not existed or had never been contacted by Europeans and Asians."

But what else can he say? To acknowledge otherwise would be an admission that slavery had in fact played a "decisive" role in world development — that Africa "mattered" — a conclusion not at all consistent with the White pride message he's been filling his Harvard students' heads with. But how is it Europe can occupy an exalted historical position, based upon a supposed "epiphany" of discovery, when exploration only became viable from the brutal, inhumane and immoral exploitation of the people and resources of Africa?

"In the beginning, people murmured very loudly against" Henry the Navigator's "buccaneering" in Africa, we're told, but

> when the way had been fairly opened and the fruits of those lands began to be seen in Portugal in much greater abundance, men began, softly enough, to praise what they had so loudly decried. Great and small alike had declared that no profit would ever come of these ventures, but when the cargoes of slaves and gold began to arrive, all were forced to turn their blame into flattery, and to say that the Infant was another Alexander the Great, and as they saw the houses of others full of new servants from the new discovered lands and their property always increasing, there were few who did not long to try their fortune in the same adventures.[498]

Six caravels of "merchant adventurers" subsequently set out for the coast of Africa in early 1444, "on the first *exploring* voyage that we can call national," wrote Beazley, "evidence that the cause of trade and political ambition had become thoroughly identified with that of exploration."[499]

The so-called "European epiphany" Landes identifies was nothing more than a realization that the road to wealth and riches lay in the exploitation of Africa and Africans.[500] He characterizes this encounter and exchange as asymmetric, because the "further developments" of discovery in the Western Hemisphere, sparked by European adventures in Africa, "on an operative level," he says, were "a one-way business." But what truly was asymmetric was the inhumanity and barbarism Europeans "exchanged" in gaining their African and New World riches. Rather than normalize those immoral means as decadent and even, God forbid, shameful European avarice, however, they are instead offered as symbolic of a supposed inherent, virtuous superiority of European culture. The spoils of that immorality included the opportunity to develop and perpetuate a social system that inculcates the glorification and exhaltation of Eurocentrism.

Thus, Landes is lauded as the "Historian of Our Time" for his Eurocentric perspective of *history*.[501]

Well, does anyone honestly believe *The Wealth And Poverty Of Nations* would be considered such a "wonderful read" if it promoted the African Diaspora as the single most important element of Western wealth and development? Such an admission automatically carries a tacit understanding of a debt owed. And since we know Black slaves didn't do anything Europeans wouldn't have done themselves, like working the sugar-cane fields, rice paddies and, oh, pick all that cotton, slavery's contributions should in no way be acknowledged as uniquely significant, right? Certainly not, at least not in any way that disparages the legendary Anglo-Protestant work ethic. Of course not.

Northern Europeans, says Landes, eschewed agricultural and mineral exploitation and focused instead on "renewable harvests and continuing industry" coming out of the middle ages,[502] rather than sitting back and enjoying the wealth created by slaves as the Spanish had.

Okay. But, what was it they did, exactly?

"They built on work," he says.

How's that?

Well, "they caught fish, tapped and refined whale oil, grew and bought and resold cereals, wove cloth, cast and forged iron, cut timber and mined coal."[503]

Oh? Well, which one of those was responsible for the wealth that made industrialization so inevitable, independent of the African slave trade and the resulting explosion of Western wealth from sugar, tobacco and cotton, notwithstanding the fact that, as we've seen, the cereals, cloth and iron pursuits in northern Europe, even at that time, were not independent of critical connections to sub-Saharan Africa? The answer, of course, is none. Because nothing else has compared to or facilitated the leaps made in population and industrialization spurned by the prodigious wealth lifted from the bloodied backs of Black slaves in the Western Hemisphere!

Landes wants us to believe, and he may even have convinced himself, that the wealth of Spain, Italy and Portugal garnered from Africa and Africans did not touch northern Europe, or that it operated in an economic vacuum, when in reality they were the direct beneficiaries of the New World wealth based on slave labor. Sixteenth century Spain was in fact the center of a network of intercontinental trade, described by Henry Kamen, in *Empire*, as "a commercial chain that connected Amsterdam, Antwerp, London and

Hamburg with La Rochelle, Nantes, Rouen, Livorno, Venice, Genoa and Naples, and beyond them with Africa, Brazil, Goa and the whole of Spanish America."[504] In the sixteenth and seventeenth centuries, moreover, when "Africa came to be regarded preeminently as a vast reservoir of labor for New World plantations,"[505] the various manufactured goods exchanged for those slaves were in fact, derived from all Europe. Cloth traded in Africa, for example,

> came from Flanders, France, even England . . . wheat was carried from Northern Europe. Brass goods came from Germany — especially "armilles," bracelets, which began to be made in Bavaria specifically for this trade, and there was also a demand for monstrous ornaments of solid brass, and brass pots and basins, often later melted down and recast according to indigenous tastes. Glass came from Venice in the form of beads. Spiced wine from the Canaries or Jerez in Spain, was also popular, as were knives, hatchets, Spanish swords, iron bars, conch shells from the Canaries and, especially, copper rods, for which the appetite of some African communities was insatiable. Candles were as interesting to Africans as they later were to the Mexicans, and many African monarchs became fond of trumpets. Finally, one of the great favorites in many harbors of West Africa in the early days of the slave trade were "lambens," striped woolen shawls made in Tunis or Oran, which had been known to the West Africans before, thanks to the Sahara caravans. All these goods were easily obtained in Lisbon or, if not, in Antwerp, and carried from there . . .[506]

Producing these items "stimulated European capitalism, provided employment . . . , and brought great profits,"[507] particularly in the cases of the southern Netherlands — considered Europe's "industrial heartland" — northern Italy and southern Germany, also noted for having "concentrations of manufactures for long distance trade."[508]

Continuing with his attempt to establish European industrialization as having predated African slavery and the Atlantic slave trade, Landes nevertheless claims, incredibly — and erroneously — the "crucial changes in energy (coal and the steam engine) and metallurgy (coke-smelted iron) *were largely independent of the Atlantic* [slave] *system*, [and] so was the attempt initially to mechanize wool spinning."[509]

Uh, no, in fact, they were not. But if so, then how so, since we've already established that Prince Henry the Navigator's ventures to the new world — down the Atlantic coast of Africa for slaves — dates to the early *fifteenth* century? Blacks were first brought directly to Portugal from Africa in 1441, spawning the Age of Discovery and the all-important "opening" Landes identifies as the doorway to modern times. As explained by Beazley,

> if the industrial element rules modern development; if the philosophy of utility, as expressing this element, is now our guide in war and peace; and if the substitution of this for the military spirit is to be dated from that dominion in the Indian seas which realized the designs of Henry—if this be so, the Portuguese become to us, through him, something like the founders of our commercial civilization.[510]

As we've seen, without African slaves, those Portuguese ventures were of little value, if any, and would have otherwise died dead in their tracks. The subsequent transport of African slaves across the Atlantic, as a distinct branch of trade, to work the fruitful mines of Mexico and South America, began around 1500, less than a decade after Columbus.[511]

What's more, we've also seen how the growth of Europe's money supply, supplemented by gold from Africa, facilitated "the change to a money agriculture"[512] and to the growth of cities and towns, signaling the beginning of the end for manorialism and White slavery, providing an impetus to Europe's industrial spirit, since, according to at least one estimate, 80 to 90 percent of the population in the middle ages "was engaged in raising food" with little or no time for much else.[513]

Successful coke smelting, says Landes, dates to 1709; the "first steam engine proper" to 1705; and the innovations of Hargreaves, Arkwright and Whitney in woolen manufacturing "came together in the last third of the eighteenth century."[514] After 1765, that is, by which time the English had in fact been prosecuting the African slave trade for two centuries — since the voyages of John Hawkins in 1562 — and some three hundred years after Portugal had been so involved, engaging the business that distinguished them as a wealthy, respected world power. Come on, man, let's be real.

After more than fifty years of watching the Spanish and Portuguese emerge as world powers, on the backs of African labor, England's slave-trading ambitions saw the establishment of the Company of Adventurers of London Trading to Cynney and Bynney (Guinea and Benin), in 1618; the Company of Merchants Trading to Guinea, in 1630; the Company of Royal Adventurers Trading to Africa with a reported one thousand year monopoly; the mighty Royal African Company, in 1672, employing all the powers of the royal government, and finally, the South Sea Company, which, in 1713, at long last secured for Britain the Asiento contract calling for 4,800 slaves annually over thirty years following the War of the Spanish Succession. The conflict was in fact precipitated when Britain feared being cut off from the lucrative, illicit trade with Spain's New World colonies following the death of Spain's King, Charles II.[515]

The riches from England's Caribbean sugar colonies, on the other hand, started pouring into Britain as early as the second quarter of the seventeenth century, and by the third quarter the mainland Chesepeake was well on its way towards being a wholly slave-based, tobacco plantation economy. "There were English settlers in Bermuda by 1609, and an official colony on St. Kitts in 1624," according to Hazlewood. Shortly thereafter the English acquired Barbados, "followed quickly by Antigua, Nevis, and Montserrat. By 1640 the English West Indies had a population in excess of twenty thousand," and in 1641 the first sugar refinery was built on Barbados. By 1645 six thousand Black slaves worked in the sugar fields there, while "five years later the island could boast three hundred plantations, and more than thirty-five thousand African slaves" by 1673.[516] Jamaica, moreover, became the base from which England illicitly sold slaves to dealers under the Asiento before securing the contract for itself following Queen Anne's War, in 1713.[517] "Through the sale of slaves and other commodities to the Spanish colonists," records Curtis P. Nettles, in *The Money Supply of the American Colonies Before 1720*, "silver in its various forms flowed into Jamaica," the center for Britain's slave traffic, and from there into Britain, with a single fleet in the year 1691 reportedly carrying to England, according to the island's British governor, some "£100,000 in bullion."[518] By 1752, more than 150,000 Black slaves had been imported into the island, and nearly 500,000 by 1774. When Britain finally ended its human trafficking from Africa, in 1807, more than 1,125,000 slaves had been brought to Jamaica, with some 350,000 of those having been re-exported. "Nearly all the *commercial wealth of England*," wrote Kettell in 1860, "*is due to those negroes.*"[519]

In the eighteenth century there were imported into Jamaica "1,128,400 blacks, selling at an average, by official tables, of £30 each," while the number

in the 140 years up to the 18th century is put at 600,000, and into all other [British] colonies at 1,000,000; making, together, 2,728,400 negroes; which, at £30 each, realized £81,852,000, or $450,000,000; but if each black produced, during his life, but 8 times his own cost, the amount of wealth sent to England was 3,600 millions of dollars, or a sum exceeding the [1860] national debt. In estimating the value of the island in 1788, the commercial export value was put down at £5,400,000; and 12 years' purchase gave £64,600,000 as the value of the island. That rate, for 100 years, gives £540,000,000, and at half the rate for the previous 170 years, the aggregate would be £810,000,000, or 4,000 million dollars [roughly 88 billion dollars in today's money].[520]

"This vast wealth," wrote Kettell, together with that gained from Britain's exploitation of India, which amounted to more than half as much "poured into the lap of England, was the source of its greatness and of the sudden development of power and wealth" from the mid-eighteenth century. The effect upon England's population, he shows us, were dramatic:

up to the close of the 18th century, the population of England and Wales was stationary. It required 700 years to rise from one to five millions, showing the severe struggles for life the people had, until the wealth we have pointed out flowed in upon them. That wealth stimulated industry of all kinds, and aided by inventions, has so improved the condition of the people, that the population gained more in the first 50 years of the present [nineteenth] century, 15 of them of war, than in the previous 800 years.[521]

"Slavery rapidly became the country's biggest, most profitable business," says Hazlewood, Africans "were the fuel that drove the Industrial Revolution, powered the empire, and fired the nation's economy."[522]

England's prodigious sugar riches in fact prompted establishment of the Acts of Trade & Navigation (1660), requiring all foreign trade of the colonies be conducted in English or colonial ships and to physically touch English soil "to encourage manufactures, and to increase the commerce of Great Britain," according to Adam Smith, who concluded, "the wealth of Great Britain has increased very much since [their] establishment."[523] Smith also observed, moreover, that the monopoly of colonial trade created by the Acts, "raised the ordinary rate of British profit higher than it otherwise would have been both in that and in all the other branches of British trade."[524] The monopoly of trade with the colonies "is more advantageous to Great Britain than any other;" he wrote, "by forcing into that trade a greater proportion of the capital of Great Britain than what would otherwise have gone to it, has turned that capital into an employment more advantageous to the country than any other which could have found."[525] Landes nevertheless maintains, "cogently," according to him, but ridiculously, I think, "these gains were simply not big enough in total, let alone that part that went back into trade and industry, to alter the path of British development."

Well, let's let the people decide for theyself. Ahhh-ight?

As early as 1695, a generation after chartering the Royal African Company, and more than a full century after the first slaving voyages of John Hawkins, the African slave trade was considered "the best and most profitable branch of British commerce" by the Board of Trade, as symbolized by the Guinea coin, a "melancholy omen" of the human traffic's "immense significance" reportedly "used even more than the sovereign as a unit of common prices."[526] At the turn of the century, moreover, Britain's largest trading partner was Holland at £2,635,000, followed by its American colonies at £1,760,000. Of the total for the American colonies, the Caribbean sugar island of Barbados provided for £460,000, and the mainland Chesapeake tobacco colonies of Virginia and Maryland accounted for £435,000, fully 25% of Britain's entire American colonial trade. Not coincidentally, both Barbados and the Chesapeake utilized slave labor, as opposed to trade with the New England colonies, which amounted to only £119,000 by comparison.[527] By 1763, the American colonies had vaulted to the number one position as Britain's largest trading partner on commerce totaling £7,500,000, with the Chesapeake area following only Jamaica in value.[528]

Tables III and IV show Britain's top trade relationships worldwide and with its ten colonies, in 1763, revealing the overwhelming influence of African slavery on British and overall world trade, as its top American traders all utilized slave labor, with the top seven colonies almost exclusively dependent upon it. As such, slave labor accounted for virtually all of Britain's trade value with its American colonies, and virtually half its total world trade value.

A mid-eighteenth century British businessman described his country's involvement with slavery this way:

the trade to Africa is the Branch which renders our American Colonies and Plantations so advantageous to Great Britain: that Traffic only affording our Planters a constant supply of Negro Servants for the Culture of their Lands in the Produce of Sugars, Tobacco, Rice, Rum, Cotton, Fustick, Pimento, and all other our Plantation Produce: so that the extensive Employment of our Shipping in, to, and from America, the great Brood of Seamen consequent thereupon, and the daily

Table III: Top Five British Trading Partners, 1763
(British Pounds)

American Colonies	7,500,000
Germany	3,360,000
Ireland	2,410,000
Holland	2,385,000
E. India	1,950,000
Total	17,605,000

Middleton, *Tobacco Coast.*

Table IV: British Colonial Trade, 1763 (British Pounds)

Jamaica	1,744,000
Chesapeake Colonies	1,197,000
The Carolinas	532,000
Barbados	467,000
Guadaloupe	423,000
Martinique	356,000
St. Christopher	340,000
New England	334,000
Pennsylvania	322,000
New York	293,000
Total	6,008,000

Middleton, *Tobacco Coast.*

Bread of the most considerable Part of our British Manufactures, are owing primarily to the Labour of Negroes ...[529]

English industrialization clearly did not initially develop, nor could it, independent of the triangular trade of the Atlantic system, of which Landes claims slavery was "a crucial part." Um, no. Sorry. It was not. Slavery, in fact, was *the* crucial part.

Without slaves there likely would have been no significant New World settlement: there would have been no plantations replacing the smallholdings of early settlers in both the Caribbean and the Chesapeake[530]; without plantations there would have been no markets for manufactures, either in Africa, the Caribbean or mainland North America; without markets in which to sell manufactures there is then no demand driving the development of industry, let alone capital. Or, put another way, without slaves there is no sugar cultivation; without sugar there is no excess of capital flowing into Britain; without capital there can be no investment in industry. It makes no difference how much of the money came from slave traders, merchants, planters, industrial capitalists or even government, through bounties, drawbacks or subsidies, it all still goes back to slavery. Clearly Landes understands this, acknowledging that the advantages of slavery's capital was "to stimulate both agriculture and industry, increase wages and incomes in Britain, promote the division of labor, and encourage the invention of labor-saving devises."[531]

In any event, what otherwise makes Landes so certain of the inevitable fruition of industrialization, since for centuries, as he cites, "the world's greatest scientists wrote in Arabic, yet a flourishing science contributed nothing to the slow advance of technology in Islam?" Additionally, despite a long list of inventions, "Chinese industrial history offers examples of technological oblivion and regression."[532] Might the difference be the feigned supremacy of the almighty European?

Well — hold onto your seats — simply put, Landes' belief is based in the "predestination" of good ol' fashioned White, Anglo-Saxon "Protestantism."[533]

What . . . ? Wait a minute. Come on.

Yep. Predestination, writes Landes, "was eventually converted into a secular code of behavior," consisting of, get this, "hard work, honesty, seriousness, the thrifty use of money and time," leading to the creation of a "new kind of man—rational, ordered, diligent, productive."[534]

Please. At this point I'm laughing out loud — uproariously.

To be sure, he adds, "religion encouraged the appearance in numbers of a personality type that had been exceptional and adventitious before; and that this type created a new economy."[535]

At the same time, not coincidentally, the African slave trade began for England and supported its rise to the top of world order. This "new kind of man," then, would have been embodied in the likes of none other than Sir John Hawkins, and the "new economy" would of course have been the Atlantic system; the triangular trade with slavery as its foundation. Yet Landes has the gall to suggest superior Protestant *values* would have inevitably caused the advance of industrialization, regardless of slavery. That's just unmitigated nerve.

I'm tempted to say this Landes guy's got balls, except I'm actually beginning to think he really believes all this shit. The theoretical argument about the predestination of Protestant Christians is, in any event, far-fetched, and his attempt to empirically posit slavery as not having been "decisive" in the advance of industrialization is, clearly, just wishful thinking.

In order to truly make the claim cogent, one would have to show where the comparable sums of money for industrial investment would have come from if not from Black slavery. Landes, of course, doesn't do that. He merely states that the "argument" surrounding the precise "effects of slavery" and the slave trade, with the resulting explosion in worldwide wealth and population, led by Great Britain and the United States, "is not susceptible of factual settlement."[536]

But, slavery was nothing if not an economic institution, and since when is Economics not quantifiable? It would no doubt be a personal insult to suggest one of America's premier intellectuals is incapable of the math, so I'll interpret the position as an unwitting betrayal of race bias. Or, perhaps, a form of defiance and "political mobilization," using his logic, to relieve guilt, provoke consciences, and oppose reparations. Although, it could just be Landes is sensitive to criticism from other Whites, like that leveled at Eric Williams for "reducing slavery to purely economic motives and interests," in *Capitalism & Slavery*.[537] Fortunately, however, others have provided us with the means to illuminate the reality, most specifically in the Northeast, the center of nineteenth century American industrialization, and the area where many people so desperately want to believe slavery played no part (see Chapter 19, King Cotton). Looking just at 1859 New England, the *Boston Post* wrote the following editorial, dollar amounts quoted should be multiplied by 22 to approximate today's currency values:

What does New England buy of the South to keep her cotton and woolen mills in operation — to supply her lack of corn and flour; to furnish her with sugar, rice, tobacco, lumber, etc.? Boston alone received from Slave States in 1859, cotton valued at $22,000,000; wool worth $1,000,000; hides valued at $1,000,000; lumber $1,000,000; flour $2,500,000; corn $1,200,000; rice $500,000; tobacco estimated at $2,000,000. We thus have $31,200,000 in value, only considering eight articles of consumption. Nor have we reckoned the large amounts of portions or all of these articles which arrived at Providence, New Haven, Hartford, Portland, and other places. Nor have we reckoned the value of other articles that arrive at Boston, very considerable though it be, such as molasses, naval stores, beef, pork, lard, and other animal produce, hemp, early vegetables, oysters and other shell-fish, game, peaches, etc. May we not estimate then, with good reason, that New England buys of the South her raw materials and other products to the amount of $50,000,000 annually? In 1858, about one-third of all the flour sold in Boston was received from the commercial ports of the Southern States, and in the same year seven-fifths of all corn sold in this city was received direct from the States of Delaware, Maryland, and Virginia. The value of the product of sugar and molasses, principally produced in Louisiana, in 1858 was about $33,000,000 . . . nearly one-half the crop is consumed in the Northern States . . .[538]

Kettell similarly concluded,

A portion of every artisan's work is paid for by Southern means. Every carman draws pay, more or less, from the trade of that section. The agents who sell manufactures, the merchants who sell imported goods, the ships that carry them, the builders of the ships, the lumbermen who furnish the material, and all those who supply means of support to them and their families. The brokers, the dealers in Southern produce, the exchange dealers, the bankers, the insurance companies, and all those who are actively employed in receiving and distributing Southern produce, with the long train of persons who furnish them with houses, clothing, supplies, education, religion, amusement, transportation, &c., are dependent upon [the labor of Black slaves].[539]

And also from the *Boston Post* (again multiply by 22 to approximate the present value of dollar amounts given),

The aggregate value of the merchandise sold to the South annually we estimate at some $60,000,000. The basis of the estimate is, first, the estimated amount of boots and shoes sold, which intelligent merchants place at from $20,000,000 to $30,000,000, including a limited amount that are manufactured with us and sold in New York. In the next place, we know from merchants in the trade, that the amount of dry-goods sold South yearly is many millions of dollars, and that the amount is second only to that of the sales of boots and shoes. In the third place, learn from careful inquiry, and from the best sources, that the fish of various kinds sold realize $3,000,000, or in that neighborhood. Upwards of $1,000,000 is received for furniture sold in the South each year. It is true, since the establishment of branch houses in New York, Philadelphia, and other cities, many of the goods manufactured in New England reached the South through those houses.[540]

This would seem to indicate slavery's economic effects are indeed quantifiable. What is not in fact "susceptible to factual settlement," however, is the speculative folly about the inevitability of industrialization, and how fast or slow it would have been realized absent slavery. At best, this is irrelevant, misplaced scholarship, at worst, nothing more than feel-good, wishful-thinking that allows Europeans and Americans to think Black slavery didn't provide anything the world wouldn't have inevitably attained without it. The fact is, industrialization *did* happen on the back of Black slavery, and, as Landes himself acknowledges, it did so for a reason: Africans, he explains, "proved far more productive."[541]

In the end, the whole prosperity/poverty debate has a real stink to it, no pun intended. No doubt history will reflect the view that Europeans and European Americans prospered disproportionately because of their supposed superior values, etc., etc., since there's no shortage of people promoting that view. As I see it, superior wealth is proof positive only of superior greed. But, says Landes, "no one likes to be reminded his source of pride is a vice rather than a virtue." Therefore the whole conversation becomes a cultural comparison that allows European Americans to pompously fantasize: "we have more money, therefore we must be more virtuous."

Many European Americans, however, are clearly and deeply troubled by the reality and are in need of continual reassurance to the contrary, which explains the efforts to distort truth by historians Ira Berlin, Elizabeth Fox Genovese, Cokie Roberts, David Landes, Michael Levin, Jared Diamond, Peter Wood, Lawrence Harrison, Samuel Huntington, Stephen Thernstrom and countless others. Such celebrations, "however tactful and indirect," to use Landes' logic, "cut close to the ego and [boost] identity and self-esteem,"[542] Moreover, they create a legacy whereby pressure engenders to maintain an artificial superiority, as youth are encouraged to join "a small and fortunate elite" of "the kind of people who accentuate the positive."[543]

The barbaric, medieval adventures to the non-White World should not be promoted as proof of European supremacy, as is widely taught and celebrated. It mistakenly lends historical support and justification to American racism, both overt and subtle, thereby insuring the culture of White supremacy reigns first, last and always.

12

Black Renaissance

Query II

ichael Levin also advances the widely held belief that the "art, music, architecture, literature, and political history of Eurasia owe virtually nothing to Africans." Previous sections of this book have conclusively addressed this point, I think. Yet some readers might still be interested in looking at the question culturally, rather than from a strictly economic perspective.

The transformation in Europe that gave birth to the New World discoveries was, of course, more popularly known as the Renaissance. From its Italian origins, the Renaissance saw changes in knowledge and understanding of the arts, sciences, philosophy, politics, education, literature, religion and even business, spreading north and eventually encompassing all Europe.

As shown previously, transformation of European business in the Middle Ages was directly influenced by Italian trading with Arab merchants active in the trans-Sahara trade. Most prominent among the Italian traders of the Renaissance period were the Genoese who, according to Hugh Thomas, in *Rivers Of Gold*, were prominent sailors among the Portuguese ventures in the Atlantic and were active in both the Spanish and Portuguese commerce of the Atlantic and Mediterranean. The Genoese "were dominant in commerce at Ceuta

[Morocco] after its capture by Portugal in 1415," where "most of the gold brought from black Africa by caravan ended up" en route to Europe, but they were also slave trading "specialists," active in the Crimea, Tunis, Malaga and Granada, selling "men, women, and children of all hues and races."[544] Perhaps "the most important" Italian slave merchant in all of Portugal, however, was one Bartolomeo Marchionni, from Florence, who, along with partners that included none other than Amerigo Vespucci, also from Florence, "sold black slaves so successfully he was thought of as an honorary Portuguese."[545] According to Kamen, the "majority backers" of Columbus' voyages to the New World were also Genoese and Florentine,[546] These merchants and their families essentially comprised the ruling classes and a patrician nobility of Genoa, Florence, Milan and Venice, which, "by the fifteenth century, were effectively the capital cities of rich and prosperous states as well as commercial and industrial cities,"[547] leading the way towards the rebirth that was the Renaissance. The increased trade of Genoa, Venice, Siena, and Florence brought great medieval wealth, inspiring opulent tastes and a desire for luxury goods, including art.[548]

Members of Italy's rich merchant families, "including the Medici," for example, were naturally among the first to commission the humanist painters, sculptors and builders of the early Renaissance,[549] including sponsorship that established a "tradition" of local demand for works of art and attracted young artists to the major cities.[550] A 1376 list of 1,224 names of "almost all artisans" living in Avignon, then the papal residence, had "over 1,100 Italians, including jewelers, goldsmiths, stone-masons and sculptors.[551] There was also large support for the ivory carvers of Paris who "overwhelmingly" supplied the "medieval European carved ivory" in the world's museums,[552] much of which, no doubt, made its way from sub-Saharan Africa by way of the Arab trade, having been "bought in Acre, Alexandria and Lajazzo by Italian merchants" who shipped it to southern France or Belgium for transport to Paris.[553] And Francesco Datini indulged a "preoccupation with building" after his return to Florence, in the last decade of the fourteenth century.[554] "At least for well known artists," writes Spufford, "the larger part of their work was for. . . the ruler, the great officers of state, and the nobility at home."[555]

Also, the infusion of sub-Saharan Africa gold, and the resulting increase in the money supply, gave liquidity to Italian commerce that was otherwise much more stagnant, thereby stimulating industry and facilitating a greater movement of goods. Because "culture and art thrive on money," African gold in turn became a significant influence on art, as "new hope and self-reliance stimulated man's creative powers."[556] One consequence was the increased popularity of portraiture, as reflected in various coins exhibiting "the physical likeness of a real human being, not some abstract symbol of an idea or institution," providing both inspiration and opportunities for artists.[557]

The popular gold *ducat*, left, of Venice, Italy, struck by the Doge Pietro Gradenigo (1289-1311) and Antonio Venier (1382-1400); fifteenth century gold coin of Granada, center, right, and thirteenth century *florini*, right, of Florence, Italy.

Sources: Black, *Atlas of World History;*
Clain-Stefanelli, *The Beauty And Lore Of Coins*

To say Blacks had no influence on the cultural and political history of Eurasia is like saying the Renaissance itself was irrelevant. But for the overall influence of Black Africa, Eurasia might yet be stuck in the Dark Ages.

Query III

Mr. Levin also claims "No important discovery, invention, or world leader emerged from Africa. . . . Few blacks have achieved eminence in areas other than sports, entertainment, the demand for rights, or writing about race itself."

On the surface, these would appear to be his strongest and most factually based points. However, it's not entirely clear whether this is a promotion of the achievements of Europeans or simply another denigration of the sons and daughters of Black Africa. Does "leader" refer to an official statesman, or simply leadership personalities who command worldwide respect and admiration, inspiring generations of people from all walks of life? I know of no supposedly great European "world leaders" who haven't plundered and destroyed thousands of lives, even millions, on their way to earning their so-called greatness. Adolf Hitler comes directly to mind here. Although, arguably, the most infamous, he certainly is not alone among European despots.

But who, then, is it that would qualify for this supposed European monopoly on leadership? Mussolini? Napoleon? Queens Elizabeth and Victoria? Ferdinand and Isabella? Julius Caesar maybe? Not one has a legacy that isn't equally as infamous, if not more so, than not. The list of supposed great European "world leaders" in fact consists of nothing less than the hall of fame for fascism, imperialism, despotism, tyranny — and racism!

Nelson Mandela, however, would absolutely compare favorably to the most prominent of any world leaders, statesmen or otherwise, from Europe, Asia, or elsewhere, in any era, for the inspiration given to all peoples world-wide. And if Levin's assessment is not exclusive to statesmen, then Dr. Martin Luther King, Jr., having received the esteemed Nobel Peace Prize, should certainly be at the top of the list; when the Chinese in Beijing and Hong Kong were heard singing, "We Shall Overcome," you can be sure it is the legacy of Dr. King providing the inspiration.

Even Muhammad Ali, an athlete, has risen to become one of the most recognizable people on the planet, a fact which, by the way, was not owing simply to his preeminent athletic prowess, but rather to a much admired and respected courage and independence of character. Still, we must not forget the likes of Toussant L'Overture, leader of the first, and only, successful Black slave revolt in the Western Hemisphere. Does he then deserve a more revered historical status for having bested the mighty French armies of Napoleon Bonaparte? Moreover, if not for Europe's plunder of the African continent, carrying tens of millions into slavery, no one knows to what heights many of those tortured souls may have risen. As Blackburn reminds us,

by the latter half of the eighteenth century, when 80,000 or even 100,000 young men and women were taken from the African coast annually, the Atlantic trade was responsible for a subtraction that could have taken each year's natural population increase in West and Central Africa. Particular peoples and nations seem to have been entirely destroyed by the traffic, others greatly weakened. A large number of captives died before ever reaching the hold of a slave trader's vessel; and of course, countless others died in wars principally conducted to feed the slave traffic.[558]

The slave trade also limited the ability of Africans to reproduce and replace those untold lost souls. Blackburn cites research concluding that the slave trade "was greatly boosting the numbers of slaves being held in those regions of Africa which supplied it. Since slaves in Africa also had a lower propensity to reproduce themselves, this would have had a depressive effect on population levels."[559]

Regarding the comparative lack of "important discoveries and inventions," it can never be known which inventions credited to European Americans may in truth have been the brainchild of a Black slave. "It seems likely," to use Levin's expression, a percentage of patents historically registered to White inventors, spanning the two hundred years of slavery, and beyond, should more properly be credited to Blacks whose ideas were usurped by European Americans. In the course of Western development, notes Vandana Shiva, in *Biopiracy*, intellectual property rights have merely become synonymous with "intellectual theft and biopiracy," while much of the

Cotton gin

Compton's Interactive

patented research and development credited to Whites throughout history has been largely, if not wholly, supported by the labors of Black slaves.[560]

Credit for the cotton gin, for example, according to Albert Bolles, in *The Industrial History of the United States*, unquestionably belongs to Eli Whitney, "one of this country's greatest material benefactors."[561] There is, however, a legitimate question about whether in fact Whitney's design was merely a formal rendering of rudimentary methods suggested, or even practiced in some degree, by the Black slaves in 'Savannah, GA, where he traveled from New Haven, CT, upon graduation from Yale, in 1792, knowing nothing about the cultivation or harvesting of cotton.[562] It can never be known to what degree he collaborated with slaves, or what input, if any, he utilized in coming to his ultimate design. Obviously some measure of interaction with slaves, or exchange of ideas about the cotton-pickin' process, as it were, inspired his imagination. Despite being arguably the most significant invention since the discovery of the western hemisphere, moreover, the gin would have been utterly useless without the labor of Black slaves. The experience of history suggests that with the so-called "Protestant work ethic" of European laborers, the invention, in all likelihood, would have amounted to nothing more than an expensive waste of Whitney's time.

It's also not known which techniques used in the early days of plantation farming originated elsewhere.[563] Africans were often taken as slaves from specific regions because of their knowledge of agriculture and various other useful skills.[564] It simply seems unrealistic to think some of those skills did not develop or adapt processes that ended in the patent office under the name of some European American.[565] It's an open question, writes Edward Countryman, as to exactly "who taught whites that [rice] could grow in the Carolina lowlands," concluding it was most likely" "West Africans, to whom rice cultivation was perfectly familiar."[566] English settlers, in fact, similarly adopted the farming methods of Native Americans in North America, but very little credit is given them for the viability of European settlement on the continent.

As for Blacks having not "achieved eminence in areas other than sports, entertainment, the demand for rights, or writing about race itself," Levin seems to be grabbing for straws, obviously reluctant to acknowledge the scholarship and, dare I say, intellect, of such notable scholars as W.E.B. Du Bois, John Hope Franklin and Cornell West. Is he suggesting race scholarship is somehow inferior to other forms of scholarship? If so, how exactly does he classify his own book, *Why Race Matters*, if not as race scholarship? But, in any event, as Derrick Bell has pointedly highlighted, in *Faces At The Bottom Of The Well*, the most acclaimed scholars of race have been European Americans. It is White, writers, Bell notes, who "have dominated the recording of race relations in this country, citing heralded works by Richard Kluger, on *Brown v. Board of Education*, and by Taylor Branch, on the life of Dr. Martin Luther King, Jr."[567] "Black writers," he reminds us, "have not received the attention or the rewards of their white colleagues."[568] Does Levin mean to similarly discount the acclaim earned by these White scholars?

Query IV

And regarding the American literary legacy, Levin says: "Of the formative works of American literature, only Huckleberry Finn is

concerned significantly with race: the topic is scarcely mentioned by
Hawthorne, Melville, Poe, Whitman, Dreiser, James, Wharton,
Sinclair, Hemingway, Salinger, Heller, or Roth."

The fact that White writers did not acknowledge Blacks in their
work is presumed to be proof of Black insignificance. By extension,
Levin must also be implying that the scarce mention of White women
in history texts meant they also were not present, or played no
significant role in the formation of America. "What were the women
up to while the men were busy founding the nation?" asks Cokie
Roberts, in *Founding Mothers*. "[C]ourses in American history
provided me with glimpses," she writes, but "that was about it."[569]
Author/teacher Julie Landsman also notes how "[c]ivilization has
almost always been defined in textbooks as something built, written,
composed, and *completed* by white men."[570]

In fact, the U. S. Constitution is silent on the presence of Blacks,
but that hardly could be interpreted to mean they were of no
"significant concern," as the revenue from slave labor, the foundation
of all early American foreign trade, was the primary reason for
restructuring the government under the new constitution. And a
review of the transcript of debates at the Constitutional Convention
reveals slavery was the subject of discussion more than any other
single issue — and likely as much as all other issues combined.
Omission of the actual words "slaves," or "Blacks" (gasp!),
conspicuous by their very absence, was, we're told, owing to the fact
that embarrassed Convention delegates "sought to avoid the
admission of expressions which might be odious in the ears of
Americans."[571] Such "descriptive terms," said Roger Sherman of
Connecticut, "were not pleasing to some people,"[572] describing
America's discomfort to one day look back on the institution of
slavery with horrific embarrassment. But despite their personal
shame, says Yates, a member of the Convention contingent from New
York who departed the proceedings prematurely, delegates were
nevertheless "willing to admit into their system those things which the
expressions signified."[573]

In *Playing in the Dark*, author Toni Morrison notes how "there
seems to be more or less tacit agreement among literary scholars that,
because American literature has been clearly the preserve of white
male views, genius, and power, those views, genius, and power are
without relationship to and removed from the overwhelming presence
of black people in the United States." This "separate and
unaccountable 'Americanness,'" she observed "shaped the body
politic, the Constitution, and the entire history of the culture."[574]

POWER

13

George Washington

I'M HYPED AND I'M READY TO FIGHT
'CAUSE I'M AMPED! MOST OF MY HEROES
DON'T APPEAR ON NO STAMP!

Public Enemy: "Fight the Power"
Do The Right Thing (A Spike Lee Joint)
Motown Records

Fred Hampton 0c

For The Love Of Money

Ｗith the issue of Black contributions to overall world development being so critically questioned, it's most important to bring the focus more specifically onto America and its beginnings and ask what the legacies of Washington and the other Founding Fathers, the group most credited with the political and economic success of the country, might have been without the support of Black slaves. Since achieving Independence and developing the nation's resources contemplated the use of African slave labor from the very beginning,[575] it's very likely, even probable, most would never have been heard from.

In his review of *Africans in America*, Edmund Morgan took exception to the avaricious and immoral depiction of George Washington as unfair. He "appears always as a slaveholder with little else to his credit," says Morgan, noting the commonality of slaveowning "in the Northern Neck of Virginia where Washington grew up."[576] His Mt. Vernon lifestyle, however, was anything but common. He

> liked house parties and afternoon tea on the Mount Vernon porch ... was fond of picnics, barbecues, and clambakes; and throughout life he enjoyed dancing, frequently going to Alexandria for balls. Cards were a steady diversion, and his accounts record sums lost at them, the largest reaching nearly 10 [sic]. In bad weather, his diary sometimes states, "at home all day, over cards." Billiards was a rival amusement. Not only the theatre, when available, but concerts, cockfights, the circus, puppet shows, and exhibitions of animals received his patronage. . . . He insisted on the best clothes—coats, laced waistcoats, hats, coloured silk hose—bought in London. . . . Washington liked to do things in a large way. It has been computed that in the seven years prior to 1775, Mount Vernon had 2,000 guests, most of whom stayed to dinner if not overnight [more than five evenings each week].[577]

Only the very wealthy lived in such a grand fashion and no one lived higher and with more gusto than did Washington. So, by his example, is it any wonder owning slaves became generally accepted as the surest path to wealth and fame in the colonies. More than character, intellect or diligence, it was slavery that propelled Washington to the top of America's political hierarchy.[578]

"He was not an intellectual; he was a man of affairs, summarized Gordon S. Wood, described as the "most respected among all scholars of the colonial and revolutionary period." Washington "knew how to run his plantation and make it pay." Even as president, Wood adds, "he devoted a great amount of his energy to worrying about the fence posts of his plantation."[579]

It was beyond dispute, said John Adams, that Washington, "was too illiterate, unlearned, unread for his station and reputation," he "was not a scholar." And, according to none other than Thomas Jefferson himself, Washington's "colloquial talents were not above mediocrity," with "neither copiousness of ideas nor fluency of words."[580]

So, with unimpressive intelligence, a less than stellar work ethic and limited social skills, it seems that if Washington actually had to work for a living things likely would have turned out much differently, not just for George and his family, but for America as a whole.

Nevertheless, "being a man of affairs and running his plantation or even the federal government efficiently were not what made him a world renowned hero," Wood concludes, "Washington's genius,

Washington's greatness," he says, "lay in his character. He was . . . truly a man of virtue."

What?

"This virtue was not given to him by nature. He had to work for it," writes Wood, unabashedly omitting credit for the blood, sweat and tears of hundreds of Black slaves. Washington, get this, was "a self-made hero," he adds, incredibly, "This impressed an eighteenth-century enlightened world that put great stock in men's controlling both their passions and their destinies."[581] Yeah, right.

But since slavery played such a central role in his life, its relationship to his career and his treatment of slaves is very much relevant to any other thing Washington may be known for. Yet Edmund Morgan tells us focusing on that aspect of the man only distorts the truth. It should also be noted that, contrary to what Gordon Wood suggests, it was not entirely unnoticed among contemporaries that Washington was "immortalizing himself" at the expense of his Black slaves who had "as good a right to be free as he."[582]

Washington

Hero?

George Washington's public profile began to rise at a time when European territorial control of North America was still very much in dispute, as a Lieutenant Colonel of the Virginia militia protecting the western colonial frontier from French encroachment, during the French and Indian War. Interestingly, he was ambushed and captured in 1754 at Fort Duquesne, near what is now Pittsburgh, Pennsylvania. Luckily, it was the French who staged the ambush and he was allowed to go free. It seems fair to presume the Indians might not have been so magnanimous, in which case Washington might have met the same fate as another famous American General named George: Custer; a man remembered more for his one major failure in battle with the Indians than any successes. It was on the strength of such *heroics*, however, that Washington was named Colonel and commander of the entire Virginia militia a year later, at only 23. With the help of the British, the colonials drove out the French and took sole possession of North America east of the Mississippi river, earning Washington much respect as a military commander. But, as mentioned, we might properly wonder whether a young Washington, who needed to work the farm to feed his family, could have afforded to join the Virginia militia at all.

What's more, it's not at all certain that even with England's assistance the American colonies could have prevailed during the Seven Years' conflict without the considerable revenues accruing to the Royal Treasury from Virginia and Maryland tobacco — and, therefore, Black slavery.[583] The tobacco trade of the colonies "was the source of a large part of the commercial capital of England," according to Lewis Gray, "largely responsible for the extension of England's sea power,"[584] and "Virginia produced a larger share of the royal revenue than any other colony," noted Edmund Morgan, "[n]o other colonial product yielded so much revenue."[585] So it was her tobacco re-exports which "earned the gold and silver coin that financed [Great Britain's] armies and navies."[586]

The resulting victory against the French laid the foundation for Washington's appointment as commander and chief of colonial forces during the successful American Revolution, his most significant achievement, from where he rose to the preeminent position of American political history. It is therefore worthwhile to analyze, for the record, important factors of the Revolutionary War itself to see just how much was properly credited to General Washington, and what uncredited significance Black slaves may have had in its — and Washington's — success.

In early 1775, the colonies found themselves having to suddenly defend against the British King who declared them in rebellion for their refusal to submit to taxation, and for refusing to pay for damage done to British property at the Boston Tea Party. Having previously relied only on local militias and the British military for their defense, the colonies had no standing army. Moreover, "neither Congress nor the Colonial Governments possessed credit," noted Albert S. Bolles, in *The Financial History of The United States, From 1774-1789*, so they had no means to pay for an army and, with no formal powers, no means to organize one.[587] With no taxation and "no proper fiscal system" for the collection and disbursement of funds, records William Graham Sumner, in *The Financier and the Finances of the American Revolution*,[588] they were "obliged to collect muskets from house to house," while the total amount of gunpowder in the colonies at the time was only about a hundred pounds.[589]

Similarly, money then in the treasury amounted to only "a few thousand pounds,"[590] as Congress knew all too well. Britain's closing of America's ports in December, and seizure of supplies on the high seas made obtaining the materials and supplies of war difficult. Duties collected on imports, paid for with the proceeds from export sales, were the sole reliable means of revenue, and therefore "indispensably necessary" to conduct the war.[591] "Direct taxes upon exports," explained Davis Rich Dewey, in *Financial History of The United States*, were in effect "a system of taxation practically levied upon the productions of [indigo], rice, and tobacco, which formed the bulk of the exports,"[592] though the single most important product sold directly to Europe, "by far," was tobacco.[593]

Table V. Average Annual Value of Top Five Exports,
Continental Colonies, 1768-1772. (British lbs.)

Tobacco	£920,000
Wheat, Bread, Flour	550,000
Rice	305,000
Fish	185,000
Indigo	125,000
Total	£2,085,000

Atlas of Early American History: The Revolutionary Era

Table V shows the state of colonial commerce for the five years preceding the Revolution, where tobacco, rice and indigo, the exclusive products of slave labor for a century leading up to the War, accounted for three of the top five items of the colonies' export trade. Prior to the revolution, as highlighted by Virginia D. Harrington, in *The New York Merchant On The Eve Of The Revolution*, Virginia actually exceeded New York in exports of Wheat and flour to England, those being the main exportable staples of Pennsylvania, New York and New Jersey.[594] Agriculture in the North was largely limited to subsistence farming. The relatively small number of slaves held in those States involved in cultivating grain would have been responsible for a substantial portion of the grain output there, if not the greater portion, since grain crops were not labor intensive,[595] meaning, of course, that a large portion of total colonial grain export was also the product of slave labor.[596]

Table VI, below, additionally shows two-thirds of New England's fish, along with some 80 percent of its grain exports, were plantation bound. In fact, the most significant markets for fish exports were the slave plantations of the West Indies, and the Southern colonies of Maryland, Virginia, the Carolinas, and Georgia.[597] Southern Europe, the other major market, had additional supply options, in its "home-based" English fishery at Newfoundland, which "answered almost 80 percent of the demand from southern Europe," according to historian James G. Lydon.[598]

Table VI

Average Annual Value and Destinations of Commodity Exports from New England, 1768-1772 (Pounds Sterling)

Commodity	Great Britain	Ireland	Southern Europe	W. Indies	Africa	Total
Fish	£206		£57,195	£94,754		£152,155
Livestock, beef, pork	374		461	89,118		89,953
Wood products	5,983	£167	1,352	57,769		65,271
Whale products	40,443		804	20,416	£440	62,103
Potash	22,390	9				22,399
Grains, grain products	117	23	3,998	15,764		19,902
Rum	471	44	1,497		16,754	18,766
Other	6,991	1,018	296	247		8,552
Total	£76,975	£1,261	£65,603	£278,068	£17,194	£439,101

Source: McCusker & Menard, *The Economy of British America*

The percentage of total colonial trade directly and indirectly supported by slavery, prior to the Revolution, therefore, considering grain and fishing exports, amounted to approximately eighty-five percent — or more — annually. Between 1760 and 1769 as illustrated in *De Bow's Review*, "the southern colonies, with a population of 1,200,000, exported produce to the value of $42,297,705; while the exports of all New England, New York, and Pennsylvania, with a [combined] population of 1,300,000, were only $9,356,035" – less than one fourth the amount.[599]

It should also be noted, as mentioned previously, 90 percent of New England rum went to Africa as part of the deadly triangular trade involving West Indian sugar and molasses, for rum distillation, and slaves, exchanged, along with Southern rice, corn and tobacco for New England fish and European manufactured goods. At the close of the Seven Years' War, in 1763, Britain determined that to recoup some of the monies spent defending the colonies, as well as maintain and hold new territories won from the French and Indians, a significant contribution to the royal revenues would be needed from the colonies. She therefore decided to modify the "almost forgotten and long-neglected Molasses Act of 1733"[600] by reducing the duty on sugar and molasses and applying a renewed, more stringent enforcement. "Nearly ninety percent of the trade with the West Indies, the basis of which was the fisheries, was imperiled to the point of annihilation by the Molasses Act,"[601] according to McFarland, because of the colony's heavy importation of molasses. From this perspective the seeds of the American Revolution can be clearly identified as based in the Sugar Act,[602] which "threatened a large and profitable [rum-distilling] industry" intimately connected to the West Indies — and the African slave trade — "in which a significant proportion of the colonial mercantile elite had a stake."[603]

In rebuttal, the State House of Representatives remarked, "our pickled fish wholly, and a great part of our cod fish, are fit only for the West Indian market," the tax

> will greatly diminish its exportation [here]; and [molasses]being the only article allowed to be given in exchange for our fish, a less quantity of the latter will of course be exported. The obvious effect of which must be the diminution of the fish trade, not only to the West Indies, but to Europe; fish suitable for both these markets being the produce of the same voyage. If, therefore, one of these markets be shut, the other cannot be supplied. The loss of one is the loss of both, as the fishery must fail with the loss of either.[604]

150 of 184 Rhode Island foreign trade vessels were similarly used in the West Indian trade, importing 14,000 hogsheads of molasses to be used in the colony's thirty distilleries and sent to Africa in trade for slaves.[605] Rhode Island distilleries, therefore, as a result of the tax,

> would have to be closed to the ruin of many families, the rum trade of Africa would cease, two-thirds of their vessels would be rendered useless and perish on their hands, the nursery of seamen would be destroyed, and the mechanics who depend upon the merchants would be compelled to seek employment elsewhere.[606]

Africa and the West Indies, as shown in Table VI, were the combined destination for seventy percent of New England's export trade. This fostered a "monopoly" on shipbuilding in the North, New England, particularly, because of its deep-sea fisheries,[607] the nursery for its sailors and, more important, its merchants.[608]

The significance of these markets to New England became prominent in the debates of the Continental Congress during America's war for Independence. Delegates complained the fishing industry couldn't survive a coercion scheme against Great Britain of Non-exportation to the islands, designed with the hope of avoiding war. The protest, as John Adams recorded it, was that cutting off the Caribbean market "will annihilate the Fishery — because, that cannot afford to loose the West India Fish — and this would throw a Multitude of Families in our fishing Towns into the Arms of Famine.[609]

This was the state of commerce the Continental Congress had at its disposal at the onset of the Revolution, underscoring Edmund Morgan when he wrote, "Americans bought their independence with slave labor,"[610] in what has also aptly been referred to by Mark Kurlansky as, "the Tobacco War."[611]

Tobacco plant

Bolles, *Industrial History of The U.S.*

War Finance

Throughout the War with England, a continuous debate raged in the Continental Congress about how best to exploit American produce — and slavery — to secure the colonies' freedom from British *oppression.* "This Measure of Opening the Ports, &C. laboured exceedingly," wrote John Adams of the proceedings, "because it was considered as a bold step to Independence."[612] Typical was this protracted 1775 discussion on whether the colonies could afford to ban all imports and exports to force England to relent:

Oct. 4- *Silas Deane*:   Whether we are to trade with all nations, except Britain, Ireland, and West India, or with one or two particular nations, we cannot get ammunition without allowing some exports; for the merchant has neither money nor bills, and our bills will not pass abroad . . .

R.R. Livingston: Ammunition cannot be had, unless we open our ports . . .

Samuel Chase: We can't support the war and our taxes without trade . . . We must trade with foreign nations, at the risk indeed, but we may export our tobacco to France, Spain, or any other foreign nation.

Oct. 12- *John Zubly*:   Whether we can raise a navy, is an important question. We may have a navy, and to carry on the war, we must have a navy. Can we do this without trade? . . . Without trade our people must starve; we cannot live; we cannot feed our people.

Oct. 20- *Samuel Chase*:   I would restrain the merchant from importing any thing but powder &c. Molasses was an article of importance in the trade of the Northern Colonies. But now [without it] they can't carry on the African [slave] trade. . . .

Oct. 21- *Samuel Chase* (upraiding Zubly, suspected of loyalty to England):   Fifteen hundred seamen are employed by the tobacco Colonies—one hundred and twenty-five sail of British ships; but you may drop your staple, your tobacco . . . The best instrument we have, is our opposition by commerce. If we take into consideration Great Britain in all her glory; Commons voted eighteen, twenty millions last war; eighty thousand seamen, from her trade alone; her strength is all artificial, from her trade alone. Imports from Great Britain to the United Colonies are three millions per annum; fifteen millions to all the world; one fifth; three quarters is British manufactures. A thousand British vessels are employed in American trade; twelve thousand sailors; all out of employ [from American non-exportation]. What a stroke! I don't take into view Ireland or West India; Colonies generally indebted about one year's importation; the revenue of tobacco alone half a million, if paid. North Britain . . . employs a great number of manufacturers; [tobacco] re-exported abroad, is a million; it is more. Eighty thousand hogsheads are re-exported, and it pays British debts. The re-export employs ships, sailors, freight, commissions, insurance...[613]

Pursuant to these deliberations the Secret Committee to Import Arms was empowered, on Nov. 8, to export "produce" to the West Indies; on Nov. 29, permission was given to export flour and pork for "musquets"; on Dec. 6, lumber and naval stores from North Carolina for muskets and gunpowder, and more produce for "arms, ammunition or salt petre" on Dec. 20. The Committee to procure Articles for the Army proposes, on Dec. 23, the exportation of $160,000 of produce for procurement purposes and, on Dec. 29, Congress resolves that Virginia, Maryland, and North Carolina be permitted to export produce for supplies.[614] At the start of 1776, the Congress again authorized exportation of produce for war materials and supplies on Feb. 2, 8, 13, 23, and 28, and again on Mar. 4, and March 9, ...[615]

Generally, war financing fell into two categories of trade-centered resources: domestic and foreign. "As a resource for the treasury," domestic resources consisted essentially of commerce in support of paper currency emissions and private loans; while foreign resources arose out of trade-based security for loans and gifts from abroad, including, more importantly, "direct exchange as a means of getting things otherwise unobtainable.[616] From guns, cannons, ammunition and gunpowder, to food, clothing, transportation and soldiers' pay, virtually all the resources that were a part of the revolutionary budget, were made possible by America's slave-dominated commerce.

CASH

Thinking the conflict with England would be brief, the Continental Congress' first formal attempts to finance the war came in June, 1775, by borrowing against future taxes,[617] creating what Alexander Hamilton referred to as "artificial revenue."[618] Resolving "That the twelve confederated colonies be pledged for the redemption of the bills,"[619] the Congress essentially printed money with the hope that "the several provincial assemblies or conventions provide for laying and levying taxes," and that the "said bills be received by the collectors in payment of such taxes."[620]

England's port blockade brought import duties from commercial operations to a virtual halt, [621] and conflicts with paper emissions of individual colonies, among other things, meant they could not fully comply in their support of continental currency.[622] From this lack of support, colonial paper depreciated to the point where, as George Washington observed, in 1779, "a wagon load of money will scarcely purchase a wagon load of provisions."[623]

In 1780, the currency was valued by Congress to be "forty dollars in paper equivalent to one" in coins.[624] Some declared its true depreciation was actually "twice as much."[625] "Continental money," wrote E. James Ferguson, in *The Power Of The Purse: A History Of American Public Finance, 1776-1790*, "fell to destruction in the widening gap between income and expenditures,"[626] and was therefore of little use in financing the war.

Notwithstanding its rapid depreciation, paper currency was nevertheless an important and necessary source of funds. Early on in the war, it was printed and given to "officials who bought supplies or paid the troops."[627] $25,000 was given to seven different New York and Philadelphia merchants, on 5 percent commission, in July 1775, for example, to purchase gunpowder.[628] The money was used to obtain American produce, the only thing of marketable value overseas, which was then shipped and exchanged for the critical materials.

LOANS

The French King declined the first public request to aid the American colonies, an early 1777 plea from Benjamin Franklin for 30,000 guns, to be paid for by the Congress. Instead, the king secretly advanced an annually renewable grant of 2,000,000 livres that at that time prevented the collapse of the Revolution.[629] The American Commissioners in France first thought to use the grants "as security for domestic loans in the colonies" where Congress was desperately attempting to produce a then non-existing "major revenue" through the sale of loan certificates, in the hope of lessening its reliance on paper money emissions.[630] But, "expecting that American produce would pay for supplies," they proposed instead that the 2 million livres be used to pay the interest on the loan certificates.[631] Wanting desperately to end it's reliance on a rapidly depreciating currency in America, the Continental Congress agreed, "vot[ing] to pay interest in bills of exchange on all previous loans and on all new loans" subscribed to before March 1, 1778.[632]

The amount received in loan subscriptions the first year was $3.8 million dollars, altogether totaling $63.3 million from September 1777 to the closing of the loan offices in 1780, but with a depreciated value of only $7.7 million dollars — far short of Congress's hoped-for several hundred million target.[633] Prevailing markets at the time offered lenders six percent interest, compared to an "uncertain pledge of the government" of a low four percent rate.[634] It was subsequently raised to six percent in early 1777, though "[still] not materially aided with funds," notes Ferguson, reasoning "there was ample reason to doubt the pecuniary integrity of a government whose financial

position was already collapsing."[635] And even the $60 million
subscribed to, he explains, was because

> merchants acquired certificates in the course of business, without
> deliberate investment. When they could not collect immediately from
> government officials who bought their goods, they accepted payment
> in loan certificates rather than wait for money whose value steadily
> declined. Thus, a great number of the subscriptions issued after March
> 1778 did not represent bona fide loans, but were paid out by the
> government in purchase of supplies.[636]

With the shortage of loan subscriptions, impressment, authorized
by congress, became the means of securing "carriages, vessels, horses,
and other things necessary for carrying on the war."[637] It was
"employed through the whole war and throughout the whole United
States," according to Sumner, "in the place of finance."[638] The
government simply took what was needed to sustain the troops,
including corn, wheat, and rice, all produced by slaves, giving loan
certificates as payment.[639] If owners were unwilling to sell at a
reasonable price, says Sumner, General Washington had the power to
"arrest and confine all who refused to receive the [virtually worthless]
Continental money."[640]

Holding the loan certificates, however, were many New England
and Northern merchants from Massachusetts, New York and
Pennsylvania whose fortunes largely arose from underwriting and
shipping Southern produce, as well as from the African slave trade.[641]
In his 1790 Report On Public Credit, Alexander Hamilton placed the
outstanding domestic debt at forty million dollars, including arrears of
interest,[642] but the actual amount borrowed, in any event, was
considerably less than what was necessary to prosecute the war,
precipitating the need for French aid. The French foreign minister,
the comte de Vergennes, reportedly complained "we are astonished at
the demands which they continue to make on us, while the
Americans obstinately refuse to pay taxes, and that it seems to us
much more natural to levy on them than on the subjects of the
[French] King the taxes necessary for the defence of their cause."[643]
As a colonial government official observed, however, "an attempt to
raise money by immediate assessment upon the people would give a
disgust" that would endlessly frustrate the intentions of Congress.[644]

Tobacco

We might additionally note here that money flowing from France to
the American revolutionary cause largely derived from her taxes on

Maryland and Virginia tobacco re-exported from England that constituted a significant portion of the French revenue.[645] In fact, the motive for the support stemmed from France's position as the largest single purchaser of re-exported Chesapeake tobacco.

As Britain's Trade and Navigation Acts called for tobacco and certain other "enumerated" articles to be exported from the colonies through Britain and in British ships with British crews, this gave England significant control over the French tobacco revenue. Prevailing market rates, set by England, made the French tobacco trade less profitable, affecting their ability to wage war — mainly against hated England.[646] For some time, France had been attempting to circumvent this compromising situation. Generous assistance to the colonies, David McCullough concluded, in *John Adams*, "was because of no abiding fervor for American liberty. First, last, and always," he reasoned, the purpose "was to expand French trade in America,"[647] which, of course, centered chiefly on tobacco — and Black slavery. "It was above all their [tobacco] we wanted," the French Foreign Minister reportedly stated.[648]

The importance of the early loans and subsidies, however, "was that they opened French arsenals and warehouses, providing a quick supply of critical materials,"[649] without which, wrote James Breck Perkins in *France in the American Revolution*, "it is hard to see how [the colonies] could have been furnished with guns or clothing, with meat or bread."[650] By early September, 1776, there may have been as much as "216 Grange cannon, 209 gun carriages, 27 mortars, 28 mortar beds, 12,826 shells, 51,134 round shot, 30,000 muskets with bayonets, 4000 tents, clothing for 30,000 men, and an estimated excess of 100 tons of gunpowder" shipped to America from France.[651] Moreover, "Cornwallis could not have been captured" in the assault on Yorktown that sealed the American victory, which could not have been attempted without French aid because "the Americans had no fleet," while "one half" the forces engaged in the decisive siege "were French."[652]

THE BARBER OF SEVILLE

France had watched the American conflict with Britain closely since the loss of Louisiana and Canada to Britain following the Seven Years' War.[653] As Congress was well aware, in addition to its interest in American commerce, France was desperate to see England separated from her own American colonies, the source of her wealth and power.[654] With a significant naval fleet, the French were therefore seen as the best option for obtaining the much needed military aid.

Negotiations for foreign war support had to be discreet because of concerns about alarmed colonials reluctant to separate completely from England, and continuing hopes for a peaceful settlement,[655] leading to Congress' creation of the Secret Committee of Correspondence, in November 1775. The French agent, Bonvouloir, sent in secret to America for information and to encourage the hostilities against the hated English was immediately questioned by the Secret Correspondence Committee about France's disposition towards providing assistance upon arrival. His response was non-committal, but he sent a famously enthusiastic — but exaggerated — report on the condition and resolve of the continental army back to France encouraging French support.[656] The report reached Paris in February of 1776 and confirmed information sent from another French agent, Beaumarchais, relaying what he learned from the American representatives in London, and encouraging the King and foreign minister, the Comte de Vergennes (love that name!), to assist the American cause with a plan offering himself as agent.[657]

To help the colonies, Beaumarchais received, through his Paris business, Roderique Hortalez & Company, a million francs from the French treasury and a million francs from the French Farmers-General, as a loan for tobacco to be shipped directly from America,[658] in addition to a million livres from the Spanish government, at the request of Vergennes.[659] He subsequently informed the Committee of Secret Correspondence about the formation of his company and that he had already begun procuring supplies, stipulating return payment should be made in tobacco consigned to him.[660] And, in fact, ships arrived in the colonies from Nantes that year with war materials to be paid for by return cargos of tobacco.[661]

By the time the French formally entered the war in 1778, Beaumarchais "was employing a fleet of twelve merchant vessels" in assisting the colonies, with supplies that year valued at five million francs and totaling some 21 million between 1776 and the close of the war in 1783.[662] By the end of 1776, he had already dispatched three war cargoes plus money to pay soldiers. The British seized two of the vessels[663] but one with 10,000 muskets and another with 12,000, a thousand barrels of gunpowder and 11,000 flints reportedly made it to America safely.[664] In response, the Secret Committee directed Pennsylvania merchant Robert Morris, owner of a Mississippi plantation with more than a hundred slaves,[665] who served on nearly all the committees of the Continental Congress during the war, to "buy up tobacco" for the account of the United States.[666]

As the first Superintendent of Finance, Morris became indispensable.[667] His "plan of action" was for "a private commercial bank chartered by the government and supplied with government funds," founded on a general import tax.[668] But by the time it began operations in 1782, as the Bank of North America, "the war was practically over," reveals Joseph Dorfman, in *The Economic Mind in American Civilization*.[669] Only $70,000 had been capitalized for it's opening[670] but the bank was nevertheless of "important service at a time when the credit of the country had reached its lowest ebb and the Continental currency had become worthless,"[671] loaning $400,000 to the U.S. government and $80,000 to the State of Pennsylvania,"[672] money "borrowed from the French" that Morris deposited.[673]

THE CARIBBEAN

With the difficulty of getting supplies directly through to the mainland, the colonials turned to the Caribbean, where neutral trading with the Dutch and Spanish remained largely uninhibited.[674] Contrary to its policy of non-exportation, Congress resolved, in July 1775, that vessels importing "Gunpowder, salt petre, brass pieces, [and] muskets with bayonets," may load and export an equivalent value of "produce"[675] in payment, sending a copy of the resolution to Bermuda where the following "annual allowance," ninety-five percent of which originated from the slave states of Virginia, Maryland, and the Carolinas, was later ordered shipped:

72,000 bushels of Indian corn [from NC, VA and MD], 2,000 barrels of bread or flour [from PA and NY], 1,000 barrels of beef or pork [PA and NY], 2,100 bushels of peas or beans [from NC, VA and MD], and 300 tuerces of rice [from SC][676]

"We have letters from Guadaloupe, Martinique and the Havana," Samuel Chase explained to Congress in October, "that they will supply us with [gun]powder for tobacco."[677] The Dutch island of St. Eustatius, however, was, by far, the most important.[678] It "was made the means of an enormous export of military supplies" with merchants, the Congress and the individual colonies, each of whom commissioned war ships for their state navies,[679] all conducting trade through agents separately stationed there,[680] "as early as March, 1776," in the case of Virginia and Maryland, the colonies' two largest tobacco producers.[681] Cargoes of supplies bought from U. S. merchants often went to St. Eustatius then on to the mainland, with the Congress paying "by remitting cargoes of American produce" whenever possible.[682] In 1779, "some 12,000 hogsheads of tobacco and 1,500,000 ounces of indigo" were sent to the island to be exchanged for war materials "and other goods from Europe."[683]

The island's illicit trade continued until it was finally seized by the Royal Navy when the Dutch declared war on England.

According to one British Admiral, "Upwards of fifty American vessels, loaded with tobacco, have been taken since the capture of this island."[684] Another British officer later wrote: "The riches of St. Eustatius are beyond all comprehension; All the magazines and store-houses are filled, and even the beach covered with tobacco and sugar."[685]

The importance of slavery in cultivating the produce so critical to America's Revolutionary victory cannot be overstated. But the great American military commander, George Washington, received the credit and immortality, along with the other Founding Fathers. Black slaves, however, with their shredded backs, bore another century of exploitation and were then swept into historical oblivion, as if they never existed. The truth about America's Revolutionary start, that it did not happen, and in fact could not have, without the significant, decisive contribution of Black slavery, would, of course, be a compromise to the infallible image of America's so-called founding *heroes*, George Washington first and foremost.

14

My Dreams are censored, my Hopes is born
I'm like a fiend that finally sees
that all the Dope is gone.
My Nerves is wrecked, Heart beatin'
and my hands is swollen
Thinkin' of the Gs I'll be holdin'
Picture me rollin!

Tupac Shakur: "picture me rollin"
All Eyez On Me
Death Row/Interscope Records

Betting On Slavery

T he credit given to John Adams in America's fight for Independence centers on his role in attracting foreign assistance and in obtaining supplies and other essentials the colonials could not do without.[686] There was no question in Adams' mind about what the price should be for the needed aid, or exactly which nations America should target. He knew European desire to share in the trade that made England a wealthy world power would allow America to avoid relinquishing all political and military control as the price for Independence. In fact, he knew that American commerce, "seven millions sterling" annually prior to the war,[687] the overwhelming product of Black slave labor, was the only valuable resource available to the colonies to attract foreign assistance. Jotting down his thoughts while en route to Philadelphia, Adams noted:

Is any Assistance attainable from F[rance]?
What Connection may We safely form with her?
1st No Political Connection. Submit to none of her Authority —
receive no Governors, or officers from her.
2nd No military Connection. Receive no Troops from her.
3rd Only a Commercial Connection, i.e. make a Treaty, to receive
her Ships into our Ports. Let her engage to receive our Ships into her
Ports — furnish Us with Arms, Cannon, Salt Petre, Powder, Duck,
Steel.[688]

The need for both military and financial aid from abroad to help America's campaign of resistance was apparent to colonial political leaders from the very beginning of the conflict. The problem, however, was that America had no money, no credit or anything tangible to offer as security for borrowed funds. "Let us apply to borrow whenever we may, our mouths will always be stopped by the one word 'security'," declared Robert Morris in 1782, "the United States have nothing to give but a general national promise."[689]

Some, however, including Adams, saw the picture differently. "The peculiar quality of our staples and the scarcity of money," as one North Carolina merchant in the Congress put it, is "a good reason" to look towards loans as the best option of finanace."[690] Europe's long interest in bypassing England for the direct purchase of Chesapeake tobacco, dating from the turn of the eighteenth century,[691] is what Adams sought to exploit. He knew American commerce was sufficient in itself to attract whatever was needed, and France, with her extensive resources, fit the profile of the perfect partner. Accordingly, Adams' Plan of Treaties, drafted by the committee formed to devise a blueprint for securing foreign aid, was in fact specifically addressed to "the most serene and mighty Prince, Lewis the Sixteenth, the most Christian King" of France.[692]

Congress' Instructions to the committee made clear the significance of any treaty should lay in the protections afforded to American commerce — over and above assistance for the war. Article IV, for example, required the French King to "endeavour, by all the Means in his Power to protect and defend all Vessels . . . of the united States . . . being in his Ports . . . or on the Seas, . . . against all Attacks."[693] This article "must be insisted upon," the instructions stated.[694]

Article VII, on the other hand, requiring that the "King shall protect, defend and secure . . . the Subjects, and Inhabitants of the said United States . . . against all Attacks, Assaults, Violences, [and] Injuries, . . . as the King and Kingdom of Great Britain [had done]

before the Commencement of the present War,"[695] Congress
instructed, "should be waived, rather than that the Treaty should be
interrupted by insisting upon it."[696] The amended Plan left out
specific references to the King and France, but was nevertheless
helpful to Franklin and the other commissioners in obtaining the
initial loans, "secured by 5 million pounds of Virginian tobacco,
providing vital early supplies for the war."[697]

The colonies' successful early resistance, particularly at Saratoga,
eventually led to an open French alliance, and ultimately to American
victory. Without Chesapeake tobacco, however, "the foundation
stone" of the colonies' overseas identity,[698] it's highly unlikely America
could have attracted any foreign assistance at all, in which case,
Independence would have been unimaginable. According to
estimates, "ninety percent" of the war materials and supplies used in
1777, the first year following Independence, came from France.[699]

The Plan was also used by Adams in 1782, to secure the all-
important loans from the Dutch, "to support the credit of the United
States from the conclusion of the peace to its reorganization under the
new Constitution in 1789."[700] Writing from Holland, in 1783, he
observed that "there is not one power in Europe whose credit is so
good here as ours," while later acknowledging to Morris that the
arrival of "a few cargoes of American produce for the payment of
interest would have the best effect on American credit."[701] The
resulting Treaty of Amity and Commerce signed with the Dutch was
the second ever by the United States, after the treaty with France.
In targeting the Dutch, Adams was well aware of their secret
Caribbean trade to procure military supplies for the colonies, and that
they were the second largest purchasers of Virginia and Maryland re-
export tobacco from the England, after France,[702] and therefore had as
much interest in American Independence as did the French. Chart I
and Table VII, below, show the status of British tobacco re-exports
on the eve of the American Revolution when France and Holland
combined to consume two-thirds of the Chesapeake product. Adams
was keen to exploit this fact during his sudden dash to Holland
seeking aid, after France's early reluctance to openly enter into a
treaty with the U.S.
Perceiving failure at winning over the French, Adams had no choice
but to try his hand elsewhere. Therefore, understanding what he must
have had in mind when he boldly dashed to Amsterdam, without
prior authorization, to pitch his Plan for formal assistance in the Royal

Provinces, the trip does not seem as courageous or temerarious as has been generally credited. Adams knew:

the Dutch were aware France had already committed financial assistance to the colonies, albeit secretly, giving them a perceived favor over Holland for the trade of colonial tobacco after Independence, an advantage the Dutch could not easily stand to see realized;

the Dutch were already assisting the American cause from the Caribbean, indicating, at least, a favorable inclination towards America's eventual success against England;

Black slavery would secure any debt through tobacco production and the anticipated adoption of Free Trade upon freedom from English mercantilism.[703]

Regarding his historic Amsterdam excursion, Adams said:

Not the declaration of American independence, not the Massachusetts Constitution, not the alliance with France, ever gave me more satisfaction or more pleasing prospects for our country than this event. It is a pledge against friends and enemies. It is an eternal barrier against all dangers from the house of Bourbon as well as a present security against England.[704]

To his wife, Abigail, he wrote, "Pardon, a Vanity, which however is conscious of the Truth, and which has a right to boast."[705] He correctly understood that the money "altered the international balance of power so as to assure a century of peace for America."[706]

While seeking compensation for sacrifices made, Adams stated "It is high time that a proper discernment of spirits and distinction of character were made."[707] But James Madison asked, "For to whom are the debts to be paid?" in 1783, before proceeding to enunciate a list of those to whom gratitude — and compensation — was due, namely, the French government, the Dutch, the unpaid American army, and American men of wealth (merchants and slaveowners):

To an Ally, in the first place, who to the exertion of his arms in support of our cause, has added the succours of his Treasurer; who to his important loans has added liberal donations; and whose loans themselves carry the impression of his magnanimity and friendship [the French]. . .
To individuals in a foreign country in the next place who were the first to give so precious a token of their confidence in our justice, and of

Chart I, Table VII

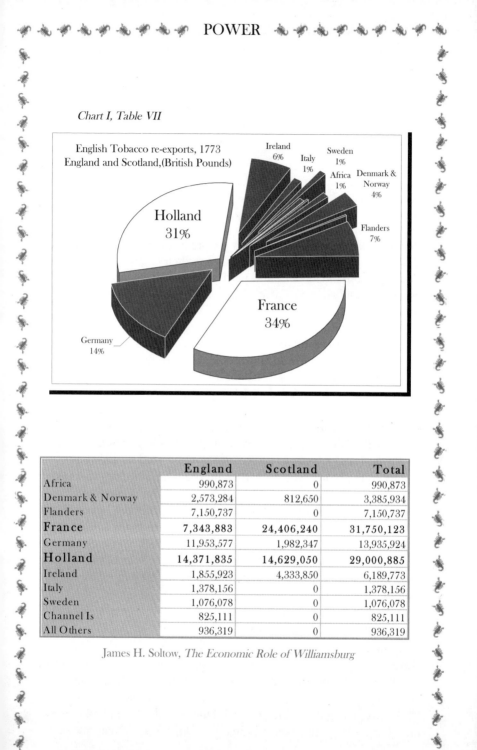

English Tobacco re-exports, 1773
England and Scotland,(British Pounds)

	England	Scotland	Total
Africa	990,873	0	990,873
Denmark & Norway	2,573,284	812,650	3,385,934
Flanders	7,150,737	0	7,150,737
France	**7,343,883**	**24,406,240**	**31,750,123**
Germany	11,953,577	1,982,347	13,935,924
Holland	**14,371,835**	**14,629,050**	**29,000,885**
Ireland	1,855,923	4,333,850	6,189,773
Italy	1,378,156	0	1,378,156
Sweden	1,076,078	0	1,076,078
Channel Is	825,111	0	825,111
All Others	936,319	0	936,319

James H. Soltow, *The Economic Role of Williamsburg*

their friendship for our cause; and who are members of a republic which was second in espousing our rank among nations [the Dutch]... Another class of Creditors is that illustrious & patriotic band of fellow Citizens, whose blood and bravery have defended the liberties of their Country, who have patiently borne, among other distresses the privation of their stipends, whilst the distresses of their Country disabled it from bestowing them; and who even now ask for no more than such a portion of their dues as will enable them to retire from the field of victory & glory into the bosom of peace & private citizenship, and for such effectual security for the residue of their claims as their Country is now unquestionably able to provide . . . [soldiers] The remaining class of Creditors is composed partly of such of our fellow Citizens as originally lent to the public the use of their funds or have since manifested most confidence in their Country by receiving transfers from the lenders; and partly of those whose property has been either advanced or assumed for the public service [merchants & planters].[708]

The slaves who ultimately made it all possible, however, were of course repaid with scarred backs, broken hearts, rape, murder, torture and terror, and nearly a century more of the same.

Adams' commitment of slave labor to American Independence additionally goes far towards explaining exactly why, as President, so little was heard from him against eradication of slavery. His and the nation's futures were tied to it; freedom for the slaves, having been already mortgaged, was out of the question. It could be allowed to dissolve in the North where, by the end of his administration, those states had emancipated virtually all their slaves. But in the South where it mattered most, to pay the bill for Independence, it could not. In fact, in the years following Independence, when many historians claim slavery was essentially dying out, it was actually going along as strong as ever.[709] Hence, the twenty years from the start of the government under the new Constitution, before even the slave trade could be abolished.

ANOTHER SCORE

Following peace with Britain in 1783, the Congress, under the Articles of Confederation, requested from the States the power to levy import taxes "as indispensably necessary to the restoration of public credit, and to the punctual and honorable discharge of the public debts," proposing that "none of said duties should be applied to any other purpose, . . . nor be continued for a longer term than *twenty* five years,"[710] the amount of time thought needed to pay off the nation's war debt. Twenty-five years from that date, not coincidently (you do the math), just happened to be the year the Framers decided on to end the importation of slaves from Africa. Coincidence? Yeah, Right. What's more, the year 1809, just one year later, as Congress was well aware, was when final payments would be due on the loans Adams negotiated in Holland.[711] Of course, he wasn't in America when Congress made its request. He was serving as ambassador in Europe at the time. Nor was he in attendance at the Constitutional Convention. His influence over the decision to extend the slave trade for twenty more years was, nevertheless, significant, even decisive (controlling?).

The reasons for the twenty-year delay in abolishing the trade in slaves from Africa were the obstinate positions taken by South Carolina and Georgia, whose citizens "would never be such fools as to give up so important an interest" and approve a Constitution abridging their right to import slaves, exclaimed John Rutledge of South Carolina.[712] It was the "eastern states," however, particularly Massachusetts, whose fortune derived directly from the West Indian cod fish trade. Pennsylvania, Connecticut and, of course, New York, "notwithstanding their aversion to slavery," were all at least as influential as the Southern States in the decision.[713]

Rutledge acknowledged though that the Convention's decision was strictly a commercial one. "Religion and humanity had nothing to do with th[e] question. Interest alone is the governing principle," he said. "If the Northern States consult their interest, they will not oppose the increase of Slaves which will increase the commodities of which they will become the carriers."[714] "The importation of slaves would be for the interest of the whole Union," noted Charles Coatsworth Pinckney, "The more slaves, the more produce to employ the carrying trade; the more consumption also, and the more of this, the more of revenue for the common treasury."[715]

The treaty Adams negotiated in Paris securing America's Independence "surpassed both the hopes of the government and the expectations of New England."[716] Because cod fish were an essential part of U.S. trade with the West Indies, territorial fishing was an important question in the peace negotiations of 1783. Congress fully expected the United States to be excluded from fishing at Newfoundland and the Gulf of St. Lawrence, as happened following the French and Indian War.[717] Adams's treaty instructions therefore did not make the territories an ultimatum in negotiating peace with England. But knowing their importance for Massachusetts fishing,

Adams made a forceful argument that the Newfoundland and St. Lawrence fisheries be included in the treaty.[718] The result was Article III, signed September 3, 1783, which began:

> It is agreed that the people of the United States shall continue to enjoy unmolested the right to take fish of every kind on the Grand Bank, and on the other banks of Newfoundland; also in the Gulph of St. Lawrence, and at all other places in the sea where the inhabitants of both countries used at any time heretofore to fish.[719]

A "great credit" is owed "to Adams in particular," observed McFarland, "for the granting of such satisfactory terms by the British government."

> The dictatorial attitude that Adams assumed during part of the negotiations, his evident transgression of his instructions as an accredited commissioner to make terms for a treaty of peace, and his bold stand for "the fisheries or no peace," undoubtedly were the means for securing the insertion of the third article in the treaty of 1783.[720]

But the rights to fish for cod were of little value without the slave markets in which to sell the catches. Following the war, Americans were barred from trading in the British West Indies and, at the same time, severely restricted in the Caribbean possessions of France and Spain, both willing to assist America towards Independence but not compete against it commercially. Desperate, New Englanders accused Britain of trying to ruin their entire fishing industry, though England was equally motivated to restore her depleted navy and merchant marine following her sea battles with France, Spain and Holland in the latter years of the war.[721] Believing its dependence on insecure West Indies markets under the control of the constantly warring European powers to be too great, increasing the number of slaves in the American South then became the extreme interest of New Englanders, whose life blood was the sale of its *refuse* fish to the southern plantations.

For Massachusetts, the Revolution itself was about the right to make money, observed Kurlansky. State "radicals sought an economic, not a social, revolution," he writes. "They were thinking of the right of every man to be middle-class, to be an entrepreneur, to conduct commerce and make money. Men of no particular skill, with very little capital, had made fortunes in the cod fishery."[722] Accordingly, we find Nathaniel Gorham, of abolitionist Massachusetts, at the Constitutional Convention matter-of-factly stating, as Madison recorded, "Eastern States had no motive to Union but a commercial one."[723]

Thereafter, Maryland, Massachusetts, New Hampshire and Connecticut joined the two Carolinas and Georgia in extending the

Figure IV. New England fishing territories

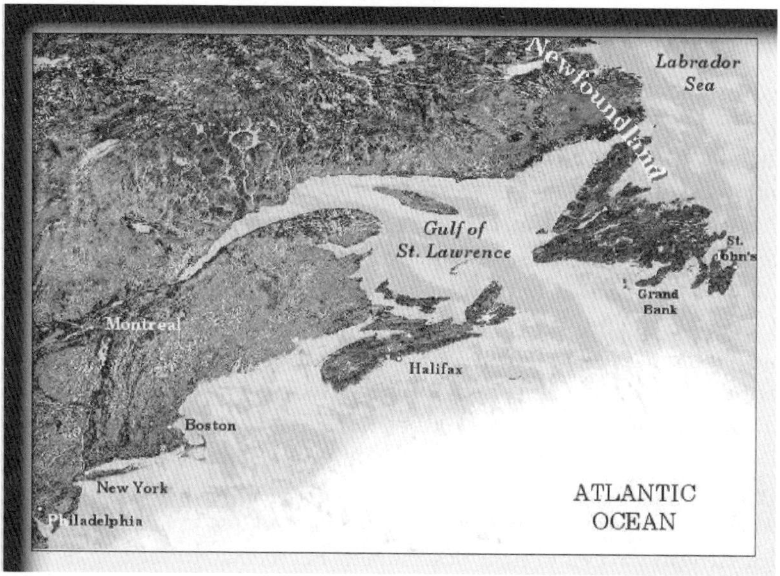

earliest date for halting African slave trafficking to 1808. A committee including one member from each state had previously agreed upon 1800 as the earliest year it might be stopped.[724] The motion to extend, initially proposed by Pinkney of South Carolina, was seconded by Ghorum.[725] New England "owned the shipping, and enjoyed the slave-trade. They accumulated capital in both" Kettell explained, it was therefore "a concession to New England interests that the trade was continued to 1808."[726] Quoting a French traveler from 1795, he further writes: "Nearly 20 vessels from the harbors of the northern States are employed in the importation of negroes to Georgia and the West India isles. The merchants of Rhode Island are the conductors of this accursed traffic, which they are determined to persevere in until the year 1808."[727] Rhode Island did not attend the Constitutional Convention, but it seems her interests were nevertheless well represented.

Table VIII, below, shows the status of America's finances during the Washington and Adams administrations, the first decade under the new Constitution. It illustrates the fact that virtually all of America's revenues during the period were derived from customs receipts. "From 1790 to 1800 inclusive," according to *DeBow's* statistics, "exports of southern plantation produce were in all 200 millions" out of $311 million dollars.[728] Imports, of course, were financed and purchased with these exports.

Table IX further shows a significant portion of the new government's expenditures, in fact the largest part, went towards paying the interest on the Revolutionary War debt. The other significant expenditures of the Adams administration were for war and naval expenses, monies dedicated to the first significant development of America's navy, primarily devoted to protecting American shipping and commercial interests on the high seas.[729] We might additionally note that the salaries of public officials: including the President, the Congress, and the entire administration of government, moreover, would have been essentially supported, through import appropriations, by the labors of Black slaves.

Adams, Of course, went on to become a national hero. But should he be identified with the supposed genius of his triumph, or more rightly for its deadly, evil pledge? America became a nation of great wealth and power, but has the stake or share in that wealth and power for African slaves and their descendants been equal to their contributions? On the contrary, those events took place in the eighteenth century; in the twenty-first century Blacks are still — as always — fighting the perpetually losing battle for full social, economic and political equality.

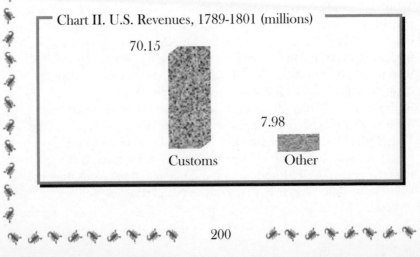

Chart II. U.S. Revenues, 1789-1801 (millions)

70.15

Customs

7.98

Other

Table VIII. U.S. Revenue, 1791 -1801

Yr.	Customs	Internal Revenue	Direct Taxes	Public Lands	Misc.	Total
1791	4,399,473				19,440	4,418,913
1792	3,443,071	203,943			9,919	3,661,932
1793	4,255,307	337,706			10,390	4,614,423
1794	4,801,065	274,090			23,799	5,128,433
1795	5,588,461	337,756			5,918	6,954,535
1796	6,567,988	475,290		4,836	16,506	7,137,630
1797	7,549,650	575,491		83,540	30,379	8,303,661
1798	7,106,062	644,358		11,953	18,693	7,820,576
1799	6,610,449	779,136			45,188	7,475,773
1800	9,080,933	809,397	734,224	444	74,712	10,777,709
1801	10,750,779	1,048,033	534,343	167,726	266,149	12,846,531

Timothy Pitkin, *A Statistical View Of Commerce*

Table IX: Expenditures, 1791 - 1801

Calendar year	War	Navy	Interest on debt	Miscellaneous	Total
1791	$633,000		$1,178,000	$1,286,000	$3,697,000
1792	1,101,000		2,373,000	4,795,000	8,269,000
1793	1,130,000		2,097,000	618,000	3,846,000
1794	2,639,000	$61,000	2,752,000	844,000	6,297,000
1795	2,481,000	410,000	2,947,000	1,471,000	7,309,000
1796	1,260,000	274,000	3,239,000	1,016,000	5,790,000
1797	1,039,000	382,000	3,172,000	1,414,000	6,008,000
1798	2,009,000	1,381,000	2,955,000	1,260,000	7,607,000
1799	2,467,000	2,858,000	2,815,000	1,155,000	9,295,000
1800	2,561,000	3,448,000	3,402,000	1,401,000	10,813,000
1801	1,673,000	2,111,000	4,412,000	1,197,000	9,393,000

Dewey, *Financial History U.S.*

The cost of Independence for Britain's American colonies, and the benefit for their Black slaves.

1783 John Singleton Copley painting of John Adams, said to be proudly pointing to a map of the new American nation. In his right hand is the Treaty of Paris ending war with England, securing Independence, for which Adams boldly pledged Death to a generation of Black slaves

15

Thomas Jefferson

Birth Of A Nation

I t seems fitting to begin a discussion of Thomas Jefferson with
some "Notes" about possibly his most curious act, among
many: his sexual relationship with the slave, Sally Hemings,
which many still refuse to accept, even with DNA corroboration,
leading to some rather half-baked explanations for the American
hero's failure to remain "beyond mixture," to use one of his own
terms.[730] Like, for example, the suggestion by author E. M. Halliday,
that the young slave girl may have actually seduced Jefferson.[731] The
nerve! Arguably one of the most powerful of Americans to ever hold
the presidency, Mr. Jefferson may have done more than any
individual in American history to permanently subjugate Black
Americans, through the "suspicions" he articulated in *Notes On The
State Of America*, his lifelong dependence on slavery and his very
public silence with regard to the institution while president. But one
major problem with the desperate theory of his seduction is of course
the young girl's age, which no less than respected historian David
McCullough determined to have likely been under sixteen when she
first conceived. "Hemings," he writes, "had arrived with little Polly
Jefferson" in London in 1787, at age fourteen, en route to be with
Thomas Jefferson in France, and "was pregnant with her first child

when she returned to Monticello," though she had been away from
Virginia little more than a year.[732]

Indeed, the shameful encounter really was, in fact, the result of a
seduction, though not by the slave girl. Polly Jefferson was apparently
supposed to be chaperoned by an "old nurse," according to
McCullough, but was instead unexpectedly accompanied by young
Hemings, the sister of Jefferson's body servant.[733] There is no
suggestion by McCullough that the change was orchestrated by
Jefferson — I'll gladly take the criticism for that outrageous, irreverent
proposition, thank you — but it's hard to imagine, with over one
hundred slaves on his Monticello plantation, a more suitable
chaperone couldn't be found for such a precarious voyage than
another adolescent. Once in France, of course, Hemings would have
been most vulnerable, making it utterly impossible for her to resist,
and impossible for Jefferson to avoid the temptation to compel her.

An act of seduction necessarily carries an element of at least a
potential rejection. But it goes without saying that Jefferson, as the
girl's owner, had the absolute ability to compel her to commit the
act.[734] Therefore, he alone possessed the power of rejection, if in fact
such an offer was forthcoming, which, in any case, was irrelevant. The
fact that the girl was likely a minor, and he her owner, override any
and all other considerations on the matter, including even the remote
possibility that another relative may have actually been the guilty party,
in which case, as her owner, Thomas Jefferson alone had the power
to stop it.

Alhough the Founding Fathers were all well served by slavery, few,
if any, benefited from the institution more than Jefferson. His
Founding legacy nevertheless manages to largely hover above his
status as a slaveowner, despite the fact, much like Washington, little in
the way of character, talent or courage leads one to the conclusion
that his success would have been just as likely absent slavery.

As for courage, Jefferson ran from the British at Monticello, while
Governor of Virginia during the Revolutionary War, displaying the
cowardice identified by contemporaries noting his apparent fear of
the American general, Aaron Burr, who killed Alexander Hamilton
and was a Presidencial rival, a man "whom, as was generally known,
Jefferson was, personally, afraid."[735]

If he actually had to work for a living and earn everything he got,
without a lifelong pampering by slaves, Jefferson likely would never
have received the same opportunities for education and renown.
Every piece of food he *ever* ate, every piece of clothing he *ever* wore,

every cent he *ever* spent, and every home he *ever* lived in, including abroad, were *all* provided for by the labors of Black slaves; even the water for every bath he ever took, was drawn for him by a Black slave. "It was not just that slaves worked his fields," observed McCullough,

> they cut his firewood, cooked and served his meals, washed and ironed his linen, brushed his suits, nursed his children, cleaned, scrubbed, polished, opened and closed doors for him, saddled his horse, turned down his bed, waited on him hand and foot from dawn to dusk.[736]

Is it any wonder he thought himself so superior to the Black race, simply by virtue of having been born with White skin? How could he not, with such pampering? Yet, there are those who intimate, with a straight face no less, slavery wasn't profitable to Jefferson in the last years of his life. Go figure! His dependence on slaves was so complete, in fact, I have serious doubts about whether he ever wiped his own ass, from the fear of possibly getting his hands dirty! A disgusting thought, I know, but slavery was a disgusting institution. And such revolting tasks were of the type invariably considered appropriate to the supposed base nature of the Black race,[737] an acceptable responsibility for a so-called "body servant,"[738] as it were.

Jefferson grew up from a baby having such things done for him by slaves and there's no reason to believe he ever progressed to the point of thinking it was an appropriate task for a supposedly respectable, higher-class White person — as many slave-owners were generally regarded. Certainly, if any were predisposed to have such an ignominious task performed for him, it would have been "T Jay."

PREDATORY BORROWING

As much as his personal life depended on slavery, Jefferson's political renown was equally supported by bonded labor. The Declaration of Independence notwithstanding, Independence-in-fact, as we've seen, became possible only on the backs of Black slaves. While the most significant act of his presidency, the Louisiana Purchase, which doubled the size of America, was also only feasible — and realized — through the fruits of slavery, though few historians, if any, acknowledge the fact.

When the Spanish suddenly cut off American access to the Gulf of Mexico at the port of New Orleans early in his Administration, Jefferson was caught between a rock and a hard place. The Mississippi River was a necessary avenue to eastern and European markets for U.S. farmers west of the Appalachian Mountains, but an attempt to force the port open would mean war with France, new owner of the entire Louisiana territory from Minnesota to New Orleans, obtained from Spain as "war booty."[739] The only way to avoid war was to purchase the port, a suddenly viable option because of America's increasing creditworthiness,[740] owing to accumulating Treasury surpluses from import customs receipts – 90 percent of the national revenues, as shown in Table X, below.[741] Imports into the United States, we must again be reminded, were paid for with the country's exports, of "which cotton came to be a very important item."[742]

Alexander Baring, of Baring Brothers Company in London, along with Pierre-Cesar Labouchere, Baring's brother-in-law, a partner at Henry Hope & Company of Amsterdam, Holland,[743] were sent to Paris "to conclude the negotiations" for New Orleans along with Livingston and Monroe.[744] He was instructed by Treasury Secretary Gallatin "to arrange if possible that the price be paid through bills on the Treasury."[745] Congress authorized $2,000,000 for the negotiations, which Monroe and Livingston guaranteed as "an advance to the French Treasury,"[746] partially "paid in the United States through Willing & Francis of Philadelphia."[747] Terms of the final treaty called for $11,250,000 of the $15 million purchase price to have 6 percent United States stock paid into the French Public Treasury, redeemable in fifteen years.[748]

© Softkey International
Jefferson: Low maintenance?

After receiving word back in Washington at the beginning of January, 1804, that the U.S. had taken formal possession of New Orleans, "Gallatin turned over one-third of the [Treasury] certificates" to Baring and Hope,[749] who made advance payments to the French in anticipation of their sale, making, in addition, "34,500,000 francs available over a period of eight months to the French Treasury in Paris and in various Baltic ports against the remaining two thirds of the certificates, delivered to Hope & Company" by Livingston,[750] who received them "by special messenger" from Gallatin, "as a precaution."[751] Interest and the remaining $3.75 million of the purchase price was paid by Gallatin directly out of the U.S. Treasury, as stipulated in the Louisiana Treaty, and appropriated by Congress "for the purpose of discharging the claims of citizens of the United States against the government of France," whereby the President was additionally authorized

> to borrow, on the credit of the United States, . . . a sum, not exceeding one million, seven hundred and fifty thousand dollars, . . . at the pleasure of the United States, or at such period, not exceeding five years from the time of obtaining the loan, as may be stipulated by contract, and it shall be lawful for the bank of the United States to lend the same [and] that so much of the duties on merchandize and tonnage, as may be necessary, be, and the same hereby is appropriated, for the purpose of paying the interest which shall accrue on the said loan.[752]

Because of their advances to the French government, the Barings acquired the Treasury bonds at the price of $78 per $100 face value, a profit estimated by Gallatin to amount to $3,000,000. The exchange of dollars for francs, moreover, was a precursor of the international exchange that would become a large and wildly profitable business of the Barings for American importers (see, "Baring It All," Chapter 17).

Believing the loan could be extinguished well before it actually became due in fifteen years, owing to the regular underestimation of revenue receipts,[753] Gallatin had specific (import) customs appropriations increased by nearly three quarters of a million dollars to redeem the debt, nearly a third coming from the New Orleans port alone.[754] With ensuing treasury constraints, however, including the Jefferson trade embargo and the War of 1812, redemption did not go speedily. In June, 1817, then Treasury secretary William H. Crawford issued an order to buy up the Louisiana bonds if it could be done affordably, but "the market price had been too high" and the Barings only "forwarded a small lot in February, 1818."[755] Final redemption did not occur until 1822,[756] yet the purchase of the Louisiana Territory set America instantly upon a stunning new destiny. Nowhere, however, will you find any mention of Black slaves, the fruits of whose labors, in fact, made it all possible. The anemic U. S. government's response to the catastrophic effects of hurricane Katrina, in 2005, particularly with regard to Louisiana's population of Black slave descendents, is therefore that much more devastating — and unacceptable!

PORT ARABS

Another financial constraint on the U. S. treasury during Jefferson's Administration was the war with the Barbary pirates of North Africa, as they were known. The United States and Europe had been paying an annual tribute to the rulers of Morocco, Algiers, Tunis and Tripoli to allow commercial shipping to ply the Mediterranean unmolested, worth several million dollars for protection and ransom from the U.S. alone in the first decade under the new Constitution.[757] After Tripoli captured the ship *Philadelphia* and condemned its crew of several hundred to hard labor, declaring war by an act of disrespect to the U. S. flag, the idea of paying additional ransom no longer seemed practical. And considering the supposed cruel treatment of prisoners held by the pirates, described below, war, no doubt, became the only option:

All those who are convicted of a conspiracy or treason are impaled; that is, a sharp spit is run up their body, on which they are left to writhe in torment till they die. Others are bound hand and foot, and cast from a high wall or tower, upon an iron hook, wherein they are sometimes staked by the belly, head, or other parts of the body, where they sometimes languish many days, till death puts an end to their tortures. Many are tied with a rope about the middle and, with four sharp spikes, fastened to a cross against the city wall; they are torn alive piecemeal; others are brayed to pieces in a mortar.
They have another mode of punishment . . .
Two hooks are fixed to a gallows, the one fastened to a short, the other to a large chain: The malefactor is forced up the ladder with the executioner, who, thrusting the hook through his left hand, hangs him by it on the shortest chain; then to the hook on the longest he fastens him by the foal of his right foot, where he hangs some days in the most insufferable torment till he dies.[758]

In preparation, Jefferson's plan was to raise naval appropriations by three quarters of a million dollars, from a special Mediterranean Fund that included, roughly, a 3 percent average increase on duties of 12½, 15 and 20 percent, with an additional 10 percent on items imported in vessels not registered to Americans.[759] This "enabled the Navy to press its operations against the Barbary powers," including, in the summer of 1804, "an effective blockade along the Tripolitan coast that remains one of the glories of our sea history."[760]

Table X: U.S. Receipts, 1801-1811

Yr	Customs	Other	Total
1801	$10,750,000	$2,185,000	$12,935,000
1802	12,438,000	2,667,000	14,995,000
1803	10,478,000	585,000	11,064,000
1804	11,099,000	727,000	11,826,000
1805	12,935,000	624,000	13,560,000
1806	14,667,000	892,000	15,559,000
1807	15,846,000	552,000	16,398,000
1808	16,363,000	697,000	17,060,000
1809	7,258,000	515,000	7,773,000
1810	8,583,000	800,000	9,384,000
1811	13,313,000	1,109,000	14,422,000

Table XI: U.S. Expenditures, 1801-1811

Yr	War	Navy	Interest	Misc.*	Total
1801	1,673,000	2,111,000	4,412,000	1,197,000	4,418,913
1802	1,179,000	915,000	4,239,000	1,642,000	3,661,932
1803	822,000	1,215,000	3,949,000,	1,965,000	4,614,423
1804	875,000	1,189,000	4,185,000	2,387,000	5,128,433
1805	713,000	1,597,000	2,637,000	4,846,000	6,954,535
1806	1,724,000	1,649,000	3,368,000	3,206,000	7,137,630
1807	1,288,000	1,722,000	3,369,000	1,973,000	8,303,661
1808	2,900,000	1,884,000	2,557,000	1,719,000	7,820,576
1809	3,345,000	2,427,000	2,886,000	1,641,000	7,475,773
1810	2,294,000	1,654,000	3,163,000	1,362,000	10,777,709
1811	2,032,000	1,965,000	2,585,000	1,594,000	12,846,531

*Includes salaries, pensions for Congress, President, civil servants, Indians, etc.
Dewey, *Financial History of the United States*

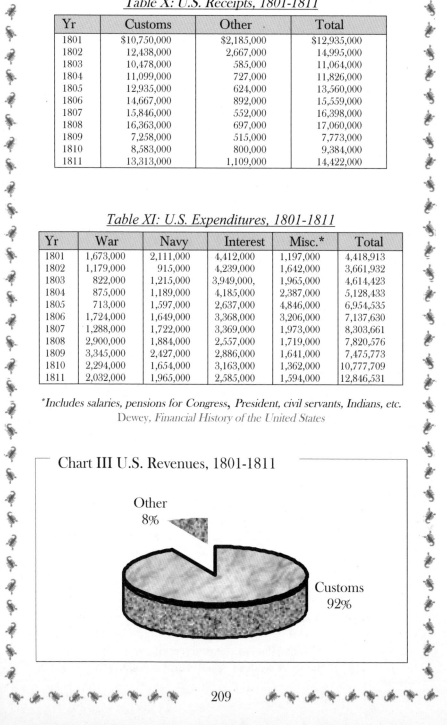

Chart III U.S. Revenues, 1801-1811

Other
8%

Customs
92%

16

James Madison

THERE CAN BE NO VICTORY,
NO WAR, WITHOUT MONEY.
SOLDIERS AND GENERALS
CAN BE CREATED BY MONEY
AND BY MONEY ONLY.

-- *STEPHEN GIRARD*

*L*ike Thomas Jefferson, his intellectual accomplishments are what establish James Madison as an American hero. But, also like Jefferson, the paper trail of his successes, including his work on the U. S. Constitution and the war that inspired the Star Spangled Banner and produced two Presidents, the War of 1812, inevitably leads one back to Black slavery. And it's not at all clear, similar to both Washington and Jefferson, that Madison possessed any inherent ability to distinguish himself if not supported by the labors of Black slaves.

The Second War For Independence

Due to lingering effects of Jefferson's trade embargo and Britain's continued menacing of American commercial interests on the seas, Treasury revenues at the start of the nineteenth century's second decade were inconsistent, at best. A government loan from the Bank

of the United States helped "tide it over the crisis," but when renewal
of the bank's charter was rejected in 1811, that option, to bankroll the
looming war with England, was no longer available.[761]

After Congress declared war on Great Britain, the treasury secretary
was authorized to borrow $11 million dollars from the public to cover
the first year's expenditures. However, only a little more than half that
amount was actually raised, prompting a request to raise an additional
$5 million from Treasury bills,[762] the first ever issued by the
government. All tolled, the $5 million was still woefully inadequate to
cover the expected $22 million needed for the Army and Navy, out of
total estimated expenses for the government of $32 million, against
just $12 million dollars in revenue – a $20 million dollar deficit.[763]

"We can expect little or nothing" from Banks to close the gap, the
secretary lamented, believing he could also expect "neither sympathy
nor aid from Congress."[764] He was authorized to borrow $16 million
dollars though, despite the fact that $5 million of the previous year's
$11 million dollar loan had not been taken. Out of what might be
properly described as desperation, the secretary offered, on March
18, a minimum commission of $250 on block subscriptions of
$100,000, and thus connected with Stephen Girard of Philadelphia
and John Jacob Astor of New York, the two richest men in America
at that time.

Because of past dealings, and the Treasury's heavy reliance on the
U. S. Bank, secretary Gallatin was intimately familiar with Girard's
wealth and stature. Girard, after all, was the bank's "largest individual
stockholder at the end of its charter in 1811."[765] In addition, a
Treasury lawsuit for bringing prohibited merchandise into the country
was still open against Girard. His ship, *Good Friends*, awaiting
expiration of the ban, was held in the waters off the coast of Spanish
Florida at Amelia Island, loaded with English goods, when suddenly
the port became the property of the United States. But, despite
seeking treble damages against Girard on the *Good Friends* cargo
valued at nearly $300,000, the Treasury Secretary nevertheless sought
his assistance for war finance. And Girard, in fact, was actually
receptive – though supposedly upon considerations of banking only.

Initially, after the $16 million loan opened, he subscribed for
$100,000 individually and received $22,000 in subscriptions through
his bank. When the loan closed on March 13, however, even at the
increased rate of 7 percent the amount taken still totaled less than $4
million dollars, and less than $6 million when extended to the 31st.[766]

Gallatin now knew his last chance to raise the money was a further
appeal to the wealthy capitalists.[767] With commissions now being

offered on block subscriptions, Girard became more interested in joining with Astor, America's second richest person, and with other investors inclined to take the risk after knowing he was involved, to complete the $16 million offering.

Investors were not generally optimistic about America's chances in a war against England, particularly as British forces increased following Napoleon's calamity in Russia; if defeated the U.S. government would likely default on its loan obligations. Girard, however, would be expecting a worthwhile return on his money. His involvement would signal that the loan was not only a safe investment, but potentially a lucrative one, materially influencing the development of a market for the loan, and for an even larger placement of $25 million the following year.[768]

On April 6, 1813, one day after loan subscriptions officially closed, and the Treasury virtually "empty and unable to honor the drafts of other departments," Gallatin concluded what has been described as "the greatest financial transaction of the War of 1812."[769] Under the loan notice of the Treasury, dated the 18th of March 1813, Girard offered to take, in syndication, "as much stock of the United States . . . as will amount to eight millions of dollars," or the remainder.[770] In total, he took $7 million, paying $88 for every $100 of face value of the loan. And at the same price, Astor, "for myself and my friends in New York," agreed to take two millions and fifty six thousand dollars of it.[771] Thus was "the credit of the United States kept high."[772]

The loans of course had an immediate effect on the war. Within six weeks of the cash infusion, the British had been defeated at Toronto, Canada, Fort Meigs, and Fort Stephenson in Ohio, Fort George and Sackets Harbor, New York, and forced to retreat from several other forts near Lake Ontario.[773] "Delight in the United States, could scarcely be equaled, when the encounter on the seas resulted in the unprecedented spectacle of a series of triumphs over the tyrant of the ocean," wrote Thomas Kettell.[774] "A power had arisen that was thenceforth to know no master upon the ocean, and submit to no insults; and this power had been born of commerce."[775]

Before the peace at Ghent, three separate issues of Treasury notes totaling $20 million had gone into the war chest, along with four public loans totaling $62,000,000.[776]

GIRARD'S AVENUE

The "frugal, avaricious" Girard, as described by one contemporary,[777] had come to Philadelphia, America's largest city, in June, 1776, from France, by way of the West Indies, just prior to the colonies' declaration of independence,[778] "illiterate, as a French common sailor must needs be, and scarcely able to write his own name."[779] He was among the pioneers of America's trade to Russia, India, China and South America, first during the Revolutionary years as a captain and officer, and later as a sedentary merchant from his home base on the Delaware River in Philadelphia, employing many ships simultaneously. His ventures generally began with a cargo of rice or cotton from Charleston, South Carolina or Savannah, Georgia; tobacco, wheat, corn or ginseng from either City Point, Broadway, Portsmouth, Petersburgh, Norfolk, Richmond or from any other various locations on the James River in Virginia; with wheat, flour or corn from Baltimore, Maryland; or with cotton from New Orleans, Louisiana, all exchanged in Europe for "cargoes worth from one to two hundred thousand dollars" of manufactured goods, provisions or wine.[780]

Biographer George Wilson correctly summed up Girard's activities thus: "The more money he made from buying and selling cargoes, the more money he had available to invest in still more cargoes. The more cargoes he acquired, the more ships he needed to carry them," at times netting a 300 percent return.[781]

A snapshot of Girard's ventures as a sedentary merchant and powerful banker provided over the next several pages, beginning in 1809, is illustrative of the critical role of Black slave labor in his accumulation of wealth, since his activities generally involved the triangular trade between America, the West Indies and Europe.[782]

Anxiously anticipating an end to Jefferson's embargo, Girard informed a Dutch correspondent of his intention "to dispatch to Europe as soon as practicable" cargoes of cotton aboard his Ships *Helvetius, Voltaire, Liberty* and *Good Friends*.[783] Two of these, *Helvetius* and *Good Friends*, were dispatched together to Goteborg, Sweden, while the *Voltaire* and *Liberty,* along with another vessel, the *Montesquieu,* also loaded with cotton, as well as indigo, coffee and other assorted produce of both India and the United States, were dispatched to Amsterdam and Rotterdam in Holland, unless under British blockade, in which case they should proceed to a port in North Germany accessible to Hamburg overland and by inland waterways. Access to the city from the North Sea was restricted by the British blockade of the Elbe River. A sixth ship, the *Rousseau,* loaded with coffee and sugar from Havana, Cuba, was also ordered to North Germany or, if blockaded, "from port to port" at the south of Spain where, "should he enter the Mediterranean, Tunis was to be his first port."

James Madison

After an eventful voyage, the *Rousseau, Voltaire,* and *Montesquieu* successfully landed their cargoes in Germany, departing October, 1809, to return to Philadelphia, the *Montesquieu* arriving in November, the *Rousseau* and *Voltaire* in December, where they were loaded once more with flour, cash and, apparently, Virginia wheat stocked from Girard's Delaware River warehouses, to begin another journey per these instructions: "the Flour is to be landed and sold at Charleston, The neat [sic] Proceeds of that article and of the two hundred Barrels shipped on board the *Rousseau,* together with the [cash] on board [the *Voltaire* and *Montesquieu*], amounting to $60,000, is to be invested in cotton as far as will be necessary to complete the loading of those two ships."[784] The vessels were also carrying cargoes of rice, though it's not clear whether they were loaded in South Carolina or in Philadelphia at Girard's waterfront warehouses.

The *Rousseau,* with 824 bales of upland cotton and total cargo worth $106,718.13, and the *Montesquieu,* with 996 bales and cargo valued at $112,224.97, were again destined for northern Europe in early January, 1810, from there on to China, west via South America and across the expansive Pacific. Leaving Philadelphia January 10, the *Voltaire* was instead headed directly to South America, her cargo valued at $201,026.36. After 55 days at sea she landed first in Monte Video, Uruguay, in early March, and on to Buenos Aires, arriving March 14, 1810, tallying total sales of $176,779 in eight months after her arrival. By January, 1811 the entire cargo had been sold and she departed for Rio de Janeiro the 11th, arriving on the 29th carrying "Forty-one thousand, four hundred dollars, twenty-two pieces of raw silver which I know not the value of."[785]

Reconnecting with the *Voltaire,* the supercargo (buyer), separated in the haste surrounding the forbidden export of money from the as yet Spanish dominions, carried with them "very near One Hundred Thousand Spanish Dollars in specie" when they arrived in Rio on April 10, 1811, to purchase goods in China, their immediate destination a few days later.[786]

Having gone to Kiel, Germany (formerly Denmark) and realized a net profit of "from 23 to 26 cents per pound" on her cotton, the *Montesquieu,* traveled to Nyborg, Denmark and Goteberg, Sweden collecting an exchange cargo of valued linens and glass,[787] procured the first week of July, 1810, in Hamburg, Germany, and was now on to South America. Soon to follow from Russia was the *Rousseau,* which, after first making Helsingor, Denmark, in the spring, had 534 bales of cotton sequestered by Napoleon in Stralsund, Germany (then belonging to Sweden), to prevent it finding its way into England. With unattractive and impossible prospects at Monte Video and Buenos Aires, however, both vessels opted for Valparaiso.

The *Montesquieu* arrived from Europe April 15th, 1811 "after a passage of 101 days." It

"Should have been in here the day before, but [Cape Horn] is so blind a place to see that alltho' we ran down the coast pretty close in we had passed it several miles before we observed it and the whole sailing powers of the *Montesquieu* were exerted to recover 15 miles against a very strong wind and ugly sea which she did by ten o'clock the next day."[788]

A comparatively easy navigation considering the *Rousseau* was blown some 250 miles south rounding the southern tip of the contintinent at Cape Horn, "after a passage of 63 days from Monte Video," reaching Valparaiso May 19. According to the captain: "We had a tedious time round Cape Horn the winds hanging much from the westward which unavoidably pushed us to the southward as far as 60° 27′ South. We experienced two smart gales with excessive cold weather."[789]

The ships forwarded their cargoes on to Santiago for sale, accumulating only $73,000 by September, complained the captain of the *Montesquieu,* who left his remaining cargo for later sale and proceeded on to China. The *Rousseau* returned around Cape Horn to Rio de Janeiro where its wheat was sold, procuring sugar and hides for the trip home.

The *Liberty*, meanwhile, was wrecked, her valuable cargo of cotton and rice salvaged and sequestered at Hamburg, Germany. The *Helvetius*, on the other hand, proceeded to Goteborg, Sweden and on June 21, 1809, while en route to Kiel, Germany, was detained in Helsingor, Denmark, its cargo similarly confiscated, after which she went on to St. Petersburg, Russia ahead of the *Rousseau*, departing Kronshtadt July, 1810, stopping again in Goteborg before her return to Philadelphia.

The *Good Friends* was detained April 30, 1809 in Farsund, Norway, and her cargo, including some 40 tons of cotton, promptly seized. The supercargo then traveled to the nearby Norwegian port of Kristiansand to lodge a protest. When no resolution had been as yet adjudicated at mid-December, he wrote in frustration, "I hope the government of the United States will show Denmark and the World that the property of its citizens is not to be sported thus unwarrantably

with impunity."[790] By mid-1810, *Good Friends* was on her way to
Russia, returning home after the New Year and embarking again for
Lisbon in August, 1811, leaving London to return home with British
goods on December 25, 1811, but was diverted to Spanish Florida
because of a U.S. ban on English imports, arriving Feb. 11, 1812.

The seizure of the *Good Friends* in Norway was the eighth
American vessel with "produce of the United States" condemned
there, and after transfer of the ship to nearby Kristiansand, Denmark,
her supercargo noted "there are now in this port twenty seven
American vessels," with produce worth approximately $1.5 million
dollars under seizure, "and they are brot daily."[791]

When the *Helvitius* was also captured in Germany one of Girard's
German correspondents wrote: "The Gent[lemen] of Helsingor
mention that four other Americans are brought in there and 18 or 19
ships carried into Norway." [792] Obviously, Girard's ventures
represented only a fraction of the business interests supported by
American slavery – world-wide.

South America

Interestingly, Stephen Girard was also a convenient vehicle through
which the labors of Black American slaves helped the cause of
Independence in South America, to the tune of an advance in the
amount of $17,801.22 for the purchase of 425 muskets and 236
"sabres with Spanish blades" procured Feb. 1811 for the assisstance
of nationalist forces in Venezuela, to the credit of the 27 yr. old
Simon Bolivar, at the request of his brother Vincent.[793] When the
revolting leaders of Chile and Argentina asked for Girard's assistance
in obtaining 20,000 muskets in November, 1811, he brought the
matter to the attention of then Secretary of State Monroe, sparking an
involvement with the southern continent that culminated in the
Monroe Doctrine in December 1823.[794]

Girard, however, was not the only vehicle through which profits
from slavery reached the cause of independence in South America.
Checks from Brazil drawn on the Baring Brothers were reportedly
issued by representatives of the U. S. State Department in 1817, and
in 1824 an Argentinean bond issue for close to $5 million dollars
(£1,000,000) was sold to British investors through Baring Brothers,
while an estimated total of the "loans marketed in England for the
Latin American states between 1822 and 1825 was £21,000,000, or
$95,000,000."[795]

ASTOR'S PLACE

New York's John Jacob Astor was another of the many shipping. merchants in early America engaged in transporting slave produce to various parts of the globe. The owner of large portions of Manhattan island, Astor was an astute investor who made great gains via the fur trade, eventually specializing in trade with China. Typical of early America, however, the fur trade, which largely involved purchasing from and contracting with Indians, could not have been prosecuted so lucratively without two great vices: tobacco and alcohol.[796]

Many European American historians would have us believe Indians parted with skins at such cheap prices because they were stupid and uneducated. The reality was more like Indians were taken advantage of because they were drunk — and high on tobacco! "Their attachment to ardent spirits is a moral phenomenon," said a contemporary, "to it they sacrifice every consideration public or private."[797] Historian Kenneth Wiggins Porter noted,

> It was not long until the Indian who had for a few times partaken of the trader's liquor had become, when not under the direct influence of the intoxicant, a pitiful sot, so enslaved to the habit as to be willing to trade his gun or his last blanket for a swallow of alcohol, [leaving] fur traders with weighty packs of furs and well-filled pocketbooks, the fruits of the ruin which their greed and their kegs of rum had brought upon the natives.[798]

Describing this infamous "fire water," a contemporary wrote: "Take two gallons of common whisky or unrectified spirits [cheap wines], add to thirty gallons of water and to this add red pepper enough to make it fiery and tobacco enough to make it intoxicating, and you have a [concoction] that will cause the Indian to give everything he possesses into the hands of the white man."[799] "Actual cost" of this fire water, he added, did not "exceed five cents a gallon and retailed to the Indians for fifty cents a bottle, of which thousands of bottles were sold every year."[800]

Of course, Astor's profitable Chinese trade was also helped considerably by the fruitful labors of Black slaves: a March 1809 cargo to China, aboard the brig *Sylph*, included 14,000 otter skins and seven tons of cotton; the August 1809 cargo aboard the *Beaver* included 63½ tons of cotton; the September 1810 voyage of the *Beaver* had 101 tons of cotton; the October, 1811 *Beaver* a cargo of Rice, Rum and cotton textiles, among other things.[801] Suffice it to say, without the many products of slave labor used in the fur trade and the trade to China, such as Kentucky and Virginia tobacco, Carolina rice and cotton, and cotton from New Orleans, Astor would likely have forever remained as poor as the day he first arrived, in 1783, at the country "where land and opportunity were to be found by all."[802]

The Fertile Crescent

This was the time Napoleon was at the peak of his power. Girard desired to be free of the whims of the ever-at-war European nations and so, beginning with his *Good Friends* cargo, he started withdrawing his assets from the keep of his agents on the continent. Whenever it was not expedient to invest the proceeds of produce sales in return cargoes, Girard directed his money be deposited with local agents or correspondents. America's "political situation with the continent of Europe is very alarming," he wrote in early 1811, consequently I have requested my correspondents there "to realize my property and to remit you my funds as fast as incashed," to be invested in American stocks.[803] "Merchants in all the leading ports" of Europe "were anxious to acquire the business brought by American merchants and sailors"[804] and also benefitted by undertaking "adventures on their own account in cotton corn, wheat, flour, coffee and other commodities" which, as a matter of course, was a routine practice with correspondents, purchasing cotton "on joint account with forwarding firms in Charleston, Savannah, and Mobile.[805] Prominent among these foreign merchants were Minturn & Champlin of St. Petersburg, Russia; Holterman & Sons of Goteborg, Sweden; Belfour, Ellah, Rainals & Co. of Helsingor, Denmark; Berenbert, Gossler & Co. and Schwartz Brothers, of Hamburg, Germany; Mahlon Hutchinson, Jr., William & Jan Willink, and Henry Hope & Co. of Amsterdam, Holland; David Parish & Co., and Ridgway, Mertens & Co. of Antwerp, Belgium; John A. Morton, Strobel & Martini, John Hourquebie and Paul Duret & Co. of Bordeaux, France; Perregaux, Lafitte & Co. and Hottinguer & Co. of Paris, France; Daniel Cornaz & Co. of Marseille, France; Millot & Toussaint of Le Havre, France; Barclay & Co., and Thellusson Bros. & Co. of London, England; John Bulkeley & Son of Lisbon, Portugal; Rey & Brandenbourg of Cadiz, Spain; John Ross of Gibraltar; Grant, Webb & Co. of Livorno (Leghorn), Italy; Holland & Co. of Trieste, Italy.

This shows the fruits of Black American slave labor were spread far across Europe, merely scratching the surface of the European firms Girard employed, saying nothing of those across Asia, South America, the Caribbean and the United States employed by him and thousands of others who traded, managed, or transported the products of slavery, providing employment, food, clothing and shelter for countless agents, wholesalers, shipbuilders, stevedores, textile workers, and many, many more, at the ports of Europe's "Fertile Crescent," if you will, stretching from St. Petersburg, Russia in the Baltic Sea, to Scandanavia and the United Kingdom, around the Iberian Peninsula with Spain and Portugal to the Mediterranean, the Balkans and the Adriatic Sea (see Figure V).

While Girard's original intention was to have all his European capital invested in United States stock, part of it was invested in English and German goods to be sold in America, leading to the voyage of the *Good Friends*, whose cargo, valued at approximately $300,000 dollars, later sold at auction in Philadelphia for nearly $600,000. Girard's remaining European capital was used "to purchase in England ... United States securities [550 shares worth $55,000], stock of the United States Bank [950 shares valued at $380,000] and $20,000 in silver."[806]

Although he arrived in this country a net debtor — absconding from a return trip to France after a failed trading venture to the West Indies[807] — by 1812 Girard had become the richest man in America. He apparently arrived in Philadelphia, in 1776, with a plan and a purpose, wasting no time on his journey of accumulating riches, not even bothering to wait out the war. After cashing in his trading profits, he became the sole owner of a bank named after him, promptly established upon expiration of the first United States Bank in Philadelphia, buying up most of its physical assets.[808]

In a 1779 response to his father in France regarding the state of his affairs following the British evacuation of Philadelphia after the war, he wrote: "When they left, all I possessed was a small estate in the country valued at ten thousand livres, in specie, and about fifteen thousand in paper money of St. Domingo. . . . I have since then finished furnishing my house, bought a small negro, [and] increased my capital to thirty-five thousand."[809] In 1803, however, he gave another personal accounting to London based Baring Brothers Company, who were proposing to cover a protested draft Girard had given treasury secretary Gallatin. The House of Baring, the British merchant bankers who arguably made more money off of American slavery, both on their own account and for the account of others, than any other European bankers, was proposing to become Girard's London agent. In response, he wrote:

I have three ships with their cargoes at sea, on their voyages to India. I expect them back next spring. Besides this I have a ship building in Philadelphia county, and another ship in this port, which arrived some time ago from Russia, with a cargo on my account, which is principally unsold. I own also two fifths of the ship *Fanny* and Cargo. This latter is expected from Sumatra in the course of two months. To this I may add the goods which I have on hand, my real estate and out-standing Debts and about $40,000 of U.S. 8pc, and Insur Compy of Pennsylv[ania] Stock. The cargoes of the ships which I have at sea, consist of Four Hundred and Forty Five Thousand Dollars in Specie, and Nineteen Thousand Fout Hundred Eighteen Dollars 71 Cents in Goods amounting together to $464,418 71/100 without comprehending the value of my ships which are all sheathed with copper, and could not be purchased for $100,000. My debts are trifling, I have at present but one note of Two Thousand Dollars out, and the Deposit I have in our Banks exceeds all I owe in the world.[810]

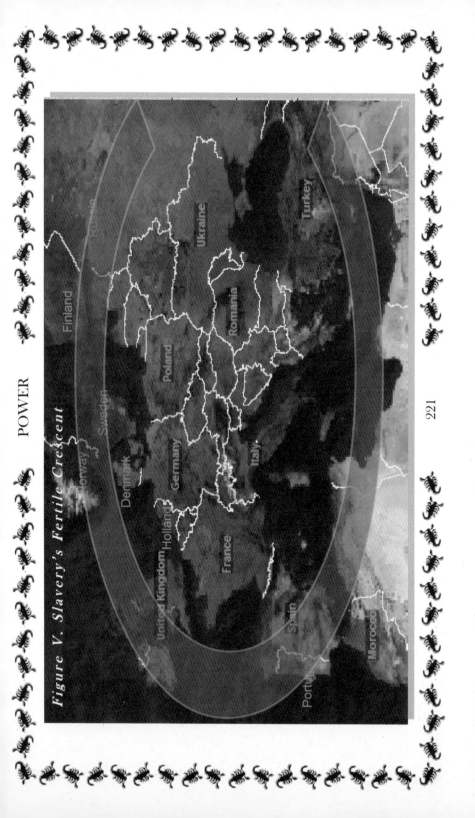

Figure V. Slavery's Fertile Crescent

Table XII: 1812 Wartime Budgets (millions)

Yr.	Total Revenue	Total Expenses	Deficit
1812	9.8	20.280	(10.4)
1813	14.3	31.681	(17.3)
1814	11.1	34.720	(23.6)
1815	15.6	32.943	(17.3)

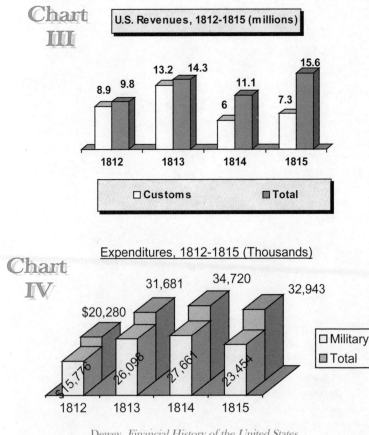

Chart III

U.S. Revenues, 1812-1815 (millions)

8.9 9.8 13.2 14.3 6 11.1 7.3 15.6

1812   1813   1814   1815

☐ Customs   ■ Total

Chart IV

Expenditures, 1812-1815 (Thousands)

$20,280   31,681   34,720   32,943

$15,776   26,098   27,661   23,454

1812   1813   1814   1815

☐ Military
■ Total

Dewey, *Financial History of the United States*

17

Baring It All

Deserving special mention among the many eighteenth and nineteenth century merchant bankers who realized extraordinary profits from the back-breaking labors of Black slaves in America was the house of Baring Brothers Company of London,[811] established 1767. Owner of London's Barings Bank, founder Sir Francis Baring "earned nearly £7 million from a business of dealing in slaves that went back 70 years. Baring Road in South East London is named after him," and he "was said to have his first money trading in slaves when he was just 16."[812]

When Stephen Girard decided to liquidate his assets from Europe, he directed agents to forward all account balances being held for him, proceeds valued at "over $1,000,000," to the Barings.[813] He expressed his desire for advice from Germany "respecting the mode of directing the sale" of his cotton held at Copenhagen, Riga and Straslund, including that salvaged from the wrecked Liberty in Hamburg, so that northern European accounts "may be finally closed and my funds remitted to Messrs. Baring Brothers as fast as practicable."[814] To Amsterdam, he also wrote, "I wish to have my business on the north of the Continent of Europe finally closed and my funds remitted to Messrs. Baring Brothers & Co. of London subject to my order."[815]

The Baring Brothers activity is significant because the effect of the cotton explosion on Europe paralleled the accelerated pace of

business in America. The firm placed loans and securities for the
U.S. government, including the Louisiana Purchase, the various
States, the United States Bank and many other banks, both public
and private. In addition to also offering currency exchange services,
the Barings generally sat at the center of a financial world that was
positively dizzying (or sickening) from the collective volume of activity
swirling mainly around American cotton, wheat, rice, sugar, indigo,
corn and tobacco. Through the Barings, profits from slavery touched
every corner of the American Union and every part of the globe. The
complete story is far beyond the scope of this book, but in no way can
justice be done to the story of American slavery without at least some
brief reference to the Barings, whose activities were "dominated by
American trade and finance" in the nineteenth century.[816] To omit
such a reference would discount the considerable international
pressure weighing heavily on the hands that directed each stinging lash
that reigned down onto the backs of tormented American and West
Indian slaves, whose labors buoyed eighteenth and nineteenth century
high finance — world-wide.

"Commissions on payments of interest to European holders of
American securities," wrote biographer Ralph Hidy, in *The House
Of Baring In American Trade And Finance*, "produced a not
inconsiderable item in the income of Baring Brothers & Company."

In 1795 foreigners held $20,288,637 of the total funded debt of the
United States and $33,041,135 in 1801. In the latter year the funded
foreign debt totaled $9,915,000 . . . foreigners also owned 13,000 of the
25,000 shares of the Bank of the United States in 1798 and 18,000 in
1809. An estimate of British capital alone invested in American
"funds" [from] a partner in Baring Brothers & Company, in 1819,
showed £4,182,000 for 1801, £5,747,000 for 1805, between 5 and 6
million pounds for 1806 and 1807, and between 4 and 5 million
pounds for the period 1808-10. . . . a large proportion of such
payments, after 1803 at least, were effected by the firm, including
more than £80,000 per year on the Louisiana Purchase bonds alone;
and through the London house after 1803 passed most all remittances
to [European] agents of both the Federal government and the Bank of
the United States.[817]

A firm policy to exploit growth opportunities in American trade
encouraged the Barings to expand their presence in America
following the peace of 1814.[818] Such opportunities occurred when the
firm intervened "to uphold the credit of the Federal government"
during its financial difficulties following the war, honoring bounced

checks and assuming accounts from failed London banker Alexander
Glennie, Son & Co., in 1814 and 1815, including the account of the
Navy Department which, by 1828, "involved an open credit of
£50,000 [nearly $230,000] from the Barings to the Bank of the
United States" for making payments to London on behalf of the U. S.
government.[819] The firm also honored a check (bill) drawn on them
by the United States Minister at Rio de Janeiro, in 1817, "without
authorization in hand from Washington."[820]

The merchant, Vincent Nolte, a German immigrant and one of the
great cotton traders of the early nineteenth century, happened to
record a rather boastful narrative of his lucrative, freewheeling
adventures that, in fact, sheds light on the nature of the heady
nineteenth century business climate. In 1812, the Barings advanced
$27,000 (£6,000) and a $45,000 (£10,000) credit line to set up a
business in New Orleans, while at the same time giving him authority
to purchase an interest for them up to "double that amount in any
safe local business" on their account.[821] In a short time, according to
Nolte, "The business of my house had very importantly increased."
He wrote,

> In opposition to the six, seven, or eight thousand bales of cotton which
> most of the houses in that city, styling themselves first class, used to
> purchase, my quota was seldom less than sixteen or eighteen thousand
> bales, which occasioned the transfer from hand to hand of at least a
> million and a half of dollars within a few weeks.[822]

Describing the advantages of having kept his bank credit "a secret,"
Nolte explains how the competition of Scottish cotton speculators, in
the dark as to "how much I would buy and how much I was to pay for
it," allowed him to play anxious planters against one another and
dominate the market, in the year 1820-21, with purchases for clients
in France, England, Boston and New York, amounting to "no less a
quantity than 40,000 bales."[823]

The Barings, it appears, were particularly interested in the "trade
potentiality" of Louisiana.[824] When Francis Baring visited New
Orleans and had "taken his quarters with me in my newly-built
residence," Nolte remembered, "We had nine large vessels receiving
cargo at that moment, and he was evidently gratified when he took his
first walk along the so-called Levee . . . and saw it strewn, from the
upper to the lower suburb, with cotton bales, on which were stamped
the marks of my firm."[825] Nolte executed a $300,000 loan to New
Orleans to pave the Rue Royale, sought by the city council, which was

"almost entirely composed of native, i.e., ignorant creoles."[826] The
money was paid in consecutive, annual installments of $150,000 "in
solid, well secured planter's notes" sold by the Barings in 1822,
netting Nolte "a profit of $65,000" and the first of separate advances
made by the Barings to New Orleans and Louisiana that "surpassed a
couple of millions."[827]

The utter casualness with which both American and international
institutions profited from the torments and misery of Black slaves
belies the frenzied, drunken hysteria that gripped individuals at the
prospect of personal gain. Vincent Nolte's narrative, most clearly,
epitomizes this dichotomy, as illustrated in the following passage
showing his actions at the prospect of gaining a preferred position in a
market expectedly short of supplies in the face of overwhelming
demand for cotton:

Men would not listen to the news that all the supply in the Atlantic
ports was exhausted, but calculated that the shipments of what
remained of the old crop, and the abundant produce of the new, from
October 1, to the end of the year, would reach 250,000 bales. . . . My
simple question, "What will be the consequence if the supply do not
transcend 100,000 bales?" was met by the reply, that a sudden rise of a
penny a pound, or fifteen to twenty per cent, was the universal
conviction.

[From] a list of all exportations . . . I perceived that instead of an
export of 150,000 bales of the old crop, scarce 30,000 had been sent
off in the months of October and November, and that the month of
December could not and would not furnish 20,000 bales. I hastened to
New Orleans. Here I found two ships in the hands of my house, which
we were to load for the account of a Quaker firm in New York. This
was done at the prices, 11, 11½, and 12 cents [per pound]. We also
sent off a cargo of 900 bales on our own account. The prices had no
direct tendency towards a rise, but the expectation of such a rise was
evident, by the willingness with which the prices demanded were paid.
I therefore determined to buy 1,000 bales more on my own account,
and to keep it ready. The prices raised but little, and we sent off
another cargo on our own account.
. . .

I possessed, in advance, the certainty, which could not be had in
Liverpool, that [the stock of American cotton on hand in Liverpool]
could not possibly surpass 100,000 bales. Already, on the 12th of
February, my fears were aroused, lest the news of the scanty condition
of the Liverpool market, at the close of the year, should find us
careless and unprepared. Driven, then, by my own impatience, I sent

our clerk, Ferriday, who was accustomed to make all our purchases with zealous diligence, to the suburbs, where the cotton market is always held, and instructed him not to return with empty hands, nor without having purchased at least 1,500 bales for our house, at the current prices. My last words were, "Do not stand upon trifles, but buy." He fulfilled the commission, and bought 2,000 bales.

Two days later, on February 14th at noon, a neat, fast sailing schooner brought me, from the two Quaker houses, Francis Thompson & Nephews, and Jeremiah Thompson, in New York, the news of the close of the Liverpool market, on December 21, 1824, and the commission to purchase 10,000 bales for them and for Cropper, Benson & Co., of Liverpool, at the current prices. The stock of American cotton in Liverpool was exactly as I had anticipated – there were but 100,000 bales there – and the consequence of so unusually small a supply was precisely the fulfilment of the knowing people's prophecies. There was a sudden rise of a penny. The first re-action on our market at New Orleans was a rise of three cents. Whosoever was engaged in the cotton trade and was a contemporary of that remarkable year, 1825, will remember the frenzy that seized all speculators, first in England, and then, by infallible consequence, in the United States. . . . [English] prices rose 110 per cent, but in the United States not more than 85. We turned most of our own local stock into money, gaining thereby $60,000; and from the first cargo sent to Liverpool, in the brig Ocean, Captain Bond, 950 bales, we received a return from the house of Cropper, with the unexampled gain of £11,460 [approx. $50,000]. Besides a share in the cargoes shipped in union with the Messrs. Cropper and Thompson, we had two other, which arrived in Liverpool about ten days after the 950 bales, but costing about ten per cent more, on which the Croppers could have gained quite as much.
. . .

The month of May, . . . was scarcely gone, when the Scottish house of James and Alexander Deniston & Co., of Glasgow, received in Liverpool 5,000 bales, from New Orleans; and under the direction of the clever head of the firm, Mr. James Deniston, then president of the bank of Scotland, in Glasgow, determined to offer the whole importation for sale. . . . The 5,000 bales were sold . . . In another five months the new American crop would be ready, and it was promising to be very abundant.[828]

In a trip to Havre, France, in late summer 1822, Nolte, understandably, was very well received. "Here I was received by the whole Exchange, not merely with distinction, but with a sort of jubilee.

In connection with all the first houses, I had executed all their commissions, sent cotton to all, and put money into the purses of all."[829]

In 1826, however, greed and jealousy conspired to bring about Nolte's insolvency. An unfortunate fate, no doubt, but how might it compare to the tortuous beatings, and even death, that resulted from the drive to supply the cotton supporting his riches?

The Baring Brothers' activity in America was hardly limited to its dealings with Nolte. They were paid $700,000 by the second Bank of the United States, in 1818, for their assistance in procuring specie, and extended a $2,000,000, 2-year loan to the Bank the following year. They also provided "an open credit of no set amount" to the Bank, feuling Baring Bros. "profits of $60,000 a year from 1826 onward" in foreign exchange, supplying "the mercantile community with sound bills to remit payments in England."[830] Because of cotton, wrote Ralph C. H. Catterall, in *The Second Bank Of The United States*, "the bank was a large buyer of foreign bills in the South and a large seller of them in the North."[831]

Eager to expand their cotton dealings in 1826, particularly after the failure of "the largest purchaser of raw cotton for export in all the southern States," Vincent Nolte, the Barings dispatched partner Thomas Baring to spread money around and expand the services that would "increase the volume of cotton and other agricultural produce consigned" to them. Thomas promptly agreed "to take shares in cargoes of cotton and other commodities shipped to the order of the Barings" from New Orleans, by William Nott & Company, and opened a credit line in New York for Nott to draw advances on sales. According to Hidy, the Barings extended credit against consignments of cotton all across the country, such as in New York, Philadelphia, Charleston, Mobile, and New Orleans, and against "rice, tobacco, and other produce" at specified prices, "usually limited to a proportion of the estimated value," recovering their money from the proceeds of sales.[832]

"The great staple by which we hope to make up for all our losses is Cotton," the Barings declared, making the decision to increase shipments on their own account before Fall, 1833. By August 1, the Liverpool office "had received 30,000 bales and had been advised of about 6,000 more on the way. The following year, "approximately one-fifth of the American cotton received by the Barings' London and Liverpool houses appears to have been for the account of the firm itself." And 1836 figures reportedly showed the firm had 100,000 bales consigned to it before the harvest season even began.[833]

"To Yeatman, Woods & Company [of New Orleans] a loan of $30,000 was extended on the security of New Orleans bonds" while, in addition, "an open credit for exchange operations" was granted the firm "to facilitate the purchase of bills on the Barings by merchants in New Orleans." Thomas Baring also agreed to buy $1,666,667 of Louisiana State bonds backing a $2.5 million loan to The Consolidated Association of the Planters of Louisiana (Consolidated Planters), who were "in search of funds easily available to the mercantile community, but lacking to [planters]." The Louisiana planters' need for credit wasn't satisfied by that loan, however, so a Union Bank was started with $7,000,000 in Louisiana bonds, $5.2 million of which was either consigned to the Barings, or purchased by the firm outright. Union Bank would also have access to a revolving credit of approximately $180,000 (£40,000) from Baring Brothers "for exchange operations," increased to $270,000 (£60,000) in autumn, 1836.[834]

In the fall of 1837, Baring Brothers "urged the Union Bank of Louisiana and the [Consolidated Planters] to each make consignments of 20,000 bales" of cotton to its Liverpool branch for the "purchasers for New England factories" there. The firm did not, however, abandon its commitment to government securities. In November, 1838, they "purchased $1,000,000 of 5 per cent bonds of South Carolina, guaranteed by the Bank of the State of South Carolina," in a joint transaction with Hope & Company of Amsterdam, "and acquired an option to purchase or sell the remaining half of the loan on commission." They additionally subscribed "to the share capital of the new Bank of Commerce, New York," in February.[835]

Thomas Baring, whose "chief concern" in the North apparently was "financial arrangements," established new agency relationships "with Oelrichs & Lurman of Baltimore and Prime, Ward, King & Company, and Goodhue & Company of New York," while maintaining existing connections, "such as with the Gilmores of Baltimore." He also "acquired a lucrative business in the sale of securities and later payment of interest" from the Bank of Pennsylvania, which "began to consign bonds of its home State for sale to Baring Brothers & Company." The Barings additionally carried a $900,000 (£200,000) loan to the Bank of New York, in 1823.[836]

Thomas Baring chose Thomas Wren Ward of Boston, onetime "member of the mercantile aristocracy of New England," to represent the House of Baring as confidential agent throughout the United States on supervision "of exchange accounts, security operations, and the forwarding of consignments from the South." He immediately boosted the flow of credit "to a continually increasing number of American merchants," resulting in a corresponding increase in exchange operations.[837]

"By the end of 1831 almost two-score firms in the United States were enjoying automatically renewable importing credits with the Barings, almost all for dry-goods operations" and bar iron products, such as those employed most successfully "with railroad companies in Massachusetts." In addition, states Hidy, the purchase of rails, chains, keys, and pins by Patrick Tracy Jackson for the Boston & Lowell Railroad Company was arranged through Baring Brothers, as were purchases by T. B. Wales for the Boston & Providence, and by Nathan Hale for the Boston & Worcester railways.

According to the Barings' own estimates, "considerably more than half the total number of accounts current, 1,500 in January, 1831, were for Americans" and credits granted to Americans, as of March, 1833, were estimated to be $50,000,000. Of the total number of merchants mentioned, "more than half were located in New York, almost half in Boston, with Philadelphia and Baltimore" having one each.[838]

18

Alexander Hamilton

Nation Time

As the architect of America's first fiscal policies, Alexander Hamilton would appear to have the strongest claim to a distinguished career independent of slavery. Though by no means original, his policies seem to indicate he had what it took to achieve fame on his own. According to the *Dictionary of American Biography*, Hamilton "must rank as one of the boldest and most farsighted of the founders of the nation."[839] He "elevated the credit of the country from a state of absolute prostration to a state of exalted pre-eminence," Bolles wrote, adding, "The darkest cloud in the firmament of the Union had disappeared. The restoration of the public credit was the beginning of a new era. The long, dreary period of neglected and broken promises was past."[840] Emory Johnson summarizes that in the early nineteenth century, Hamilton made it possible for American merchants "to gain and hold a position in the trade of the world second only to that occupied by the United Kingdom."[841]

Such praise is typical of how America's Founders are continually celebrated, with nary a mention of the pivotal contributions of Black slaves. Hamilton, however, would likely have never emigrated to America had slavery not existed here. In the West Indies, his mother, Rachel, "owned five adult female slaves and supplemented her income by hiring them out," assigning a Black boy named Ajax to Alexander as a house slave.[842] He later served an apprenticeship as clerk and agent to New York merchants Kortright and Cruger, helping to "inspect, house, groom and price the slaves about to be auctioned."[843] And he saw "a fast-paced modern world of trading ships and fluctuating markets [that] afforded valuable insights into global commerce and the maneuvers of imperial powers," an experience biographer Ron Chernow described as "the most useful part of his education."[844] What he learned in the eighteenth century was that slave-based agriculture, inextricably linked to commerce, was the key to wealth and prosperity for both nations and individuals. "The often-agitated question between agriculture and commerce," he would later write, in the Federalist Papers,

> has from indubitable experience received a decision which has silenced the rivalship that once subsisted between them, and has proved, to the entire satisfaction of their friends, that their interests are intimately blended and interwoven . . . The prosperity of commerce is now perceived and acknowledged by all enlightened statesmen to be the most useful as well as the most productive source of national wealth, and has accordingly become a primary object of their political cares.[845]

As the nation's first treasury secretary, chief among Hamilton's priorities was providing for a national revenue, because without "perpetual funds," he recognized, "a government can have no power."[846] The revenue would allow for payment of the daunting Revolutionary war debt, both domestic and foreign, estimated to be approximately 42million dollars, as presented to the House of Representatives in his 1790 Report On Public Credit.

In his Report On A National Bank, also in 1790, Hamilton proposed a uniform currency throughout the Union, to eliminate the chaos of domestic exchange then prevailing from State to State and as a vehicle to simplify and promote commercial trade. He also deemed it essential for America to stimulate expansion of domestic manufacturing, explained in his 1791 Report On The Subject of Manufacturing, examined briefly in the final chapter, King Cotton.

REVENUE BONDAGE

In *The Federalist Papers*, Hamilton noted:

A nation cannot long exist without revenue. Destitute of this essential support, it must resign its independence and sink into the degraded condition of a province. . . . the finances of the community, under such embarrassments, cannot be put into a situation consistent with its respectability or its security. Thus we shall not even have the consolations of a full treasury *to atone for the oppression of that valuable class of the citizens who are employed in the cultivation of the soil.*[847]

Frustration, confusion and animosity within and between the States caused the nation's credit to suffer and its overall financial condition to deteriorate after the Revolution. In such a state of affairs, wrote Hamilton, the nation "can neither have dignity vigour nor *credit.*"[848]

The ability to borrow was critical. "Indeed nations the most powerful and opulent are obliged to have recourse to loans," he wrote. [849] But credit "supposes specific and permanent funds for the punctual payment of interest, with a moral certainty of a final redemption of the principal,"[850] conspicuously absent in America just after its birth.

The prospect of taxes had to be cautiously avoided, "else distress and disorder must ensue," he acknowledged. We must "not suffer them, either first, or last, to fall too heavily upon *parts* of the community."[851] It is evident, Hamilton would later explain,

from the state of the country, from the habits of the people, from the experience we have had on the point itself, that it is impracticable to raise any very considerable sums by direct taxation. . . . Tax laws have in vain been multiplied; new methods to enforce the collection have in vain been tried; the public expectation has been uniformly disappointed, and the treasuries of the States have been empty. . . . the popular system of administration inherent in the nature of popular government, coinciding with the real scarcity of money. . . . has hitherto defeated every experiment for extensive collections, and has at length taught the different legislatures the folly of attempting them.[852]

To manage the federated government at that time the nation had to make recourse to the thirteen States. But with attitudes more concerned with the individual debts of their separate governments, they offered only varying degrees of compliance. With "the paltry payments on the last requisition of Congress," James Madison observed, who could not "shudder at the prospects" for the country.[853] Along with Madison, Hamilton therefore actively lobbied the States for Congressional power to lay a tax on imports, a power reserved only to the States under the existing Articles of Confederation,[854] but "by far the best system of revenue possible for the federal government," and "the only one which could be made to produce revenue consistently."[855] According to Hamilton,

> In America it is evident that we must a long time depend for the means of revenue chiefly on such duties. . . . *that state of things which will best enable us to improve and extend so valuable a resource* must be the best adapted to our political welfare. And it cannot admit of a serious doubt that this state of things must rest on the basis of a general Union [and on slavery, because as] far as this would be conducive to the interests of commerce, so far it must tend to the extension of the revenue to be drawn from that source. . . .[856]

The States, however, could not agree, to put it mildly, on a method of collections or on the appointment of revenue officers, among other things.

Recognizing disagreement as an impediment to fiscal stability, Hamilton was a leader in calling for revision of the Articles. "THE POWER OF REGULATING TRADE," is of "IMMEDIATE NECESSITY," he wrote, in 1781, to "give solidity and permanency to the union."[857] "Justice, gratitude, our reputation abroad, and our tranquility at home, require provision for [the national] debt," Madison warned Edmund Randolph, "If there are not revenue laws which operate at the same time through all the States, and are exempt from the control of each," he wrote, as a nation we "will assuredly defraud both our foreign and domestic creditors of their just claims."[858]

A request from Congress to levy a general five percent tax on imports, for 1782 expenses, was rejected by the States, led by Rhode Island, contributing to a budget shortfall of $4,460,000, not counting interest obligations.[859] Hamilton and Madison both defended the tax as one that ultimately fell on consumers rather than merchants, as Rhode Island feared. Both were wrong. It fell on Black slaves — hard!

Reintroduced by Madison in March, 1783, with the previously-mentioned, twenty-five year life, and applicable only to the principal and interest of the debt. It was passed by the Congress,[860] but again voted down by Rhode Island, along with Massachusetts, while Hamilton's "No," split New York's vote. He thought there was no chance of ratification by the States, loathe to cede the power of the purse to a central government.[861]

To sell the tax, Madison wrote the Address To The States from Congress, in which he said the levy was conceived by Congress as "necessary to render the fruits of the Revolution, a full reward for the blood, the toils, the cares and the calamities which have purchased it."[862] He was not, of course, referring to the Black slaves upon whose backs the Revolution was carried, and from whence the import tax would be gleaned.

Without the urgency of war the exigency of the tax was not readily apparent to the States and therefore floundered, leading to a 1786 Virginia proposal for a Convention at Annapolis to revise the Articles of Confederation, "to take into consideration the trade of the United States, and to report propositions for a uniform system of commercial regulation which, if unanimously ratified, will enable Congress to provide for trade."[863] The Convention was convened, but only five states actually attended, prompting Hamilton to immediately author his Address of the Annapolis Convention to the State Legislatures, calling for the Constitutional Convention in Philadelphia a year later.[864]

Putting the nation onto sound financial footing through import duties was actually expressed privately by Hamilton as early as 1780, when he recognized Congress should have the benefit of "applying to their own use the product of these duties,"[865] which, of course, were "the most agreeable species of taxes to the people."[866] Such a plan, he wrote,

would be of inconceivable utility to our affairs, its benefits would be very speedily felt. It would give new life and energy to the operations of government. Business would be conducted with dispatch method and system. A million abuses now existing would be corrected, and judicious plans would be formed and executed for the public good."[867]

The position symbolizes Hamilton's long understanding of not only the commercial value of slavery, America's exports being almost exclusively the product of Black slaves, but the institution's critical significance in facilitating the political stability of the government, further evidenced in his Report On Public Credit, clearly written in contemplation of the nation's reliance upon slave labor.

Debt Bondage

Seeing payment of the war debt as a national priority, Hamilton forecasted "a determinate period" in his Report On Public Credit for

appropriations to redeem both the principal and interest on it,
"without burthening the people" with direct taxes. That period, of
course, was the magic twenty years mentioned for extension of the
slave trade after establishment of the new government. [868] In response,
Congress passed legislation stipulating the recommended
appropriations, i.e., that the priority of import taxes should be the
payment of interest and, after the administration of government,
payment of principal on the outstanding debt, including a Sinking
Fund for revenue surpluses.[869]

There is little doubt Hamilton was among the critically influential
"eastern states" delegates at the 1787 Constitutional Convention who
acquiesced to delaying abolition of the slave trade.[870] "The true
question," said Convention delegate John Dickinson of Delaware,
"was whether the national happiness would be promoted or impeded
by the importation" of slaves.[871] Happiness obviously required slaves
be imported for at least twenty more years, since "[I]t was agreed on
all hands," wrote Madison, the national revenue "w[ould] principally
be drawn from trade."[872] Hamilton understood as clearly as anyone
that slavery was in fact the backbone of American commercial trade,
critical to supplying the U. S. Treasury, learning during his
apprenticeship years how business supported the operation of
government. Commerce, he later wrote, "must of necessity render the
payment of taxes easier, and facilitate the requisite supplies to the
treasury."[873]

BANKING ON SLAVERY

Underlying Hamilton's 1790 proposal outlining the need for a
national bank was, amng other things, "the value of a uniform
currency in stimulating trade," which of course he saw as the
foundation upon which the nation's revenues rested.[874] "The ability of
a country to pay taxes must always be proportioned, in a great
degree," he earlier wrote, "to the quantity of money in circulation and
to the [speed] with which it circulates," obvious functions of
uniformity and banking,[875] since "for every sum of money deposited in
a bank, the party making that deposit either receives the amount in
bank notes, or obtains a credit on the books of the bank . . . the
aggregate of those credits, and of the bank notes issued, constitutes
the circulating medium," as when payments and transfers are made
through drafts and checks drawn on the bank.[876]

The first United States Bank called for a $10 million dollar
operating capital, one-fifth to be contributed by the federal

government and the rest by private citizens, with one fourth of each stock subscription to be paid in gold and silver coin.[877] This bank, wrote Sumner, "was taken as a model by so many others that we must attribute to [Hamilton's] opinions on banking a predominant influence in forming the banking institutions of this country."

Buying out the initial offering in a matter of hours, plus "four thousand shares more,"[878] subscribers, three-fourths of whom were European,[879] comprised a virtual "Who's Who" of merchants, bankers, factors and planters with varying interests in slavery and/or the African slave trade, such as, among many others,[880] the Baring Brothers; the Massachusetts Bank; William Bingham, founder of Binghamton, NY, whose "extensive trade in the staples of Virginia and Maryland" made him "probably the greatest single land owner in America at the beginning of the nineteenth century," and famed Philadelphia merchant Thomas Willing, the bank's first president, whose 1784 ship, the *United States*, was "the first American vessel"[881] in the ports of India, loaded, predictably, with a cargo of Virginia tobacco and ginseng.

According to Hamilton's long-held view, "The only certain manner to obtain a permanent paper credit is to engage the monied interest immediately in it by making them contribute the whole or part of the stock and giving them the whole or part of the profits."[882] Stockholders, he understood, were mere "lenders of their own capital which is amalgamated with what they borrow to lend again."[883]

Owing to an empty treasury, the government's $2 million dollar subscription was to be paid through loans from the Bank itself, in what Hamilton described as "borrowing with one hand what is lent with the other,"[884] or "a kind of high class confidence operation," as referred to by Sumner, wondering, in *A History Of Banking*, what right the federal government had to an ownership stake in the Bank, since it "possessed no capital and the Treasury had no surplus?"

If the stockholders of a bank are debtors to it and not creditors of it, it is a swindle. They take something out [dividends and profits] where they have put nothing in. They are not lending a surplus of their own; they are using an engine by which they can get possession of other people's capital. . . . They bear no risk of their own operations, but throw all the risk on others while taking all the gain. The government had no more right to subscribe stock when it possessed nothing, and put nothing in, than an individual would have to do the same thing.[885]

As it happened, Hamilton entered the bank June 25, 1792, upon authorization from president Washington, and "subscribed for 5,000 shares of capital stock at $400, a total of $2,000,000, on which the United States would receive the usual dividends; but immediately borrowed that amount" at six percent interest payable semiannually, "so that the United States was one-fifth of the stockholders, and had the loan of a sum equal to its whole stock," due in ten years.[886] By the end of 1795, the bank had loaned the government a total of 6.2 million dollars, "almost two-thirds of the bank's capital."[887]

Of the original 5,000 share government "subscription," 2,493 shares were sold at $500 in the year 1796-97, 287 at $480 in1797, and the final 2,220 were sold to Baring Brothers of London in 1802, at $580 a share — which Baring promptly resold in England for $600[888] — bringing a total profit to the government of $671,860, with another $1,101,720 having been received in dividends, which averaged eight and a half per cent over the eighteen year period ending in 1809.[889]

Upon a close inspection of it's operational purpose: to provide a stable circulating currency throughout the country, slavery's role in making the bank profitable, aside from merely providing for it's start, becomes readily apparent. The main branch was located in Philadelphia, but, not coincidently, six of the eight other branches were located in the South: Baltimore, Washington, D.C., Norfolk, Charleston, Savannah, and New Orleans,[890] despite the fact that nine of the then sixteen States, plus the Northwest territories, were situated in the North. The significance of the Southern branch locations was as collection centers for import revenues or customs receipts, being major port exchange locations for slave crops and European manufactures.

A major feature of the United States Bank was the fact that only a quarter of its capital had to be paid in actual money, allowing three-fourths to be in United States stocks, "to enable the creation of a capital sufficiently large to be the basis of an extensive circulation, and an adequate security for it."[891] The import duties act of 1789 provided that customs receipts into the Treasury be payable only in gold or silver coin. With an eye towards a National Bank, however, Hamilton proposed, in 1790, receiving the notes of banks whose capital stock was partially in gold and silver as payment for import duties into the Treasury. The charter establishing the Bank therefore provided that its notes "be receivable in all payments to the United States," thus establishing them as a medium of circulation throughout the Union.[892]

Sumner termed the encouragement "directly mischievous," attacking, among other things, Hamilton's assertion that "the faculty of a bank to lend and circulate a greater sum than the amount of its stock in coin [is] to all the purposes of trade and industry, an absolute increase of capital."[893]

Bank notes, however, could only serve as currency if there was sufficient confidence in the nation's economic and commercial prospects to support their circulation and acceptance as such. That confidence existed only because of America's vast trade resources: it's land, agriculture – and slaves. The nation's commercial trade potential, then, was the real and true security behind the successful circulation of bank notes as currency.

The United States Bank therefore highlights Hamilton's intentions to exact the maximum economic benefit from American slavery, without which the nation could never have implemented its fiscal policies or realized its full economic potential, which, we now know, carried it to the top position of the entire world. By comparison, Germany "contain[ed] a great extent of fertile, cultivated, and populous territory and some of the best gold and silver mines in Europe," Hamilton noted, but without African slaves, her vast natural resources notwithstanding, she could realize "but slender revenues."[894]

According to Sumner, citing a detailed report released January 1811, prior to expiration of its twenty-year charter, "the bank held private deposits, $6 millions; public deposits, $2millions; bank deposits, $600,000. It had $5 millions circulation; $14.5 millions [loans outstanding]; had lent the United States $2.7 millions; was a creditor of other banks for $900,000 and held their notes for $400,000. It had $5 millions in [gold and silver coin]."[895]

Upon retirement from the presidency of the bank in 1807, having suffered a stroke, Thomas Willing acknowledged

"the great assistance it has afforded to the agricultural and manufacturing interests, and to the internal trade and improvement of our country – in the great advancement, resulting from its operations, to our public credit, with the greatest trading nations of Europe – in the necessary and useful aid and extension it has afforded to the American commerce, whereby the public revenue has been produced and supported, the individual adventurers enriched, and the community at large much benefited.[896]

The benefits of slavery to America were enormous. The institution allowed the Founding Fathers to bequeath a stable, vibrant structure that reached to the very top of world order. But by indulging the institution of slavery so heavily, the Founders also strapped Americana with a burden so heavy it threatens to cave in the roof of the very structure built on the bowed backs of crying slaves.

Present day Americans, it seems, revel in the benefits bequeathed from slavery, yet wish to disown the burdens associated with their inheritance, one of which is an acknowledgement that without Black slavery, the Founding Fathers would have been utterly lost.

19

King Cotton

Industrial Revolution

T he third major initiative in Alexander Hamilton's plan for American growth and fiscal stability was "the introduction and advancement of American manufactures."[897] His Report On The Subject of Manufactures therefore encouraged the government's active promotion of the nation's nascent manufacturing industry, newly free of Britain's mercantilist prohibitions, as a means of increasing the development and productive output of this country's vast natural resources and overall wealth. "A maxim well established by experience," he explained, is "that the aggregate prosperity of manufactures, and the aggregate prosperity of Agriculture are intimately connected," in that separating "the occupation of the cultivator, from that of the Artificer," tends to increase overall productivity and thus "the total mass of the produce or revenue of a Country."[898] Specifically,

> The establishment of manufactures is calculated not only to increase
> the general stock of useful and productive labour . . . but even to
> improve the state of Agriculture in particular, [and] must be admitted
> to have a tendency to promote a more steady and vigorous cultivation
> of the lands occupied than would happen without them, . . . serv[ing]
> to increase both the capital value and the income of [the] lands.[899]

Among those resources most likely to succeed in stimulating
American industry, in combination, Hamilton correctly predicted, "a
bounty on the national cotton" will be particularly "encouraging to
domestic production," both for "home manufactory" and for
export.[900] Increased demand for cotton, however, could only be met
through an expansion of slavery, which, "upon the whole," he wrote,
"must increase in proportion, as a certain and extensive domestic
demand shall induce the proprietors of land to devote more of their
attention to the production of [that article]."[901] In turn, slave labor
lowers the price of the product which, as a result, "seldom or never
fails to be sold Cheaper" than that of foreign competitors,[902] allowing
the farmer "to procure with a smaller quantity of labour, the
manufactured produce of which he stands in need, and consequently
increases the value of his income and property."[903]

Congress thereafter "gave to [cotton] and its manufactures new and
zealous attention" with a series of bounties and other legislative
initiatives between 1794 and 1830,[904] Bolles observed, leading directly
to the invention of the cotton gin, increasing U.S. export cotton
produce from just 138,328 lbs. in the year immediately following
Hamilton's report, 1792, to more than 6,000,000 lbs. in 1795.[905]
Following Whitney's invention, cotton output increased "from 2
million lbs to 48 million lbs in the course of the 1790s."[906]

Assessing which areas of the country would most adequately host
America's promising industrial development, Hamilton explained that
certain "districts" with "fewer attractions to agriculture than other parts
of the Union," such as New England, for example, "may be
discerned, no inconsiderable maturity for manufacturing
establishments."[907] Thus, while only one cotton mill existed in
America in 1791, there were more than eighty-seven by the end of
1810, mostly centered in New England with over eighty thousand
spindles in operation.[908]

NORTHERN EXPOSURE

Aside from privateering by a small number of its membership, the decade-long Independence War was a period of little activity for New England's fishing industry. Wharves, vessels and equipment were in disrepair and decay, there was a loss of manpower from casualties, and valuable training of youth had been lost.[909] When added to British, French and Spanish restrictions on exports to the Caribbean, the desperation of New Englanders became extreme.

The embargo of 1809 and the War of 1812 dealt an additional blow to New England shipping, since both the slave trade, officially ended in 1808, and the carrying trade, due to embargo and war, "were lost together."[910] By 1814, the tonnage of shipping engaged in the codfishery was reduced "to the lowest point recorded since the establishment of the Federal Government."[911] As a result, "the large capital accumulated in that trade," was driven from commerce, writes Kettell, and "betook itself to manufacturing."[912] Thus, New England, with its "swift streams for power and a humid climate, suitable for spinning and weaving cotton fibers," quickly developed a significant cotton textiles industry.[913]

Development

Unlike during the height of the industrial revolution, when "whole communities were designed and created for the specific purpose of manufacturing textiles,"[914] the first efforts to manufacture cotton in New England were made in small factories at Beverly and Bridgewater, Mass, in 1787.[915] Reportedly induced by a notice in an early 1790's Pennsylvania newspaper of a bounty being offered,[916] the English apprentice Samuel Slater thereafter introduced to America, "with his own hands [and] from recollection" through a partnership to open mills at Providence and Pawtucket,[917] innovative textiles manufacturing machinery then in use in Europe, within four years of Eli Whitney's cotton gin.

As the rush was on to increase plantation production across the South, the North, led by New England, was engaging in a similar rush to build manufacturing facilities, cotton factories being "one of the passions of the age,"[918] giving birth to the region's enormous industrial cotton textiles economy.

"Factories were built on the large and powerful mill-streams of Eastern Connecticut, at different places in Massachusetts, and elsewhere in New England and the Middle States," with eighty-seven having been erected by 1810, averaging, with the help of protective tariffs, 20 new facilities a year over the next forty years. By 1831, "of the 795 active and profitable cotton-mills built and operating in the United States, 508 were in New England alone, while ninety-three percent (738) were located in New England and the Middle States."[919]

Table XIII: Cotton Textile Mills (1831)

"The Connecticut river valleys had virtually no industry until the early 19ᵗʰ century when cotton mill owners from Rhode Island sited operations along fast-moving streams. By the Civil War, texstile mills dotted virtually every stream in eastern Connecticut north of Norwich. To the north, the Slaters operated mills in Oxford and Webster, Mass. Other families—the Tiffanys [yes, those Tiffanys], the Youngs and the Ballous—built mills in Killingly and its villages."

STATE	Mills
Maine	8
N. H.	40
Massachusetts	250
Rhode Island	116
Connecticut	94
New York	112
Pennsylvania	67
New Jersey	51
Maryland	23
Delaware	10
Virginia	7
Other	17
TOTAL	795

Source: *The Hartford Courant*

By estimation, in 1809 "37 mills near Providence were in operation or in the process of erection," and "by 1850 there were 140."[920] By January, 1814, "newspaper columns were filled with lists of manufacturing companies the Massachusetts and Connecticut legislatures were incorporating,"[921] leading to a sudden spurt of new banking establishments: the Boston State Bank and the Merchants Bank of Salem, founded in 1811; the New England Bank, in 1813; the Phoenix Bank of Hartford, and the Boston Manufacturers' and Mechanics' Bank, both in 1814.[922] "Total paid in capital stock of Massachusetts banks alone" nearly doubled in five years, "increas[ing] from $6,685,000, in 1810, to $11,462,00 in 1815."[923]

The resulting development of manufacturing in New England closely resembled that of Chicopee, MA, and was directed by a tight-knit group informally known as the "Boston Associates," operating as "a large-scale business enterprise."[924] After a piece of town property was purchased at Chicopee Falls, along with water privileges at the Chicopee River, in 1823, the Springfield Manufacturing Company was incorporated with a capitalization of a half million dollars. "Work was immediately started on a dam, a canal, a cotton mill . . . and houses for the workers," all completed in 1825.[925]

"Rows of new tenements arose in the vicinity alongside the mill. Not ordinary houses surrounded by decent plots, but long blocks of buildings, edging right up to the street and pressed closely together, looking as though a section of a distant city had been lifted and transplanted bodily to Chicopee Falls."[926] Work started on a second mill in the same year, while "[a] third unit was erected in 1826, and a fourth in 1831, when the capital of the company was increased to $600,000, and then to $700,000 in 1835," by which time the Springfield Company had changed its name to the Chicopee Manufacturing Company.[927]

> This new corporation was more than a cotton manufacturing company. It owned a large tract of land, water power, and the tenements which housed the operatives, so that it was in the real estate business. It was also in the construction business, for it had erected all the buildings, and built the dam and the canal. It operated a machine shop for the construction and repair of cotton machinery, and was prepared to continue all these activities for new mills which were planned for the region. After a time the owners of this hybrid company decided to separate its manufacturing functions from the construction and machine building business . . . planning to incorporate some new companies in Chicopee . . . In 1831, then, they incorporated the Springfield Canal Company, with a capital of $90,000. As owners of the cotton company, they transferred to themselves, as owners of the canal company, title to the water privilege at the lower site, the construction business and the machine shops. In the future the canal company would accept all orders for the construction of mills, dams, canals, and tenements. The owners of the Chicopee Manufacturing Company and the Springfield Canal Company were practically identical.[928]

The two companies, in fact, shared ownership with a number of other cotton-related manufacturing concerns. The spread of new factories meant a flood of investment opportunities for those with money to lend who, in the early nineteenth century, were *only* men from the fishing, shipping, and slave trades, which left "large aggregates of capital accumulating in the hands of the leading merchants."[929] Thomas Cutts and Josiah Calef, for example, successful merchants from Maine and Massachusetts, entered into a partnership that spurred development in southern Maine. Over four decades in the early nineteenth century, "they organized the Saco Manufacturing Co., which bought the property of the Saco Iron Works and built a large mill for cotton goods" on the Saco River.[930] Incorporated for the purpose of "holding real estate, the development of water power, the building of mills and the manufacture of textile machinery," among other things, the company, destroyed by fire, was succeeded by the York Manufacturing Co. and, according to Evelyn Knowlton, in *Pepperell's Peogress*, "sold some of its holdings of property to the Saco Water Power Co."[931] After putting up some of its buildings in Biddeford, ME, the company "built machinery for York's fourth mill," and subsequently "promoted the Laconia Co.," a new cotton textile company with a capitalization of $2,000,000, that would eventually become the Pepperell Manufacturing Company.[932]

Very influential to the growth of New England textiles was of course the pioneering partnership that included Francis C. Lowell of Boston who, with the Merrimack Manufacturing Company, incorporated in 1822, gave birth to the city of Lowell, MA on the Merrimack River. While introducing waterpower into the cotton manufacturing process, theirs were the first mills to include "all the operations of converting the cotton-lint into cloth under the same roof."[933]

The Merrimack Company bought out the assets of the "Locks and Canals on the Merrimack," . . . and in 1825 reorganized it as a separate canal and machine shop company to which it transferred the land and water power not in its own immediate use. For the next twenty years this canal company sold land and furnished power, built machinery and mills and tenements for the various Lowell companies as they were organized under the leadership of the Boston Associates, just as the Springfield Canal Company fulfilled a similar function in Chicopee. In 1845, the same year that the Ames Manufacturing Company took over the Springfield Canal Company, the Lowell Machine Shops were organized by Abbott Lawrence, J.A. Lowell and Nathan Appleton to buy the assets of the Merrimack Canal Company. These activities established the modern city of Lowell. Company after company was incorporated, the capitalizations ranging from $500,000 to $1,000,000. After the Merrimack Company came the Boott Mills, the Tremont Mills, the Lawrence, Appleton, Suffolk, Hamilton, Massachusetts and Prescott Manufacturing companies in Lowell; the Chicopee, Cabot, Perkins and Dwight mills in Chicopee; the Hopewell and Whittenden mills in Taunton; the Lyman mills in

Holyoke; the textile mills in Lawrence; the Laconia and York mills in
Maine. In New Hampshire the Boston Associates controlled the
Cocheco Manufacturing Company in Dover, the Salmon Falls and
Great Falls companies in Somersworth, the Stark, Manchester and
Amoskeag mills in Manchester, and others in Nashua. In Manchester
the Amoskeag company bought the land, laid out the city, did the
construction, and operated the machine shops. It was the parent
company. All of these companies, except the Lyman Mills in Holyoke
were in operation before 1850. All were patterned after the Waltham
model. The Boston Associates were the prime movers in the
enterprises and constituted the heart of a wider group of companies
knit together by duplication of stockholders. [934]

In the face of this formative growth financed with profits from
slavery and cotton cultivation, misguided (ignorant?) authors Stephen
and Abigail Thernstrom incredibly assert, in *America In Black And
White,* that American slavery was only "marginal to the economies"
of the North. "So far as the greater part of the working population was
concerned," contrasts Vera Shlakman, in *Economic History of a
Factory Town: A Study of Chicopee, Massachusetts,* "the cotton mills
constituted the heart of [Northern] economic life," the very existence
of which "is dependent on the continued and steady operation of the
[Massachusetts] cotton mills."[935]

Employment & Immigration

In the 20-year period ending in 1850, the number of immigrants to
enter America was 2,466,200, with nearly 80 percent living in the
North. Their employment, Kettell concluded, "comes almost
altogether from the South. Indeed, without the growing capacity of the
South to absorb larger amounts of goods annually, the North would
be utterly unable to keep employed the crowds of foreign artisans
which arrive each week."[936]

David Christy observed, in *Cotton Is King:*

Our dry goods' merchants and grocers constitute an immense army of
agents for the sale of fabrics and products coming, directly or
indirectly, from the hand of the slave; and all the remaining portion of
the people . . . are exerting themselves, according to their various
capacities, to gain the means of purchasing the greatest possible
amount of these commodities.[937]

In essence, the transfer of cotton weaving and spinning to factories,
previously done by families, created a great factory-industry and

provided employment that fueled the rush of early nineteenth century European immigration,[938] as had been correctly predicted by Alexander Hamilton. One of seven enumerated circumstances by which manufactures "occasioned a positive augmentation of the Produce and Revenue" of America, he noted in his Report On Manufactures, was the "promotion of emigration."[939] If the interest of the United States "is to open every possible avenue to emigration from abroad," he wrote, then "it affords a weighty argument for the encouragement of manufactures, which will have the strongest tendency to multiply the inducements to it," namely, employment and jobs.[940]

By 1840, according to Robert Zevin, in *The Growth of Manufacturing in Early Nineteenth Century New England,*

[cotton textiles] factories had become familiar landmarks at hundreds of New England water power sites; large cities such as Lowell and Holyoke had been created entirely by the advance of industrial activity while Fall River, Pawtucket, Worcester and the like had been greatly enlarged and transformed by the same advance. About 100,000 people were employed by large scale manufacturing enterprises with 20 or 30 [factories supporting] up to 1,500 employees each.[941]

By 1832, wrote Shlakman, "the Chicopee Manufacturing Company had in its employ 781 persons," while "the Cabot, Perkins and Dwight mills, which went into operation between 1834 and 1841, were to employ another 1,600 workers."[942] Men in large numbers worked in "constructing and installing new equipment,"[943] Kettell observed, while cloth production in the factories was "largely performed by females [and] supplied by immigration in nearly its whole extent, a very large proportion . . . being Irish."[944] "At the very beginning," writes Shlakman further, "some of the laborers engaged in the construction work were of local and near-local origin. . . . However, when the time came to dig the canal for the Cabot Manufacturing Company in 1832-34 a group of Irishmen were imported to do the work [and] another group came in 1841 to work on the Dwight Canal."[945]

Capital

Table XIV shows a snapshot of the excess of imports (purchases/expenditures) over exports (sales revenue/income) for

Top, painting of type used by New England textile mills to recruit immigrant employment, showing the billowing factories and rows of barracks to shelter the recruited labor, Bottom, a depiction of Southern cotton plantation slavery that provided raw materials for the North's mills.[946]

North

Source: *The Hartford Courant*

South

Source: *Compton's Interactive Encyclopedia*

New York, New England and Pennsylvania, versus that of the South, for the year 1764, highlighting an early Northern dependence that continued throughout the tenure of American slavery. The North, which consumed 70 percent more of England's manufactures than did the South, had only a fraction of total colonial exports — just over 15 percent — with which to pay for them, making up the difference by

carrying a large bulk of Southern produce to England, and by selling slaves obtained on the coast of Africa in the return trip, in the Caribbean and the American South. According to the table, Northern imports of manufactured goods exceeded exports nearly tenfold, while the Southern colonies, using slave labor, enjoyed a surplus of exports over imports.

Moreover, as a result of freight charges accruing to Northern merchants from shipping Southern produce, between 1790 and 1800, the North "had the use and command of 182 and a half millions of the productions of southern labor," an average of 16½ million a year ($363 million in today's dollars).[947]

Table XIV.
Colonial Imports and Exports, 1764 (Pounds Sterling)

	Imported from England	Exported to England
New England	459,765	88,157
New York	515,416	53,697
Pennsylvania	435,191	36,258
Total	1,410,372	178,112
VA & MD	515,192	559,408
Carolina	305,808	341,727
Georgia	18,388	31,325
Total	889,388	932,460
Grand Total	2,249,760	1,110,572

Source: Kettell, *Southern Wealth and Northern Profits*.

One organization, formed by the Boston Associates to invest this money for wealthy northern merchants, was responsible for the spread of slavery profits and cotton capital in the North more than any other single entity: the Massachusetts Hospital Life Insurance Company (Hospital Life). According to author Gerald T. White, in *A History of The Massachusetts Hospital Life Insurance Company*, members of it's Committee of Finance "were mainly mercantile capitalists whose fortunes derived primarily from trade," and were succeeded by a group made up of "predominately" cotton textiles manufacturers.[948] One of the largest financial institutions in Boston, wrote White, the company was "probably the most important single source of intermediate term credit for the Massachusetts textile industry during the nineteenth century," lending large sums to several of New England's cotton textile mills, and, sharing in their management and ownership.[949]

Chartered in 1818 to fund Boston's Massachusetts General Hospital, the company quickly branched off into investment management as "the savings bank of the wealthy."[950] Hospital Life also invested heavily in farm mortgages in western Massachusetts, with the largest numbers in the counties of Franklin (124), Suffolk (64), Berkshire (51), and Worcester (12).[951] The discriminating lending policy of the company was "designed to permit only the best mortgages to sift through," declining applications on expensive homes not easily sold upon foreclosure, and properties whose value was subject to rapid decline; no second mortgages; no property with clouded title, and "no mortgages to women, unless there were sureties." So eager was the company to compound its cotton returns, however, it ignored its own strict lending guidelines, extending funds on what Taylor described as "completely inadequate security," such as a $20,000 loan to the Boston Manufacturing Company secured by just "five shares of the Suffolk Bank."[952] "Especially with textile companies," says White, Hospital Life ignored the statutory prescription against placing loans in excess of one-third a company's capital.

Individual loans, however, "were mainly to the merchant group responsible for [funding] the company," and the individual given the most loans prior to 1840, "William Appleton, borrowed some 30 times," not including loans extended to his various businesses interests, including "textile companies, a real estate company, and a sugar refinery."[953]

The first significant cotton textiles loan was placed with the Boston Manufacturing Company of Waltham for $20,000, in 1826, marking the beginning of a series of loans before 1840 to interests of the "Boston Associates," including $200,000 to the Dover Manufacturing Company of Dover New Hampshire, owned, coincidentally, by William Appleton and David Sears; the Amesbury Flannel Company; Boott Cotton Mills; Eliot Manufacturing Company; Hamilton Manufacturing Company; Proprietors of the Locks and Canals on the Merrimack River; Lowell Manufacturing Company; and Merrimack Manufacturing Company, all but three of which, says Taylor, were located in Lowell, MA. In one instance, when a group representing a Chicopee cotton mill borrowed $25,000 from Hospital Life, "practically every member of the group sat on the board."[954]Other prominent borrowers were the City of Boston, Mass General Hospital, the Commonwealth of Massachusetts, and various local commercial banks, including "the City, Commonwealth, Commercial, Globe, American, Atlantic, Columbian, State, Merchants, Traders, Oriental and Eagle banks."[955] All together, "this group of men," according to Shlakman, "shared largely in the control of about 40 per cent of the Boston banking capital in 1848. Only natural since the cotton mills banked exclusively with the institutions in which their sharehlders had a financial interest."[956] For example, "one of the Chicopee companies transacted business with the Merchants', Columbian, and State Banks, . . . Another dealt with the Merchants' and the Globe Banks."[957]

Among Hospital Life's "Associate" investors were owners of the Ames Manufacturing Company, incorporated in 1834 with a capital of $30,000, "increased to $75,000 in 1841 and again to $200,000 in 1845"; the Cabot Manufacturing Company, established in Chicopee "for the purpose of manufacturing cotton" and other goods, "with an authorized capital of $1,000,000," finally set at $500,000; the Perkins Mills, incorporated in 1836, also with a half million dollar capitalization; the Dwight Manufacturing Company, in 1841, with another half million dollar capitalization, all in addition to the previously mentioned Springfield Canal Company and Chicopee Manufacturing Company, and "all under the same management."[958]

Hospital Life was capitalized at $500,000, selling 5,000 shares of stock at $100 each to an exclusive group of prominent figures from Boston's former merchant community, including, for an investment of $10,000 dollars, William Prescott, Josiah Quincy, John Lowell, Gardiner Greene, John Phillips, Joseph Head, T.H. Perkins, Joseph Coolidge, David Sears, William Pratt, John Parker, Israel Thorndike, Thomas M. Jones, Theodore Lyman, James Perkins, among others, and Thomas Wren Ward, George Cabot, Amos Lawrence, William

Sturgis, John Bryant, Thomas Motley, Thomas Wigglesworth, Harrison Gray Otis, Nathan Appleton, Charles Jackson, Joseph May, Daniel Parker, Henry Codman, Patrick Tracy Jackson, William Appleton, Samuel P. Gardner, George Ticknor, John C. Gray, Benjamin Guild, and Nathaniel Silsbee at just under $5,000.[959]

Illustrative of the returns realized by textiles investors, Boston Manufacturing paid a 12.5 percent dividend in 1817, with 16 to 21 percent paid in succeeding years. By 1822, "104.5 per cent had been paid in all," exceeding in dividends the original investments of merchant stockholders, causing one Associate to gleefully exclaim, "your profits will make people delirious."[960]

Transportation

Because of the need for connections between Boston and their various manufacturing concerns, the Boston Associates also became heavily interested in the construction of transportation facilities.[961] An amendment to the Massachusetts statute of incorporation thereafter allowed for an investment of company funds in railroad securities, and "to make loans to cities and towns," or "other corporations and individuals on the basis of railroad, manufacturing, or other corporate securities issued within the Commonewalth."[962] Consequently, the first Massachusetts railway "of any length," the Boston and Lowell, was incorporated in 1830 by Boston Associates Kirk Boott, P.T. Jackson and G.W. Lyman, among others.[963] Opened in 1835, the road subsequently named to its board of directors such Hospital Life and Boston Associate operatives as "Joseph Tilden, Wiliam Appleton, William Sturgis, and E. Chadwick," with Associates directing various other rail lines, such as T.B. Wales, J. K. Mills, William Sturgis and G.W. Pratt with the Taunton Branch railroad; Samuel Batchelder and George H. Kuhn with the Maine railroad, "which, in 1843, brought railway transportation to Dover and Somersworth, New Hampshire.[964] With Associate participation, the Boston and Worcester and the Western railroads "provided the connecting link from Boston to Springfield via Worcester," and the Connecticut River railroad, "a project that received the management and investment of some of the Associates, brought Chicopee and Holyoke into the chain." The result, summarized Shlakman, "was that in the late forties the associates, through their directorates, shared in the control of some 25 to 30 per cent of the railway mileage in Massachusetts."[965]

The importance of Hospital Life funds to New England and overall American development, is truly mind boggling, particularly in light of the fate of the Black slaves who made it all possible, since the Company invested and managed the profits of slavery long after the original businesses had vanished. But, as we've seen, virtually all the immigration, employment, transportation food, clothing, shelter, and capital in the North were either directly or indirectly provided for in the South. Black slavery, consequently, through cotton cultivation, was the very lifeblood of Northern economic life.

Table XV: MASS HOSPITAL LIFE INS CO. TEXTILES INDUSTRY LOANS

Company	Location	Capital (000's)	AS OF DECEMBER 31, 1855			Earliest	Selling Agent Group
			No.	Amt (000's)			
Mass. Cotton Mills	Lowell	$1,800	7	$300		Mar. '49	A & A Lawrence & Co.
Atlantic Cotton Mills	Lawrence	1,800	1	200		Sept. '49	A & A Lawrence & Co.
Boott Cotton Mills	Lowell	1,200	6	200		Jan. '49	A & A Lawrence & Co.
Lowell Mfg. Co.	Lowell	2,000	2	200		Jul. '49	A & A Lawrence & Co.
Middlesex Co.	Lowell	1,000	6	195		Aug. '45	Lawrence, Stone & Co.
Tremont Mills	Lowell	600	3	150		Jun. '55	A & A Lawrence & Co.
Hadley Falls Co.	Holyoke	1,470	5	145		Sept. '52	(George W. Lyman)
Bay State Mills	Lawrence	1,800	3	130		Jan. '51	Lawrence, Stone & Co
Essex Co.	Lawrence	1,500	3	122		Feb. '53	(Abbott Lawrence, et al.)
Appleton Co.	Lowell	600	2	100		Aug. '53	J.W. Paige & Co.
Hamilton Co.	Lowell	1,200	2	100		Jun. '53	J.W. Paige & Co.
Lawrence Machine Shop	Lawrence	900	2	100		Sept. '53	(Abbott Lawrence, et al.)
Lowell Machine Shop	Lowell	600	4	100		Jul. '54	(Abbott Lawrence, et al.)
Suffolk Mills	Lowell	600	2	100		Nov. '54	J.W. Paige & Co.
Lyman Mills	Holyoke	1,470	2	90		Jul. '55	Charles H. Mills & Co.
Chicopee Mfg. Co.	Chicopee	700	2	70		Jun. '55	Charles H. Mills & Co.
Lancaster Mills	Clinton	900	3	70		Aug. '51	(G. W. Lyman, et al)
Boston Mfg. Co.	Waltham	450	4	60		Apr. '54	J.W. Paige & Co.
Dwight Mfg. Co.	Chicopee	700	1	50		Apr. '54	Charles H. Mills & Co.
Perkins Mills	Chicopee	1,000	1	50		Apr. '53	Charles H. Mills & Co.
Merrimack Mfg. Co.	Lowell	2,500	1	48		Jun. '54	J.W. Paige & Co.
Pemberton Mills	Lawrence	500	1	20		Feb. '54	Lawrence, Stone & Co
Ames Mfg. Co.	Springfield	250	1	15		Dec. '55	Charles H. Mills & Co

Source: White, *A History of The Massachusetts Hospital Life Insurance Company*

Conclusion

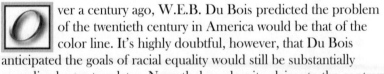

We have concluded to test your sincerity by asking you
to send us our wages for the time we served you.
If you fail to pay us for faithful labors in the past,
we can have little faith in your promises in the future.
We trust the good Maker has opened your eyes
to the wrongs which you and your fathers have done . . .
in making us toil for you for generations without recompense.

*Ex-slave Jourdan Anderson's reply to former owner's request
for his return to work, with pay, following Emancipation.*

O ver a century ago, W.E.B. Du Bois predicted the problem
of the twentieth century in America would be that of the
color line. It's highly doubtful, however, that Du Bois
anticipated the goals of racial equality would still be substantially
unrealized a century later. Nevertheless, despite claims to the contrary
by several scholars and intellectuals, and token political gains, it
appears the problem for America in the twenty-first century remains
largely the same: racial inequality.

While many Black Americans have of course enjoyed so-called
"mainstream" success, there remains an unanticipated, and
unacceptable, schism between the European American experience
and that of Black Americans, particularly those native-born with
historical ties to the nation's history of slavery. The reasons for the
differences are certainly debatable, and in fact are the subject of the
endless White supremacy promotions touting a uniquely Western or
European "culture" as inherently lending itself to success. My feeling,

however, is that the same way Whites controlled immigration to insure a majority White population in America, Governmental and non-governmental powers have been overtly and covertly active insuring an essentially White power structure continues to exercise economic and political control over institutions which influence social mobility and the prospects for realization of equality in America. Those same overt and covert forces, I believe, will seek to continually maintain a certain economic and political domination over non-White/non-Europeans, as has been practiced throughout the world for the better part of a thousand years.

It does not seem reasonable that achieving full equality might take more than a century, much less two centuries. Therefore, it's difficult to avoid the inevitable conclusion that if full equality hasn't been realized in the four hundred years of Blacks in this country, another generation or two, or even three, following current strategies, isn't likely to get it done, contrary to the belief of the U.S. Supreme Court, as expressed in the recent University of Michigan Affirmative Action case. And as Malcolm X famously stated: 'if you're not on the right road, you're certainly not going to get where you're trying to go.'

The important question then becomes what, if anything, can or should be done differently to achieve equality-in-fact in America. Given the desperately disenfranchised state of Black youth needlessly dying at alarming rates across this country everyday,[966] full social equality appears unacceptably absent from the nation's agenda, as evidenced by the billions of dollars (trillions?) arbitrarily spent in Iraq where policy makers somehow believe the security of America's future rests, much more so than with our youth here at home. The humiliating and painfully deliberate makeover of New Orleans following hurricane Katrina, with the permanent displacement of so many of its poorest residents, being further evidence.[967]

America nevertheless has no misgivings about declaring that the ultimate solution to Iraqi apathy, violence and instability lies in money and jobs.[968] Journalist Fareed Zakaria observed how "Unemployment in non-Kurdish Iraq remains close to 50 percent, which helps explain why so many young men are joining gangs, militias and insurgent groups," a dilemma for which he proposed a $100 million solution.[969] Ivy league researchers, however, determined that unemployment for twenty-something Black men rose to 50 percent in 2004, 72 percent for those without a high school diploma, versus 34 and 19 percent unemployment for Hispanic and White non-graduates.[970] Yet we mostly hear strident conservative opposition to "throwing money at the problem" in this country, where "culture" supposedly makes money irrelevant, the preferred solution being, of course, to build more prisons, which, in turn, requires, well, money. Thus the greater American investment in prisons than higher education.

The primary road followed to equality, during much of the twentieth century, has been that of integration, largely through policies of Affirmative Action where, it was thought, unfettered access to so-called "equal opportunity" — and the elimination of Jim Crow — would translate into equal enjoyment of the fruits and benefits of American capitalism and democracy. Obviously, the view was somewhat shortsighted.

It now seems clear that as long as Blacks are forced to rely on the conscience of European Americans for rationing out full political and economic equality, we must forever occupy a relative subordinate, inferior and subjugated position. It is therefore also clear that something must supplant the status quo in order to achieve the desired result. The merits of integration may be debatable, but Affirmative Action, given its convenient perception as a program of "preferences" for non-Whites, and the consequent overwhelming opposition to it, clearly is not and, in its current form, can never be the answer to the problem of American racial inequality.

I believe Reparations are the proper solution to effectively address the need of contemporary Black Americans to fully and equally share the benefits that sprang from the labors of toiling slaves, , by empowering Blacks to be judged independent of the perpetually damning control and influence of White supremacy.

An alternate premise of Reparations, in addition to their underlying atonement for past wrongs, is the inescapable reality that America as we now know it is fast heading towards the point that is no more, in which case the toil and trouble of Black slaves will have been squandered, with their descendants having been significantly precluded from enjoying the advantages of those labors. Salvaging something for the thankless labors that built America therefore seems not only prudent, but also imperative.

Value

Underlying the need for and the utility of Reparations, however, are questions of what form they should take, and how they might best be promoted. As to form, the value must not be trivial, short-lived or minimal. That is, it should respectfully reflect the generations of lives exploited, discounted and destroyed, both during slavery and after, a period spanning three centuries, and measured by the growth and development of not only America, but also the entire Western world. From these parameters we can see that the final settlement in view must be prodigious and, as a practical matter, must have permanency. Injustice lies only in an insufficiency of consideration.

This question is of such gravity and so perplexing, however, it invariably brings a complete halt to any and all deliberations on the matter, even for its advocates. For this reason, I offer a potentially realistic solution in the form of two separate options. One being land, which will no doubt be seen as prohibitively controversial. The other being money, which symbolizes the more conventional perception of Reparations, and therefore likely to be viewed as the more practical alternative.

LAND

Any proposal seeking land as compensation will, of course, be immediately seized upon as advocating a militant, separatist movement of Black Nationalism. This will no doubt be the preferred perception of White supremacy, just as Affirmative Action is generally interpreted to be a policy of preferences or "reverse discrimination." I prefer to view the situation, rather, as a choice between a dignified autonomy and perpetual subjugation. Granted, a geographic partition is most often applied as an option of last resort in cases where people cannot respectfully live together in peace, and where one group refuses to subjugate itself to the other simply for the sake of peace. But the fact that Black America has, thus far, accepted its subordinate status peacefully, does not mean they should do so indefinitely. Both timing and circumstance, however, suggest the time has come for Black America to definitively reject their subjugated position in this country as a statement of that condition being contrary to the natural order, and with an understanding that it does not take 500 years, or even 150 years, to realize the founding principles of our national creed. Otherwise, it's very likely another 500 years will see the relative status of Blacks in America, and the world, unchanged.

Most importantly, the justice of land consideration lies in the basic doctrines on property, which hold that proper title rests with those whose labor adds to its productive utility and value, labor being by far the greater part of its worth, with such title remaining vested in the descendents of its rightful owners, whatever force, conquest or usurpation used to obtain it from their ancestors, notwithstanding.[971]

Delta State

Given the significance to America of the Louisiana Purchase, financed on the bowed, bloodied backs of Black American slaves, combined with the humiliation and suffering experienced by the many Black slave descendents in New Orleans following hurricane Katrina, the first considerations (see Appendix for alternates) of land for Reparations should fittingly be given to the region of the Mississippi Delta.

The contiguous States of Louisiana, Mississippi, and Arkansas comprise an area that certainly can support a viable, prosperous, independent Black American State. The area covers approximately 143,000 square miles with a population of roughly some 10 million, pre-Katrina. Led by Louisiana's manufacturing and mining industries; natural gas and petroleum deposits beneath virtually all of the State's 64 parishes; strong manufacturing and service economies in both Arkansas and Mississippi, including gaming and the region's thriving agriculture and fishing industries, a foundation exists for long-term economic stability and sustainable growth.

Alternative considerations for Reparations should include some combination of initiatives designed to not only atone for the past, but to set the right course for a future of permanent Black self determination and racial equality.

TRUTH

Because slavery was a central cornerstone of America's founding identity, its institutional importance should be firmly established right alongside the Founding Fathers and the American Revolution. Reparations should therefore include a national holiday that allows Americans to reflect, learn about and commemorate the importance of slavery to this country — and the West — essential if we are to exist in a state of full equality. Continued misrepresentations of the origins of Europeans in the Western hemisphere, by praising the supposed heroic deeds of America's slavery contemporaries while discounting their shortcomings, facilitates the sense of White entitlement that encourages such compromising opposition to full equality. The view that American wealth and power grew predominantly from the genius of European settlers and their superior Anglo-Protestant work ethic should be appropriately augmented to celebrate slavery and its importance to the success and prosperity of early America. We might therefore replace Black History month with a month-long Black slavery commemoration instead.

RACE

With the mark of race being slavery's most damning and perplexing legacy, similarly critical to Reparations should be some initiative to adopt a zero tolerance attitude towards race discrimination, i.e., a War on Racism, where such inclinations risk exposure to criminal liability. This should necessarily include a comprehensive plan or strategy to address covert and de facto, institutional, race-based injustices that effectively nullify current, ineffectual policies intended to neutralize race hatred and bias.

Education

An extensive study of slavery as an institution, through the narratives of slaves and the writings of other slavery contemporaries, should be a requirement of American grade school education. Young people should not have to wait until college to read Frederick Douglass, for example, to learn what the American slave experience really was from the slaves' perspectives.

Reparations might additionally address the financial instability threatening the future of America's Historically Black Colleges and Universities (HBCUs) that served such a vital purpose following slavery, and who symbolize the centuries of education denied the slaves who built America. These institutions should not be allowed to crumble and perish. They serve as important a role in today's anti-diversity climate, where many of the promises and gains of the historic *Brown v. Board* decision have been unfulfilled or rolled back, as during legalized segregation, a role equal to that of America's single gender institutions.[972] As has been correctly recognized, the African American community "will not succeed in America, has not succeeded in America, without the contribution of historically black colleges and universities."[973]

From an historical perspective, many institutions of higher learning across America were built by slaves and/or the resources springing from slave labor, but for generations refused admission to Black Americans, while at the same time educating generations of European Americans, exclusively, for a century following Emancipation, laying an intellectual foundation that benefited all Americans and created a debt that might best be extinguished through an equally race based solution: an annual fund to benefit HBCU schools and contributed to by the accredited, otherwise mainstream, post-secondary institutions across America who would commit a nominal percentage of their endowments. Or a fund for HBCU capital projects similarly contributed to from capital budgets of the so-called mainstream schools.

Pursuant to a pre-determined formula, accreditation might also require post-secondary educators to teach one year at HBCU schools, with one additional semester per fixed period thereafter, say, every five or ten years, for example, as a prerequisite of tenure, towards the end of potentially boosting HBCU enrollments.

Further, as a way of helping American students of European descent understand the complexities minorities face in a White dominated culture, towards eliminating the ignorance that breeds racism, schools might require students, as an alternative or supplement to Study Abroad programs, to spend a year at an HBCU school as a condition of graduation. The president and CEO of the National Association for Equal Opportunity in Higher Education, Lezli Baskerville, refers to this as an ideal way for Whites to "prepare for an 'increasingly black and brown world.'" According to Baskerville, "If you want to know how to live in one, you can't grow up in an all-white neighborhood, go to a predominantly white school, white cultural and social events, go to a predominantly white university and then thrive in a world that is today more black, more brown than before."[974]

Employment

Nothing is more essential to full equality in America than unfettered access to employment. Many leading corporations owe their beginnings to slavery, yet experience reveals far too many Whites willing to actively control, frustrate and interfere with the efforts of Black Americans to earn a living and accumulate wealth. It is therefore plain that unless we are uniquely empowered to own, operate, manage, and staff businesses on a scale that provides viable alternatives to White control and domination,[975] economic equality can never exist.

It is inconceivable, for example, that at the opening decade of the twenty-first century, despite the length of time Blacks have been in this country, only two Black owned and operated corporations generate sufficient sales to rank among the top 1,000 of the nation's largest businesses, according to research compiled recently by both *Black Enterprise* and *Fortune* magazines. Neither of those would rank higher than number 825, and only one competing at number 985.

CONCLUSION

With respect to corporate America, one seeming equitable consideration for Reparations would be the transfer of management and control of various operations at the corporate entities identified as allegedly having had connections to slavery, such as FleetBoston Financial (now BankAmerica) , CSX, Aetna,[976] R.J. Reynolds, Brown Brothers Harriman, American International Group (AIG), Lloyd's of London, Loews Corp., New York Life, Royal & Sun Alliance, J.P. Morgan Chase & Co. , Lehman Brothers Holdings, Inc., Union Pacific Corp., Norfolk Southern Corp., WestPoint Stevens Inc., Brown & Williamson, and Liggett Group Inc., among many others. These corporations might either be broken up according to the precedent of AT&T, or required to spin off subsidiary operations to be run by Black American directors, officers and managers,[977] but under the same corporate identity, and with the same suppliers and markets. These "satellite" operations would maintain an organizational relationship with the parent company for purposes of training and consultation during an unspecified period when officers might seat an "Enterprise Board" for example, to map operations, after which each entity may become autonomous, pursuant to specific benchmarks and guidelines.

Credit

A major feature of slavery, both before and after the Revolution, was widespread borrowing against the value of slaves, as well as against the value of projected crop yields, particularly tobacco and cotton. Traders also regularly sold slaves on credit. With little or no cash, planters were able to obtain land, equipment and supplies, including seed, and even transport crops to market, all secured in the body and/or labors of slaves. This was the practice that for generations (two centuries) provided capital to immigrant settlers during a time when money was scarce. It therefore seems appropriate — and just — that a component of Reparations should be directed towards helping to balance the inequities of this historical record.

Those firms unable to accommodate subsidiary spin-offs under the above outline should meet an alternate financial obligation or otherwise participate in a program designed to facilitate Black access to credit, offset by a corporate "Reparations tax" on discriminatory representation of minorities and women in employment and salary outside stipulated parameters. Such monies should be reserved for new business development and home ownership, well-established staple elements of wealth accumulation.[978] Acceptance and participation, however, should not be limited to the traditional standards for creditworthiness, but instead to a more creative process, such as that introduced by GMAC, Wells Fargo to assist Mexican immigrants in obtaining mortgages, qualifying a collective household income, including extended relatives, etc., rather than just a single individual or couple.[979]

MONEY

As illustrated in a Modern Marvels episode, broadcast on cable television's History channel, "our money expresses our national identity and our cultural character." Currency generally honors institutions and icons of significance to a nation's early history and/or development, as illustrated in our analysis of coins from the Renaissance. A component of Reparations, therefore, might similarly see slavery memorialized in the currency of the United States on a scale equal to that of the Founding Fathers, many of whom were in fact slaveholders themselves.

New currency designs should be introduced with a commissioned symbol of slavery that might grace various denominations singularly, and also added to existing designs. Each unit of currency should be a statement or permanent reminder that acknowledges slavery as among the most vital of America's economic and historical institutions.

POWER

The continued, determined opposition to diversity and equality, as expressed by the persistent majority in America through its many diligent, powerful and sophisticated White supremacy interests, and the consequent, disproportionate disenfranchisement of Black Americans of slave descent, highlights a fundamental flaw in the governing compact that comprises this civil society: that being the fact that, under the current Constitution, as it relates to a consenting and acknowledged governing union of diverse interests, it is an unlawful, despotic government never consented to by Black Americans who, through their de facto exclusion from considerations of equality, are not deemed to have done so, making plain that a new Constitutional convention must convene, where all America's varied interests are freely and equally represented, in order to establish legitimacy to the government as a compact of equals.

It is manifestly plain that, according to the conditions necessary for establishing political societies, as expressed by John Locke, not being freemen at the time of the formation of the U.S. Constitution, Black slaves and their descendents cannot be charged with ever having expressly consented to the American union, or having "submit themselves to the determination of the majority," the forcible capture, transport and servitude forclosing even a tacit consent.[980]

The primary issue to be addressed at such a Convention therefore relates to the inherent diversity that is America. Evolution of this society calls out loudly for a new governing document to define the country going forward, with express language outlining whether we are in fact a melting pot of equals, as we claim, or simply just another White European country.

A second issue that might be visited at the proposed Convention concerns military service. The all-volunteer enlistment policy means economic necessity, particularly as it arises from limited career alternatives, generally outweighs patriotism. The well-to-do actually have a disincentive to indulge such a high-risk occupation, i.e. presidential and congressional offspring (what in hell prevented Jenna & Barbara Bush or Chelsea Clinton from serving in Iraq?). Those enjoying the greatest benefits of the system can generally avoid the responsibility of protecting and defending it, which effectively amounts to their exploitation of the poor and minorities. The responsibility for defending America should be shared equally by all citizens, regardless of financial status. The wealthy should not enjoy the luxury of voluntarily foregoing that obligation, while daunting financial pressures compel poorer classes to disproportionately imperil their lives. Mere patriotism, according to experience, is less a motivating factor than is the desire for pecuniary gain.

Thirdly, there might also be a constitutional requirement that those responsible for sending America to war, namely the President and members of Congress, should have qualified offspring enlisted into service as a precondition of the right to cast a vote sending the children of others into harm's way. Specifically, a prerequisite of holding office should be that eligible children of elected federal representatives *must* serve in America's armed forces. Approximately two percent of current congressmen and congresswomen have children serving in active duty. One can readily see how much easier it therefore becomes to cast a "Yes" vote for war, particularly for an ill-advised, meaningless war.

Also regarding military incursions, fourthly, there should also be Constitutional language specifically outlining the necessary criteria for appropriately engaging the nation in a war, where preemptive, unilateral military actions, for example, would be prohibited.

NOTES ON THE STATE OF AMERICA

As a fifth issue, the Constitution might further balance the process for attaining elective office, which has absurdly evolved to assume a somewhat pornographic nature, seemingly outside the foresight and intentions of the framers. Those with the greatest financial resources are the most viable candidates, effectively barring an overwhelming majority of Americans, particularly poor Blacks, from the process. To get more young people enthusiastic about the political process, and about America's future, we might try to bring the process more within reach of every citizen by making it more about leadership and ideas than money and influence.

Additionally, with the increasing national debt burden on future generations, younger Americans should have greater participation in the deliberations that create the various liabilities they will eventually be responsible for extinguishing. As such, I see no reason why term limits, as a sixth issue, should apply only to the nation's chief executive. Limiting terms of service for Representatives and Senators, for example, might allow for greater overall participation in the process of government deliberations, and potentially prevent outdated ideologies from continuing to hamstring more contemporary policy approaches. As we have been publicly reminded about the braintrust largely responsible for cooking the half-baked Iraq invasion scheme more common to an earlier, misguided imperialist agenda:

> Donald Rumsfeld, chief of staff at the White House, secretary of defense, CEO, member of Congress; Dick Cheney, member of Congress, leader of the Congress, White House chief of staff, secretary of defense; vice president, Colin Powell, national security adviser, Joint Chiefs of Staff chairman, secretary of state, arguably the most experienced foreign policy, national security team we've ever had, and a disaster of epic, historic proportions.[981]

There should also be, as a seventh consideration, some uniform, Constitutionally defined, national policy protecting the citizenship rights of criminal ex-offenders who have paid their debt to society and seek to once again participate on an equal footing with other law abiding citizens. The right to vote, for example, should not be withheld from anyone endeavoring to live within the bounds of the law and paying taxes like everyone else. It has also become an accepted practice to continually bar ex-offenders from employment, housing and other rights of citizenship long after having paid for their transgressions. Society as a whole might benefit from a discussion of open-ended punishment versus allowing ex-offenders to permanently put their past behind them.

Lastly, the highly contentious Second Amendment right to bear arms might also be revisited. The current need for an armed militia might be fairly debated at a Convention as it is amidst the episodic mass shootings across the country.[982]

Promotion

The best way to promote Reparations is of course of critical importance. There is, in my opinion, a role for each and every interested citizen to play, since nothing less than the future of America is at stake. A segment of the Black American community, however, believes the promotion of Reparations should be limited to efforts already undertaken by established *elites* within the community (the "Talented Tenth"), with at least one presumption being, as a prominent, Black law school professor in the Boston area cautioned, certain efforts would be defeatist or detrimental to the overall prospects for success, and potentially even viewed as "pimping Reparations." If we've learned anything from the varied struggles in Ameria, however, it should be that great leaders, no matter how energized, do not make for a successful movement in and of themselves. Once they are cut down, the movement is cut down right along with them.

First and foremost, the very population that stands to benefit the most must drive the promotion of Reparations. Namely, in addition to the critical role of students, the working poor and community activists who, during earlier civil rights struggles influenced some of the most significant social reforms ever in America, those overwhelmingly unemployed, disenfranchised and institutionalized Black youth, including the ones on lockdown or otherwise entangled in the "system" who very much influence people and events on the outside.

Whether student, executive, or yes, even gang member — leaders especially — the entire community should understand that without their sustained active ownership, true equality, and Reparations, will never be realized. People need to recognize the extent to which they can best contribute, and assert themselves accordingly, whether through student organization, civil disobedience, public activism, etc..

Specifically, individuals and groups should engage in activities that will be felt, understood and profoundly acknowledged throughout all America, . . . "BY ANY MEANS NECESSARY!" as Malcolm famously advised. Those hovering outside the so-called "mainstream" should direct their energies in contravention of the system and its institutions, meaning the police, the courts and other discriminating symbols of America's capitalist hierarchy, i.e. Madison Avenue and corporate America, as a rejection of the status quo, and in support of justice. Prison, to quote none other than Dr. Martin Luther King, Jr. , for those forced to endure it as the price of justice, would then be "transformed from a dungeon of shame to a haven of freedom and dignity."

It is unacceptable in our third century to expect another generation of Black Americans to continue living under compromised citizenship rights in the country so disproportionately built up on the blood, sweat and tears of their ancestors.

Give me Equality, damnit, . . . or give me Death!

It's time for Reparations!

Appendix

lternative Land Considerations

The inclusive area contained by Alabama, Georgia and Florida, comprising approximately 163,000 square miles and a population of nearly 28 million, would be similarly desirable as the location of an independent, autonomous, *Las Floridas* compensatory State, whose capitol might be seated, appropriately, at the location of the first capitol of the Confederacy, in 1861, in the "Heart of Dixie," Montgomery, Alabama. Significant ports at Miami, Savannah and Mobile, the diverse industrial mix of service, manufacturing and agricultural economies, with world-class cities at Atlanta and Miami, make this area easily the most attractive of possibilities for successful, sustainable Black independence.

Thirdly, an area bounded by the contiguous States of Virginia, Tennessee and the Carolinas, is another geographical alternative, with respect to permanency and value, offering similarly attractive features and merits. *Old Dominion* The enclosed territory is approximately 160,000 square miles and supports a current population of some 24 million people.

Lastly, the Northeast region of the country, plus New York (not shown), is an area covering *Rockin' Plymouth* approximately 110,000 square miles, supporting a population in excess of thirty million. The advantages of this area, relative to those already mentioned, are obvious, potentially providing the most accommodating of all, long term, for the growth and prosperity of a separate, autonomous State.

SELECT 18th CENTURY SLAVING VOYAGES

No.	SHIP	Registration	VESSEL/CARGO OWNER		Date	Captain	SLAVES			
			Last	First			From	To	load	unload
1	Anne and Mary	New York	Linch	Anthony	1715	Jacobs, Tho	Africa n/s	New York	47	38
2	Anne and Mary	New York	Moore	Allex	1715	Jacobs, Tho	Africa n/s	New York	47	38
3	Anne and Mary	New York	Rutgers	Anthony	1715	Jacobs, Tho	Africa n/s	New York	47	38
4	Anne and Mary	New York	Vandam	Rip	1715	Jacobs	Africa n/s	New York	47	38
5	Anne and Mary	New York	Gerbransen	Frances	1716	Jacobs	Africa n/s	New York	53	43
6	Anne and Mary	New York	Moore	Allex	1716	Jacobs	Africa n/s	New York	53	43
7	Anne and Mary	New York	Rutgers	Anthony	1716	Jacobs	Africa n/s	New York	53	43
8	Anne and Mary	New York	Vandam	Rip	1716	Jacobs	Africa n/s	New York	53	43
9	Anne and Mary	New York	Gerbransen	Frances	1716		Africa n/s	New York	53	43
10	Cath. and Mary	New York	Fresneau	Andrew	1717	Cracraft, John	Africa n/s	New York	74	60
11	Cath. and Mary	New York	Vanhorne	Jno, Gart, Abr	1717	Cracraft, John	Africa n/s	New York	74	60
12	Cath. and Mary	New York	Fresneau	Andrew	1718	Cracraft, John	Africa n/s	New York	78	64
13	Cath. and Mary	New York	Vanhorne	Jno, Gart, A	1718	Cracraft, John	Africa n/s	New York	78	64
14	Phillipsburg	New York	Phillips	Adolf	1718	Jarrat, Allane	Africa n/s	Barbados	293	239
15	Burnet	New York	Chuyler	Henry	1723	Sanders, Edward	Africa n/s	Jamaica		
16	Burnet	New York	Robinson	Jos	1723	Sanders, Edward	Africa n/s	Jamaica		
17	Burnet	New York	Thong	Walter	1723	Sanders, Edward	Africa n/s	Jamaica		
18	Burnet	New York	Vandam	Rip	1723	Sanders, Edward	Africa n/s	Jamaica		
19	Anne	New York	Hopkins	Thomas	1725	Garretse, Garret	Africa n/s	New York	72	59
20	Katherine	Boston	Bant	Wm	1729	Atkinson, William	Gold Coast	Antigua		
21	Katherine	Boston	Belcher	Jona	1729	Atkinson, William	Gold Coast	Antigua		
22	Katherine	Boston	Foy	Willm	1729	Atkinson, William	Gold Coast	Antigua		
23	Katherine	Boston	Hough	Ebenr	1729	Atkinson, William	Gold Coast	Antigua		
24	Katherine	Boston	Janvill	Andrew	1729	Atkinson, William	Gold Coast	Antigua		
25	Katherine	Boston	Pusulton	Peter	1729	Atkinson, William	Gold Coast	Antigua		
26	Dorcas	Rhode Island	Newton	Thos S	1729	Newton, Thomas	Africa n/s	Barbados	175	143
27	Dorcas	Rhode Island	Sims	William	1729	Newton, Thomas	Africa n/s	Barbados	175	143
28	Frnd's Adventure	Britain	Green		1730	Moore, Samuel	Gambia	Barbados	163	142
29	Frnd's Adventure	Britain	Moore	Samuel	1730	Moore, Samuel	Gambia	Barbados	163	142

Source: Eltis, Behrendt, Richardson, Klein, *The Transatlantic Slave Trade: A Database on CD-ROM* (Cambridge U. Press, 1999).

| No. | SHIP | VESSEL/CARGO OWNER | | Registration | Date | Captain | SLAVES | | | |
		Last	First				To	From	load	unload
30	Frnd's Adventure	Pearce	Jos	Britain	1730	Moore, Samuel	Barbados	Gambia	163	142
31	Frnd's Adventure	Walker		Britain	1730	Moore, Samuel	Barbados	Gambia	163	142
32	Frnd's Adventure	Weeks	Sa	Britain	1730	Moore, Samuel	Barbados	Gambia	163	142
33	Frnd's Adventure	Wibord	Ricd	Britain	1730	Moore, Samuel	Barbados	Gambia	163	142
34	James	Hopkins	John	Pennsylvania	1731	Douglas, William	Barbados	Africa n/s	141	115
35	James	Jones	Jas, Phillip	Pennsylvania	1731	Douglas, William	Barbados	Africa n/s	141	115
36	Catherine	Schuyler	Arnot	New York	1731	Farmer, Jaspr	New York	Africa n/s		
37	Catherine	Watter	Jo	New York	1731	Farmer, Jaspr	New York	Africa n/s		
38	Gambia	Moore	Samuel		1732	Major, John	New York	Gambia		
39	Catherine	Schuyler	Arnot	New York	1733	Farmer, Jaspr	New York	Angola	146	133
40	Catherine	Watter	Jo	New York	1733	Farmer, Jaspr	New York	Angola	146	133
41	Dispatch	Malbone	Godfrey	Newport, RI	1733	Hammond, Pollipus	unspecified	Africa n/s		
42		Bours	Peter	Newport, RI	1733	Scott, Geo	Antigua	Africa n/s	172	154
43		Goulding	Geo	Newport, RI	1733	Scott, Geo	Antigua	Africa n/s	172	154
44	Fox	Goulding		Newport, RI	1735	Scott	Antigua	Africa n/s	96	86
45	Fox	Scott		Newport, RI	1735	Scott	Antigua	Africa n/s	96	86
46	Marigold	Bours	Peter	Newport, RI	1735	Taylor, Thom	Antigua	Africa n/s	142	127
47	Marigold	Goulding	Geo	Newport, RI	1735	Taylor, Thom	Antigua	Africa n/s	142	127
48	Marigold	Scott	George	Newport, RI	1735	Taylor, Thom	Antigua	Africa n/s	142	127
49	Haddock	Malbone	Godfrey	Newport, RI	1736	Aldridge	n/s			
50		Ayrault	Steph	Newport, RI	1736	Cahoone, John (Jr)	unspecified	Gold Coast		
51		Malbone	Godfrey	Newport, RI	1737	Godfrey, Caleb		Africa n/s		
52	Mary	Brown	James, Obediah	Providence	1737		Godfrey, John	Rhode Island		
53	Olive Branch	Vernon	Wm, Sam	Newport, RI	1737	Godfrey, John		Africa n/s		
54	Norfolk	Bouch	Saml, (Jr/Sr)	Virginia	1737	Tindall, Saml	Barbados	Africa n/s	135	110
55	Diamond	Malbone	Godfrey	Newport, RI	1739	Hammond, Pollipus	unspecified	Africa n/s	55	
56	Prudent Abigail	Jones	John	New England	1739	Thurston, Jos		Africa n/s		
57	Prudent Abigail	Thurston	Jos	Rhode Island	1739	Thurston, Jos		Africa n/s		
58	Mary Anne	Boutin	John	Boston	1740	Cutler, John	Upper James, Va	Africa n/s	86	70

Select Eighteenth Century African Slaving Voyages

No.	SHIP	VESSEL/CARGO OWNER			Date	Captain	SLAVES			
		Registration	Last	First			To	From	load	unload
59	Martha and Jane	Newport, RI	Redwood	Abraham	1740	Pope, Francis	Antigua	Gold Coast		
60		Newport, RI	Malbone	Godfrey	1740	Wickham	Rhode Island	Africa n/s		
61	Charming Betty	Newport, RI	Malbone	Godfrey	1742	Brewer, Thomas	unspecified	Africa n/s		
62	Jolly Batchelor	Boston	Cutler	John	1743	Cutler, John	Newport, RI	Sierra Leone	20	20
63	Jolly Batchelor	Boston	Jones	John	1743	Cutler, John	Newport, RI	Sierra Leone	20	20
64	Jolly Batchelor	Boston	Faneuil	Peter	1743	Wickham, Charles	Newport, RI	Sierra Leone	20	20
65	Anstis	Newport, RI	Ellery	Wm	1746	Hammond, Pollipus	Rhode Island	Africa n/s		
66	Anstis	Newport, RI	Tillinghast	Philip	1746	Hammond, Pollipus	Rhode Island	Africa n/s		
67	Betsy	Boston	Anyon	Timothy, A	1747	Anyon, Timothy	Kingston, Jam	Bight/Biafra	297	240
68	Bonetta	Newport, RI	Thurston	John	1747	Jepson, John	Barbados, Antig	Africa n/s	123	100
69	Fanny	Newport, RI	Barstow	Michael	1749	Barstow, Michael				
70	Fanny	Newport, RI	Coggeshall	Nat	1749	Barstow, Michael				
71	Fanny	Newport, RI	Durfey	Benj	1749	Barstow, Michael				
72	Fanny	Newport, RI	Hammond	Jos	1749	Barstow, Michael				
73	Fanny	Newport, RI	Rhodes	Simon	1749	Barstow, Michael				
74	Fanny	Newport, RI	Salter	Elisha	1749	Barstow, Michael				
75		Providence	Comstock	Gideon	1749	Brown, Wm	Rhode Island	Africa n/s		
76		Providence	Sessions	Darius	1749	Brown, Wm	Rhode Island	Africa n/s		
77		Providence	Smith	Elias	1749	Brown, Wm	Rhode Island	Africa n/s		
78		Providence	Smithfield		1749	Brown, Wm	Rhode Island	Africa n/s		
79		Providence	Spague	Nehemiah	1749	Brown, Wm	Rhode Island	Africa n/s		
80		Providence	Waterman	Resolved	1749	Brown, Wm	Rhode Island	Africa n/s		
81	Success	Newport, RI	Ellery	Wm	1749	Hammond	Rhode Island	Africa n/s		
82	Elizabeth	Newport, RI	Chaloner		1750	Cahoone	Rhode Island	Africa n/s		
83	Elizabeth	Newport, RI	Channing		1750	Cahoone	Rhode Island	Africa n/s		
84	Stork	New York	Livingston	Philip / others	1750	Lindsay, David	Antigua	Africa n/s	293	239
85	Wolf	New York	Livingston	Philip / others	1751	Wall, Gurnay	New York	Gold Coast	75	73
86	Two Friends	Newport, RI	Chase	Ammi*	1752	Hammett, Abraham	South Carolina	Gold Coast	69	60
87	Potomack Merch	Virginia	Douglass	Thomas*	1752	Hartley, Richard	S Potomac, Va	Bight/Biafra	244	197

273

No.	SHIP	VESSEL/CARGO OWNER			Date	Captain	SLAVES		load	unload
		Registration	Last	First			To	From		
88		Newport, RI	Ayrault		1752	Lindsay, David	Barbados	Gold Coast	65	56
89	Westmoreland	Newport, RI	Willson	Joseph*	1752	Wilson, Joseph	Kingston, Jam	Senegambia	165	144
90	Sanderson	Newport, RI	Brown	Peter	1753	Lindsay, David	Barbados, RI	Gold Coast	61	57
91	Sanderson	Newport, RI	Johnston	Wm	1753	Lindsay, David	Barbados, RI	Gold Coast	61	57
92	Rainbow	Newport, RI	Chase	Ammi*	1753	Pinegar, William	Jamaica	Seneg/Wndwrd	94	78
93	Rainbow	Newport, RI	Thurston	Peleg	1753	Pinegar, William	Jamaica	Seneg/Wndwrd	94	78
94		Barbados	Merivielle	Sus	1753		Barbados	Gambia	155	135
95		Barbados	Merivielle	Elias	1753		Barbados	Gambia	155	135
96	Sherbro	Newport, RI	Rivera	Jacob	1754	Brown, Wm	Guianas	Africa n/s		
97	Sherbro	Newport, RI	Vernon	Wm	1754	Brown, Wm	Guianas	Africa n/s		
98	Elizabeth	Newport, RI	Challoner	Walter	1754	Carpenter, James	Kingston, Jam	Gold Coast	70	62
99	Elizabeth	Newport, RI	Channing	John	1754	Carpenter, James	Kingston, Jam	Gold Coast	70	62
100	Elizabeth	Newport, RI	Thurston	Peleg	1754	Carpenter, James	Kingston, Jam	Gold Coast	70	62
101	Elizabeth	Newport, RI	Thurston	Peleg*	1754	Carpenter, Thomas	Kingston, Jam	Gold Coast	98	85
102	Sarah and Elizabeth	New York		Browan,Tho	1754	Corne, Peter	New York	Africa n/s	11	9
103	Sarah and Elizabeth	New York		Livingston, P.	1754	Corne, Peter	New York	Africa n/s	11	9
104	Sarah and Elizabeth	New York		Waddie, John	1754	Corne, Peter	New York	Africa n/s	11	9
105	Anstis	Newport, RI	Wanton	John*	1754	James, Peter	Kingston, Jam	Africa n/s	152	124
106	Young Batchelor	Newport, RI	Shearman	Robert*	1754	Johnson, Samuel	Kingston, Jam	Gold Coast	133	115
107	York	New York	Greenel	Thomas	1754	Mercier, Wm	New York	Gambia	35	26
108	York	New York	Robart	Christopher	1754	Mercier, Wm	New York	Gambia	35	26
109	Polly	New York	Farmer	Jasp'r	1754	Miller, Paul	New York	Africa n/s	9	7
110	Polly	New York	Marston	Nath'l	1754	Miller, Paul	New York	Africa n/s	9	7
111	Rainbow	Newport, RI	Chase	Ammi*	1754	Reader, Thomas	St. Lucia	Africa n/s	68	61
112	Rainbow	Newport, RI	Crooke	Robert	1754	Reader, Thomas	St. Lucia	Africa n/s	68	61
113	Angola	Newport, RI	Stoddard	Robert*	1754	Stoddard, Robert	Kingston, Jam	Africa n/s	124	101
114	Rebeccah	New York	Bridge	Samuel	1754	Thorn, Daniel	New York	Gambia	36	23
115	Rebeccah	New York	Couzine	Garrat	1754	Thorn, Daniel	New York	Gambia	36	23
116	Rebeccah	New York	Griffith	William	1754	Thorn, Daniel	New York	Gambia	36	23

Select Eighteenth Century African Slaving Voyages

No.	SHIP	VESSEL/CARGO OWNER			Date	Captain	SLAVES			
		Registration	Last	First			To	From	load	unload
117	Rebeccah	New York	Thorn	Daniel	1754	Thorn, Daniel	New York	Gambia	36	23
118	Hare	Newport, RI	Vernon	Saml, Wm	1755	Godfrey, Caleb	Charleston	Sierra Leone	65	56
119	Sierra Leone	Newport, RI	Johnston	Wm	1755	Lindsay, David	Barbados	Africa n/s	57	58
120	Camelion	Newport, RI	Hart	Naphtaly*	1755	Molton, Michael	Kingston, Jam	Africa n/s	67	55
121	Polly	Newport, RI	Dennis	John*	1755	Taylor, John	Kingston, Jam	Africa n/s	93	76
122	Africa	Newport, RI	Tipson	John*	1755	Taylor, Teackle	Kingston, Jam	Africa n/s	146	119
123	Hare	Newport, RI	Vernon	Saml, Wm	1756	Godfrey, Caleb	Charleston	Sierra Leone	80	63
124	Young Batchelor	Newport, RI	Shearman	Robert*	1756	Johnson, Samuel	Jamaica	Cape Coast	120	117
125	Annamabo	Newport, RI	Grant	Alex	1756	Keith, James	Jamaica	Africa n/s	126	113
126	Annamabo	Newport, RI	Healy	Andrew	1756	Keith, James	Jamaica	Africa n/s	126	113
127	Sierra Leone	Newport, RI	Ayrault	D	1756	Lindsay, David	St. Kitts (Christ)	Cape Coast	57	44
128	Sierra Leone	Newport, RI	Wilkinson	Philip	1756	Lindsay, David	St. Kitts (Christ)	Cape Coast	57	44
129	Titt Bitt	Newport, RI	Redwood	Jonas, W (Jr)	1756	Rogers, Thom	n/s	Gold Coast		
130	Titt Bitt	Newport, RI	Vernon	Wm	1756	Rogers, Thom	n/s	Gold Coast		
131	Marygold	Newport, RI	Scott	Edw	1756	Taylor, William	French Carib	Gold Coast	92	80
132	Marygold	Newport, RI	Taylor	Teackle	1756	Taylor, William	French Carib	Gold Coast	92	80
133	Marygold	Newport, RI	Thurston	Jon	1756	Taylor, William	French Carib	Gold Coast	92	80
134	Africa	Newport, RI	Collins	Henry	1757	Gardner, John	Antigua, Martnq	Senegambia	127	111
135	Africa	Newport, RI	Engs	Sam	1757	Gardner, John	Antigua, Martnq	Senegambia	127	111
136	Africa	Newport, RI	Flagg	Ebenezer	1757	Gardner, John	Antigua, Martnq	Senegambia	127	111
137	William	New York	Griffith	David	1757	Griffith, David	Eastern N Jersey	Gambia	57	50
138	William	New York	Williams	Rice	1757	Griffith, David	Eastern N Jersey	Gambia	57	50
139	Success	Newport, RI	Mason	Benj	1757	Harvey, Seth	Martinique	Africa n/s	118	96
140	Anstis	Newport, RI	James	Peter	1757	James, John	Kingston, Jam	Gold Coast	147	127
141	Anstis	Newport, RI	Watson	John*	1757	James, John	Kingston, Jam	Gold Coast	147	127
142	Young Batchelor	Newport, RI	Johnson	Sam	1757	Johnson, Samuel	Jamaica	Africa n/s	140	114
143	Sierra Leone	Newport, RI	Wilkinson	Philip*	1757	Lindsay, David	Guadeloupe	Cape Coast	70	61
144	Venus	Newport, RI	Stevens	Robt	1757	Pinnegar, William	Kingston, Jam	Gold Coast	120	130
145	Venus	Newport, RI	Vernon	Willm	1757	Pinnegar, William	Kingston, Jam	Gold Coast	120	130

NOTES ON THE STATE OF AMERICA

No.	SHIP	VESSEL/CARGO OWNER			Date	Captain	SLAVES			
		Registration	Last	First			To	From	load	unload
146	Cassada Garden	Newport, RI	Redwood	Jonas, W (Jr)	1757	Taylor, Thom		Gold Coast	202	175
147	Cassada Garden	Newport, RI	Vernon	Wm	1757	Taylor, Thom		Gold Coast	202	175
148	Dolphin	Newport, RI	Robinson	Nich, Thom	1757	Weaver, Jos	Barbados	Cape Coast	80	69
149	Gambia	Newport, RI	Grant	McCloud, R	1757		St. Kitts	Africa n/s	58	47
150	Gambia	Newport, RI	Healy	McCloud, R	1757		St. Kitts	Africa n/s	58	47
151	Prince George	Newport, RI	Wilkinson	Philip*	1758	Lindsay, David	Barbados, S.C.	Gold Coast	170	133
152	Othello	Newport, RI	Redwood	Jonas, W (Jr)	1758	Malbone, Francis	Barbados	Africa n/s	299	244
153	Othello	Newport, RI	Vernon	Wm	1758	Malbone, Francis	Barbados	Africa n/s	299	244
154	Catherine	Newport, RI	Pease	Simon (Jr)	1759	Carpenter, Thom	Rhode Island	Cape Coast	39	34
155	Wheel of Fortune	Providence	Brown	Nicholas, Obadiah	1759		Earl, Wm	n/s	Africa n/s	
156	Elizabeth	Newport, RI	Elliot	Robert	1759	Elliott, Robert	Charleston	Windwl Coast	50	45
157	Elizabeth	Newport, RI	Miller	John	1759	Elliott, Robert	Charleston	Windwl Coast	50	45
158	Venus	Newport, RI	Redwood	Jonas, W (Jr)	1759	Johnson, Saml	Martiniq, S. Car	Cape Coast	150	150
159	Venus	Newport, RI	Vernon	Wm	1759	Johnson, Saml	Martiniq, S. Car	Cape Coast	150	150
160	Three Friends	Newport, RI	Pease	Simon (Jr)	1760	Carpenter, James	Rhode Island	Cape Coast	78	63
161	John	Britain	Guerard	John	1760	Cherry, George	Savannah	Gambia	80	70
162	John	Britain	Jolliffe	William	1760	Cherry, George	Savannah	Gambia	80	70
163	Betsey	Charleston	Boyd	Augustus	1760	Deas, Robert	St. Kitts	Africa n/s		
164	Betsey	Charleston	Grant	Nayr	1760	Deas, Robert	St. Kitts	Africa n/s		
165	Betsey	Charleston	Oswald	Robert	1760	Deas, Robert	St. Kitts	Africa n/s		
166	Betsey	Charleston	Sergent	John*	1760	Deas, Robert	St. Kitts	Africa n/s		
167	Agnes	Boston	White	John*	1760	Duthie, Robert	Upper James, Va	Sierra Leone	226	202
168	Phillis	Boston	Fitch	Timothy	1760	Gwyn, Peter	Boston	Windward Coast		
169	Charming Betty	Newport, RI	Thurston	Peleg	1760	James, Peter	Rhode Island	Cape Coast	117	101
170	Salisbury	Boston	Ivers	Thomas*	1760	Martin, Thomas	Hampton, Va	Africa n/s	93	76
171	Marygold	Newport, RI	Taylor	Thom	1760	Taylor, Thom	Antigua	Gold Coast	135	112
172	Marygold	Newport, RI	Vernon	Saml, Wm	1760	Taylor, Thom	Antigua	Gold Coast	135	112
173	John	UK	Guerard	John	1760		Charleston	Senegambia	80	70
174	John	UK	Jolliffe	William	1760		Charleston	Senegambia	80	70

Select Eighteenth Century African Slaving Voyages

No.	VESSEL/CARGO OWNER				Date	Captain	SLAVES			
	SHIP	Registration	Last	First			To	From	load	unload
175	Phillis	Boston	Fitch	Timothy	1761	Gwyn, Peter	New England	Windward Coast	83	75
176	Dolphin	Newport, RI	Hazard	Thom	1761	Kean, Wm	unspecified	Gold Coast		300
177	Bance Island	Charleston	Boyd	Aug, Jno	1761	Stephens, John	South Carolina	Sierra Leone	336	300
178	Bance Island	Charleston	Grant	Alex (Sir)	1761	Stephens, John	South Carolina	Sierra Leone	336	300
179	Bance Island	Charleston	Mill	Jno	1761	Stephens, John	South Carolina	Sierra Leone	336	300
180	Bance Island	Charleston	Oswald	Rd	1761	Stephens, John	South Carolina	Sierra Leone	336	300
181	Bance Island	Charleston	Sargent	Jno	1761	Stephens, John	South Carolina	Sierra Leone	336	300
182	Friendship	Newport, RI	Grant	Wm	1762	Bull, Nathan		Africa n/s		
183		Annapolis, MD	Galloway	Samuel	1762	Craig	Antigua	Gambia	112	98
184		Annapolis, MD	Ringgold	Thomas	1762	Craig	Antigua	Gambia	112	98
185		Annapolis, MD	Symmes	Andrew, Alex	1762	Craig	Antigua	Gambia	112	98
186	Pitt	New York	Cruger	John*	1762	Elder, Robert	Kingston, Jam	Africa n/s	88	72
187	Prince George	Newport, RI	Elizer	Isaac	1762	Peck, John	Bahamas	Africa n/s		
188	Prince George	Newport, RI	Moses	Sam	1762	Peck, John	Bahamas	Africa n/s		
189	Africa	Newport, RI	Guyse	Wm	1762	Searing, James	Guadeloupe	Africa n/s	60	49
190	Africa	Newport, RI	Hagger		1762	Searing, James	Guadeloupe	Africa n/s	60	49
191	Africa	Newport, RI	King	Benj	1762	Searing, James	Guadeloupe	Africa n/s	60	49
192	Charming Abigail	Newport, RI	Wanton	Joseph, Wm	1762	Wanton, Peter	Barbados, Guad	Cape Coast	145	126
193		Philadelphia	Galloway	Samuel	1762		Antigua	Senegambia	112	98
194		Philadelphia	Ringgold	Thomas	1762		Antigua	Senegambia	112	98
195		Philadelphia	Symmes	Alexander, A	1762		Antigua	Senegambia	112	98
196	Reynard	Newport, RI	Vernon	Saml, Wm	1763	Dordin, Peter	Barbados	Bight / Benin	204	182
197	Pompey	New London, CT	Easton, John	Easton, John	1763	Easton, John	Upper James, Va	Windwrd Coast	89	81
198	Apollo	Newport, RI	DBlois	Louis*	1763	Morris, Owen	Kingston, Jam	Gambia	90	101
199	Greyhound	Newport, RI	Lopez	Aaron	1763	Pinnegar, Wm	Charleston, N. O	Cape Coast	150	134
200	Greyhound	Newport, RI	Rivera	Rod	1763	Pinnegar, Wm	Charleston, N. O	Cape Coast	150	134
201	Charming Sally	New York	Bridge	Samuel	1763	Richards, Roger	New York	Gold Coast	126	103
202	Charming Sally	New York	Dwight	Samuel	1763	Richards, Roger	New York	Gold Coast	126	103
203	Whydah	Newport, RI	Vernon	Wm	1763	Rogers, Thom	Barbados	Cape Coast	60	31

No.	SHIP	Registration	Last	First	Date	Captain	To	From	load	unload
204	Durnell	Boston	Davis	Elijah*	1763	Spear, Gresham	Upr James, Va	Africa n/s	98	80
205	Elizabeth n Mary	Philadelphia	Bradford	Cornelius*	1763	Taylor, William	Rappahan, Va	Africa n/s	98	80
206	Little Sally	Newport, RI	Taylor	Thom	1763	Taylor, William	Rhode Island	Africa n/s	67	61
207	Little Sally	Newport, RI	Vernon	Saml, Wm	1763	Taylor, William	Rhode Island	Africa n/s	67	61
208	Royal Charlotte	Newport, RI	Taylor	Thom	1763	Taylor, Wm	Rhode Island	Cape Coast	70	15
209	Royal Charlotte	Newport, RI	Vernon	Saml, Wm	1763	Taylor, Wm	Rhode Island	Cape Coast	70	15
210	Thomas	Virginia	Newton	Thomas*	1763	Thomas, Charles	Hampton, Va	Gld/Wndwd	69	60
211	Three Friends	Newport, RI	Pease	Simon	1764	Carpenter, Willett	Mntego Bay, Jam	Gold Coast	78	53
212	Fanny	Newport, RI	Mumford	Nat	1764	Morris		Africa n/s		
213	Shiprah	Newport, RI	Hart	Napt (Jr)	1764	Peck		Africa n/s		
214	Three Friends	Newport, RI	Greene	Jos	1765	Carpenter, Willett	n/s	Africa n/s	53	47
215	Three Friends	Newport, RI	Pease	Simon	1765	Carpenter, Willett	n/s	Africa n/s	53	47
216	Three Friends	Newport, RI	Simons	John	1765	Carpenter, Willett		Africa n/s	53	47
217	King George	Bristol, RI	Potter	Simeon	1765	Earl, Wm	St. Dominque	Cape Coast	200	173
218	Polly	New York	Wanton	Joseph	1765	Eldridge, Benjn	Kingston, Jam.	Africa n/s	123	100
219	Triton	Newport, RI	Gardner	Caleb	1765	Gardner, Caleb	St. Kitts (Christ)	Cape Coast	100	87
220	Sally	Providence	Brown	Nicholas	1765	Hopkins, Esek	Antigua	Gambia	178	90
221	Sally	Providence	Brown	James, Moses	1765	Hopkins, Esek	Antigua	Gambia	178	90
222	Nancy	Newport, RI	Turney	Edward	1765	Keast, John	Charleston	Gambia	34	30
223	King George	Bristol, RI	Potter	Simeon	1765	Knowles, Henry	Mntego Bay, Jam	Cape Coast	200	140
224	King George	Bristol, RI	Wharton	Jos*	1765	Knowles, Henry	Mntego Bay, Jam	Cape Coast	200	140
225	Sharpe	New York	Durham	Thomas*	1765	Leavcraft, Viner	Kingston, Jam	Africa n/s	260	212
226	Ospray	Newport, RI	Hart	Nephthali	1765	Potter, Nathaniel	St. Donin, Jam	Cape Coast	100	80
227	Othello	Newport, RI	Vernon	Saml, Wm	1765	Rogers, Thomas	Antigua	Bight / Benin	66	42
228	Newport Packet	Newport, RI	Bourse	John	1765	Sherman, James	Charleston	Gold Coast	172	154
229	Newport Packet	Newport, RI	Cranston	Thomas	1765	Sherman, James	Charleston	Gold Coast	172	154
230	Newport Packet	Newport, RI	Hicks	Benjamin	1765	Sherman, James	Charleston	Gold Coast	172	154
231	Newport Packet	Newport, RI	Lawton	Isaac	1765	Sherman, James	Charleston	Gold Coast	172	154
232	Alice	Rappahan.. VA	Hunter	James	1765	Sinclair, Arthur	S. Potom, Va	Senegambia	85	71

Select Eighteenth Century African Slaving Voyages

No.	SHIP	VESSEL/CARGO OWNER			Date	Captain	SLAVES			
		Registration	Last	First			To	From	load	unload
233	Alice	Rappahan., VA	Mills	James	1765	Sinclair, Arthur	S. Potom, Va	Senegambia	85	71
234	Black Prince	Virginia	Newton	Thomas, Jr.	1765	Thomas, Charles	Upper James, Va	Windwd Coast	139	120
235	Africa	Newport, RI	Lopez	Aaron	1766	All, Abraham	Kingston, Jam	Africa n/s	65	45
236	Africa	Newport, RI	Rivera	Jacob	1766	All, Abraham	Kingston, Jam	Africa n/s	65	45
237	Molly	Newport, RI	Goldthwaite	Samuel*	1766	Barden, William	Kingston, Jam	Africa n/s	37	30
238	Betsey	Newport, RI	Lopez	Aaron	1766	Briggs, Nathaniel	Kingston, Jam	Briggs, Nath	46	40
239	Betsey	Newport, RI	Rivera	Jacob	1766	Briggs, Nathaniel	Kingston, Jam	Briggs, Nath	46	40
240	Katy	Newport, RI	Pease	Simon*	1766	Carpenter, James	Mntego Bay, Jam	Africa n/s	102	83
241		Boston	Boylston	Thomas	1766	McCarthy, Dan	Barbados	Africa n/s		
242	Peggy	Newport, RI	Moore	Charles	1766	Moore	Mntego Bay, Jam	Africa n/s	165	135
243	Spry	Newport, RI	Lopez	Aaron	1766	Pinfeger, William	Kingston, Jam	Gold Coast	66	57
244	Spry	Newport, RI	Rivera	Jacob	1766	Phineger, William	Kingston, Jam	Gold Coast	66	57
245	Harlequin	Newport, RI	Richardson	Thom	1766		n/s	Africa n/s		
246	Sally	Newport, RI	Lopez	Aaron	1767	Briggs, Nat	Barbados	Cape Coast	120	104
247	Sally	Newport, RI	Rivera	Jacob	1767	Briggs, Nat	Barbados	Cape Coast	120	104
248	Othello	Newport, RI	Vernon	Samuel, Wm	1767	Duncan, John	Virginia	Africa n/s	97	87
249	Eagle	Newport, RI	Vernon	James	1767	Easton, James	unspecified	Africa n/s		
250	Queen of Barra	Newport, RI	Elliot	Robert	1767	Elliot, Robert	Jamaica	Africa n/s		
251	Prosperity	Newport, RI	Potter	Simeon	1767	Martindale, Silas	Barbados	Cape Coast	100	87
252	Greyhound	Newport, RI	Levy	Moses	1767	Thurston, John	Jamaica	Africa n/s	103	84
253	Adventure	Newport, RI	Vernon	Joseph	1767	Tillinghast, Jos		Africa n/s		
254	Polly	Newport, RI	Wanton	Joseph	1767	Wanton, Peter	Barbados	Cape Coast	180	160
255	Two Friends	Philadelphia	Drinker	Henry	1767	Woodhouse, James	Kingston, Jam.	Gambia	80	77
256	Africa	Newport, RI	Lopez	Aaron	1768	All, Abraham	Kingston, Jam.	Africa n/s	85	69
257	Africa	Newport, RI	Rivera	Jacob	1768	All, Abraham	Kingston, Jam.	Africa n/s	85	69
258	Hannah	Newport, RI	Lopez	Aaron	1768	Briggs, Nathl	Barbados	Cape Coast	165	133
259	Hannah	Newport, RI	Rivera	Jacob	1768	Briggs, Nathl	Barbados	Cape Coast	165	133
260	Polly	Newport, RI	Wanton	John	1768	Child, Thomas	Barbados	Cape Coast	130	104
261	Polly	Newport, RI	Mason	Benj	1768	Ferguson, Robt	Barbados	Cape Coast	130	132

NOTES ON THE STATE OF AMERICA

| No. | SHIP | VESSEL/CARGO OWNER | | | | | SLAVES | | |
		Registration	Last	First	Date	Captain	To	From	load	unload
262	Ruth	Newport, RI	Wanton	Jos	1768	Fowler, Gideon	Barbados	Africa n/s	45	37
263	Sally	Boston	Boylston	Thomas	1768	McCarthy, Dan	Barbados	Windwd Coast	220	180
264	Betsey	Newport, RI	Wanton	Jos	1768	Remington, Benj	Barbados	Cape Coast	115	120
265	Royal Charlotte	Newport, RI	Taylor	Thom	1768	Taylor, Wm	V. I. St. Croix	Gold Coast	105	95
266	Royal Charlotte	Newport, RI	Vernon	Saml, Wm	1768	Taylor, Wm	V. I St. Croix	Gold Coast	105	95
267	Africa	Newport, RI	Wanton	Jos	1768	Warner, James				
268	Two Friends	Philadelphia	Drinker	Henry	1768	Woodhouse, James	Kingston, Jam.	Africa n/s	87	71
269		Newport, RI	Lopez	Aaron	1768	Barden, Wm	Barbados	Africa n/s	112	100
270	Shelburne	Newport, RI	Clark	Jas (Capt)	1769	Clark, James	Charleston	Senegal	155	138
271	Polly	Newport, RI	Mason	Benj	1769	Coddington, John	Barbados	Cape Coast	154	146
272	Othello	Newport, RI	Vernon	Saml. Wm	1769	Duncan, John	Uppr Jas, Va	Gold Coast	86	72
273	King George	Bristol, RI	Potter	Simeon	1769	Earl, Wm	n/s	Gold Coast	230	199
274	Polly	Newport, RI	Robinson	James	1770	Godfrey, Isaac	Barbados	Africa n/s	74	60
275	Polly	Newport, RI	Vernon (2)		1770	Godfrey, Isaac	Barbados	Africa n/s	74	60
276	Cleopatra	Newport, RI	Lopez	Aaron	1771	Briggs, Nat	Barbados	Gold Coast	108	96
277	Cleopatra	Newport, RI	Rivera	Jacob	1771	Briggs, Nat	Barbados	Gold Coast	108	96
278	Sutton	Providence	Brown	John	1771	Cook, Silas	Barbados	Gold Coast		
279	Sutton	Providence	Sabins	Jos	1771	Cook, Silas	Barbados	Gold Coast	99	86
280	Sutton	Providence	Smith	Hayward	1771	Cook, Silas	Barbados	Gold Coast	99	86
281	Othello	Newport, RI	Vernon	Saml. Wm	1771	Duncan, John	Rappa., Va	Gold Coast	71	61
282	Grossle	Boston	Mason	Benj	1771	Elliot, Robert	Barbados	Gold Coast	148	128
283	Polly	Newport, RI	Lopez	Aaron	1771	English, Wm	Grenada	Gold Coast	101	90
284	Mary	Newport, RI	Rivera	Jacob	1771	English, Wm	Barbados	Africa n/s		
285	Mary	Newport, RI	Caesar		1771	Jencks, Silas	Barbados	Africa n/s		
286	Royal Charlotte	Newport, RI	Wanton	Jos, Wm	1771	Remington, B	Barbados	Africa n/s	37	30
287	Betsey	Newport, RI	Champlin	Christ, Geo	1771	Rogers, Thomas	Barbados	Gold Coast	103	89
288	Adventure	Newport, RI	Jouanne	de StMartin	1771		St. Domingue	Gold Coast	101	101
289	Saint André	France			1771		Barbados	GC/Guinee	552	530
290	Cleopatra	Newport, RI	Lopez	Aaron	1772	Briggs, Nat	Barbados	Gold Coast	257	240

Select Eighteenth Century African Slaving Voyages

| No. | SHIP | VESSEL/CARGO OWNER | | | Date | Captain | SLAVES | | | |
		Registration	Last	First			To	From	load	unload
291	Active	Newport, RI	Mason	Benj	1772	Elliot, Robert	Barbados	Africa n/s	100	82
292	Active	Newport, RI	Vernon	Saml, Wm	1772	Elliot, Robert	Barbados	Africa n/s	100	82
293	Black Prince	Newport, RI	Gardner		1772	Gardner, Dan	Barbados	Gold Coast	139	120
294	Black Prince	Newport, RI	Wickham		1772	Gardner, Dan	Barbados	Gold Coast	139	120
295	George	Newport, RI	Lopez	Aaron	1772	Greene, Peleg	n/s	Africa n/s		
296	Africa	Newport, RI	Wanton	Colo	1772	Mowatt, Geo	Barbados	Africa n/s	71	58
297	Neptune	Boston	Boylston		1773	Bennett	Grenada	Gold Coast	242	210
298	Cleopatra	Newport, RI	Lopez	Aaron	1773	Briggs	St. Domingue	Gold Coast		
299	Thomas	Newport, RI	Fletcher		1773	Clarke	Jamaica	Gold Coast		
300	Ann	Newport, RI	Lopez	Aaron	1773	English, Wm	Jamaica	Gold Coast	108	102
301	Ann	Newport, RI	Rivera	Jacob	1773	English, Wm	Jamaica	Gold Coast	108	102
302	Black Prince	Newport, RI	Gardner		1773	Gardner	Jamaica	Africa n/s		
303	Fanny	Newport, RI	Wanton	John, Edward	1773	Hicks, Benj	Charleston	Gold Coast	231	206
304	Polly	Newport, RI	Wanton		1773	Rogers, Thomas	Barbados	Gold Coast	141	122
305	Charlotte	Newport, RI	Lopez	Aaron	1773	Shearman	Jamaica	Africa n/s		
306	Active	Newport, RI	Lopez	Aaron	1773	Taggart	Barbados	Africa n/s		
307	Adventure	Newport, RI	Champlin	Christ, Geo	1773	Tuell, Sam	Barbados	Gold Coast	94	94
308	Royal Charlotte	Newport, RI	Lopez	Aaron	1773	Wright, Benj	Jamaica	Africa n/s		
309	Friendship		MacKenzie		1773		South Carolina	Gold Coast	162	140
310	Cleopatra	Newport, RI	Lopez	Aaron	1774	Bourke, James	Jamaica	Gold Coast	104	90
311	Cleopatra	Newport, RI	Rivera	Jacob	1774	Bourke, James	Jamaica	Gold Coast	104	90
312	Africa	Newport, RI	Wanton	Jos, Wm	1774	Boutin, John		Africa n/s		
313	Africa	Newport, RI	Lopez	Aaron	1774	Briggs, Nat	Barbados	Gold Coast	183	171
314	Africa	Newport, RI	Rivera	Jacob	1774	Briggs, Nat	Barbados	Gold Coast	183	171
315	Adventure	Newport, RI	Champlin	Christ, Geo	1774	Champlin, Robt	Grenada, St. Kitts	Gold Coast		
316	Nancy	Newport, RI	Clarke	Peleg	1774	Clarke, Peleg	Jamaica	Africa n/s	191	180
317	Nancy	Newport, RI	Fletcher	John	1774	Clarke, Peleg	Jamaica	Africa n/s	191	180
318	Othello	Newport, RI	Vernon	Saml, Wm	1774	Duncan, John	VA, RI	Gold Coast	58	52
319	Russell	Boston	Shoolbred*		1774	Dunn	Kingston, Jam	Gold Coast	318	275

No.	SHIP	VESSEL/CARGO OWNER			Date	Captain	SLAVES			
		Registration	Last	First			To	From	load	unload
320	Africa	Bristol, RI	Potter	Simeon	1774	DWolf, Mark Anthony	Jamaica	Africa n/s		
321	Polly	Newport, RI	Mason		1774	Elliot, Robert	Grenada	Africa n/s	101	90
322		Newport, RI	Lopez	Aaron	1774	Greene, Peleg		Windwd/Gold Coast		
323	Mill	Boston	Mill		1774	Hay	Jamaica	Gold Coast		
324	Mill	Boston	Ross*		1774	Hay	Jamaica	Gold Coast		
325	Fanny		Bruton*		1774	Mayne	So. Car.	Gold Coast	320	277
326	Thomas	Boston	Boylston		1774	McCarthy, Dan	Barbados	Gold Coast	208	180
327	Sally	Newport, RI	Gardner	Caleb	1774	Scarberry, Benjamin	Barbados	Africa n/s	75	61
328	Fanny	Newport, RI	Ayrault	Steph	1774	Stanton, John	Charleston	Gold Coast	112	60
329	Africa	Newport, RI	Collins	John	1774	Toman, Draper		Africa n/s	43	38
330	Betsey	Newport, RI	Wanton	Jos., Wm	1775	Auld, Abraham	St. Vincent	Gold Coast	150	133
331	Adventure	Newport, RI	Champlin	Christ, Geo	1775	Champlin, Robt	Jamaica	Gold Coast	103	92
332	Thames	Newport, RI	Clarke	Peleg	1775	Clarke, Peleg	Lucea, Jamaica	Gold Coast	348	297
333	Thames	Newport, RI	Fletcher	John	1775	Clarke, Peleg	Lucea, Jamaica	Gold Coast	348	297
334	Ann	Newport, RI	Lopez	Aaron	1775	English, Wm	Jamaica	Cape Coast	125	112
335	Wanton	Newport, RI	Wanton	Wm, Jos	1775	Mowatt, Geo	Barbados	Gold Coast	200	157
336	Fortune	Newport, RI	Wanton		1775	Remington, Benj		Gold Coast	150	130
337	Fletcher	Newport, RI	Clarke	Peleg	1775	Stockford	Kingston, Jam	Gold Coast		
338	Fletcher	Newport, RI	Fletcher	John	1775	Stockford	Kingston, Jam	Gold Coast		
339	Fletcher	Newport, RI	Pett	Jn	1775	Stockford	Kingston, Jam	Gold Coast		
340	Othello	Newport, RI	Vernon	Saml, Wm	1775	Sweet, George D	Mutego Bay, Jam	Sierra Leone	66	61
341	Mill	Boston	Ross*		1776	Hay	Grenada	Gold Coast	500	400
342	Mill	Boston	Shoolbred*		1776	Hay	Grenada	Gold Coast	500	400
343	Anthony	Salem, MA	Grafton	Jos, Joshua	1782	Nelson, Geo		Senegambia		
344	Gambia	Newpt / Salem	Grafton	Jos, Joshua	1785	Champlin, Robt	Charleston	Gold Coast	112	100
345	Prudence	Providence (RI)	Clark	Peleg	1785	Greene, Peleg	Georgia	Africa n/s	88	79
346	Prudence	Providence (RI)	Greene		1785	Greene, Peleg	Georgia	Africa n/s	88	79
347	Prudence	Providence (RI)	Nightingale		1785	Greene, Peleg	Georgia	Africa n/s	88	79
348	Prudence	Providence (RI)	Power	Nich	1785	Greene, Peleg	Georgia	Africa n/s	88	79
349	Prudence	Providence (RI)	Sterry	Cyprian	1785	Greene, Peleg	Georgia	Africa n/s	88	79

Select Eighteenth Century African Slaving Voyages

No.	SHIP	Registration	Last	First	Date	Captain	To	From	load	unload
		VESSEL/CARGO OWNER					SLAVES			
350	Africa	Salem, MA	Grafton	Jos.,Joshua	1785	Robinson		Gold Coast/Guinee	133	127
351	Don Galvez	Newport, RI	Brown	Sam	1785		unspecified	Africa n/s		
352	Favorite	Salem, MA	Grafton	Jos.,Joshua	1785		Martinique	Africa n/s	18	15
353		Grenada	Seymour		1785		UK	Africa n/s		
354	Don Galvez	Rhode Island	Vernon	Wm	1785		unspecified	Africa n/s	133	127
355	Gambia	Salem, MA	Grafton	Jos.,Joshua	1786	Boss, Ed	So. Car.	GC/Guinee	100	87
356	Collector	New England	Cabot		1786	Carnes, John	So. Car.	Sierra Leone	243	217
357	Collector	New England	Pierce		1786	Carnes, John	So. Car.	Sierra Leone	243	217
358		Newport, RI	Grafton	Jos.,Joshua	1786	Chilcutt	Charleston	Gold Coast	114	99
359	America	Providence	Cooke	John	1786	Cooke, Jos	n/s	Africa n/s	66	54
360	Don Galvez	Newport and Salem	Brown	Brown, Sam	1786	Grey	Trinidad	Africa n/s	114	93
361	Don Galvez	Newport and Salem	Brown	Vernon,Wm	1786	Grey	Trinidad	Africa n/s	114	93
362	Providence	Providence (RI)	Brown	John	1786	Wanton, Peter	n/s	Africa n/s	83	68
363	Louisa	Newport, RI	Spooner	Andrew	1787	Champlin, Robt	n/s	Africa n/s	121	99
364	Whim	Newport, RI	Clarke	Peleg	1787	Clarke, Peleg	n/s	Africa n/s	66	54
365	Providence	Providence (RI)	Brown		1787	DWolf, James	n/s	Africa n/s	88	72
366	Providence	Providence (RI)	Francis		1787	DWolf, James	n/s	Africa n/s	88	72
367	Enterprize	Bristol, RI	DWolf	Chas	1787	DWolf, John	St. East (Dutch Carib)		80	71
368	Washington	Newport, RI	Briggs	Nat	1787	Gardner, Wm	n/s	Africa n/s	55	45
369	Washington	Newport, RI	Gardner	Caleb	1787	Gardner, Wm	n/s	Africa n/s	55	45
370	Washington	Newport, RI	Taber	Constant	1787	Gardner, Wm	n/s	Africa n/s	55	45
371	Hannah	Newport, RI	Boss	John	1787	Remington, Benj	n/s	Africa n/s	66	54
372	Hannah	Newport, RI	Newman	Augustus	1787	Remington, Benj	n/s	Africa n/s	66	54
373	Hannah	Newport, RI	Topliam	John	1787	Remington, Benj	n/s	Africa n/s	66	54
374	Favorite	Salem, MA	Grafton	Jos.,Joshua	1787	Robinson, William	Martinique	Africa n/s		
375	Three Friends	Newport, RI	Briggs	Nat	1787	Shearman, Ebenezer	n/s	Africa n/s	116	95
376	Three Friends	Newport, RI	Rivera	Jacob*	1787	Shearman, Ebenezer	n/s	Africa n/s	116	95
377	Louisa	Newport, RI	Spooner	Andrew	1788	Carr, Isaac	n/s	Africa n/s	121	99
378	Whim	Newport, RI	Clarke	Peleg	1788	Clarke, Peleg	n/s	Africa n/s	66	54

NOTES ON THE STATE OF AMERICA

No.	SHIP	VESSEL/CARGO OWNER			Date	Captain	SLAVES			
		Registration	Last	First			To	From	load	unload
379	Nancy	Bristol, RI	Wardwell	Sam	1788	DWolf, James		Gold Coast	114	93
380	Washington	Newport, RI	Briggs	Nat	1788	Gardner, Wm	n/s	Africa n/s	55	45
381	Washington	Newport, RI	Ellery	Christ	1788	Gardner, Wm	n/s	Africa n/s	55	45
382	Washington	Newport, RI	Gardner	Caleb	1788	Gardner, Wm	n/s	Africa n/s	55	45
383	Washington	Newport, RI	Taber	Constant	1788	Gardner, Wm	n/s	Africa n/s	55	45
384	Washington	Newport, RI	Taber	Constant	1788	Gardner, Wm	n/s	Africa n/s	55	45
385	Washington	Newport, RI	Vernon	Sam	1788	Gardner, Wm	n/s	Africa n/s	55	45
386	Industry	Providence	Murray	John	1788	Hicks, Benj	n/s	Africa n/s	66	54
387	Industry	Providence	Sterry	Cyprian	1788	Hicks, Benj	n/s	Africa n/s	66	54
388	Hannah	Newport, RI	Boss	John	1788	Shearman, Ebenezer	Caribbean		114	93
389	Hannah	Newport, RI	Newman	Augustus	1788	Shearman, Ebenezer	Caribbean		114	93
390	Hannah	Newport, RI	Topham	John	1788	Shearman, Ebenezer	Caribbean		114	93
391	Hope	Newport, RI	Briggs	Nat	1788	Stanton, John	Martinique	Africa n/s	90	80
392	Hope	Newport, RI	Briggs	Nat	1788	Stanton, John	Caribbean	Africa n/s	130	116
393	Hope	Newport, RI	Gardner	Caleb	1788	Stanton, John	Martinique	Africa n/s	90	80
394	Hope	Newport, RI	Gardner	Caleb	1788	Stanton, John	Caribbean	Africa n/s	130	116
395	Marianne	France	Fatures	(Dame)	1788		n/s	Senegambia	116	101
396	Marianne	France	Gachinard	(Vve)	1788		n/s	Senegambia	116	101
397	Dove	Newport, RI	Briggs	Nat	1789	Batty, Jos			114	93
398	Dove	Newport, RI	Briggs	Nat	1789	Batty, Jos	n/s	Africa n/s	114	93
399	Dove	Newport, RI	Gardner	Caleb	1789	Batty, Jos			114	93
400	Nancy	Bristol, RI	Bourne	Shearjashub	1789	DWolf, John	n/s	Africa n/s	55	45
401	Felicity	Salem, MA	White	Jo	1789	Fairfield, William	Guianas	Sierra Leone	35	31
402	Pacific	Newport and Salem	Brown, Sam		1789	Gardner, Dan	St. Eustatius (Dutch Caribbean)		157	140
403	Pacific	Newport / Salem	Gardner	Dan	1789	Gardner, Dan	St. Eustatius (Dutch Caribbean)		157	140
404	Pacific	Newport / Salem	Tabor	Constant	1789	Gardner, Dan	St. Eustatius (Dutch Caribbean)		157	140
405	Pacific	Newport / Salem	Vernon	Wm	1789	Gardner, Dan	St. Eustatius (Dutch Caribbean)		157	140
406	Washington	Newport, RI	Gardner	Wm	1789	Gardner, Wm	Caribbean	Africa n/s	147	120
407	Betsey	Newport, RI	Gardner	Caleb	1789	Lawton, Sam	Caribbean	Africa n/s	114	93

284

Select Eighteenth Century African Slaving Voyages

No.	SHIP	VESSEL/CARGO OWNER Registration	Last	First	Date	Captain	To	From	SLAVES load	unload
408	Betsey	Newport, RI	Gibbs	Geo	1789	Lawton, Sam	Caribbean	Africa n/s	114	93
409	Ganganelli	Newport, RI	Benson	Martin	1789	Thurston, John	n/s	Africa n/s	114	93
410	Providence	Providence (RI)	Clark	John	1790	Bowen, Oliver	Havana	Africa n/s	87	78
411	Providence	Providence (RI)	Nightingale	Jos	1790	Bowen, Oliver	Havana	Africa n/s	87	78
412	Whim	Newport, RI	Clarke	Audley	1790	Briggs, Willard	Havana	Gold Coast	110	88
413	Abigail	Warren (RI)	Cole	Ebenezer	1790	Collins, Chas	n/s	Africa n/s	64	52
414	Abigail	Warren (RI)	Collins	Chas	1790	Collins, Chas	n/s	Africa n/s	64	52
415	Abigail	Warren (RI)	Level	Maxwell	1790	Collins, Chas	n/s	Africa n/s	64	52
416	Abigail	Warren (RI)	Maxwell	James	1790	Collins, Chas	n/s	Africa n/s	64	52
417	Nancy	Bristol, RI	DWolf	John, Jas	1790	DWolf, John	Havana	Gold Coast	58	52
418	Nancy	Bristol, RI	DWolf	Levi, Wm	1790	DWolf, John	Havana	Gold Coast	58	52
419	Betsey	Newport, RI	DWolf	Wm	1790	DWolf, Wm	n/s	Africa n/s	99	81
420	Betsey	Newport, RI	Gardner	Caleb	1790	DWolf, Wm	n/s	Africa n/s	99	81
421	Charlotte	Bristol, RI	DWolf	Wm	1790	Gorham, Isaac	n/s	Africa n/s	46	38
422	Betsey	Boston	Elliot	Simon	1790	Hallet, Allen	Saint-Domingue	Africa n/s	39	32
423	Nancey	Newport, RI	Huntington	David	1790	Huntington, Jos	n/s	Africa n/s		
424	Hope	Newport, RI	Briggs	Thom	1790	Stanton, John	Caribbean	Africa n/s	99	81
425	Polly	Bristol, RI	DWolf	James	1791	DWolf, James	Havana, Cuba	Africa n/s	122	121
426	Dove	Newport, RI	Briggs	Nat	1791	Gardner, Jos	Havana		97	91
427	Dove	Newport, RI	Gardner	Caleb	1791	Gardner, Jos	Havana		97	91
428	Abeona	Salem, MA	Sinclair	John	1791	Sinclair, John	Cuba	Sierra Leone	93	68
429	Abeona	Salem, MA	Waters	John	1791	Sinclair, John	Cuba	Sierra Leone	93	68
430	Sally	Providence	Graves	James	1791	Taber, Jeremiah	n/s	Africa n/s		
431	Sally	Providence	Valentine	Wm	1791	Taber, Jeremiah	n/s	Africa n/s		
432	Whim	Newport, RI	Clarke	Audley, P.	1792	Briggs, Willard	n/s	Africa n/s	110	90
433	Nancy	Bristol, RI	DWolf	John, Jas	1792	DWolf, Levi	n/s	Gold Coast	84	73
434	Nancy	Bristol, RI	DWolf	Levi, Wm	1792	DWolf, Levi	n/s	Gold Coast	84	73
435	Sally	Bristol, RI	DWolf	Wm	1792	DWolf, Wm	Havana	Africa n/s	120	98
436	Fanny	Newport, RI	Gardner	Caleb, Wm	1792	Gardner, Jos	n/s	Africa n/s		

285

NOTES ON THE STATE OF AMERICA

No.	SHIP	VESSEL/CARGO OWNER			Date	Captain	SLAVES			
		Registration	Last	First			To	From	load	unload
437	Mary	Newport, RI	Lassalle	Chas	1792	Geoffrey, Andrew	Havana	Africa n/s	221	197
438	Mary	Newport, RI	Lassalle	Chas	1792	Godfrey	n/s	Africa n/s	110	90
439	Don Galvez	Newport/Salem	Brown	James	1792	Grey	St. Eustatius, Dutch Caribb			114
440	Don Galvez	Newport/Salem	Vernon	Wm	1792	Grey	St. Eustatius, Dutch Caribb			114
441	Desire	Tiverton (RI)	Cook	John	1792	Hicks, Gabriel	Havana	Africa n/s	135	134
442	Patty	Bristol, RI	Bourn	Shearjashu	1792	Jacobs, Wilson	n/s	Africa n/s		
443	Patty	Bristol, RI	DWolf	John, Wm	1792	Jacobs, Wilson	n/s	Africa n/s		
444	Patty	Bristol, RI	Wardwell	Sam	1792	Jacobs, Wilson	n/s	Africa n/s		
445	Fair Eliza	Bristol, RI	DWolf	Chas	1792	Remington, Benj	Havana	Africa n/s	127	104
446	Fair Eliza	Bristol, RI	Ingraham	Jeremiah	1792	Remington, Benj	Havana	Africa n/s	127	104
447	Willing Quaker	Boston	McNeil	Daniel	1793	Adamson	Guianas	Sierra Leone	110	98
448	Willing Quaker	Boston	Perkins	J, & T H	1793	Adamson	Guianas	Sierra Leone	110	98
449	Sukey	Bristol, RI	DWolf	John	1793	Collins, Chas	Havana	Bight of Benin	128	104
450	Katy	Chastwn, MA	McNeil	Daniel	1793	Connelly (a) Conolly	Cuba	Sierra Leone		
451	Nancy	Providence (RI)	Allen	Zachariah, Ph	1793	Cooke, Jos	n/s	Africa n/s	121	99
452	Sally	Bristol, RI	DWolf		1793	DWolf	Havana	Africa n/s	120	98
453	Sukey	Bristol, RI	DWolf	John	1793	DWolf, John	Havana	Africa n/s	128	104
454	Diana	Bristol, RI	DWolf	Chas	1793	Gorham, Isaac	Savannah	Africa n/s	35	29
455	Diana	Bristol, RI	Gorham	Isaac	1793	Gorham, Isaac	Savannah	Africa n/s		
456	Diana	Bristol, RI	Ingraham	Jeremiah	1793	Gorham, Isaac	Savannah	Africa n/s	35	29
457	Washington	Newport, RI	Gardner	Caleb	1793	Hicks, Barney	Havana	Africa n/s	156	139
458	Susannah	Providence	Allen	Zachariah, Ph	1793	Jenckes, John	n/s	Africa n/s	112	91
459	Sally	Newport, RI	Clarke	Peleg	1793	Shearman, Geo	Havana	Gold Coast	69	62
460	Fair Eliza	Bristol, RI	DWolf	Chas	1793	Smith, Benedict	Havana	Africa n/s	127	44
461	Ascension	Newport/Salem	Brown	Sam	1793	Stanton, John	Havana	Africa n/s	240	214
462	Ascension	Newport/Salem	Clarke	Peleg	1793	Stanton, John	Havana	Africa n/s	240	214
463	Ascension	Newport/Salem	Gardner	Caleb	1793	Stanton, John	Havana	Africa n/s	240	214
464	Ascension	Newport/Salem	Vernon	Wm	1793	Stanton, John	Havana	Africa n/s	240	214
465	Enterprize	Providence (RI)	Sterry	Cyprian	1793	Sterry, Nathan	Savannah	Africa n/s	177	144

Select Eighteenth Century African Slaving Voyages

No.	SHIP	VESSEL/CARGO OWNER		Date	Captain		To	From	SLAVES		
		Registration	Last	First		Last	First		load	unload
466	Nancy	Bristol, RI	DWolf	John, Jas	1793	Usher, Hezekiah	Havana	Africa n/s	84	54
467	Nancy	Bristol, RI	DWolf	Levi, Wm	1793	Usher, Hezekiah	Havana	Africa n/s	84	54
468	Peatt	Newport, RI	Clarke	Peleg	1798	Vilett, John	Havana	Africa n/s	71	63
469	Hope	Newport, RI	Briggs	Nat	1793	Wood, Peleg (Jr)	Havana	Africa n/s	83	74
470	Hope	Newport, RI	Gardner	Caleb	1793	Wood, Peleg (Jr)	Havana	Africa n/s	83	74
471	Elizabeth	Newport, RI	Champlin	Christ, Geo	1793	Wood, Wm	n/s	Africa n/s	138	113
472	Hannah	Newport, RI	Briggs	Willard	1794	Almy, John	Havana	Gold Coast	110	116
473	Whim	Newport, RI	Clarke	Audley	1794	Ambrose, Robert	Havana	Gold Coast	221	197
474	Ascension	Newport/Salem	Brown	Sam	1794	Chace, Sam	Havana		221	197
475	Ascension	Newport/Salem	Clarke	Peleg	1794	Chace, Sam	Havana		221	197
476	Ascension	Newport/Salem	Gardner	Caleb	1794	Chace, Sam	Havana		221	197
477	Ascension	Newport/Salem	Vernon	Wm	1794	Chace, Sam	Havana		221	197
478	Dolphin	Providence	Mitchell	Edward	1794	Fuller, Gilbert	Savannah	Goree(Senegam)	52	49
479	Dolphin	Providence	Sterry	Cyprian	1794	Fuller, Gilbert	Savannah	Goree(Senegam)	52	49
480	Nancy	Charleston, S.C.	Macleod	William	1794	Hyer, Vincent	Savannah	Sierra Leone	69	62
481	Patty	Bristol, RI	Bourn	Shearjashub	1794	Jacobs, Wilson	Virgin Is, Cuba	Gold Coast	162	139
482	Patty	Bristol, RI	DWolf	John, Wm	1794	Jacobs, Wilson	Virgin Is, Cuba	Gold Coast	162	139
483	Patty	Bristol, RI	Wardwell	Sam	1794	Jacobs, Wilson	Virgin Is, Cuba	Gold Coast	162	139
484	Dove	Bristol, RI	DWolf	Chas	1794	Perry, James	Havana	Africa n/s	113	101
485	Dove	Bristol, RI	Ingraham	Jeremiah	1794	Perry, James	Havana	Africa n/s	113	101
486	NY Packet	Newport, RI	Hazard	Rowland	1794	Shaw, Wm	n/s	Africa n/s	64	52
487	NY Packet	Newport, RI	Robinson	John	1794	Shaw, Wm	n/s	Africa n/s	64	52
488	NY Packet	Newport, RI	Shaw	Wm	1794	Shaw, Wm	n/s	Africa n/s	64	52
489	Louisa	Providence	Sterry	Cyprian	1794	Sterry, Nathan	n/s	Africa n/s		89
490	Peatt	Newport, RI	Clarke	Peleg	1794	Villet, John	Havana	Africa n/s	99	88
491	James	Providence	Sterry	Cyprian	1795	Boss, Edward	Savannah	Windwrd Coast	110	98
492	Abigail	Warren (RI)	Bowen	Jon	1795	Bowen & Pardon	n/s	Gold Coast	64	55
493	Abigail	Warren (RI)	Hail	Pardon	1795	Bowen & Pardon	n/s	Gold Coast	64	55
494	Dolphin	Providence	Mitchell	Edw	1795	Fuller, Gilbert	Savannah	Senegambia	53	46
495	Dolphin	Providence	Sterry	Cyprian	1795	Fuller, Gilbert	Savannah	Senegambia	53	46

287

NOTES ON THE STATE OF AMERICA

No.	SHIP	VESSEL/CARGO OWNER			Date	Captain	SLAVES			
		Registration	Last	First			To	From	load	unload
496	Blackney	Bristol, RI	Bourn		1795	Gardner, Edward	n/s	Senegambia	47	41
497	Blackney	Bristol, RI	Wardwell		1795	Gardner, Edward	n/s	Senegambia	47	41
498	Polly	Providence	Sterry	Cyprian	1795	Gorham, Isaac	Savannah	Africa n/s	40	33
499	Washington	Newport, RI	Briggs	Nat	1795	Hicks, Barney	n/s	Gold Coast	147	127
500	Washington	Newport, RI	Clarke	Peleg	1795	Hicks, Barney	n/s	Gold Coast	147	127
501	Washington	Newport, RI	Gardner	Caleb	1795	Hicks, Barney	n/s	Gold Coast	147	127
502	General Greene	Providence (RI)	Packard	Sam	1795	Stanton, John	Savannah	Sierra Leone	99	88
503	General Greene	Providence (RI)	Sterry	Cyprian	1795	Stanton, John	Savannah	Sierra Leone	99	88
504	Enterprize	Providence (RI)	Sterry	Cyprian	1795	Sterry, Nathan	Savannah	Senegambia	167	149
505	Peatt	Newport, RI	Clarke	Audley, Peleg	1795	Vilett, John	n/s	Gold Coast	74	64
506	William	Newport, RI	Gardner	Caleb	1795	Wood, Peleg (Jr)	Savannah	Gold Coast	153	132
507	Whim	Newport, RI	Clarke	Audley	1796	Ambrose	Savannah	Gold Coast	110	95
508	Hannah	Newport, RI	Briggs	Willard	1796	Cook, Thaddeus	Havana	Sierra Leone	136	141
509	Charleston	Charleston, S.C.	Martin	Thomas	1796	Harris, Charles	Savannah	Windwrd Coast	364	330
510	Charleston	Charleston, S.C.	Price	John	1796	Harris, Charles	Savannah	Windwrd Coast	364	330
511	Nancy	Charleston, S.C.	Macleod	William	1796	Hewit, James	Savannah	Goree/Senegam	70	61
512	Friend's Adventure	Charleston, S.C.	Macleod	William	1796	Hyer, Vincent	Savannah, GA	Gambia	73	64
513	Sally	Bristol, RI	DWolf	John, Wm	1796	Manchester, Isaac	Savannah	Gold Coast	167	149
514	Fair Eliza	Bristol, RI	DWolf	Chas	1796	Smith, Benedict	Savannah	Gold Coast	127	110
515	Fair Eliza	Bristol, RI	Ingraham	Jeremiah	?	Smith, Benedict	Savannah	Gold Coast	127	110
516	General Greene	Providence (RI)	Sterry	Cyprian	1796	Stanton, John	Savannah	(Iles de)/Sierra L.	99	88
517	Fame	Charleston, S.C.	Benson	Martin	1797	Benson, Martin	Charleston	Sierra Leone		
518	Fame	Charleston, S.C.	Brown		1797	Benson, Martin	Charleston	Sierra Leone		
519	Fame	Charleston, S.C	Ives		1797	Benson, Martin	Charleston	Sierra Leone		
520	Liberty	Providence (RI)	Potter	Abijah	1797	Prentice, Thomas	Savannah	Africa n/s	116	9.5
521	Liberty	Providence (RI)	Smith	Amassa	1797	Prentice, Thomas	Savannah	Africa n/s	116	9.5
522	Ascension	Newp/ Salem	Brown	Sam	1798	Chace, Samuel	Montevideo	Mozambique	250	217
523	Ascension	Newp/ Salem	Clarke	Peleg	1798	Chace, Samuel	Montevideo	Mozambique	250	217
524	Ascension	Newp/ Salem	Gardner	Caleb	1798	Chace, Samuel	Montevideo	Mozambique	250	217
525	Ascension	Newp/ Salem	Vernon	Wm	1798	Chace, Samuel	Montevideo	Mozambique	250	217

Notes

Introduction

[1] See Reza Aslan, "He Could Care Less About Obama's Story," *The Washington Post*, December 30, 2007, p. B03.

Chapter One:
All In The Family

[2] James W. Loewen, *Lies My Teacher Told Me: Everything Your American History Textbook Got Wrong* (New York: Touchstone/Simon & Schuster, 1995), p. 15.

[3] Elizabeth Fox-Genovese, *Within the Plantation Household: Black and White Women of the Old South* (Chapel Hill: Univ. of No. Car. Press, 1988), p. 315 (emphasis added).

[4] James Mellon, ed., *Bullwhip Days: The Slaves Remember: An Oral History.* (New York: Weidenfeld & Nicolson, 1988), p. 55.

[5] Harriet Jacobs, *Incidents in the Life of a Slave Girl* (New York: Penguin/Signet Classic, 2000), pp. 3, 5.

[6] Mellon, *Bullwhip Days*, p. 15.

[7] Christine Stansell, *The Nation*, March 27, 1989, v.248, no. 12, p. 417-23; Winthrop D. Jordan, *Civil War History*, Dec. 1991, vol. 37, no. 4, p. 350.

[8] Stansell, *The Nation*, p. 417-23; Jacqueline Jones, "One Big Happy Family?" *Women's Review of Books*, vol. 6, no. 5, Feb. 1989, p. 4.

[9] Jacobs, *Life of a Slave Girl*, pp. 30-37.

[10] Frederick Douglass, "Narrative Of The Life of Frederick Douglass, An American Slave, Written By Himself," in *The Classic Slave Narratives,* Henry Louis Gates, Jr., ed. (New York: Signet, 1987), pp. 341-42.

[11] Fox-Genovese, p. 302.

[12] Quoted in *The Founding Fathers: James Madison, A Biography In His Own Words*, Merrill D. Peterson, ed. (New York: Newsweek/Harper Row, 1974), p. 216.

[13] *The Founding Fathers: James Madison, A Biography In His Own Words*, Merrill D. Peterson, ed. (New York: Newsweek/Harper Row, 1974), p. 215.

[14] Frances Anne Kemble, *Journal of a Residence on a Georgian*

Plantation in 1838-1839, ed. John A. Scott (New York: Alfred A. Knopf 1961), p. 4.

[15] Frances Kemble, *Journal*, p. 234. See also, Harriet Martineau, Retrospect Of Western Travel, 1838, quoted in *The Founding Fathers: James Madison*, p. 379.

[16] Fox-Genovese, p. 332.

[17] Fox-Genovese, p. 392.

[18] Fox-Genovese, p. 394.

[19] *Encarta World English Dictionary* (New York: St. Martin's, 1999); Compton's Interactive Dictionary © 1998 The Learning Company, Inc.; *American Heritage Dictionary of the English Language*, 3d. Edition (Houghton Mifflin, 1992).

[20] Peter H. Wood, Black Majority: Negroes in Colonial South Carolina, From 1670 through the Stono Rebellion (New York: Knopf, 1974), p. 286.

[21] Wood, *Black Majority*, pp. 221-24, 238.

[22] Friedrich Nietzsche, *Beyond Good and Evil: Prelude To A Philosophy Of The Future* (New York: e, 1990), p. 67.

[23] Captain Theophilus Conneau, *A Slaver's Log Book, Or 20 Years' Residence in Africa* (Englewood Cliffs, NJ: Prentice-Hall 1976), p. 55.

[24] George Bourne, *Slavery Illustrated in its Effects Upon Woman and Domestic Society* (Boston: Isaac Knaap, 1937/1972, ISBN: 0-8369-9174-5), pp. 57-58.

[25] Captain Conneau, *A Slaver's Log Book*, p. 81-86.

[26] Fox-Genovese, p. 206.

[27] Neal M. Rosendorf, "American Slavery Was Never Simple or Stable," *The Christian Science Monitor*, October 15, 1998, vol. 90, no. 225, p. B6.

[28] Ira Berlin, Marc Favreau, and Steven F. Miller, eds., *Remembering Slavery: African Americans Talk About Their Personal Experiences of Slavery* (New York: The New Press, 1998), p. xliv.

[29] Ira Berlin, "Before We Apologize, We Should Learn What Slavery Means." *The Washington Post*, June 29, 1997, p. C5.

[30] *Remembering Slavery*, p. xxviii.

[31] Ira Berlin, *Many Thousands Gone: The First Two Centuries of Slavery In North America* (Cambridge: Harvard Press, 1998), p. 137 (emphases added).

[32] "Diary of John Harrower, 1773-1776," *American Historical Review*, October 1900, p. 91.

[33] Edmund S. Morgan, "The Big American Crime," *The New York Review of Books*, Dec. 3, 1998, vol. 45, no. 19, p. 14; Jon Sensbach,

"Many Thousands Gone" (Book review), *The Journal of Southern History*, May 2001, vol. 67, no.2, p. 428;.

[34] *Many Thousands Gone*, p. 158 (emphasis added).

[35] Beth Day, *Sexual Life Between Blacks and Whites* (World Publishing, New York 1972), p. 145.

[36] Coco Fusco, "Hustling For Dollars," *Ms. Arlington*, Sept./Oct. 1996, vol. 7, no. 2, pp. 62-71.

[37] Beth Day, *Sexual Life*, p. 37.

[38] Theodore Weld, *American Slavery As It Is* (New York: Arno Press, 1968), p. 97.

[39] *Slavery Illustrated*, pp. 59-60 (emphasis added).

[40] *The Negro American Family* (1908), W.E.B. Du Bois, ed. (Negro Universities Press, NY 1969 reprint edition), p.25, citing Will Goodsell (NY 1853), *The American slave code in theory and practice. Judicial decisions and illustrative facts*.

[41] *Many Thousands Gone*, p. 158.

[42] Robin Blackburn, *The Making of New World Slavery: From the Baroque to the Modern, 1492-1800* (New York: Verso, 1997), pp. 10, 82.

[43] Captain Conneau, *A Slaver's Log Book*, pp. 69-70, quote on 104-05. See also, Edward Countryman, *Americans: A Collision of Histories* (London: LB Tauris & Co. Ltd., 1997), p. 27; David Richardson, "West African Consumption Patterns and Their Influence on the Eighteenth-Century English Slave Trade" in, *The Uncommon Market: Essays of the Economic History of the Atlantic Slave Trade*, Henry A Gemery and Jan S. Hogendorn, eds. (New York: Academic Press, 1979), pp. 303-330.

[44] Joseph C. Miller, "Commercial Organization of Slaving at Luanda, Angola — 1760-1830," in *The Uncommon Market: Essays of the Economic History of the Atlantic Slave Trade*, Henry A Gemery and Jan S. Hogendorn, eds. (New York: Academic Press, 1979), pp. 89, 94.

[45] Miller, "Slaving at Luanda," p. 97 (citations omitted).

[46] Thomas Pakenham, *The Scramble For Africa: The White Man's Conquest of the Dark Continent from 1876 to 1912* (New York: Random House, 1991), p. 17.

Chapter Two:
Negotiations

[47] Lerone Bennett, Jr., *The Shaping of Black America: The Struggles and Triumphs of African-Americans, 1619 to the 1990s* (New York:

Penguin Books, 1993), p. 146.

[48] Dorothy Sterling, (book review) *The Journal of Southern History*, August 1990, vol. 56, no. 3, p. 528.

[49] *Many Thousands Gone*, p. 265.

[50] Frederick Douglass, "Narrative," pp. 352-53 (emphasis added).

[51]"Narrative of William W. Brown, An American Slave, Written By Himself," London, 1849, in *The Civitas Anthology of African American Slave Narratives* (Washington, D.C.: Civitas/Counterpoint, 1999), William L. Andrews and Henry Louis Gates, eds. pp 218-19

[52] Cornel West, *Race Matters* (Boston: Beacon, 1993), p. 15.

[53] Winthrop Jordan, *White Over Black: American Attitudes Toward the Negro, 1550-1812* (Chapel Hill: Univ. N. Car. Press, 1968), pp. 55-56.

[54] John Locke, *Two Treatises Of Government*, Ian Shapiro ed. (Yale, 2003), p. 110.

[55] Louis Hughes, *Thirty Years A Slave: From Bondage To Freedom* (Montgomery: NewSouth, 2002), pp. 17-18, 25-29, 42, 60-61. See also, Jacobs, *Life of a Slave Girl.*

[56] Morgan, *The New York Review of Books*, p. 16.

[57] Jordan, *White Over Black*, pp. 55-56 (emphasis added); Howard Zinn, *A People's History of the United States, 1492-Present* (New York: Harper Collins, 1999, Perennial Classics edition), p. 35; James Oliver Horton and Lois E. Horton, *Slavery and the Making of America* (New York: Oxford Univ. Press, 2005), p. 11.

[58] Countryman, *Collision of Histories*, p. 13.

[59] Morgan, *American Slavery*, p. 312.

[60] Morgan, *American Slavery*, p. 312.

[61] Morgan, *American Slavery*, p. 313; *Hening II*, p. 270.

[62] Howard Zinn, *A People's History of the United States, 1492-Present* (New York: Harper Collins, 1999, Perennial Classics edition), p. 35.

[63] Robert McColley, *Slavery And Jeffersonian Virginia* (Urbana: Univ. of Ill., 1964), p. 98; See *A Narrative Of The Adventures And Escape Of Moses Roper From American Slavery, With a Preface By The Rev. T. Price, D.D., Philadelphia, 1838*, pp. 48-49; "Narrative of William W. Brown," pp 261-263; "Burning of a Negro at the Stake," *Harpers's Weekly*, February 5, 1859, p.86; Theodore Weld (1839), *American Slavery As It Is: Testimony of a Thousand Witnesses* (New York: Arno Press, 1968), pp. 66, 77-82; Blackburn, *New World Slavery*, p. 324.

[64] Yael Danieli, PhD, ed. "International Handbook of Multigenerational Legacies of Trauma," in *PTSD Research Quarterly*,

Winter 1997, vol. 8, no. 1, issn 1050-1835, pp. 2, 5.

[65] Thomas Jefferson, "Notes On The State Of Virginia," (1784), in *The Complete Jefferson, Containing His Major Writings, Published and Unpublished, Except His Letters,* Saul K. Padover, ed. (New York. Duell, Sloan, & Pearce, 1943 War Edition), p. 677.

[66] Martineau, *Retrospect,* quoted in *The Founding Fathers: James Madison,* p. 378.

[67] Madison to Robert J. Evans, June 15, 1819, in *The Founding Fathers: James Madison,* p. 372.

[68] Martineau, *Retrospect,* quoted in *The Founding Fathers: James Madison,* p. 377.

[69] Madison to Robert J. Evans, June 15, 1819, in *The Founding Fathers: James Madison,* p. 372.

[70] Martineau, *Retrospect,* quoted in *The Founding Fathers: James Madison,* p. 378.

Chapter Three:
Racism Matters

[71] Morgan, *N.Y. Review of Books,* p. 16.

[72] Morgan, *N.Y. Review of Books,* p. 15.

[73] Morgan, *N.Y. Review of Books,* p. 15.

[74] David Frum, "How The West Was Won: History That Feels Good Usually Isn't," *Foreign Affairs,* Sep/Oct 1998. Vol. 77, no. 5, pp. 132-35.

[75] Morgan, *N.Y. Review of Books,* p. 16, emphases added.

[76] Morgan, *N.Y. Review of Books,* p. 15.

[77] Morgan, *N.Y. Review of Books,* p. 16.

[78] Morgan, *N.Y. Review of Books,* p. 16.

[79] Morgan, *N.Y. Review of Books,* p. 18.

[80] OpinionJournal, CNBC, April, 2002.

[81] Allan Kulikoff, *Tobacco and Slaves: The Development of Southern Cultures in the Chesapeake, 1680-1800* (Chapel Hill: UNC Press, 1986), p38.

[82] Earle Shorris, "Our Next Race Question: The Uneasiness Between Blacks And Latinos." *Harper's Magazine,* April, 1996, p. 62.

[83] Morgan, *New York Review of Books,* pp. 16, 18.

[84] David S. Landes, *The Wealth And Poverty Of Nations: Why Some Are So Rich And Some So Poor* (New York: W.W. Norton, 1999), p. 118.

[85] James W. Loewen, *Lies My Teacher Told Me: Everything Your American History Textbook Got Wrong* (New York:

Touchstone/Simon & Schuster, 1995), pp. 25, 44, 50-53, 72.

[86] James W. Loewen, *Lies My Teacher Told Me: Everything Your American History Textbook Got Wrong* (New York: Touchstone/Simon & Schuster, 1995), pp. 299-311.

[87] Julie Landsman, *A White Teacher Talks About Race* (Lanham, MD: Scarecrow Press, Inc., 2001), p. 34.

[88] Peter Wood, *Diversity: The Invention Of A Concept* (San Francisco: Encounter, 2003), pp. 13, 16.

[89] *Notes of Debates in the Federal Convention of 1787: Reported by James Madison* (Ohio University Press, 1966), pp. 76-7.

[90] James Madison, "Federalist no. 10", *The Federalist Papers*, Clinton Rossiter, ed. (New York: Penguin, 1961), pp. 78-81.

[91] Peter Wood, *Diversity: The Invention Of A Concept* (San Francisco: Encounter, 2003), p. 13.

[92] *Debates in the Federal Convention*, p. 224 (emphasis added).

[93] Madison, "Federalist no. 51", The Federalist Papers, pp. 323-24; *Debates in the Federal Convention*, p. 77.

[94] Address to the Virginia Convention, December 2, 1829, in *The Founding Fathers: James Madison, A Biography In His Own Words*, Merrill D. Peterson, ed. (New York: Newsweek/Harper Row, 1974), pp. 390-91.

[95] Madison to Lafayette, February 1, 1830, in *The Founding Fathers: James Madison,* p. 395.

[96] See Loewen, *Lies My Teacher Told Me*; Julie Landsman, *A White Teacher Talks About Race* (Lanham, MD: Scarecrow Press, Inc., 2001).

[97] Michael Levin, *Why Race Matters: Race Differences and What They Mean* (Westport: Praeger, 1997), pp. 194-95 (citations omitted).

[98] Countryman, *Collision of Histories*, p. 9.

[99] Loewen, *Lies My Teacher Told Me*, p. 68.

[100] Bennett, *Black America*, pp. 68-73.

[101] Paul Gottfried, "Why Race Matters." (Book review) *Society*, Nov.-Dec. 1998, vol. 36, no. 1, p. 91-94.

[102] Reginald Horsman, *Race and Manifest Destiny: The Origins of American Racial Anglo-Saxonism* (Cambridge: Harvard, 1981), p. 191.

Chapter Four:
Media & Politics

[103] Alexandra Starr and Paul Magnasson, "After Sharpton: The Great Black Hopes," *BusinessWeek*, April 12, 2004, p. 47.

[104] Henry Louis Gates, Jr., "The Powell Perplex" in, *Thirteen Ways of Looking at a Black Man,* (New York: Random House, 1997), p. 74.

[105] July 31, 2000 at the Republican National Convrntion, (url: www.msnbc.com/news/440123.asp).

[106] Beth Potier, "Abolish prisons, says Angela Davis." *Harvard University Gazette,* March 13, 2003, p. 9.

[107] Jewell Handy Gresham (1989), "The Politics of Family in America," in *Experiencing Race, Class, and Gender in the United States* (Mountain View, CA: Mayfield Publishing Co., 1993), p. 197; see also Gerald Markowitz and David Rosner, *Children, Race and Power* (Charlottesville, 1996), pp. 134-35. cf Patricia J. Williams, "Rush Limbaugh's Inner Black Child," *The Nation,* October 23, 2003, vol. 277, no. 13, p. 11.

[108] Frank Rich, "The Weight of an Anchor." *The New York Times Magazine,* May 19, 2002, p. 37.

[109] Frank Rich, "The Weight of an Anchor." *The New York Times Magazine,* May 19, 2002, p. 66.

[110] Jack Mccallum, "Citizen Barkley," *Sports Illustrated,* March 11, 2002, p. 37.

[111] "White House: Bush misstated report on Iraq." *MSNBC,* September 7, 2002.

[112] Fox Butterfield, "Study Finds Big Increase in Black Men as Inmates Since 1980." *The New York Times,* August 28, 2002; Beth Potier, "Abolish prisons, says Angela Davis." *Harvard University Gazette,* March 13, 2003, p. 9.

[113] Joshua Hammer, "How Two Lives Met In Death," *Newsweek,* April 15, 2002, pp. 20-22.

[114] See Lara Jakes Jordan, "Big-city murders jump more than 10 pct." Associated Press, Thu Mar 8, 2007.

[115] Lynne Duke, "How Big a Stretch?" *The Washington Post,* Monday May 7, 2007, p. C01.

[116] Michael Ignatieff, "The Burden," *The New York Times Magazine,* January 5, 2003.

[117] W.E.B. Du Bois (1898). "The Study Of The Negro Problems," in *The Annals of The American Academy of Political and Social Science,* v.568 (March 2000), p. 14; Orlando Patterson, *Rituals of Blood: Consequences of Slavery in Two American Centuries* (Washington D.C.: Civitas/Counterpoint, 1998), passim; Robert Brent Toplin, *Freedom And Prejudice, The Legacy of Slavery in the United States and Brazil.* (Westport, Conn, Greenwood Press 1981), p. 113; Eugene D. Genovese, *The World The Slaveholders Made,* (New

York: Pantheon, 1972), p. 430.

[118] Cornel West, *Race Matters* (Boston: Beacon, 1993), p. 14.

[119] Audrey F. Saftlas, Lisa M. Koonin and Hani K. Atrash, "Racial Disparity in Pregnancy-related Mortality Associated with Livebirth: Can Established Risk Factors Explain It?" *American Journal of Epidemiology*, 2000, 152(5): 413-419.

[120] Beth Day, *Sexual Life*, p. 38, citing Kenneth M. Stampp, *The Peculiar Institution: Slavery in the Antebellum South* (New York: Random House, 1956), p. 319-20.

[121] Frances Kemble, *Journal*, pp.229-30,.244-48; *Many Thousands Gone*, p. 111-12, 149; Daniel H. Usner, "From African Captivity to American Slavery: The Introduction of Black Laborers to Colonial Louisiana." *Louisiana History*, vol. 20, 1979, p. 38.

[122] "Blacks Get Poorer Care Than Whites Even In Similar Health Plans." *Associated Press*, March 12, 2002. see also, Madeline Drexler, "The People's Epidemiologists," *Harvard Magazine*, March/April 2006, vol. 108, no. 4, pp. 25-33.

[123] Audrey F. Saftlas, Lisa M. Koonin and Hani K. Atrash, "Racial Disparity in Pregnancy-related Mortality Associated with Livebirth: Can Established Risk Factors Explain It?," *American Journal of Epidemiology*, 2000, 152(5): 413-419; see also, "Breaking The Chains," *Essence*, Jan. 12, 2005 (url: http://www.essence.com/essence/lifestyle/voices/0,16109,1016958,00.html.).

[124] Judith Gaines, "3 Questions, 3 Answers," *Yankee*, Sept. 2004, vol. 68, no. 7, p. 126.

[125] Fox NFL Sunday, October 5, 2003.

[126] Charles J. Ogletree, Jr., *All Deliberate Speed: Reflections on the First Half Century of Brown v. Board of Education* (New York: W.W. Norton, 2004), pp. 72, 73.

[127] The Today Show, August 1, 2000 (url: www.msnbc.com/news/438365.asp).

[128] "Our law, your law" in "Present at the Creation: A survey of America's world role." Special supplement to *The Economist*, June 29th, 2002, p. 20.

[129] July 31, 2000 at the Republican National Convrntion, (url: www.msnbc.com/news/440123.asp).

[130] Hugh Price on The NewsHour with Jim Lehrer, August 27, 2001.

[131] The NewsHour, August 27, 2001.

[132] "The Powell Perplex," pp. 80-81.

[133] "The Powell Perplex," pp. 82-84.

[134] See Reza Aslan, "He Could Care Less About Obama's Story," *The Washington Post*, December 30, 2007, p. B03.

Chapter Five:
Employment

[135] Stephan Thernstrom & Abigail Thernstrom, *America in Black and White, One Nation Indivisible: Race in Modern America* (New York: Simon & Shuster 1997), pp. 253, 256.

[136] Charles Stein, "Our invisible dropouts." *The Boston Globe*, Dec.10, 2002, p. C1 (emphasis added).

[137] Joe R. Feagin, Melvin P. Sikes, *Living With Racism: The Black Middle-Class Experience* (Boston: Beacon, 1994), p. 153-54.

[138] "Why Teens Aren't Finding Jobs, and Why Employers Are Paying the Price," *Knowledge@Wharton*, March 07, 2007

[139] See, Steven Greenhouse, "Forced to Work Off the Clock, Some Fight Back," *The New York Times*, November 19, 2004; George Lipsitz, *The Progressive Investment in Whiteness: How White People Profit from Identity Politics* (Phila.: Temple University, 1998), p. 51.

[140] David S. Landes, *The Wealth And Poverty Of Nations: Why Some Are So Rich And Some So Poor* (New York: W.W. Norton, 1999), p. 63.

[141] Thernstrom, *America in Black and White,* pp. 247-50.

[142] "The kamikazes of poverty: Mexico's immigration problem." *The Economist,* January 31, 2004, vol. 370, no. 8360, p. 33.

[143] Thernstrom, *America in Black and White,* p. 251.

[144] Deborah Mathis, *Yet A Stranger: Why Black Americans Still Don't Feel At Home* (New York: Time Warner, 2002), pp. 117-121; John P. Fernandez, *Race, Gender & Rhetoric: The True State of Race and Gender Relations in Corporate America* (New York: McGraw Hill, 1999), p. 39; Jody David Armour, *Negrophobia and Reasonable Racism: The Hidden Costs of Being Black in America* (New York: NYU, 1997), p. 46; Lawrence Blum, *"I'm Not A Racist But..." The Moral Quandry of Race* (Ithace: Cornell, 2002), pp. 85-90.

[145] See Yvonne Abraham, "Diversity still lagging in Bay State boardrooms," *The Boston Globe,* May 11, 2007; Adam Liptak, "Lawyers Debate Why Blacks Lag At Major Firms," *The New York Times*, Nov. 29, 2006; Marcella Bombardieri and Andrew Ryan, "MIT dean of admissions resigns for falsifying resume," *The Boston Globe,* April 26, 2007; Lisa Takeuchi Cullen, "Getting Wise to Lies," *TIME,* Apr. 24, 2006.

[146] Linda Lee Small, "What White Women Are Really Saying About

Us!" *Essence*, March 2003, vol. 33, no.11, p. 154.

[147] Ella L. J. Edmondson Bell and Stella M. Nkomo, *Our Separate Ways: Black and White Women and The struggle For Professional Identity* (Boston: Harvard Business School, 2001), p. 145; David K. Shipler, *A Country Of Strangers: Blacks and Whites In America* (New York: Knopf, 1997), pp. 409-20; Joe R. Feagin, Melvin P. Sikes, *Living With Racism: The Black Middle-Class Experience* (Boston: Beacon, 1994), p. 145.

[148] Ayelet Shachar (2007) "The Worth of Citizenship in an Unequal World," *Theoretical Inquiries in Law*: Vol. 8 : No. 2, Article 2, pp. 369-77 (http://www.bepress.com/til/default/vol8/iss2/art2) emphasis in original.

[149] Ayelet Shachar (2007) "The Worth of Citizenship in an Unequal World," *Theoretical Inquiries in Law*: Vol. 8 : No. 2, Article 2, p. 385 (http://www.bepress.com/til/default/vol8/iss2/art2) emphasis in original.

[150] Jennifer Loven, "Diversity Lags in Most Newsrooms," Associated Press, April 11, 2002.

[151] Ellen Christian, "ASNE Keeps Pushing For Diversity," *The Quill*, Dec. 2004, vol. 92, no. 9, p. 16.

[152] Bill Dedman, "Newspapers Fall Short Of Diversity Goal," *The Boston Globe*, April 11, 2002.

[153] Ellen Christian, "ASNE Keeps Pushing For Diversity," *The Quill*, Dec. 2004, vol. 92, no. 9, p. 16.

[154] Anonymous, "Journalists of Color Work Toward Increasing Newsroom Diversity," *Black Issues in Higher Education,* May 5, 2005, vol. 22, no. 6, p. 11.

[155] Anonymous, "Journalists of Color Work Toward Increasing Newsroom Diversity," *Black Issues in Higher Education,* May 5, 2005, vol. 22, no. 6, p. 11.

[156] See, "L.A. Times, Philadelphia Inquirer Face Pressure of Newsroom Job Cuts," The NewsHour with Jim Lehrer, Nov. 10, 2006 (url: http://www.pbs.org/newshour/bb/media/july-dec06/press_11-10.html).

[157] See, Fischer, Hout, Jankowski, Lucas, Swindler, and Voss, *Inequality by Design* (Princeton, 1996).

[158] John Leo, "Conventional Diversity," *U.S. News & World Report*, July 26, 1999 (url: www.usnews.com/usnews/opinion/articles/990726/archive_001512.htm).

[159] Jawanza Kunjufu, *State of Emergency: We Must Save African*

American Males (Chicago: AAI, 2001), p. 65.

160 Rhonda M. Williams, "Culture as Human Capital: Methodological and Policy Implications, " *Praxis International*, July 1987, vol. 7, no. 2, p. 156.

161 Suzanne C. Ryan, "Brokaw to pass 'Nightly News' baton to Williams." *The Boston Globe*, May 29, 2002, p. D1.

162 Kim Masters, "Mo' News is Bad News." *Esquire*, January, 2002, pp. 42-44.

163 Williams, "Man of the Hour," *Vanity Fair*, p. 95.

164 Williams, "Man of the Hour," *Vanity Fair*, p. 95.

165 Suzanne C. Ryan, "Brokaw to pass 'Nightly News' baton to Williams." *The Boston Globe*, May 29, 2002, p. D5.

166 Frank Rich, "The Weight of an Anchor." *The New York Times Magazine*, May 19, 2002, p. 36.

167 "Man of the Hour," p. 92.

168 Frank Rich, "The Weight of an Anchor." *The New York Times Magazine*, May 19, 2002, p. 66.

169 "Man of the Hour," p. 95.

170 Frank Rich, "The Weight of an Anchor." *The New York Times Magazine*, May 19, 2002, p. 66.

171 "Man of the Hour," p. 95.

172 "Man of the Hour," p. 95 (emphasis added).

173 "Man of the Hour," p. 93 (emphasis added).

174 Fernandez, *Race Relations in Corporate America*, p. 23-32.

175 Claude S. Fischer, Michael Hout, Martin Sanchez Jankowski, Samuel R. Lucas, Ann Swindler, and Kim Voss, *Inequality by Design: Cracking The Bell Curve Myth* (Princeton 1996), p.103; see also Beverly Daniel Tatum, *Why Are All the Black Kids sitting Together in the Cafeteria?: And Other Conversations About Race.* (New York: Basic Books, 1999), p. 126; Stephen L. Carter, *Reflections of an Affirmative Action Baby* (New York: Basic/Harper Collins, 1991), p. 18.

176 Frank Rich, "The Weight of an Anchor." *The New York Times Magazine*, May 19, 2002, p. 66.

177 J. Max Robins, "Chaos At ABC News," *Variety*, Jan. 1994, vol. 353, no. 10, p.45.

178 Judith Gaines, "3 Questions, 3 Answers," *Yankee*, Sept. 2004, vol. 68, no. 7, p. 126.

179 "To The News Biz Born," *People Weekly*, July 12, 1993, vol. 40, no. 2, p.93.

180 "To The News Biz Born," *People Weekly*, July 12, 1993, vol. 40,

no. 2, p.93.

[181] Landsman, *A White Teacher*, p. 28, quote on p. 65, 66.

[182] Rhonda M. Williams, "Culture as Human Capital: Methodological and Policy Implications, " *Praxis International*, July 1987, vol. 7, no. 2, p. 156.

[183] Landsman, *White Teacher*, p. 26.

[184] See Beverly Daniel Tatum, *Why Are All the Black Kids sitting Together in the Cafeteria?: And Other Conversations About Race.* (New York: Basic Books, 1999)

[185] Katherine S. Newman, *No Shame In My Game: The Working Poor IinThe Inner City* (New York: Knopf, 1999), pp. 155-56.

[186] Huntington, *Who Are We?* p. 157.

[187] Huntington, *Who Are We?* p. 150.

[188] Huntington, *Who Are We?* p. 23.

[189] Michael Elliott, "New Patriots In Our Midst," *Time*, April 12, 2004, v. 163, no. 15, p. 52.

[190] Daniel Lazare, "Diversity And Its Discontents," *The Nation*, June 14, 2004, v. 278, no. 23, p. 18.

[191] Geraldine Hawkins, "American Legal System Is Corrupt Beyond Recognition, Judge Tells Harvard Law School." MassNews.com, *http://www.massnews.com/2003_Editions/3_March/030703_mn_ame rican_legal_system_corrupt.shtml*

[192] Nate Blakeslee, "The Worst Judges In Texas," *The Texas Observer*, February 10, 2006 (url: http://www.texasobserver.org/article.php?aid=2132).

[193] Geraldine Hawkins, "American Legal System Is Corrupt Beyond Recognition, Judge Tells Harvard Law School." MassNews.com, *http://www.massnews.com/2003_Editions/3_March/030703_mn_ame rican_legal_system_corrupt.shtml*

[194] Charles A. Beard, *An Economic Interpretation Of The Constitution Of The United States* (New York: Free Press, 1913/1986), p. 161.

[195] "A Bigot in Congress," *The Washington Post*, December 22, 2006; p. A32 (url:http://www.washingtonpost.com/wp-dyn/content/article/2006/12/21/AR2006122101612.html.

Chapter Six:
Criminal Just-Us

[196] Randy Cohen, The Ethicist: "The Prosecution Rests," *The New York Times Magazine*, May 23, 2004, p. 15.

197 Mark Fazlollah, Dylan Purcell and Keith Herbert, "Suburban Cops, Tough Tactics," *The Philadelphia Inquirer*, Dec. 15, 2007.
198 Fox Butterfield, "Despite Drop In Crime, An Increase In Inmates," *The New York Times*, Nov. 8, 2004, P. A14.
199 Richard Delgado, "Rodrigo's Eighth Chronicle: Black Crime, White Fears—On The Social Construction Of Threat," *80 Virginia Law Review 503* (1994).
200 See Bill Dedman, "Police chiefs decry profiling study," *The Boston Globe*, May 5, 2004.
201 See Kevin Joy, "Roxbury, Mattapan rap police in survey," *The Boston Globe*, May 12, 2004.
202 Michael W. Lynch, "Battlefield Conversions: Reason talks with three ex-warriors who now fight against the War on Drugs." *Reason*, Jan. 2002, vol. 33, no. 8, pp. 37-46; Wendy Kaminer, "Ordinary Abuses," in *And Justice For All* (Boston: Beacon, 2002), p. 116.
203 Dana Canedy, "Ex-Miami Officer Testifies in Police Corruption Case." *The New York Times*, January 29, 2003.
204 Dana Canedy, "4 Miami Officers Convicted of Conspiracy in Shootings." *The New York Times*, April 10, 2003.
205 Susan Sontag, "Regarding The Torture Of Others," *The New York Times Magazine*, May 23, 2004, p. 26.
206 Wendy Davis, "Simpson trial cast a long shadow on Skakel verdict," *The Boston Globe*, June 9, 2002, p. B1.
207 1984 figures from, Walter L. Updegrave, Gale Thompson McMullin, Veronica Byrd, and Miriam A. Leuchter, "Race and Money," *Money*, Dec. 1989, v.18, n.12, p.152; see also Barbara Hagenbaugh, "Nation's wealth disparity widens," *USA TODAY*, Jan. 22, 2003; Edmund L. Andrews, "Economic Inequality Grew in 90's Boom, Fed Reports," *The New York Times*, Jan. 23, 2003.
208 See, Fox Butterfield, "Study Finds Big Increase in Black Men as Inmates Since 1980." *The New York Times*, August 28, 2002.
209 Bryan Gruley, "Why Did Mississippi Agree to Pay for 'Ghost Inmates'?" *Wall Street Journal*, September 6, 2001.
210 Gruley, *Wall Street Journal*, September 6, 2001.
211 Gruley, *Wall Street Journal*, September 6, 2001.
212 Joseph Hallinan, "Shaky Private Prisons Find Vital Customer In Federal Government." *Wall Street Journal*, November 6, 2001.
213 Bruce Porter, "A Long Way Down," *The New York Times Magazine*, June 6, 2004, p. 53.
214 Porter, *The New York Times Magazine*, June 6, 2004, p. 52. (emphasis added).

NOTES

[215] Porter, *The New York Times Magazine*, June 6, 2004, p. 52.

[216] Joshua Green, "Life After Death in the Boardroom," *Corporate Board Member*, May/June 2002, vol. 5, no. 3, pp. 8-10.

[217] Maureen Dowd, "The Dream Is Dead," *The New York Times*, December 12, 2007.

[218] Michael W. Lynch, "Battlefield Conversions: Reason talks with three ex-warriors who now fight against the War on Drugs." *Reason*, Jan. 2002, vol. 33, no. 8, pp. 37-46; see also, Deborah Small. "The War On Drugs is a War On Racial Justice," *Social Research*, Fall 2001, vol. 68, no. 3, p. 896-905.

[219] Michael W. Lynch, "Battlefield Conversions: Reason talks with three ex-warriors who now fight against the War on Drugs." *Reason*, Jan. 2002, vol. 33, no. 8, pp. 37-46.

[220] Matthew Brzezinski, "Re-engineering the Drug Business," *The New York Times Magazine*, June 23, 2002.

[221] Fox Butterfield, "Study Finds 2.6% Increase in U.S. Prison Population." *The New York Times*, July 28, 2003.

[222] "A Stigma That Never Fades." *The Economist*, August 10-16, 2002, pp. 25-27.

[223] *United Sates v. R. Enterprises, Inc.*, 498 U.S. 292, 111 S.Ct. 722 (1991).

Chapter Seven:
Why Racism Matters

[224] See, Robert Westley, *Many Billions Gone: Is It Time To Reconsider The Case For Black Reparations?*, 40 Boston College Law Review 429, 443-444 (Dec. 1998); Howard McGary, "The Black Underclass and The Question of Values," in *The Underclass Question*, ed. Bill E. Lawson (Philadelphia1992), pp. 63-64.; Rhonda M. Williams, "Culture as Human Capital: Methodological and Policy Implications, " *Praxis International*, July 1987, vol. 7, no. 2 p. 152-63; Pettigrew, *New Patterns of Racism*, p. 691-93. Cf. Orlando Patterson, *The Ordeal of Integration: Progress and Resentment in America's "Racial" Crisis* (Washington D.C.: Civitas/Counterpoint, 1997), pp. 64-65 David K. Shipler, *A Country Of Strangers: Blacks and Whites In America* (New York: Knopf, 1997), pp. 344-55; Madeline Drexler, "The People's Epidemiologists," *Harvard Magazine*, March/April 2006, vol. 108, no. 4, pp. 25-33.

[225] Alexis de Tocqueville 1835, *Democracy In America*, J. P. Mayer and Max Lerner, eds. (New York: Harper & Row, 1966), vol. 1, Ch. 10, p. 294.

[226] Dinesh D'Souza, *The End Of Racism: Principles For A Multiracial Society* (New York: The Free Press, 1995), p.287.

[227] Lawrence E. Harrison & Samuel P. Huntington, eds., *Culture Matters: How Values Shape Human Progress* (New York: Basic Books, 2000), p. xxi (emphases added).

[228] *Culture Matters*, p. xxi.

[229] Samuel P. Huntington, *Who Are We? The Challenges To America's National Identity* (New York: Simon & Schuster, 2004), p. 40.

[230] Huntington, *Who Are We?* p. xvii.

[231] *Culture Matters*, p. xiv.

[232] Huntington, *Who Are We?* p. 17.

[233] Huntington, *Who Are We?* p. xvii.

[234] Huntington, *Who Are We?* p. 68.

[235] Cokie Roberts, *Founding Mothers: The Women Who Raised Our Nation* (New York: Harper Collins, 2004), p. xvii (emphasis added).

[236] Paul G.E. Clemens, *The Atlantic Economy and Colonial Maryland's Eastern Shore: From Tobacco To Grain* (Ithaca: Cornell, 1980), p. 29.

[237] Lewis C. Gray, *History of Agriculture in the Southern United States To 1860* (Gloucester: Peter Smith, 1958), I, p. 362

[238] Abbott Emerson Smith, "The Indentured Servant and Land Speculation in Seventeenth-Century Maryland," *American Historical Review*, April 1935, vol. 40, no. 3, p. 472

[239] E.T. Thompson, "The Climatic Theory of the Plantation," *Agricultural History*, January 1941, pp. 58-9, quoting Earl Hanson, "Are the Tropics Unhealthy?" *Harper's Magazine*, October 1933, v.167, no. 563.

[240] Alexis de Tocqueville, *Democracy In America*, J. P. Mayer and Max Lerner, eds. (New York: Harper & Row, 1966), vol. 1, Ch. 10, p. 324; see also, Eric Williams, *Capitalism & Slavery* (New York: Capricorn, 1966), p. 22.

[241] William B. Weeden, *Economic And Social History Of New England, 1620-1789* (Williamstown, MA: Corner House, 1890/1978), v. II, p. 451.

[242] E.T. Thompson, "The Climatic Theory of the Plantation," *Agricultural History*, January 1941, p. 57.

[243] Kulikoff, *Tobacco and Slaves*, p. 40.

[244] Clemens, *The Atlantic Economy: From Tobacco To Grain*, p. 60

[245] Kulikoff, *Tobacco and Slaves*, pp. 40-41.

[246] Morgan, *American Slavery*, pp. 164-66.

[247] Morgan, *American Slavery*, pp. 83-84.

[248] Blackburn, *New World Slavery*, p. 220.

[249] Wood, *Black Majority*, p. 42.

[250] Kulikoff, *Tobacco and Slaves*, p. 41.

[251] Kulikoff, *Tobacco and Slaves*, p. 41.

[252] Blackburn, *New World Slavery*, p. 387.

[253] Lewis C. Gray, *History of Agriculture in the Southern United States To 1860* (Gloucester: Peter Smith, 1958), I, pp. 88-89.

[254] Gray, *History of Southern Agriculture, I*, p. 350; Paul G.E. Clemens, From Tobacco To Grain, p. 59.

[255] Lewis C. Gray, *History of Agriculture in the Southern United States To 1860* (Gloucester: Peter Smith, 1958), I, pp. 88-89

[256] Blackburn, *New World Slavery*, p. 255.

[257] Gray, *History of Southern Agriculture, I*, pp. 354-55; Morgan, American Slavery, pp. 307-08.

[258] Gray, *History of Southern Agriculture, I*, p. 369.

[259] Gray, *History of Southern Agriculture, I*, p. 368; Clemens, From Tobacco To Grain, p. 62.

[260] Stephen Innes, "Fulfilling John Smith's Vision," in *Work and Labor in Early America*, Stephen Innes, ed. (Chapel Hill: UNC Press, 1988), p. 5.

[261] John McCusker and Russell Menard, *The Economy of British America, 1607-1789* (Chapel Hill: UNC, 1985), p. 122.

[262] Clemens, *From Tobacco To Grain*, p. 32.

[263] Clemens, *From Tobacco To Grain*, pp. 47-59, 79, 85, quotes pp. 29, 32.

[264] Eric Williams, *Capitalism & Slavery* (New York: Capricorn, 1966), p. 26.

[265] Lorena S. Walsh, "Slave Life, Slave Society, and Tobacco Production in the Tidewater Chesapeake, 1620-1820," in *Cultivation and Culture: Labor and The Shaping of Slave Life in the Americas*, Ira Berlin and Philip D. Morgan, eds. (Charlottesville: UVA Press, 1993), p. 176.

[266] Lorena S. Walsh, "Slave Life, Slave Society, and Tobacco Production in the Tidewater Chesapeake, 1620-1820," in *Cultivation and Culture: Labor and The Shaping of Slave Life in the Americas*, Ira Berlin and Philip D. Morgan, eds. (Charlottesville: UVA Press, 1993), p. 176.

[267] John McCusker and Russell Menard, *The Economy of British America, 1607-1789* (Chapel Hill: UNC, 1985), p. 124.

[268] Clemens, *From Tobacco To Grain*, p. 85.

[269] Jordan, *White Over Black*, pp. 44-98.

[270] N.S.B. Gras, *Business & Capitalism: An Introduction to Business History* (New York: F.S. Crofts & Co., 1939), pp. 113-14.

[271] N.S.B. Gras, *Business & Capitalism: An Introduction to Business History* (New York: F.S. Crofts & Co., 1939), p. 113.

[272] Blackburn, *New World Slavery*, pp. 187, 188.

[273] Nick Hazlewood, *The Queen's Slave Trader: John Hawkyns, Elizabeth I, And The Trafficking In Human Souls* (New York: William Morrow, 2004), p. 313.

[274] Bennett, *Black America*, p. 11; Jordan, *White Over Black*, p. 45. As noted above, others have placed mortality as high as 75 and 80 percent, see for example, Thomas J. Wertenbaker, *The Planters of Colonial Virginia* (Princeton, 1922), p. 39; Gray, *History of Southern Agriculture, I*, p. 363.

[275] Zinn, A *People's History of the U.S.*, p. 24.

[276] James H. Soltow, *The Economic Role of Williamsburg* (Charlottesville: UVA Press, 1965), pp. 21-22; Arthur Pierce Middleton, PhD, *Tobacco Coast: A Maritime History of Chesapeake Bay in the Colonial Era* (Newport News: Mariners' Museum, 1953), pp. 94-95.

[277] *The Economy of British America*, p. 134.

[278] Blackburn, *New World Slavery*, p. 11.

[279] Thomas Wertenbaker, *The Planters of Colonial Virginia* (Princeton: Princeton Univ., 1922), p. 137.

[280] Carlos Fuentes, "Huntington And The Mask Of Racism," *New Perspecttives Quarterly*, Spring 2004, vol. 21, no. 2, p. 79.

[281] Daniel Lazare, "Diversity And Its Discontents," *The Nation*, June 14, 2004, v. 278, no. 23, p. 18.

[282] Carlos Fuentes, "Huntington And The Mask Of Racism," *New Perspecttives Quarterly*, Spring, 2004, vol. 21, no. 2, p. 80.

[283] Gunnar Myrdal, *An American Dilemma: The Negro Problem and Modern Democracy* (New York: Harper & Brothers, 1944), pp.81-112.

[284] Thernstrom, *America in Black and White*, pp. 253-57.

[285] Thernstrom, *America in Black and White*, p. 233.

[286] Thernstrom, *America in Black and White*, p. 242.

[287] Thernstrom, *America in Black and White*, pp. 253-57.

[288] Stephanie Coontz and Nancy Folbre, "Marriage, Poverty, and Public Policy: A Discussion Paper from the Council on Contemporary Families." Prepared for the Fifth Annual CCF Conference, April 26-28, 2002; Kathryn Edin, "Few Good Men: Why Poor Women Don't

Remarry." *The American Prospect*, vol. 11, no. 4, January 3, 2000; Jawanza Kunjufu, *State of Emergency: We Must Save African American Males* (Chicago: AAI, 2001), p. 152.

[289] Robert Frank, "Marrying for Love ... of Money," *Wall Street Journal,* December 14, 2007.

[290] Ralph Gardner, Jr., "Alpha Women, Beta Men," *New York*, vol. 36, no. 40, pp. 24-29.

[291] Gunnar Myrdal, *An American Dilemma: The Negro Problem and Modern Democracy* (New York: Harper Brothers, 1944), p. 214 (emphases added).

[292] Julianne Malveaux, "More Jobs, Not More Marriages, Lift Poor." *USA TODAY,* Feb. 22, 2002, p. 15A; Stephanie Coontz and Nancy Folbre, "Marriage, Poverty, and Public Policy: A Discussion Paper from the Council on Contemporary Families," Prepared for the Fifth Annual CCF Conference, April 26-28, 2002, (url: www.prospect.org/webfeatures/2002/03/coontz-s-03-19.html); Ronald B. Mincy, "Marriage, Child Poverty, and Public Policy. *American Enterprise Quarterly*, Summer 2001, pp. 68-71.

[293] Thernstrom, *America in Black and White,* p. 243.

[294] Ellis Cose, "The Black Gender Gap," *Newsweek*, March 3, 2003, p. 46; .

[295] Stephan Thernstrom, from The NewsHour with Jim Lehrer, March 2, 1998, url: www.pbs.org/newshour/bb/rare_relations/jan-june98/commission_3-2.html

[296] Andrew Hacker, *Two Nations: Black and White, Separate, Hostile, Unequal* (New York: Ballantine 1995), pp. 75-76.

[297] Frances Kemble, *Journal*, pp. 111.

[298] "The Challenge of Facts" in *The Challenge of Facts and Other Essays by William Graham Sumner*, Abert Galloway Keller, ed. (New Haven: Yale Press, 1914), p. 37.

[299] Levin, *Why Race Matters*, p. 164.

[300] *Why Race Matters*, p. 165.

[301] Frances Kemble, *Journal*, p. 94.

[302] Frances Kemble, *Journal*, pp. 95-96. See also, Chancellor Harper, "Slavery In The Light Of Social Ethics," in *Cotton Is King, And Other Pro-Slavery Arguments*, E.N. Elliott, L.L.D., ed. (New York: Negro Universities Press), pp. 580-85.

[303] Derrick Bell, "The Sexual Diversion: The Black Man/Black Woman Debate in Context" in, *Black Men On Race, Gender, and Sexuality: A Critical Reader*, Devon W. Carbado, ed. (New York: NYU Press, 1999), p. 239.

[304] *Slavery Illustrated*, pp. 60-61; see also, Harriet Beecher Stowe, *Uncle Tom's Cabin* (New York: Signet Classic, 1998), pp. 384-85.

[305] Jacobs, *Life of a Slave Girl*, pp. 40-42, emphasis mine.

[306] "Narrative of William W. Brown," pp 208-19.

[307] Martineau, Retrospect, quoted in *The Founding Fathers: James Madison*, p. 377.

[308] *Remembering Slavery*, p. xxxv.

[309] Alexis de Tocqueville 1835, *Democracy In America*, J. P. Mayer and Max Lerner, eds. (New York: Harper & Row, 1966), vol. 1, Ch. 10, p. 292.

[310] Kemble, p.95. cf John Locke, *Two Treatises Of Government*, Ian Shapiro ed. (Yale, 2003), p. 126.

[311] *Why Race Matters*, p. 168 (emphasis added).

[312] *Why Race Matters*, p. 178.

[313] Joseph E. Le Doux, "Emotion Memory and the Brain." *Scientific American*, June 1994, p. 57.

[314] *Why Race Matters*, p. 186.

[315] U.S. Department of Health and Human Services (2001). *Mental Health: Culture, Race, and Ethnicity–A Supplement to Mental Health: A Report of the Surgeon General.* Rockville, MD: U.S. Department of Health and Human Services, Public Health Service, Office of the Surgeon General. citations omitted.

[316] Stephan Thernstrom, from "The NewsHour with Jim Lehrer," March 2, 1998, url: www.pbs.org/newshour/bb/rare_relations/jan-june98/commission_3-2.html

[317] Arthur Schlesinger, Jr., *War And The American Presidency* (New York: W.W. Norton, 2004), p. 117.

Chapter Eight:
Africa

[318] David Landes, "Culture Makes Almost All The Difference," in *Culture Matters: How Values Shape Human Progress*, Lawrence E. Harrison and Samuel P. Huntington, eds. (New York: Basic, 2000), p. 13.

[319] Weeden, *Economic And Social History Of New England*, v. II, p. 452.

[320] Weeden, *Economic And Social History Of New England*, v. II, p. 457 (citation omitted).

[321] Ralph D. Paine, *The Ships And Sailors Of Old Salem: The Record of A Brilliant Era Of American Achievement* (Chas. E. Lauriat Co., Boston, 1927), pp. 189, 192.

[322] James Duncan Phillips, *Salem And The Indies*, (Boston: Houghton Mifflin, 1947), pp. 38-39.

[323] James Duncan Phillips, *Salem And The Indies*, pp. 38-39.

[324] Samuel Eliot Morison, *The Maritime History of Massachusetts, 1783-1860* (Cambridge: Riverside Press, 1961), p. 85.

[325] George E. Brooks, *Yankee Traders, Old Coasters & African Middlemen* (Boston U., 1970), p. 19 (emphasis added, citation omitted).

[326] Morison, *Maritime History of Massachusetts*, p. 154.

[327] Paine, *Ships And Sailors*, pp. 141- 164.

[328] Paine, *Ships And Sailors*, p. 145.

[329] Paine, *Ships And Sailors*, p. 145.

[330] Paine, *Ships And Sailors*, p. 151.

[331] Paine, *Ships And Sailors*, p. 152.

[332] Paine, *Ships And Sailors*, p. 152 (emphasis added.).

[333] Brooks, *Yankee Traders,* pp. 94-5.

[334] Brooks, *Yankee Traders,* p. 79.

[335] Phillips, *Salem And The Indies*, pp. 15-6.

[336] Morison, *Maritime History of Massachusetts*, pp. 84-85.

[337] Brooks, *Yankee Traders,* p. 105.

[338] Morison, *Maritime History of Massachusetts*, pp. 160-61.

[339] See, David E. Kaplan, "A Smokin' Old Time In Tehran," *U.S. News & World Report*, March 19, 2007, p. 34

[340] Brooks, *Yankee Traders,* p. 11.

[341] Pakenham, *The Scramble For Africa*, p. 17; *Atlas Of World History,* Jeremy Black, ed. American edn. (New York: Dorling Kindersley, 2005), p. 66..

[342] Peter Spufford, *Power And Profit: The Merchant In Medieval Europe* (New York: Thames & Hudson, 2003), p. 310; Albert Hourani, *A History Of The Arab Peoples* (Harvard, Belknap, 2002), p. 44; David S. Landes, *The Wealth And Poverty Of Nations: Why Some Are So Rich And Some So Poor* (New York: W.W. Norton, 1999), p. 130.

[343] Lapidus, *Islamic Societies*, p. 433; *Atlas Of World History,* Jeremy Black, ed. American edn. (New York: Dorling Kindersley, 2005), pp. 66, 162-63.

[344] Iris Origo, *The Merchant of Prato: Francesco Di Marco Datini – 1335-1410* (Boston: Nonpareil, 1986), p. 72.

[345] Albert Hourani, *A History Of The Arab Peoples*, p. 45.

[346] Hourani, *Arab Peoples*, p. 44.

[347] Spufford, *Power And Profit: The Merchant In Medieval Europe*, p.

20.

[348] Iris Origo, *The Merchant of Prato: Francesco Di Marco Datini*, p. 80.

[349] Peter Russell, *Prince Henry 'the Navigator': A Life* (New Haven: Yale, 2000), p. 118; Pakenham, *The Scramble For Africa*, p. 17.

[350] Spufford, *Power And Profit*, p. 358.

[351] Spufford, *Power And Profit*, pp. 360-61.

[352] Spufford, *Power And Profit*, pp. 344-45, 348; Iris Origo, *The Merchant of Prato: Francesco Di Marco Datini - 1335-1410* (Boston: Nonpareil, 1986), p. 94; Hourani, *Arab Peoples*, p. 44; Pakenham, *The Scramble For Africa*, p. 17.

[353] Hourani, *Arab Peoples*, p. 111.

[354] Ira M. Lapidus, *A History Of Islamic Societies* (United Kingdom: Cambridge University, 2002), p. 405; *Atlas Of World History*, Jeremy Black, ed. American edn. (New York: Dorling Kindersley, 2005), pp. 162-63.

[355] Lapidus, *Islamic Societies*, p. 405; *Atlas Of World History*, Jeremy Black, ed. American edn. (New York: Dorling Kindersley, 2005), pp. 162-63.

[356] C. Raymond Beazley, *Prince Henry The Navigator: The Hero Of Portugal And Of Modern Discovery, 1394-1460* (New York: Barnes & Noble, 1901/1968), p. 272.

[357] Spufford, *Power And Profit*, p. 349.

[358] Pakenham, *The Scramble For Africa*, p. 17.

[359] Spufford, *Power And Profit*, p. 12.

[360] Spufford, *Power And Profit*, pp. 22-46, 59.

[361] *Atlas Of World History*, Jeremy Black, ed. American edn. (New York: Dorling Kindersley, 2005), pp. 190-91.

[362] Iris Origo, *The Merchant of Prato: Francesco Di Marco Datini - 1335-1410* (Boston: Nonpareil, 1986), p. 6; Peter Spufford, *Power And Profit*, pp. 60, 63, 66.

[363] Origo, *The Merchant of Prato*, pp. 10-11, 73.

[364] *Atlas Of World History*, Jeremy Black, ed. American edn. (New York: Dorling Kindersley, 2005), p. 191; Spufford, *Power And Profit*, p. 95.

[365] *Atlas Of World History*, Jeremy Black, ed. American edn. (New York: Dorling Kindersley, 2005), p. 66; Spufford, *Power And Profit*, pp. 346, 353-54.

[366] Spufford, *Power And Profit*, p., 112.

[367] Spufford, *Power And Profit*, pp. 134, 136.

[368] Spufford, *Power And Profit*, pp. 146-48.

[369] Lapidus, *Islamic Societies*, p. 438.

[370] Thomas Prentice Kettell, *Southern Wealth and Northern Profits* (U. of Alabama, 1860/1965), pp. 10-11.

[371] Blackburn, *New World Slavery*, p. 79.

[372] Origo, *The Merchant of Prato*, p. 90.

[373] Spufford, *Power And Profit*, pp. 340-41 (citation omitted).

[374] Hugh Thomas, *The Slave Trade: The Story of the Atlantic Slave Trade: 1440-1870* (New York: Simon & Schuster, 1997), pp. 23, 41-60. (quote p.60).

[375] Origo, *The Merchant of Prato*, pp. 91-92, 123.

[376] Origo, *The Merchant of Prato*, p. 121.

[377] Origo, *The Merchant of Prato*, pp. 86-89; Spufford, *Power And Profit*, pp. 288-89.

[378] Origo, *The Merchant of Prato*, p. 78.

[379] Origo, *The Merchant of Prato*, p. 130.

[380] Spufford, *Power And Profit*, p. 341.

[381] Pakenham, *The Scramble For Africa*, p. 17.

[382] Thomas, *The Slave Trade*, p. 210. Citation omitted.

[383] Origo, *The Merchant of Prato*, pp. 124-25.

[384] Origo, *The Merchant of Prato*, p. 113.

Chapter Nine:
The Virgin Prince

[385] Citations to Beazley, *Prince Henry The Navigator*, include references to Azurara, *Chronicle of the Discovery of Guinea*.

[386] Beazley, *Prince Henry*, p. 138.

[387] Beazley, pp. 123, 125.

[388] Beazley, p. 146.

[389] Beazley, pp. 160-61, 168.

[390] Beazley, p. 170.

[391] Russell, *Prince Henry*, p. 111.

[392] Beazley, p. 171.

[393] Beazley, pp. 171-72.

[394] Beazley, p. 173.

[395] Beazley, p. 174.

[396] Russell, p. 113, quote on p. 124.

[397] Russell, p. 132.

[398] Beazley, pp. 174-75.

[399] Russell, p. 131.

[400] Beazley, pp. 175-76.

[401] Beazley, pp. 177-78.

[402] Russell, p. 134.

[403] Russell, p. 110.

[404] Beazley, p. 208.

[405] Beazley, p. 218.

[406] Beazley, p. 209.

[407] Russell, p. 213.

[408] Russell, p. 213 (citations omitted).

[409] Beazley, p. 193.

[410] Russell, p. 132.

[411] Beazley, pp. 193-95.

[412] Beazley, p. 195.

[413] Beazley, pp. 196-97.

[414] Beazley, p. 197.

[415] Beazley, p. 200.

[416] Russell, p. 120.

[417] Beazley, pp. 197-201.

[418] Russell, p. 115.

[419] "Henry the Navigator," Encyclopædia Britannica, Inc., Encyclopædia Britannica Concise Edition CD-ROM., Copyright © 2006.

[420] Beazley, pp. 201-04 (emphasis added).

[421] Beazley, pp. 206-06.

[422] Russell, p. 210.

[423] Sugata Bose and Ayesha Jalal, *Modern South Asia: History, Culture, Political Economy* (New York: Routledge, 1997), p. 34.

[424] Russell, p. 212.

[425] Paul E. Lovejoy and Jan S. Hogendorn, "Slave Marketing In West Africa," in *The Uncommon Market*, p. 222; Zinn, *A People's History of the U.S.*, p. 26; Blackburn, *New World Slavery*, p. 129; Pakenham, *Scramble For Africa*, p. xxiii. See also, Sugata Bose and Ayesha Jalal, *Modern South Asia: History, Culture, Political Economy* (New York: Routledge, 1997), p. 34; Adam Smith, *An Inquiry Into The Nature and Causes of The Wealth of Nations* (New York: Knopf, 1991, Everyman edition), Vol. II, Bk IV, p. 130.

[426] Russell, p. 197 (citation omitted).

[427] Russell, p. 211.

[428] Beazley, p. 217.

[429] Beazley, pp. 218, 226.

[430] Beazley, p. 213.

[431] Beazley, pp. 214-15.

[432] "Bring Me My Machine Gun."

[433] Beazley, pp. 204-05.

[434] Hugh Thomas, *Rivers Of Gold: The Rise Of The Spanish Empire, From Columbus To Magellan* (New York: Random House, 2003), pp. 48-9.

[435] George Scelle, "The Slave Trade in the Spanish Colonies of America: The Assiento." *The American Journal of International Law*, Vol. IV, 1910, p. 628.

[436] Pakenham, *The Scramble For Africa*, p. 17; Joe R. Feagin, *Racist America: Roots, Current Realities, and Future Reparations* (New York: Routledge, 2000). p. 48.

[437] Blackburn, *New World Slavery*, pp. 192-3.

[438] Blackburn, *New World Slavery*, pp. 107-08.

[439] Blackburn, *New World Slavery*, p. 193.

[440] W.E.B. Du Bois, *Supression of the African Slave Trade to the United States, 1638-1870* (LSU, 1896/1965), p. 17.

[441] Du Bois, *Supression of the Slave Trade*, p. 17.

Chapter Ten:
Sir John Hawkins

[442] Hazlewood, *The Queen's Slave Trader*, p. xvi.

[443] Morgan, *American Slavery*, pp. 4-6; Pakenham, *The Scramble For Africa*, p. 17.

[444] Blackburn, *New World Slavery*, p. 220.

[445] *Wealth And Poverty Of Nations*, pp. 174-75.

[446] "The First Voyage Of The Right Worshipfull And Valiant Knight Sir John Hawkins," in *The Portable Hakluyt's Voyages: The Principle Navigations*, Irwin R. Blacker, ed. (New York: Viking, 1965), p. 114.

[447] Hazlewood, *The Queen's Slave Trader*, p. 66.

[448] Hazlewood, *The Queen's Slave Trader*, p. 100.

[449] "The Voyage Made By M. John Hawkins Esquire, To The Coast Of Guinea, And The Indies Of Nova Hispania," in *The Portable Hakluyt's Voyages: The Principle Navigations*, Irwin R. Blacker, ed. (New York: Viking, 1965), p. 122.

[450] *The Portable Hakluyt's Principle Navigations*, p. 125.

[451] *The Portable Hakluyt's Principle Navigations*, p. 125; Hazlewood, *The Queen's Slave Trader*, p., 106.

[452] Russell, p. 213.

[453] *The Portable Hakluyt's Principle Navigations*, pp. 125-26.

[454] *The Portable Hakluyt's Principle Navigations*, pp. 126-27.

[455] *The Portable Hakluyt's Principle Navigations*, pp. 130-31.

[456] *The Portable Hakluyt's Principle Navigations*, p. 125.

[457] Hazlewood, *The Queen's Slave Trader*, pp. 166-67.

[458] "The Third Voyage To Guinea, And The West Indies By M. John Hawkins," in *The Portable Hakluyt's Principle Navigations*, p. 163.

[459] Hazlewood, *The Queen's Slave Trader*, pp. 275-76.

[460] Arthur Pierce Middleton, PhD, *Tobacco Coast: A Maritime History of Chesapeake Bay in the Colonial Era* (Newport News: Mariners' Museum, 1953), p. 137.

[461] Ralph W. Hidy, *The House Of Baring In American Trade and Finance: English Merchant Bankers At Work, 1763-1861* (Harvard, 1949), p. 37.

[462] Middleton, *Tobacco Coast*, p. 135.

[463] Middleton, *Tobacco Coast*, p. 136-7.

[464] Countryman, *Collision of Histories*, pp. 9, 12.

[465] Countryman, *Collision of Histories*, p. 12.

[466] Gray, *History of Southern Agriculture, I*, quote, p. 354.

[467] Emory R. Johnson, ed., *History of Domestic and Foreign Commerce of the United States, vol. I* (New York: Burt Franklin, 1915), p. 102.

[468] Du Bois, *Supression of the Slave Trade*, p. 5.

[469] Zinn, *A People's History of the U.S.*, p. 29.

[470] Pakenham, *The Scramble For Africa*, p. 17; Zinn, *A People's History of the U.S.*, p. 29.

[471] Blackburn, *New World Slavery*, pp. 389-90.

[472] Captain Conneau, *A Slaver's Log Book*, p. v.

[473] Middleton, *Tobacco Coast*.

[474] Middleton, *Tobacco Coast*, pp. 136, 139.

[475] Middleton, *Tobacco Coast*, p. 136.

[476] Gray, *History of Southern Agriculture, I*, quote, p. 358.

[477] Middleton, *Tobacco Coast*, p. 140.

[478] W.E.B. Du Bois, *Supression of the African Slave Trade to the United States, 1638-1870* (LSU, 1896/1965), p. 5.

[479] Diamond, pp. 16-17.

Chapter Eleven:
Rich Land, Poor Land

[480] Jared Diamond, *Guns, Germs, and Steel: The Fates of Human Societies* (New York: W.W. Norton & Co., 1997, '99), p. 27.

[481] Diamond, *Guns, Germs, and Steel*, p. 18, emphasis added.

[482] James M. Blaut, "Environmentalism and Eurocentrism," *Geographical Review*, vol. 89, no. 3, pp. 391-409.

[483] Diamond, p. 410.

[484] James M. Blaut, "Environmentalism and Eurocentrism,"

Geographical Review, vol. 89, no. 3, pp. 391-409.

485 Blackburn, *New World Slavery,* p. 14.

486 Joe R. Feagin, *Racist America: Roots, Current Realities, and Future Reparations* (New York: Routledge, 2000). p. 48.

487 Blackburn, *New World Slavery,* p. 23.

488 *Wealth And Poverty Of Nations,* p. 62 (emphasis added).

489 *Wealth And Poverty Of Nations,* p. 63.

490 *Wealth And Poverty Of Nations,* p. 62 (emphasis added).

491 *Encarta World English Dictionary* (New York: St. Martin's, 1999).

492 *Wealth And Poverty Of Nations,* p. 71.

493 Christopher Columbus, Tuesday, October 16, 1492, *The Log Of Christopher Columbus,* translated by Robert H. Fuson (Camden, ME: Int'l Marine Pub. Co., c1987), p. 80.

494 Christopher Columbus, October 12, 13, 14, 1492, *The Log Of Christopher Columbus,* translated by Robert H. Fuson (Camden, ME: Int'l Marine Pub. Co., c1987), p. 80.

495 Hugh Thomas, *Rivers Of Gold: The Rise Of The Spanish Empire, From Columbus To Magellan* (New York: Random House, 2003), p. 51

496 *Wealth And Poverty Of Nations,* p. 117.

497 *Wealth And Poverty Of Nations,* p. 121.

498 Beazley, p. 206. (citation omitted)

499 Beazley, p. 206. (citation omitted)

500 Beazley, p. 211.

501 David Warsh, "The Historian Of Our Times," *The Boston Globe,* March 22, 1998. See also, Daniel Lazare, "Diversity And Its Discontents," *The Nation,* June 14, 2004, v278, n.23, p18.

502 *Wealth And Poverty Of Nations,* p. 173.

503 *Wealth And Poverty Of Nations,* p. 173.

504 Henry Kamen *Empire: How Spain Became A World Power, 1492-1763* (New York: Harper Collins, 2003), p. 197.

505 George E. Brooks, Jr., *Yankee Traders, Old Coasters & African Middlemen* (Boston U., 1970), p. 9.

506 Thomas, *The Slave Trade,* p. 69.

507 Eric Williams, *Capitalism & Slavery* (New York: Capricorn, 1966), p. 65.

508 Spufford, *Power And Profit,* p. 228.

509 *Wealth And Poverty Of Nations,* pp. 120-21 (emphasis added).

510 Beazley, p. 125.

511 See, Henry Kamen *Empire.*

512 Nathan Rosenberg & L.E. Birdzell, Jr., *How The West Grew Rich:*

The Economic Transformation Of The Industrial World (New York: Basic Books, 1986), p. 49.

513 Nathan Rosenberg & L.E. Birdzell, Jr., *How The West Grew Rich: The Economic Transformation Of The Industrial World* (New York: Basic Books, 1986), p. 39.

514 *Wealth And Poverty Of Nations*, pp. 187-90.

515 Gray, *History of Southern Agriculture, I*, quote, p. 352. see also, George Scelle, "The Slave Trade in the Spanish Colonies of America: The Assiento." *The American Journal of International Law*, Vol. IV, 1910, pp. 612-61; Marthe Allain, *Not Worth A Straw: French Colonial Policy and the Early Years of Louisiana* (Lafayette: U of SW Louisiana, 1988), Ch. 4, pp. 55-56; Kettell, *Southern Wealth and Northern Profits*, p. 13.

516 Hazlewood, *The Queen's Slave Trader*, p. 310.

517 Curtis P. Nettles, *The Money Supply of the American Colonies Before 1720* (New York: Sentry Press, 1934), pp. 15-30.

518 Curtis P. Nettles, *The Money Supply of the American Colonies Before 1720* (New York: Sentry Press, 1934), p. 21.

519 Kettell, *Southern Wealth and Northern Profits*, p. 12 (emphasis his).

520 Kettell, *Southern Wealth and Northern Profits*, pp. 13-14.

521 Kettell, *Southern Wealth and Northern Profits*, p. 14.

522 Hazlewood, *The Queen's Slave Trader*, p. 311.

523 Adam Smith, *Wealth of Nations*, pp. 112, 93.

524 Adam Smith, *Wealth of Nations*, p. 95.

525 Adam Smith, *Wealth of Nations*, p. 97.

526 Weeden, *Economic And Social History Of New England, v. II*, p. 451 (citation omitted).

527 Middleton, *Tobacco Coast*, p. 176.

528 Middleton, *Tobacco Coast*, p. 176-77.

529 Joe R. Feagin, *Racist America: Roots, Current Realities, and Future Reparations* (New York: Routledge, 2000). p. 50; J. H. Parry and P. M. Sherlock, *A Short History of the West Indies, 3d Ed.* (New York: St. Martin's Press, 1971), pp. 110-11.

530 Hazlewood, *The Queen's Slave Trader*, p. 310.

531 *Wealth And Poverty Of Nations*, p. 120.

532 *Wealth And Poverty Of Nations*, p. 55.

533 *Wealth And Poverty Of Nations*, p. 175.

534 *Wealth And Poverty Of Nations*, pp. 175, 177.

535 *Wealth And Poverty Of Nations*, p. 178.

536 *Wealth And Poverty Of Nations*, p. 122.

[537] *Wealth And Poverty Of Nations*, p. 119, citing Sheridan, in *British Capitalism*.

[538] Quoted in Guy Stevens Callender, ed., *Selections From the Economic History of the United States* (Boston: Ginn & Co., 1909), pp. 281-82; Kettell, *Southern Wealth and Northern Profits*, p. 49.

[539] Kettell, *Southern Wealth and Northern Profits*, p. 75.

[540] Kettell, *Southern Wealth and Northern Profits*, p. 60.

[541] *Wealth And Poverty Of Nations*, p. 123.

[542] David Landes, "Culture Makes Almost All The Difference," p. 2.

[543] David Landes, "Culture Makes Almost All The Difference," p. 13.

Chapter Twelve:
Black Renaissance

[544] Thomas, *Rivers Of Gold*, pp. 48-9.

[545] Thomas, *Rivers Of Gold*, p. 49.

[546] Quoted in Henry Kamen *Empire: How Spain Became A World Power, 1492-1763* (New York: Harper Collins, 2003), p. 41.

[547] Origo, *The Merchant of Prato*, pp. 18-9; Spufford, *Power And Profit*, pp. 274-76.

[548] Clain-Stefanelli, *The Beauty And Lore Of Coins*, p. 113.

[549] Spufford, *Power And Profit*, p. 82. (citation omitted).

[550] Origo, *The Merchant of Prato*, pp. 18-9; Spufford, *Power And Profit*, pp. 274-76.

[551] Origo, *The Merchant of Prato*, p. 8.

[552] Spufford, *Power And Profit*, p. 280.

[553] Spufford, *Power And Profit*, p. 280.

[554] Origo, *The Merchant of Prato*, p. 148.

[555] Spufford, *Power And Profit*, p. 276.

[556] Elvira & Vladimir Clain-Stefanelli, *The Beauty And Lore Of Coins, Currency And Medals* (Newton Abbot, UK: David & Charles, 1975), p. 113.

[557] Clain-Stefanelli, *Coins*, p. 113.

[558] Blackburn, *New World Slavery*, pp. 81, 387.

[559] Blackburn, *New World Slavery*, pp. 81, 388.

[560] Vandana Shiva, *Biopiracy: The Plunder of Nature and Knowledge* (Boston: South End, 1997), pp. 10, 17.

[561] Albert Bolles, *Industrial History of the United States, 3d. edn* ((New York: Augustus Kelly, 1966), p. 52.

[562] Bolles, *Industrial History of the U.S.*, p. 52, emphasis added.

[563] James M. Clifton, "The Rice Industry In Colonial America." *Agricultural History*, 1981, vol. 55, p. 274; Wood, *Black Majority*, pp.

59-61, 201.

[564] Countryman, *Collision of Histories*, pp. 4-5, 11.

[565] Wood, *Black Majority*, p. 62.

[566] Countryman, *Collision of Histories*, p. 10.

[567] Derrick Bell, *Faces At The Bottom Of The Well: The Permanence of Racism* (New York: Basic Books, 1992), p. 113.

[568] Derrick Bell, *Faces At The Bottom Of The Well*, p. 113.

[569] Cokie Roberts, *Founding Mothers*, p. xvi.

[570] Landsman, *White Teacher*, p. 29, 33-34 (emphasis hers, quote on 33).

[571] Robert Yates, *Secret Proceedings and Debates of the Convention Assembled at Philadelphia, in the Year 1787* (Birmingham Public Library, Bicentennial Edition, 1821/1987), p. 63.

[572] *Debates in the Federal Convention*, p. 531.

[573] Yates, *Secret Proceedings of the Convention at Philadelphia*, p. 63.

[574] Toni Morrison, *Playing in the Dark: Whiteness and the Literary Imagination* (Cambridge, MA: Harvard Univ. Press, 1992), pp. 4-5;. See also, Beth Day, *Sexual Life*, emphasis added.

Chapter Thirteen:
George Washington

[575] Morgan, *American Slavery*, p. 4.

[576] Morgan, *The New York Review of Books*, p. 18.

[577] *Encyclopædia Britannica*, 1996.

[578] Bernard Bailyn, "Politics and Social Structure in Virginia," in *Essays in American Colonial History*, Paul Goodman, ed. (New York: Holt, Rineheart & Winston, 1967), pp.272-95.

[579] Gordon S. Wood, *Revolutionary Characters: What Made The Founders Different* (New York: Penguin, 2006), p.33.

[580] Quoted in, Wood, *Revolutionary Characters*, p.33.

[581] Wood, *Revolutionary Characters*, p.35.

[582] *Debates and Proceedings of the Convention of the Commonwealth of Massachusetts, Held in the Year 1788* (Boston: Wm. White, 1856), p. 208.

[583] Morgan, *American Slavery*, p. 197.

[584] Gray, *History of Southern Agriculture*, I, p. 368. Duties from tobacco exports that went directly to the support of the Royal military amounted to approximately £3000 in Maryland and £6000 in Virginia at the time of the French and Indian War. Middleton, *Tobacco Coast*, p. 112. See also Davis Richard Dewey, PhD, *Financial History of The United States* (New York: Longmans, Green & Co., 1903), pp. 9, 12;

Kettell, *Southern Wealth and Northern Profits*, pp. 11-19.

585 Morgan, *American Slavery*, p. 198.

586 Robert J. Samuelson, "The End of Free Trade," *The Washington Post,* December 26, 2007, p. A21.

587 Albert S. Bolles, *The Financial History of The United States, From 1774-1789, vol. 1* (New York: D. Appleton & Co., 1879), p. 8.

588 William Graham Sumner, *The Financier And The Finances Of The American Revolution* (New York: Dodd, Mead, and Co., 1891), v.1, p5; Bolles, *Financial History of The U.S., vol. 1*, p. 44; Morgan, *American Slavery*, p. 5.

589 Sumner, *Finances Of The Revolution, v.1*, p. 106.

590 Bolles, *Financial History of The U.S., vol. 1*, p. 8.

591 Sumner, *Finances Of The Revolution, v.1*, p. 108.

592 Dewey, *Financial History of The U.S.*, p. 195.

593 *Selections From The Economic History of The United States, 1765-1860*, Guy Stevens Callender, ed. (New York: Ginn & Co., 1909), p. 8.

594 Virginia D. Harrington, Ph.D, *The New York Merchant On The Eve Of The Revolution* (Gloucester: Peter Smith, 1964), p. 172.

595 *History of Domestic and Foreign Commerce I*, p. 102 ; See, "Narrative of Sojourner Truth, A Northern Slave Emancipated From Bodily Servitude By The State Of New York, In 1828." (Boston, 1850), in *Slave Narratives* (NY: Lib. of Amer./Penguin Putnam, 2000), p. 587.

596 See, David Klingaman, "The Significance of Grain in the Development of the Tobacco Colonies," *Journal of Economic History*, 1969, vol. 29, p. 275; Clemens, *From Tobacco To Grain.*

597 Mark Kurlansky, *Cod: A Biography Of The Fish That Changed The World* (NY: Penguine, 1997), p. 86; *Selections From The Economic History of The United States, 1765-1860*, Guy Stevens Callender, ed. (New York: Ginn & Co., 1909), pp. 8, 795, citation omitted.

598 James G. Lydon, "Fish For Gold: The Massachusetts Fish Trade With Iberia, 1700-1773," *New England Quarterly*, 1981, v. 54, p. 541, 549.

599 Garnett, "The South and the Union, Part II," *De Bow's Review*, March 1855, vol. 18, no. 3, p. 293.

600 *History of Domestic and Foreign Commerce I*, p. 156.

601 McFarland, *New England Fisheries*, p. 106.

602 *History of Domestic and Foreign Commerce I*, p. 156.

603 *Atlas of Early American History: The Revolutionary Era 1760-*

1790, Lester J. Cappon, ed. (Princeton, 1976), p. 103.

[604] McFarland, *New England Fisheries*, p. 107.

[605] McFarland, *New England Fisheries*, p. 105.

[606] McFarland, *New England Fisheries*, p. 106.

[607] McFarland, *New England Fisheries*, p. 17.

[608] *The Economy of British America*, p. 99.

[609] L.H. Butterfield, ed., *The Adams Paper: Diary and Autobiography of John Adams* (Belknap/Harvard, 1961), v. 2, p. 149.

[610] Morgan, *American Slavery*, p. 5.

[611] Kurlansky, *Cod*, p. 94.

[612] James Bishop Peabody, ed., *The Founding Fathers: John Adams, A Biography in His Own Words* (New York: Newsweek, 1973), p. 195; *Journals of Congress IV*, Feb. 16, 1776, p. 159, Adams' notes on debates in Congress.

[613] *Journals of Congress, III*, Oct. 1775, pp. 477, 479, 491, 495-6, 502, Adams' notes on debates in Congress.

[614] *Journals of Congress, III*, Oct., Nov., Dec. 1775.

[615] *Journals of Congress, IV*, Feb., March., 1776.

[616] Sumner, *Finances Of The Revolution, v.1*, p. 103.

[617] Sumner, *Finances Of The Revolution, v.1*, p42; Bolles, *Financial History of The U.S., vol. 1*, pp. 42-45; E. James Ferguson, *The Power Of The Purse: A History Of American Public Finance, 1776-1790* (Chapel Hill: UNC, 1961), p 8.

[618] Hamilton to James Duane, September 3, 1780, in *Alexander Hamilton, Writings*. Joanne B. Freeman, ed. (New York: Literary Classics, 2001), p. 81.

[619] *Journals of Congress II*, June 22, 1775, p. 103

[620] *Journals of Congress II*, July 29, 1775, p. 222.

[621] Paul A. Varg, *Foreign Policies Of The Founding Fathers* (Michigan State Univ. Press 1963), p. 22.

[622] Ferguson, *The Power Of The Purse*, p 30-31; William Graham Sumner, *The Financier And The Finances Of The American Revolution* (New York: Dodd, Mead, and Co., 1891), v.1, p. 129.

[623] Sumner, *Finances Of The Revolution, v.1*, p. 132.

[624] Sumner, *Finances Of The Revolution, v.1*, p. 135; *Journals of Congress*.

[625] Sumner, *Finances Of The Revolution, v.1*, p. 135.

[626] Ferguson, *The Power Of The Purse*, p 27; Joseph Dorfman, *The Economic Mind in American Civilization, 1606-1865* (New York: Viking, 1946), vol. 1, pp. 235-36.

[627] Ferguson, *The Power Of The Purse*, p 8.

[628] *Journals of Congress II,* July 27, 1775.

[629] Ferguson, *The Power Of The Purse,* p. 36; James Breck Perkins, *France in the American Revolution* (Boston: Houghton Mifflin, 1911), p. 9; Labaree, Fowler, Jr., Hattendorf, Safford, Sloan, and German, *America and the Sea: A Maritime History* (Mystic, CT, Seaport Museum, 1998), p. 147; *The Founding Fathers: John Adams,* p. 209; *The American Revolution 1775-1783.*

[630] Ferguson, *The Power Of The Purse,* pp 36-40, quotes on 36; Dewey, *Financial History of The U.S.,* pp. 45-47; Bolles, *Financial History of The U.S., vol. 1,* p. 44.

[631] Ferguson, *The Power Of The Purse,* p. 36.

[632] Ferguson, *The Power Of The Purse,* p. 36.

[633] Dewey, *Financial History of The U.S.,* p. 46; E. James Ferguson, *The Power Of The Purse: A History Of American Public Finance, 1776-1790* (Chapel Hill: UNC, 1961), p. 39.

[634] Bolles, *Financial History of The U.S., vol. 1,* p. 46.

[635] Ferguson, *The Power Of The Purse,* p. 38; Bolles, *Financial History of The U.S., vol. 1,* pp. 47-48; Dewey, *Financial History of The U.S.,* p. 46.

[636] Ferguson, *The Power Of The Purse,* pp 39-40.

[637] *Journals of Congress III,* Nov 4, 1775, p. 323.

[638] Sumner, *Finances Of The Revolution, v.1,* p. 141.

[639] Based on one pre-war estimate, available grain surplus would have been approximately one million bushels of corn and wheat annually. David Klingaman, "The Significance of Grain in the Development of the Tobacco Colonies," *Journal of Economic History,* 1969, vol. 29, p. 275.

[640] Sumner, *Finances Of The Revolution, v.1,* p. 121; *Journals of Congress III,* Nov 4, 1775, p. 323.

[641] Kettell, *Southern Wealth and Northern Profits,* p. 72.

[642] "Report On Public Credit," *Alexander Hamilton, Writings,* Joanne B. Freeman, ed. (New York: Literary Classics, 2001), pp. 549-50.

[643] Sumner, *Finances Of The Revolution, v.2,* p. 39.

[644] Quoted in *The Power Of The Purse,* p 30, note 15; Sumner, *Finances Of The Revolution,* v.1, p. 38.

[645] Sumner, *Finances Of The Revolution,* v.1, pp. 159, 164-5.

[646] Middleton, *Tobacco Coast,* pp. 126-132; Jacob M. Price, "The French Farmers-General in the Chesapeake: The Mackercher-Huber Mission of 1737-38." *William & Mary Quarterly,* 3d ser., vol. XIV, 1957, pp. 125-53.

[647] David McCullough, *John Adams* (New York: Simon & Schuster,

2001), p. 233.

[648] Quoted in David McCullough, *John Adams* (New York: Simon & Schuster, 2001), p. 233.

[649] Ferguson, *The Power Of The Purse*, p. 36.

[650] James Breck Perkins, *France in the American Revolution* (Boston: Houghton Mifflin, 1911), p. 9.

[651] *The American Revolution 1775-1783: An Encyclopedia*, Richard L. Blanco, ed. (New York: Garland, 1993), p. 108.

[652] James Breck Perkins, *France in the American Revolution* (Boston: Houghton Mifflin, 1911), pp. 10-11; see also, Catherine Drinker Bowen, *Miracle at Philadelphia: The Story of the Constitutional Convention, May to September, 1787* (Boston: Little, Brown, & Company, 1986), p. 132, acknowledging importance of French aid at Yorktown.

[653] James Breck Perkins, *France in the American Revolution* (Boston: Houghton Mifflin, 1911), p. 13; Sumner, *Finances Of The Revolution*, v.1, p156.

[654] Labaree, Fowler, Jr., Hattendorf, Safford, Sloan, and German, *America and the Sea: A Maritime History* (Mystic, CT, Seaport Museum, 1998), p. 146; James Breck Perkins, *France in the American Revolution* (Boston: Houghton Mifflin, 1911), p. 42.

[655] Paul A. Varg, *Foreign Policies Of The Foundign Fathers* (Michigan State Univ. Press 1963), p14; Labaree, Fowler, Jr., Hattendorf, Safford, Sloan, and German, *America and the Sea: A Maritime History* (Mystic, CT, Seaport Museum, 1998), p. 135.

[656] James Breck Perkins, *France in the American Revolution* (Boston: Houghton Mifflin, 1911), p. 45-8.

[657] James Breck Perkins, *France in the American Revolution* (Boston: Houghton Mifflin, 1911), p. 54; Blanche Evans Hazard, *Beaumarchais and the American Revolution* (Boston: Daughters of the Revolution/Slocum, 1910), p. 13.

[658] Blanche Evans Hazard, *Beaumarchais and the American Revolution* (Boston: Daughters of the Revolution/Slocum, 1910), p. 13.

[659] James Breck Perkins, *France in the American Revolution* (Boston: Houghton Mifflin, 1911), p. 57-9.

[660] Sumner, *Finances Of The Revolution*, v.1, p. 163.

[661] James Breck Perkins, *France in the American Revolution* (Boston: Houghton Mifflin, 1911), p. 57-9; *America and the Sea*, p. 133; *The American Revolution 1775-1783: An Encyclopedia*, Richard L. Blanco, ed. (New York: Garland, 1993), p. 107.

[662] Blanche Evans Hazard, *Beaumarchais and the American Revolution* (Boston: Daughters of the Revolution/Slocum, 1910), p. 14.

[663] Sumner, Finances Of The Revolution, v.1, p. 165.

[664] *The American Revolution 1775-1783: An Encyclopedia*, Richard L. Blanco, ed. (New York: Garland, 1993), p. 108.

[665] Clarence L. Ver Steeg, *Robert Morris: Revolutionary Financier* (New York: Octagon, 1976), p. 5.

[666] Clarence L. Ver Steeg, *Robert Morris: Revolutionary Financier* (New York: Octagon, 1976), p. 4; quote in William Graham Sumner, *The Financier And The Finances Of The American Revolution* (New York: Dodd, Mead, and Co., 1891), v.1, p. 198.

[667] Eugene R. Slaski, "Thomas Willing: a study in moderation, 1774-1778," *Pennsylvania Magazine of History & Biography*, vol. 100, 1976, pp. 491-506.

[668] Dorfman, *The Economic Mind* 1, pp. 224-25. See also, Sumner, *Finances Of The Revolution*, v.2, pp. 64-5, quote on p. 70.

[669] Dorfman, *The Economic Mind* 1, p. 225.

[670] Dorfman, *The Economic Mind* 1, p. 225.

[671] *History of Domestic and Foreign Commerce I*, p. 303.

[672] Bolles, *Industrial History of the U.S.*, p. 785.

[673] *History of Domestic and Foreign Commerce I*, p. 303.

[674] Ferguson, *The Power Of The Purse*, p. 42.

[675] *Journals of Congress II*, July 15, 1775.

[676] *Journals of Congress III*, Oct. 20, 1775, pp. 362-63.

[677] John Adams' notes of debates in Congress, *Journals of Congress III*, Oct. 20, 1775, p. 495.

[678] *America and the Sea*, p. 134; J. Franklin Jameson, "St. Eustatius In The American Revolution." *American Historical Review*, vol. 8, 1902-3, pp. 684-85.

[679] *America and the Sea*, p. 141.

[680] J. Franklin Jameson, "St. Eustatius In The American Revolution." *American Historical Review*, vol. 8, 1902-3, pp. 687.

[681] J. Franklin Jameson, "St. Eustatius In The American Revolution." *American Historical Review*, vol. 8, 1902-3, p. 685; *America and the Sea*, p. 134; Sumner, *Finances Of The Revolution*, v.2, p. 60.

[682] Ferguson, *The Power Of The Purse*, p. 42.

[683] J. Franklin Jameson, "St. Eustatius In The American Revolution." *American Historical Review*, vol. 8, 1902-3, p. 686; Ferguson, *The Power Of The Purse*, p. 42.

[684] J. Franklin Jameson, "St. Eustatius In The American Revolution."

American Historical Review, vol. 8, 1902-3, p. 700.
[685] J. Franklin Jameson, "St. Eustatius In The American Revolution." *American Historical Review,* vol. 8, 1902-3, p. 700.

Chapter Fourteen:
John Adams

[686] *The Founding Fathers: John Adams,* p. 163.
[687] Sumner, *Finances Of The Revolution, v.1,* p105.
[688] L.H. Butterfield, ed., *The Adams Papers: Diary and Autobiography of John Adams* (Belknap/Harvard, 1961), v.2, p. 236.
[689] Sumner, *Finances Of The Revolution, v.2,* p. 65.
[690] Dorfman, *The Economic Mind 1,* p. 225.
[691] Jacob M. Price, *France and the Chesapeake: A History of the French Tobacco Monopoly, 1674-1791, and of Its Relationship to the British and American Tobacco Trades, Volume 1* (U. of Michigan, 1973), pp. 173-89.
[692] *Journals of Congress V,* July. 18, 1776, p. 576 (url: http://memory.loc.gov/ll/lljc/005/01610576.gif).
[693] "Plan of Treaties," *Journals of Congress V,* September 17, 1776, p. 769.
[694] "Instructions," *Journals of Congress V,* September 24, 1776, p. 814 (url: http://memory.loc.gov/ll/lljc/005/0300/03990814.gif).
[695] "Plan of Treaties," *Journals of Congress V,* September 17, 1776, p. 770.
[696] "Instructions," *Journals of Congress V,* September 24, 1776, p. 814 (url: http://memory.loc.gov/ll/lljc/005/0300/03990814.gif).
[697] Toby & Will Musgrave, *An Empire of Plants: People and Plants That Changed The World* (London: Cassell, 2000), p.30.
[698] Iain Gately, *Tobacco: A Cultural History of How an Exotic Plant Seduced Civilization* (New York: Grove Press, 2001), p. 140; Many Thousands Gone, p. 31.
[699] Paul A. Varg, *Foreign Policies Of The Foundign Fathers* (Michigan State Univ. Press 1963), p. 22.
[700] *The Founding Fathers: John Adams,* pp. 266, 289.
[701] Sumner, *Finances Of The Revolution,* v.2, p113 (citations omitted, emphasis added).
[702] Middleton, *Tobacco Coast,* pp. 126-27.
[703] *History of Domestic and Foreign Commerce I,* p. 134.
[704] John Adams at The Hague, Sept. 6, 1782, in *The Founding Fathers: John Adams,* p. 290.
[705] Shaw, *John Adams,* p. 156.

[706] Peter Shaw, *The Character of John Adams* (New York: Norton, 1976), p. 155.

[707] Shaw, *John Adams*, pp. 157-58.

[708] Address and Recommendations To The States (Philadelphia, 1783), in *The Founding Fathers: James Madison*, pp. 76-77.

[709] William W. Freehling, "The Founding Fathers and Slavery," *American Historical Review*, LXXVII, Feb., 1972, pp. 81-93.

[710] *Journals of Congress*, April 18, 1783, v. 24, p.257, 258, (url: www.memory.loc.gov/ll/llc/024/0200/02650257.gif) emphasis added.

[711] Timothy Pitkin, *A Statistical View of the Commerce of the United States* (New Haven: Durrie & Peck, 1835), p. 280.

[712] *Debates in the Federal Convention*, p. 507.

[713] Yates, *Secret Proceedings of the Convention at Philadelphia*, p. 64.

[714] *Debates in the Federal Convention*, p. 502.

[715] Francis Leigh Williams, *A Founding Family: The Pinckneys of South Carolina* (New York: Harcourt, Brace, Jovanovich, 1978), p. 260.

[716] *History of Domestic and Foreign Commerce I*, p. 159.

[717] McFarland, *New England Fisheries*, p. 125.

[718] McFarland, *New England Fisheries*, p. 126.

[719] McFarland, *New England Fisheries*, p. 127.

[720] McFarland, *New England Fisheries*, p. 128.

[721] *History of Domestic and Foreign Commerce I*, pp. 125-31, 159.

[722] Kurlansky, *Cod*, p. 93.

[723] *Debates in the Federal Convention*, p. 508.

[724] *Debates in the Federal Convention*, p. 530.

[725] *Debates in the Federal Convention*, p. 530.

[726] Kettell, *Southern Wealth and Northern Profits*, p. 18.

[727] Kettell, *Southern Wealth and Northern Profits*, p. 18.

[728] Garnett, "The South and the Union, Part II," in *De Bow's Review*, March 1855, vol. 18, no. 3, p. 295.

[729] *America and the Sea*, p. 184.

Chapter Fifteen:
Thomas Jefferson

[730] Jefferson, "Notes on Virginia," p. 666.

[731] E. M. Halliday, *Understanding Thomas Jefferson*, Harper Collins, 2001, p. 99

[732] David McCullough, *John Adams* (New York: Simon & Schuster, 2001), pp. 577, 580.

[733] David McCullough, *John Adams* (New York: Simon & Schuster, 2001), p. 372.

[734] DeWayne Wickham, "Hemings, Jefferson: No free will, no love," *USA TODAY*, Feb. 01, 2000; Roger Wilkins, *Jefferson's Pillow* (Boston: Beacon Press, 2001), p. 136.

[735] Vincent Nolte, *Fifty Years In Both Hemispheres: or, Reminiscences Of The Life Of A Former Merchant* (Freeport, NY: Books For Libraries Press, 1954/1972), p. 92.

[736] David McCullough, *John Adams* (New York: Simon & Schuster, 2001), p. 116.

[737] Wood, *Black Majority*, p. 230.

[738] "Narrative of William W. Brown," p 210.

[739] Raymond Walters, Jr., *Albert Gallatin: Jeffersonian Financier and Diplomat* (Univ. of Pittsburgh, 1969), p. 152.

[740] Alexander Balinky, *Albert Gallatin: Fiscal Theories and Policies* (New Brunswick: Rutgers, 1958), p. 93.

[741] Alexander Balinky, *Albert Gallatin: Fiscal Theories and Policies* (New Brunswick: Rutgers, 1958), p. 64; Pitkin, *A Statistical View of Commerce*, p. 342.

[742] Ralph W. Hidy, *The House Of Baring In American Trade and Finance*, p. 25; Dewey, *Financial History of The U.S.*, p. 121.

[743] Algar Labouchere Thorold, *The Life of Henry Labouchere* (New York: Putnam & Sons, 1913), p. 2; Nolte, *Fifty Years In Both Hemispheres*, p. 159.

[744] Hidy, *House Of Baring*, p. 34.

[745] Walters, *Gallatin*, p. 153.

[746] Walters, *Gallatin*, p. 153.

[747] Hidy, *House Of Baring*, p. 34.

[748] Walters, *Gallatin*, p. 153; Hidy, *House Of Baring*, p. 33.

[749] Walters, *Gallatin*, p. 154.

[750] Hidy, *House Of Baring*, p. 34.

[751] Walters, *Gallatin*, p. 154.

[752] Act of Congress, Oct. 27, 1803; Hidy, *The House Of Baring*, p. 33.

[753] Walters, *Gallatin*, p. 154.

[754] Walters, *Gallatin*, p. 154.

[755] Hidy, *House Of Baring*, p. 69.

[756] Hidy, *House Of Baring*, p. 69.

[757] George Wilson, *Stephen Girard: America's First Tycoon* (Conshohocken: Combined Books, 1995), p. 139; Walters, *Gallatin*, p. 150.

[758] *Pennsylvania Packet and Daily Advertiser*, January 2, 1788,

reprinted in Wilson, *Stephen Girard*, p. 139.

[759] Walters, *Gallatin*, p. 151.

[760] Walters, *Gallatin*, p. 151.

Chapter Sixteen:
James Madison

[761] Walters, *Gallatin*, p. 237.

[762] Walters, *Gallatin*, pp. 248-49.

[763] Walters, *Gallatin*, p. 254.

[764] Walters, *Gallatin*, pp. 254-55.

[765] Wilson, *Stephen Girard*, p. 245.

[766] Wilson, *Stephen Girard*, p. 266; Walters, *Gallatin*, p. 256.

[767] Porter, *John Jacob Astor, vol. I*, p. 330.

[768] Wilson, *Stephen Girard*, pp. 271-72.

[769] Walters, *Gallatin*, p. 258.

[770] Girard to Gallatin, April 5, 1813, in McMaster, *The Life and Times of Stephen Girard, vol. 2*, p. 248.

[771] Astor to Gallatin, April 5, 1813, in McMaster, *The Life and Times of Stephen Girard, vol. 2*, p. 249.

[772] Walters, *Gallatin*, p. 258; McMaster, *The Life and Times of Stephen Girard, vol. 2*, p. 250.

[773] Wilson, *Stephen Girard*, pp. 278-79.

[774] Quoted in Bolles, *Industrial History of the U.S.*, p. 865.

[775] Quoted in Bolles, *Industrial History of the U.S.*, p. 865.

[776] Dewey, *Financial History of The U.S.*, pp. 133, 135-8.

[777] Nolte, *Reminiscences of a Former Merchant*, p. 144.

[778] John Bach McMaster, *The Life and Times of Stephen Girard: Mariner and Merchant), vol. 1* (Philadelphia: J.B.Lippincott Co., 1918, p. 7.

[779] Nolte, *Reminiscences of a Former Merchant*, p. 144.

[780] Nolte, *Reminiscences of a Former Merchant*, p. 144.

[781] Wilson, *Stephen Girard*, pp. 183, 192-94.

[782] Unless otherwise indicated, information regarding ships and cargoes of Stephen Girard taken from John Bach McMaster, *Life and Times of Stephen Girard: Mariner and Merchant , vol. 2* (Philadelphia: J.B.Lippincott Co., 1918), pp. 42-171.

[783] Girard to Mahlon Hutchinson, Jr., Amsterdam, 1809, in McMaster, *Life and Times of Stephen Girard, vol. 2*, p. 78.

[784] Instructions to Titon Grelaud, in McMaster, *The Life and Times of Stephen Girard, vol. 2*, p. 111.

[785] Captain Bowen to Girard, Feb. 4, 1811, in McMaster, *Life and*

Times of Stephen Girard, vol. 2, p. 158.

[786] Edward George and Samuel Nicholson to Girard, Feb. 1811, in McMaster, *Life and Times of Stephen Girard, vol. 2*, p. 159.

[787] The actual value was recorded to be Bo.326,054., possibly the abbreviation for Groats Banco of the period, placing the value, of about 4 cents each, at approx. $13,000. It's more likely the number instead refers to dollars, given the profits obtained for the cotton and the value of the ship's total cargo.

[788] Captain Wilson to Girard, April, 1811, in McMaster, *Life and Times of Stephen Girard, vol. 2*, p. 161.

[789] Captain McLeveen to Girard, April, 1811, in McMaster, *Life and Times of Stephen Girard, vol. 2*, p. 161.

[790] Wm. Adgate to Girard, Dec. 16, 1809, in McMaster, *Life and Times of Stephen Girard, vol. 2*, pp. 87-91.

[791] Wm. Adgate to Girard, July 18, 1809, in McMaster, *Life and Times of Stephen Girard, vol. 2*, pp. 90, 91.

[792] Hope and Co. to Girard, July, in McMaster, *Life and Times of Stephen Girard, vol. 2*, p. 87.

[793] McMaster, *Life and Times of Stephen Girard*, vol. 2, pp. 165-66.

[794] Wilson, *Stephen Girard*, p. 225.

[795] *House Of Baring*, pp. 65-66.

[796] Kenneth Wiggins Porter, *John Jacob Astor: Business Man* (New York: Russell & Russell, 1966), vol. I, p. 173.

[797] Porter, *John Jacob Astor, vol. II*, p. 795.

[798] Porter, *John Jacob Astor, vol. II*, p. 792.

[799] Porter, *John Jacob Astor, vol. II*, pp. 802-03.

[800] Porter, *John Jacob Astor, vol. II*, p. 802.

[801] Porter, *John Jacob Astor, vol. I*, pp. 151-53, 200.

[802] Porter, *John Jacob Astor, vol. I*, p. 8.

[803] Girard to Baring Brothers, 1811, in McMaster, *Life and Times of Stephen Girard, vol. 2*, pp. 173-74.

[804] Hidy, *House Of Baring*, p. 25.

[805] R.W. Hidy, "The Organization and Functions of Angle-American Merchant Bankers, 1815-1860," *Journal of Economic History, I*, supplement, 1941, p. 57.

[806] Kenneth L. Brown, "Stephen Girard's Bank," *Pennsylvania Magazine of History and Biography*, vol. 66, pp.31-32, see also note 4.

[807] McMaster, *Life and Times of Stephen Girard, vol. 1*, p. 4.

[808] Brown, "Stephen Girard's Bank," pp.29-55.

[809] McMaster, *Life and Times of Stephen Girard, vol. 1*, p. 19.

[810] McMaster, *Life and Times of Stephen Girard, vol. 1*, pp. 429-30.

Chapter Seventeen:
Baring It All

[811] Unless otherwise noted, references to operations of Baring Brothers Company are from Ralph W. Hidy, *The House Of Baring In American Trade and Finance: English Merchant Bankers At Work, 1763-1861* (Harvard, 1949).

[812] Seán Mac Mathúna, *Slavery and London*.

[813] Brown, "Stephen Girard's Bank," vol. 66, pp.30-31; Hidy, *House Of Baring*, p. 49.

[814] Girard to Schwartz Brothers, Hamburg, 1811, in McMaster, *The Life and Times of Stephen Girard, vol. 2*, p. 172.

[815] Girard to Mahlon Hutchinson, Jr., Amsterdam, 1811, in McMaster, *The Life and Times of Stephen Girard, vol. 2*, p. 173.

[816] Hidy, *House Of Baring*, p. 1.

[817] Hidy, *House Of Baring*, pp. 34-35.

[818] Hidy, *House Of Baring*, p. 65.

[819] Hidy, *House Of Baring*, p. 68.

[820] Hidy, *House Of Baring*, p. 68.

[821] Nolte, *Reminiscences of a Former Merchant*, p. 258; Hidy, *House Of Baring*, p. 74.

[822] Nolte, *Reminiscences of a Former Merchant*, p. 277.

[823] Nolte, *Reminiscences of a Former Merchant*, pp. 277-280.

[824] Hidy, *House Of Baring*, p. 70.

[825] Nolte, *Reminiscences of a Former Merchant*, p. 277.

[826] Nolte, *Reminiscences of a Former Merchant*, p. 298; Ralph W. Hidy, *The House Of Baring In American Trade and Finance: English Merchant Bankers At Work, 1763-1861* (Harvard, 1949), p. 70.

[827] Nolte, *Reminiscences of a Former Merchant*, p. 299.

[828] Nolte, *Reminiscences of a Former Merchant*, pp. 314-18.

[829] Nolte, *Reminiscences of a Former Merchant*, p. 290.

[830] Hidy, *House Of Baring*, pp. 71-72, quotes on p. 73; Ralph C. H. Catterall, *The Second Bank Of The United States* (U. of Chicago, 1968), p. 111.

[831] Ralph C. H. Catterall, *The Second Bank Of The United States* (U. of Chicago, 1968), p. 111.

[832] *House Of Baring*, pp. 75, 93-95, 131-32.

[833] *House Of Baring*, pp. 185, 189-90, 233, 255 (Citation omitted).

[834] *House Of Baring*, pp. 95, 96, 110-12, 200.

[835] *House Of Baring*, pp. 255, 266.

[836] *House Of Baring*, pp. 72, 96.

[837] *House Of Baring*, pp. 98-100.

[838] *House Of Baring*, pp. 102-03, 173.

Chapter Eighteen:
Alexander Hamilton

[839] *Dictionary of American Biography*; William Graham Sumner, "Banks In The United States," in *A History Of Banking In All The Leading Nations, vol. I*, William Graham Sumner, ed. (New York: Augustus M. Kelly, 1896/1971), p. 28; C. F. Dunbar, "Some Precedents Followed by Alexander Hamilton," *Quarterly Journal of Economics*, October, 1888.

[840] Bolles, *Financial History of The U.S., vol. 2*, pp. 33, 41. See also, Alexander Hamilton, *Works*, vol. 6, p. 640.

[841] *History of Domestic and Foreign Commerce I*, p. 185.

[842] Ron Chernow, *Alexander Hamilton* (New York: Penguine, 2004), p. 23.

[843] Ron Chernow, *Alexander Hamilton* (New York: Penguine, 2004), p. 32.

[844] Ron Chernow, *Alexander Hamilton* (New York: Penguine, 2004), p. 29 (citation omitted).

[845] Hamilton, Federalist no. 12, *The Federalist Papers*, pp. 91-92. See also, "The Continentalist No. VI," in *Alexander Hamilton, Writings*. Joanne B. Freeman, ed. (New York: Literary Classics, 2001), pp. 113-14.

[846] Hamilton to James Duane, September 3, 1780, in *Alexander Hamilton, Writings*. Joanne B. Freeman, ed. (New York: Literary Classics, 2001), p. 78.

[847] Hamilton, Federalist no. 12, *The Federalist Papers*, p. 96 (emphases added).

[848] "The Continentalist No. IV," in *Alexander Hamilton, Writings*. Joanne B. Freeman, ed. (New York: Literary Classics, 2001), p. 108 (emphasis his).

[849] "The Continentalist No. IV," in *Alexander Hamilton, Writings*. Joanne B. Freeman, ed. (New York: Literary Classics, 2001), p. 109.

[850] "The Continentalist No. IV," in *Alexander Hamilton, Writings*. Joanne B. Freeman, ed. (New York: Literary Classics, 2001), p. 108 (emphasis his).

[851] "The Continentalist No. VI," in *Alexander Hamilton, Writings*. Joanne B. Freeman, ed. (New York: Literary Classics, 2001), pp. 112-13, 115 (emphasis added).

[852] Hamilton, Federalist no. 12, *The Federalist Papers*, pp. 92-93.

853 Madison to Edmund Randolph, November 26, 1782, in *The Founding Fathers: James Madison*, p. 72.
854 Dorfman, *The Economic Mind* 1, p. 227.
855 Sumner, *Finances Of The Revolution, v.2*, p. 198.
856 Hamilton, Federalist no. 12, *The Federalist Papers*, p. 93 (emphases added).
857 "The Continentalist No. IV," in *Alexander Hamilton, Writings*. Joanne B. Freeman, ed. (New York: Literary Classics, 2001), p. 107 (emphasis his).
858 Madison to Edmund Randolph, November 26, 1782, in *The Founding Fathers: James Madison*, p. 73.
859 Sumner, *Finances Of The Revolution*, v.2, pp. 64-65.
860 See n. 710.
861 *Alexander Hamilton, Writings*. Joanne B. Freeman, ed. (New York: Literary Classics, 2001), p. 1039; Merrill D. Peterson, ed., *The Founding Fathers: James Madison*, pp. 73-74; Sumner, *Finances Of The Revolution*, v.2, pp. 68-9; Pitkin, *A Statistical View of Commerce*, p. 30; *Journals of Congress*, April 18, 1783, v. 24, p. 257, 258 (www.memory.loc.gov/ll/lljc/024/0200/02650257.gif).
862 Address and Recommendations To The States (Philadelphia, 1783), in *The Founding Fathers: James Madison*, p. 76.
863 Quoted in Sumner, *Finances Of The Revolution*, v.2, pp. 196-97.
864 "Address of the Annapolis Convention," in *Alexander Hamilton, Writings*. Joanne B. Freeman, ed. (New York: Literary Classics, 2001), p. 143, see also pp. 1039-40.
865 Hamilton to James Duane, September 3, 1780, in *Alexander Hamilton, Writings*. Joanne B. Freeman, ed. (New York: Literary Classics, 2001), p. 77.
866 "The Continentalist No. VI," in *Alexander Hamilton, Writings*. Joanne B. Freeman, ed. (New York: Literary Classics, 2001), p. 112.
867 Hamilton to James Duane, September 3, 1780, in *Alexander Hamilton, Writings*. Joanne B. Freeman, ed. (New York: Literary Classics, 2001), p. 79.
868 "The Continentalist No. IV," in *Alexander Hamilton, Writings*. Joanne B. Freeman, ed. (New York: Literary Classics, 2001), pp. 108, 110.
869 Pitkin, *A Statistical View of Commerce*, p. 269; Dewey, *Financial History of The U.S.*, p. 114; Report On Public Credit," 1790, in *Alexander Hamilton, Writings*, Joanne B. Freeman, ed. (New York: Literary Classics, 2001), pp. 531-74.
870 Yates, *Secret Proceedings of the Convention at Philadelphia*, p. 64.

[871] *Debates in the Federal Convention*, p. 506.

[872] *Debates in the Federal Convention*, p. 500.

[873] Hamilton, Federalist no. 12, *The Federalist Papers*, pp. 91-92 (emphasis added). See also, "The Continentalist No. VI," in *Alexander Hamilton, Writings*. Joanne B. Freeman, ed. (New York: Literary Classics, 2001), pp. 113-14.

[874] Ron Chernow, *Alexander Hamilton* (New York: Penguine, 2004), p. 27.

[875] Hamilton, Federalist no. 12, *The Federalist Papers*, pp. 91-92 (emphasis added). See also, "The Continentalist No. VI," in *Alexander Hamilton, Writings*. Joanne B. Freeman, ed. (New York: Literary Classics, 2001), pp. 113-14.

[876] *Selected Writings of Albert Gallatin*, p. 267.

[877] "Report On A National Bank," 1790, in *Alexander Hamilton, Writings*, Joanne B. Freeman, ed. (New York: Literary Classics, 2001), pp. 575-612.

[878] Sumner, *A History Of Banking I*, p. 33.

[879] Albert Gallatin, "Report On The Bank Of The United States," March 3, 1809, in *Selected Writings of Albert Gallatin*, E. James Ferguson, ed. (New York: Bobbs-Merrill, Co., 1967), pp. 264-74.

[880] Margaret I. Brown, "William Bingham, Eighteenth Century Magnate," *Pennsylvania Magazine of History and* Biograpy, vol. 61, pp. 387-434; Burton Alva Konkle, *Thomas Willing And The First American Financial System* (Univ. of Pa., 1937), pp. 141-43; *House Of Baring*, p. 30.

[881] Holden Furber, "The Beginnings of American Trade With India," *The New England Quarterly*, June 1938, vol. XI, p. 236.

[882] Hamilton to James Duane, September 3, 1780, in *Alexander Hamilton, Writings*. Joanne B. Freeman, ed. (New York: Literary Classics, 2001), p. 83.

[883] Sumner, *A History Of Banking* I, p. 29. see also, Alexander Hamilton, "Report On A National Bank," in *Alexander Hamilton, Writings*, Joanne B. Freeman, ed. (New York: Literary Classics, 2001), pp. 575-612.

[884] Hamilton, "Report On A National Bank," *Writings*, pp. 575-612.

[885] Sumner, *A History Of Banking* I, pp. 23, 32-33.

[886] Burton Alva Konkle, *Thomas Willing And The First American Financial System* (Univ. of Pa., 1937), p. 149.

[887] Konkle, *Thomas Willing*, p. 153.

[888] Sumner, *A History Of Banking I*, p. 49.

[889] Albert Gallatin, "Report On The Bank Of The United States,"

March 3, 1809, in *Selected Writings of Albert Gallatin*, E. James
Ferguson, ed. (New York: Bobbs-Merrill, Co., 1967), pp. 266, 274;
Konkle, *Thomas Willing*, p. 154; Bolles, *Industrial History of the
U.S.*, pp. 786, 788.

[890] *Selected Writings of Albert Gallatin*, pp. 264-74.

[891] Sumner, *A History Of Banking I*, pp. 31-32. Hamilton, "Report On
A National Bank," *Writings*, pp. 575-612.

[892] Konkle, *Thomas Willing*, p. 157; Sumner, *A History Of Banking I*,
p. 27.

[893] Sumner, *A History Of Banking I*, p. 23. Hamilton, "Report On A
National Bank," *Writings*, pp. 575-612.

[894] Hamilton, Federalist no. 12, *The Federalist Papers*, p. 92.

[895] Sumner, *A History Of Banking I*, p. 49 (citations omitted).

[896] Konkle, *Thomas Willing*, p. 190.

Chapter Nineteen:
King Cotton

[897] Albert Gallatin, "Report On Manufactures," in *Selected Writings of
Albert Gallatin*, Ferguson, ed., p. 263.

[898] Hamilton, 1791, "Report On Manufactures," *Selected Writings*, pp.
659-669.

[899] Hamilton, 1791, "Report On Manufactures," *Selected Writings*, pp.
659-669.

[900] Hamilton, "Report On Manufactures," *Selected Writings*, p. 725.

[901] Hamilton, "Report On Manufactures," *Selected Writings*, p. 676.

[902] Hamilton, "Report On Manufactures," *Selected Writings*, p. 688.

[903] Hamilton, "Report On Manufactures," *Selected Writings*, p. 688.

[904] Bolles, *Industrial History of the U.S.*, pp. 410, 865.

[905] Bolles, *Industrial History of the U.S.*, p. 408.

[906] Blackburn, *New World Slavery*, p. 483.

[907] "Report On The Subject of Manufactures," December 1791, in
Alexander Hamilton, Writings, Joanne B. Freeman, ed. (New York:
Literary Classics, 2001), p. 673.

[908] Albert Gallatin, "Report On Manufactures," April 19, 1810, in
Selected Writings of Albert Gallatin, E. James Ferguson, ed. (New
York: Bobbs-Merrill, Co., 1967), p. 246.

[909] Raymond McFarland, *A History of the New England Fisheries*
(Univ. of PA, 1911), p. 130.

[910] Kettell, *Southern Wealth*, p. 19.

[911] McFarland, *New England Fisheries*, p. 139.

[912] Kettell, *Southern Wealth and Northern Profits*, p. 19.

[913] Compton's Interactive Encyclopedia Deluxe © 1998 The Learning Company, Inc.

[914] Vera Shlakman, *Economic History of a Factory Town: A Study of Chicopee, Massachusetts,* (Northampton: Smith College, 1935), p. 15.

[915] Bolles, *Industrial History of the U.S.,* p. 405.

[916] Evelyn H. Knowlton, *Pepperell's Progress: History of a Cotton Tesxtile Company, 1844 – 1945* (Harvard, 1948), p. 24.

[917] Bolles, *Industrial History of the U.S.,* p. 406.

[918] Bolles, *Industrial History of the U.S.,* p. 411.

[919] Bolles, *Industrial History of the U.S.,* pp. 410-11, 412.

[920] Knowlton, *Pepperell's Progress,* p. 27.

[921] Robert A. East, "Economic Development and New England Federalism, 1803-1814," *New England Quarterly,* Sept. 1937, pp. 445, 444.

[922] Robert A. East, "Economic Development and New England Federalism, 1803-1814," *New England Quarterly,* Sept. 1937, pp. 439-42.

[923] Robert A. East, "Economic Development and New England Federalism, 1803-1814," *New England Quarterly,* Sept. 1937, p. 439.

[924] Shlakman, *Factory Town,* p. 15.

[925] Shlakman, *Factory Town,* p. 25.

[926] Shlakman, *Factory Town,* p. 48.

[927] Shlakman, *Factory Town,* p. 25.

[928] Shlakman, *Factory Town,* p. 26.

[929] Gerald T. White, *A History of The Massachusetts Hospital Life Insurance Company* (Harvard U. Press, 1953), p. 3.

[930] Knowlton, *Pepperell's Progress,* p. 10.

[931] Knowlton, *Pepperell's Progress,* p. 10.

[932] Knowlton, *Pepperell's Progress,* pp. 10-11.

[933] Shlakman, *Factory Town,* pp. 27-33, 36; Bolles, *Industrial History of the U.S.,* p. 411.

[934] Shlakman, *Factory Town,* pp. 36-37 (citations omitted).

[935] Shlakman, *Factory Town,* p. 88.

[936] Kettell, *Southern Wealth,* pp. 64-65.

[937] David Christy, "Cotton Is King," in *Cotton Is King, And Other Pro-Slavery Arguments,* E.N. Elliott, L.L.D., ed. (New York: Negro Universities Press), p. 124.

[938] Bolles, *Industrial History of the U.S.,* p. 413.

[939] "Report On The Subject of Manufactures," December 1791, in *Alexander Hamilton, Writings,* Joanne B. Freeman, ed. (New York: Literary Classics, 2001), p. 658.

[940] "Report On The Subject of Manufactures," December 1791, in *Alexander Hamilton, Writings*, Joanne B. Freeman, ed. (New York: Literary Classics, 2001), p. 662.

[941] Robert Brooke Zevin, *The Growth of Manufacturing in Early Nineteenth Century New England* (New York: Arno Press, 1975), p. 10-1.

[942] Shlakman, *Factory Town*, p. 64.

[943] Robert Brooke Zevin, *The Growth of Manufacturing in Early Nineteenth Century New England* (New York: Arno Press, 1975), p. 10.

[944] Kettell, *Southern Wealth*, p. 61.

[945] Shlakman, *Factory Town*, p. 49.

[946] Bottom photo: *Compton's Interactive Encyclopedia Deluxe*, © Copyright 1998, The Learning Company, Inc.

[947] Garnett, "The South and the Union, Part II," *De Bow's Review*, March 1855, vol. 18, no. 3, p. 295 (emphasis added).

[948] White, *Hospital Life*, pp. 5-6.

[949] White, *Hospital Life*, pp. xiii, 5.

[950] Letter of John Lowell to Samuel Appleton, Dec. 26, 1834, reprinted in White, *Hospital Life*, p. 200.

[951] White, *Hospital Life*, p. 47.

[952] White, *Hospital Life*, pp. 50-51.

[953] White, *Hospital Life*, p. 48.

[954] Shlakman, *Factory Town*, p. 45.

[955] White, *Hospital Life*, pp. 49-50.

[956] Shlakman, *Factory Town*, p. 44.

[957] Shlakman, *Factory Town*, p. 44.

[958] Shlakman, *Factory Town*, pp. 27-28.

[959] White, *Hospital Life*, pp. 12-13.

[960] Quoted in, Shlakman, *Factory Town*, pp. 27-33, 36.

[961] Shlakman, *Factory Town*, p. 43.

[962] White, *Hospital Life*, p. 51.

[963] Shlakman, *Factory Town*, p. 43.

[964] Shlakman, *Factory Town*, p. 43.

[965] Shlakman, *Factory Town*, pp. 43-44.

Conclusion

[966] See Karen Matthews, "Murders up in New York, other big cities," Associated Press, Dec 27, 2006.

[967] See David Leonhardt, "What $1.2 Trillion Can Buy" *The New York Times*, Jan. 17, 2007

[968] Jonathan Karl, "Baghdad Factory Reopens, Four Years After Invasion. Employment Opportunites Could Help Cure Terrorism," ABC News.com, Jan. 31, 2007.

[969] Fareed Zakaria, "Iraq Needs an 'Economic Surge,'" *Newsweek*, March 5, 2007 (URL: http://www.msnbc.msn.com/id/17316434/site/newsweek/?from=rss)

[970] Erik Eckholm, "Plight Deepens For Black Men, Studies Warn," *The New York Times*, March 20, 2006.

[971] John Locke, *Two Treatises Of Government*, Ian Shapiro ed. (Yale, 2003), pp. 110-185.

[972] Joanne V. Creighton, "Why we need women's colleges," *The Boston Globe*, May 21, 2007.

[973] See, "Saving Black Colleges," Online NewsHour, from February 25, 2004, www.pbs.org/newshour/bb/education/jan-june04/college_02-25.html.

[974] Katrina A. Goggins, "At black colleges, door open for whites," Associated Press, May 29, 2007

[975] Malcolm X, at Cory Methodist Church, Cleveland, OH, April 3, 1964, in *Malcolm X Speaks*, ed. George Breitman (New York 1965), p39.

[976] *Deadria Farmer-Paellmann v. FleetBostonFinancial, et. al.*, New York class action complaint, March 26, 2002.

[977] See "Comrade Capitalist," CBS.com

[978] George Lipsitz, *The Progressive Investment in Whiteness: How White People Profit from Identity Politics* (Phila: Temple University, 1998), p. 32.

[979] Brian Grow, "Hola, Amigo! You're Approved." *BusinessWeek*, April 12, 2004, p. 84.

[980] John Locke, *Two Treatises Of Government*, Ian Shapiro ed. (Yale, 2003), pp. 141-54, quote on p. 142.

[981] "Analysts Discuss Rumsfeld Resignation and Iraq Study Group Report," The NewsHour with Jim Lehrer, December 15, 2006 (url: http://www.pbs.org/newshour/bb/politics/july-dec06/sb_12-15.html).

[982] See Adam Freedman, "Clause and Effect" *New York Times*, December 16, 2007.

D